# Politics and the Intellectual

# Shofar Supplements in Jewish Studies

# Politics and the Intellectual

## Conversations with Irving Howe

Edited by John Rodden and Ethan Goffman

Purdue University Press / West Lafayette, Indiana

Printed in the United States of America.

**Library of Congress Cataloging-in-Publication Data**

Politics and the Intellectual : Conversations with Irving Howe / edited by John Rodden and Ethan Goffman.

p. cm.

Includes bibliographical references and index.

ISBN 978-1-55753-551-1

1. Howe, Irving--Interviews. 2. Howe, Irving--Political and social views. 3. Politics and literature. 4. Socialism. 5. New Left. 6. Dissenters--United States. 7. Jews--United States--Intellectual life. I. Rodden, John. II. Goffman, Ethan, 1961-

PS29.H68P66 2009

974.7'1004920092--dc22

2009022320

# Dedication

to Walter H. Sokel
Mentor and *Mensch*

AND

to Marianne for her love and unwavering support

# Contents


Preface ix

Acknowledgments xiii

Chronology xv

Introduction. *Affirming Dissent, or Irving Howe in His Interviews* 1

1 William Novak, "The Lost Worlds of Our Fathers and of Yiddish Literature," *Moment*, March 1976, 24-27. 25

2 Sol Stern, "Israel, American Jews, and the Peace Now Camp," *Jerusalem Post Weekly*, 24 August 1976. 34

3 Sandra Greenberg, "Fiction, Society, and the Literary Critic," *Book Forum: An International Transdisciplinary Quarterly*, 1981, 534-40. 41

4 Maurice Isserman, "*Dissent* in the Fifties and Sixties," 24 January 1982; 21 October 1982 (unpublished transcripts). 52

5 Grace Schulman, "A Margin of Hope at the 92nd Street Y," 7 November 1983 (unpublished audiotape). 82

6 Stephen Lewis, "From the Thirties to the Rise of Neoconservatism: Politics and Intellectual Life Across a Half-Century," Radio Interview with the Canadian Broadcasting Company, Toronto, December 1983. 107

7 Editorial Board of *The New York Times*, "Howe and Harrington on the Future of Democratic Socialism Beyond the Reagan Era," *New York Times Magazine*, 17 June 1984, 24. 120

8 John Rodden, "A 'Partisan' View of Orwell," October 1983 and April 1987 (unpublished transcript). 137

9 Todd Gitlin, "Looking Back on the New Left and the Counterculture," 15 April 1985 (unpublished audiotape). 151

10 Neil Jumonville, "Socialism, Communism, and the New York Intellectuals," 6 June 1985 (unpublished transcript). 198

11 Susanne Klingenstein, "Thoughts on Jewish Intellectual Life and the American Academy," 12 December 1988 (unpublished audiotape). 206

12 Irving Howe, "The First 35 Years Were the Hardest: Interview with Myself," *Dissent*, Spring 1989, 133-36. 232

13 William Cain, "Making of a Modern Critic," *American Literary History*, Fall 1989, 554-64. 243

14 Jim Holt, "'Howe Now': on Politics, Art, and the Critic," *Thesis: The Magazine of the Graduate School and University Center*, Fall 1990, 4-11. 256

15 Robert Negin, "Fraternal Dissents on Max Shachtman and American Trotskyism," November 1990 (unpublished audiotape). 270

16 Maurice Isserman, "'My Recollections of Mike': Harrington the Thinker and Socialist Activist," 26 March 1991 (unpublished transcript). 281

17 Joseph Dorman, "Irving Howe, New York Intellectual," Selections from *Arguing the World* (New York: The Free Press, 2000). 310

Postscript. Interview with Robert Silvers on the Death of Irving Howe, CBC Radio, "As It Happens," May 5, 1993 323

Afterword by Nina Howe 327

Bibliography 332

Index 335

Photographs follow page 145

# Preface

## I

This book brings to life Irving Howe (1920-93), the indefatigable radical intellectual and editor of *Dissent* who helped shape the history of the postwar American Left. Focusing on his evolving thought around his trio of loves—Socialism, literature, and Judaica—during his late career, this collection of interviews spans the last seventeen years of Howe's life. The volume addresses in detail Howe's views of the 1960s, and his staunch critique of Reaganism. More than that, the collection illuminates how his life history contributed to the principled intellectual he became.

Howe discusses at length how his parents' poverty and his radical youth deeply influenced his psyche, how his Socialist commitments affected his work, and how he managed to befriend (and alienate) many of America's leading postwar intellectuals. He gives tribute to writers and intellectuals with whom he worked (and especially to his literary heroes), and he talks enthusiastically about topics ranging from the fiction of Sherwood Anderson to the conventions of popular Yiddish theatre.

Beginning with a 1976 conversation in which Howe shares reflections on his "fifteen minutes of fame" as a result of the brief celebrity that he experienced as the author of his literary bestseller, *World of Our Fathers*, these interviews reveal Howe as a natural in the interview genre. He emerges as a witty raconteur and a well-read, inspiring advocate for democratic Socialism. With pleasure, insight, and depth, these interviews reveal Howe's struggles as a critic-intellectual, the manifold influences that shaped him, and the creative process that formed him. The volume contains both previously unpublished material and interviews that first appeared in minor and major publications.

## II

Who was Irving Howe? The interviews marvelously illuminate the biographical facts, which can be quickly summarized here. He was a 1940 City College of

New York (CCNY) graduate whose parents struggled through the Depression. He came to his Socialist beliefs through the direct experience of his working-class parents' hard life. First published in the mid-1940s in *Partisan Review,* Howe penned more than fifty books during his lifetime. While most prolific writers tend to concentrate almost exclusively on a single topic, Howe wrote widely on a variety of subjects. He published an autobiography, histories, biographies, literary criticism, student anthologies, and collections of Socialist prose.

From the 1940s until his death, Howe was a major literary and social critic who acknowledged the legacy of Socialism yet also was adept at taking the pulse of contemporary American culture. Howe was unlike many of his colleagues in his unbending commitment to a vision of Socialism, albeit an increasingly qualified one. Unlike most prominent intellectuals, he did not veer rightward in the 1950s. Instead he founded the only radical quarterly of the decade, *Dissent,* whereby he aimed to revitalize American radical thinking. *Dissent* paved the way for Socialist journalism that was more speculative and philosophical than had been previously seen in American radical publications.

Yet Howe excelled in all three of his beloved genres—not just Socialist analysis and literary criticism, but also Jewish cultural criticism. With Eliezer Greenberg, he revolutionized how Yiddish literature was taught and studied in the academy. Their 1954 collection, *A Treasury of Yiddish Fiction*, remains the template for English language commentary on Yiddish fiction.

Irving Howe became one of America's most respected literary-cultural critics and vocal Left intellectuals during the conservative middle decades of the twentieth century. His literary commentary represents the flowering of the period (1945-75) when literary criticism was considered a vitally important form of cultural and social engagement. During this era, Howe exerted enormous influence on other intellectuals, especially on the left, not only through his own writings, but also through his editing of numerous volumes of the best work from *Dissent* in the mid-1960s through the mid-1980s. Though his literary reputation may have faded in the last quarter-century, the originality of his voice, and his championing of American authors as an idiosyncratically provincial extension of European tradition, ensure that his books remain vital. Because of his literary merits and his status as the voice of *Dissent,* Howe remains a significant presence among Left intellectuals today. These facts and his varied interests established Howe as a premier public intellectual of his time, one who was frequently called upon to clarify political and cultural debates. Indeed *Irving Howe: Politics and the Intellectual* collects interviews with a man considered to be—along with Edmund Wilson, Lionel Trilling, and Alfred Kazin—the leading American literary intellectual of the postwar era.

## III

The interviews in *Irving Howe: Politics and the Intellectual*—some in print for the first time—disclose a candid, cultivated, and unselfish man, genuinely but also strategically self-critical, who is also a skilled conversationalist. There are few writers about whom it can be said that they write just like they speak, but Irving Howe was one of them. Like his writing, his manner in these interviews is crisp and lucid, his tone engaging, and his observations enlightening. Howe is revealed to be subtle, graceful, prophetic, complex, stylish, and lucid. In an intellectual career that spanned five decades, he did not cease to experiment and explore. These conversations show his ideas ripening along with the work he was writing.

The book also shows Howe's progression from a passionately engaged dissenter to a contemplative thinker and intellectual elder. In the last interviews, he opens up about another, late love: ballet. He discusses how it affects his temperament, disclosing a man who remained active on the public scene while maintaining the distinctive quirks of a quixotic spirit.

Howe's critical acumen is present in every selection here, as he talks forthrightly about literature's place in American culture, the role of American history in his political development, and the specific cultural debates that raged during his lifetime. Featuring interviews conducted by literary-cultural historians and intellectuals for public forums, for notable journals and newspapers, and as independent research for books, the collection's breadth and depth exhibit the consistency and integrity of Howe's vision.

Because it covers the last flowering of Howe's political engagements and literary output, the volume ultimately serves as the sequel that Howe never wrote to his autobiography, *A Margin of Hope* (1982), which took the story of his life up to the 1970s. This collection begins where his memoirs end, rounding out the dream of his life's journey and allowing the reader to hear the remaining chapters of the story in his own words and his own eloquent, undying voice.

# Acknowledgments

The impetus for this book emerged more than a quarter century ago, when I first met and interviewed Irving Howe. My first thanks thus go to him, an exemplary elder representing so much of the best from the ever receding world of my intellectual fathers. More immediately, I am grateful to Nina Howe, who not only wrote the Afterword but also gave me photos of her father and the Howe family for this volume. Later she also interceded with Robert Silvers to acquire his memorial tribute to Irving Howe for the collection. It was a great pleasure to spend a wintry evening in November 2009 in the warmth of her Montreal home, where she and her husband Bill Bukowski shared with me their personal memories of Irving Howe.

I owe an equal debt of gratitude to Nina's older brother, Nick Howe, who enthusiastically supported this collection as it was conceived and took early shape. I had come to know Nick when we worked together on my two previous books devoted to his father, *Irving Howe and the Critics* (2004) and *The Worlds of Irving Howe* (2005), to which Nick generously contributed personal essays and family photographs. Nick's premature death at 53 from leukemia in September 2006 was a cruel tragedy, occurring just at the moment when he was entering a period not only of his full powers as a writer but also of professional recognition as a scholar-critic, having recently accepted a position at the University of California at Berkeley.

The interviews with Irving Howe in this volume could not have been gathered without the generous cooperation of the interviewers. I am grateful to them for permission to include their interviews and to edit them selectively in order to make them more accessible. Several of the contributors—especially Todd Gitlin, Maurice Isserman, and Neil Jumonville—were not only supportive but also helpful with clarifying an obscure reference, deciphering a garbled phrase on audiocassette, or placing a remark of Howe in historical and political context.

Other colleagues and friends read parts of the manuscript as it progressed and offered sage advice: Morris Dickstein, Steve Longstaff, Neil McLaughlin, and Jonathan Imber. Dan Klein entered late in the day and distinguished himself as copyeditor and proofreader extraordinaire, catching several howlers with virtuoso last-minute saves. Above all, I wish to thank my co-editor, Ethan Goffman, who joined to work with me on this project as it struggled toward maturity, reinvigorating it in a collaboration that has been both wonderfully enjoyable and richly edifying.

Finally, I thank my old colleague and friend Walter H. Sokel, a onetime student and colleague of Lionel Trilling at Columbia University, an acquaintance of Hannah Arendt, and a long-time admirer of Irving Howe and other New York intellectual elders. I became acquainted with Walter, first as a Ph.D. student and later as a junior colleague, during the last two decades of his academic career at the University of Virginia. Now in his mid-90s, his energy still undimmed, Walter is another emissary from Howe's "world of our fathers"—indeed a brilliant exemplar of that dying species, a consummate intellectual, a man of erudition and *Bildung*. For me, he shines forever forth as mentor and Mensch.

For all these reasons and more, I dedicate this book to Walter.

-John Rodden

Grateful thanks to Daniel Klein for his editing prowess, Susan Klingenstein for her helpful advice, Maxine Phillips for her support, and Carolyn Mitchell for her intellectual guidance. Thanks to Karen Eilenberg for her insightful conversations and to Lisa Goffman for her astounding good spirits. I especially wish to thank John Rodden, who conceived of this book and whose vast intellectual resources and hard work made it what it is. And I thank Callie and Thelma for being there.

-Ethan Goffman

# Chronology

**1920** Irving Arthur Horenstein, who later adopted the name Irving Howe (IH) is born on June 11, at 139th Street in the Bronx, New York City, a Yiddish-speaking neighborhood, to David and Nettie (Goldman) Horenstein.

**1922** IH's father and mother, both of whom were born in Russia, are naturalized as U.S. citizens.

**1930** The family's grocery store in the West Bronx goes bankrupt. David Horenstein works as a peddler and later as a presser in a dress factory. Nettie Horenstein also works in the dress trade as a machine operator.

**1935** IH reads Edmund Wilson's *Axel's Castle* and first encounters literary criticism and history.

**1936** IH graduates from DeWitt Clinton High School in June and matriculates to City College of New York in September.

- IH majors in English at CCNY, spending most of his college days in the CCNY cafeteria, in Alcove 1, which he later calls "the home of heresy, left sectarianism, independent thought, and sheer fanaticism and intolerance." Alcove 1 houses the Trotskyist students, consisting of approximately fifty CCNY members. Alcove 2 is occupied by the pro-Stalinist Left, which numbers roughly four hundred students. Other members of Alcove 1 included Irving Kristol, Seymour Martin Lipset, Daniel Bell, Nathan Glazer, and Melvin J. Lasky.

**1938** The CCNY Trotskyists organize "a strike against imperialist war," which features a rally led by James Burnham, James Farrell, and Sidney Hook.

- IH edits a mimeographed publication, *The CCNY Red Book.*
- IH becomes widely regarded as Max Shachtman's most promising protégé.
- IH joins and remains in the Socialist Workers Party until 1940.

**1939** Officially registered at CCNY under the name Horenstein, IH begins to use the Trotskyist party name of "Hugh Ivan." He also acquires the nickname of "Fangs" because of his zest for polemics. The pseudonym conveniently resembles one of his party names, R. Fangston, which he was dubbed by a comrade because of his protruding eyeteeth. (These were later filed down.)

**1940** IH is elected as member of the National Executive Board of the Young People's Socialist League.

- IH, along with classmate Irving Kristol, graduates from City College of New York with a B.S. in social science. (He graduates as Irving Horenstein but uses the name Irving Howe for speeches and articles.)
- In the spring, a faction led by Max Shachtman, and including IH, splits from the Socialist Workers Party to form the Workers Party. (Shachtman had been one of the chief lieutenants of James Cannon, whose Socialist Workers Party had a membership of 645; Max Shachtman's Workers Party membership was slightly smaller.)

**1941** On June 15, IH marries Anna Bader in the Bronx, the first of his four marriages. The couple resides in Greenwich Village.

- In early December, IH becomes managing editor, under Emanuel Garrett (pseudonym of Emanuel Geltman), of the Workers Party weekly, *Labor Action*. Later the same month he becomes editor, continuing in this position until drafted into the army in mid-1942.

**1942** IH is inducted into the U.S. Army on July 27, at Fort Dix, New Jersey (army serial no. 32-404-986), thus beginning a term of military service that lasts about three and a half years.

**1946** On January 18, at Fort Dix, IH is honorably discharged from the U.S. Army with the rank of corporal, having held the position of clerk in the enlistment center at Camp Upton, New York. Following his release from the army, he moves back to the Bronx.

- In the spring, IH contributes to the journals *politics*, edited by Dwight Macdonald, and *Tomorrow*. Writing for *politics* using the pseudonym Theodore Dryden, IH is hired as a part-time assistant to Macdonald for $15 per week.
- In November, IH begins contributing to *Partisan Review*. His first review is of a collection of stories by Sholom Aleichem translated from the Yiddish, *The Old Country*.

**1947** On April 12, IH marries Thalia Phillies, an archeologist from Buffalo, New York, who is doing graduate studies at Columbia University.

**1948** In the spring, IH writes a full-page article in the journal *Labor Action*, reacting with despair to the Stalinist takeover of Czechoslovakia. After this time, he confines his contributions to the theoretical magazine *New International.*

- IH moves to Princeton in September, when his wife gets a job teaching Greek and Latin at Miss Fine's Day School, a private school for girls. During his Princeton years, he becomes acquainted with faculty members in the English Department such as R. P. Blackmur, Delmore Schwartz, Saul Bellow, and John Berryman.
- IH rewrites the British translation of Leo Baeck's *Essence of Judaism*, published in the United States by Schocken Books.

**1949** *The UAW and Walter Reuther* (with B. J. Widick) is published by Random House. The Workers Party reorganizes itself as the Independent Socialist League (ISL).

**1951** *Sherwood Anderson* is published by William Sloane Associates in the American Men of Letters Series.

**1952** IH teaches a summer session at the University of Washington, Seattle.

- On October 12, IH resigns from the Independent Socialist League (ISL) in a statement jointly issued with Stanley Plastrik. The letter criticizes "the intellectual incompetence of the ISL," its "political split personality" between Trotskyism and "a new view of American Socialism," and its "state of floating anxiety covered up by a doctrinal rigidity." Howe and Plastrik add: "We are and intend to remain democratic Socialists. Our motive in leaving the ISL is a conviction that it has ceased to be useful for advancing the cause of democratic Socialism or for providing a lively center in which its problems can be discussed."

**1953** In January, IH is invited to present his views at the New York membership meeting of the ISL, shortly after which his resignation letter is published.

- IH leaves Princeton to begin teaching in the fall at Brandeis University, where he remains until 1961. He participates in Brandeis campus debates with Howard Fast (on the USSR) and with Herbert Marcuse and Oscar Handlin (on the Israeli capture of Adolf Eichmann in Argentina).
- In the spring, IH assembles a group of fifty people, many of them former Shachtmanites, to discuss the viability of launching a new left-wing magazine. Dwight Macdonald agrees to allow *Dissent* to use his subscribers list to solicit funds from supporters of *politics* magazine. IH and Lewis Coser are joined in the planning of *Dissent* by Stanley Plastrik, Emanuel Geltman, Bernard Rosenberg, Meyer Schapiro, Norman Mailer, and Harold Orlans.

**1954** IH publishes an essay, "This Age of Conformity," in the January/February issue of *Partisan Review*. In this article he accuses Lionel Trilling, who had helped IH publish *Sherwood Anderson*, of "indulging in a pleasant fantasy" about the quality of American life. This leads to a seven-year break in their relationship.

- IH co-founds *Dissent* along with Lewis Coser, publishing its first issue in January. IH does most of the line-by-line editing and rewriting of the articles. Emanuel Geltman does the technical work of makeup and general editing.
- IH edits *A Treasury of Yiddish Stories* (with Eliezer Greenberg), published by Viking Press and dedicated "to the six million."

**1957** *Politics and the Novel* is published by Horizon Press.

**1961** IH leaves Brandeis and moves to California to teach at Stanford University. He is the first tenured Jewish full professor at Stanford.

**1963** IH and some *Dissent* editors meet Tom Hayden and other members of Students for a Democratic Society (SDS).

**1963** *A World More Attractive* is published by Horizon Press.

- IH edits Orwell's *Nineteen Eighty-Four: Text, Sources, Criticism*, published by Harcourt Brace.
- IH leaves California to begin teaching at Hunter College and the Graduate Center of City University of New York (CUNY), where he remains until retirement in 1986.

**1964** IH marries Arien Mack, a widow and a member of the New School psychology faculty. Arien later becomes editor of *Social Research*.

**1966** *Steady Work: Essays in the Politics of Democratic Radicalism, 1953-66* is published by Harcourt Brace.

**1968** In April and May, student riots erupt at Columbia. IH finds himself on the side of the alleged "reactionaries," such as Trilling.

- In October, IH publishes his seminal essay "The New York Intellectuals" in *Commentary*.

**1969** *The Decline of the New* is published by Harcourt.

- IH edits *A Treasury of Yiddish Poetry* (with Eliezer Greenberg), published by Holt, Rinehart and Winston.

**1970** IH is named Distinguished Professor at CUNY.

- In December "The Middle-Class Mind of Kate Millett," IH's critique of the author of *Sexual Politics*, is published in *Harper's*.

**1973** *The Critical Point* is published by Horizon Press.

- *Thomas Hardy* is reissued by Collier Books in the Masters of World Literature Series.
- IH joins Michael Harrington's Democratic Socialist Organizing Committee, of which he later becomes vice president.

**1974** IH edits *Selected Stories: I L. Peretz*, published by Schocken Books.

- IH edits *The New Conservatives: A Critique from the Left* (with Lewis Coser), published by Quadrangle Books.
- IH makes his first trip to Israel, during which he meets Ilana Wiener, an Israeli.

**1976** *World of Our Fathers*, published by Harcourt Brace Jovanovich, reaches number seven on the *New York Times* bestseller list and wins the National Book Award in history.

- IH marries Ilana Wiener.
- In August, IH visits Israel with his new wife as a guest of the Israeli Labor Party.
- In November, IH's father and stepmother become gravely ill and are hospitalized. In December, his father dies at age eighty-five.

**1978** *Leon Trotsky* is published by Viking.

- IH's name appears in ads from the American Friends of Peace Now, urging Prime Minister Menachem Begin to show greater flexibility on peace negotiations with the Arabs.

**1982** *A Margin of Hope* (originally titled *A Chronicle of Our Times*) is published by Harcourt Brace Jovanovich.

- IH edits *The Portable Kipling*, published by Viking.
- IH edits (with Ilana Wiener-Howe) *Short Shorts: An Anthology of the Shortest Stories*, published by Godine.

**1983** IH edits *1984 Revisited: Totalitarianism in Our Century*, published by Harper & Row.

**1985** *Socialism and America* is published by Harcourt Brace Jovanovich.

- At Harvard, IH delivers the William E. Massey, Sr. Lectures on the history of civilization, which form the basis of *The American Newness: Culture and Politics in the Age of Emerson*.

**1986** IH retires from CUNY.

- *The American Newness: Culture and Politics in the Age of Emerson* is published by Harvard University Press.

**1987** IH is named a MacArthur Fellow, receiving the highest award possible ($375,000) from the foundation.

**1990** *Selected Writings: 1950-1990* is published by Harcourt Brace Jovanovich.

**1991** IH republishes *William Faulkner* (with Ivan R. Dee).

- IH begins an aggressive defense of the traditional literary canon in the American academy.

**1992** *Politics and the Novel* is reissued by Columbia University Press with a new preface.

- IH successively undergoes heart-bypass surgery, prostate surgery, and an operation for an abdominal aneurysm. He spends the first four months of the year in the hospital.

**1993** On May 5, in New York City, IH dies of a burst aorta, a month short of his seventy-third birthday. In his will, he leaves parts of his estate to *Dissent* and to the Democratic Socialists of America. Memorial services for IH are held at the 92nd Street YMCA in New York City.

- *Dissent* publishes a special fall issue devoted to the memory of IH. The contributors include his son Nicholas and his daughter Nina Howe, along with numerous old friends from *Dissent* and other writers and intellectuals.

**1994** A memorial conference, "Irving Howe and His World," is held at CUNY on April 15. Featured speakers include Mitchell Cohen, Michael Walzer, Marshall Berman, John Hollander, Morris Dickstein, Richard Rorty, Allen Mandelbaum, and Celia Morris.

- *A Critic's Notebook*, edited by Nicholas Howe, is published by Harcourt Brace.

**1997** *Arguing the World*, a documentary about New York Intellectuals, features CCNY graduates IH, Daniel Bell, Nathan Glazer, and Irving Kristol.

- *Short Shorts* is reissued by Bantam.

**2002** *Politics and the Novel* is republished by Ivan R. Dee.

**2003** IH's edited volume *Classics of Modern Fiction: Twelve Short Novels*, originally published in 1968, is reprinted by Harcourt.

**2004** *Dissent* celebrates its fiftieth anniversary.

**2005** *Irving Howe and the Critics*, edited by John Rodden, appears from the University of Nebraska Press.

- *The Worlds of Irving Howe*, edited by John Rodden, is published by Paradigm Press.

# Introduction. *Affirming Dissent, or Irving Howe in His Interviews*

## Politics and the Intellectual

Irving Howe's intellectual autobiography, *A Margin of Hope* (1982), closes as the 1980s open, the so-called dawn of Reaganism and the political ascendancy of the American Right, an era in which U.S. radicalism arguably reached its nadir. Despite Howe's success as an author, editor, literary critic, social commentator, public intellectual, and radical activist, his political life as a Socialist tribune was marked by a series of failures that reflected the declining prospects of American Socialism itself as the twentieth century proceeded. As his vision of a Socialist future dissolved into a dream, Howe's right-wing enemies mocked him as a hopeless utopian: his stern critique of Communism failed to ingratiate him with conservatives. Meanwhile, the far Left attacked him as a wavering accommodationist; Howe's brand of moderate democratic Socialism seemed all but forgotten. By the conclusion of *A Margin of Hope,* Howe admits that "the years of my life coincided with the years of Socialist defeat."[1]

Yet *A Margin of Hope* is not Howe's final word. In a series of interviews granted during the last seventeen years of his life, which the editors have collected in the present volume, he reflects further on the main intellectual currents that sustained him: literature, Jewish culture, and radical politics. This book thus represents the closest we have to an autobiographical record of Irving Howe's thought at the time of his greatest prominence and success, during the years of his bestselling *World of Our Fathers,* his reception of the MacArthur Award (known colloquially as the "genius" grant), and his much-discussed late essays on topics ranging from the politics of multiculturalism to the literature of the Holocaust. By the mid-1980s—after the deaths of Edmund Wilson, Lionel Trilling and other New York Intellectual elders—he was widely regarded as both the leading liberal-radical voice and (except among some conservatives and on the far Left) the foremost literary intellectual in America.

Paradoxically, Howe's professional triumphs came despite a series of disastrous political failures that befell the cause to which he had dedicated much of his life, as the seemingly solid radical alternatives of his youth all melted into air. Yet an experience of loss and defeat may give rise to a period of reflection, perhaps of learning. Although the tone of these interviews is often embattled and somber, they also are studded with flashes of insight. Howe lived through, and meditated intently on, the major political, social, and cultural events that dominated the international scene in the last half of the twentieth century. In these conversations Howe reflects on the conservative, business-oriented character of American society during this era. He also muses on larger historical patterns and on the dramatic upheavals on the Left, particularly those in the 1960s that suddenly crested and just as quickly receded.

Whether this quintessentially American pattern of abrupt ebb and flow amid conservative stability marks an essentially static or an evolving society—and, if evolving, in what directions—is largely beyond the scope of this volume yet surfaces indirectly in several interviews. To his credit, Howe does not dodge it in these conversations, but rather advances a number of tantalizing clues and suggestions. The Howe of the 1980s and 1990s was far more temperate and indeed wiser than the precocious young polemicist of the 1940s who banged the drum loudly for Leon Trotsky, the Soviet Communist leader who was ousted from power, thrust into exile, and ultimately murdered by Joseph Stalin and his henchmen. The elder Howe nevertheless refused to abandon the radical vision of transformation that enflamed his Socialist youth, even though he qualified and modified his utopian vision in countless ways in light of his deepened understanding about America and the changing climate of the postwar West.

Acknowledging a form of "American exceptionalism," Howe ultimately came to prize both the endless complexity of the United States—that creative, impetuous, individualistic, conservative, radical, capitalist riddle that had long baffled him, partly due to his European-oriented intellectual inclinations—and America's bracing distinctiveness, a revaluation that extended to a mature admiration for Ralph Waldo Emerson and the native "Emersonian tradition."

So this collection of interviews contributes not only to an appreciation of the intellectual biography of a leading American literary-political figure of the twentieth century, nor merely illuminates the historical period in which he wrote, but also bears relevance to the role of America in our own time, one in which ideological polarization has reached extremes, one that replays numerous old historical patterns yet adds strange new twists. Just as Howe's political innocence matured into both more nuanced understanding and deepened ambivalence, so might present-day America need to move beyond our youthful idealism in order to find a sober mix that balances principle and pragmatism.

Indeed, reading these conversations from Howe's last seventeen years, one is struck by how the trends of the 1980s have returned in the new millennium. Living through a period of right-wing activism aiming to scale back the liberal domestic initiatives of the New Deal and the Great Society, Howe preserves a margin of hope for a revived Left at some unidentified future time, a coming wave of changes promising greater social justice. This idealism—amid what Howe recognizes as an imperfect world in which progress is invariably partial, piecemeal, and often temporary—represents a recurrent theme. As blunt and acrid as Howe can be, he never abandons his vision of a better world. For this reason he clings to the term "Socialism," as misused and vilified as the word may be.

Howe's conservative adversaries saw him as struggling naively to maintain the viability of a radical alternative in a world that has passed it by and rendered it an historical anachronism. These include his colleagues among the New York Intellectuals, that largely Jewish group affiliated with *Partisan Review* who came to prominence beginning in the 1930s and have come to embody the ideal of the public intellectual. Some of these colleagues, several of whom have since formed the nucleus of the neoconservative movement, have expressed scathing criticism and withering ridicule of Howe's so-called utopianism. Yet Howe was also subjected to vicious and relentless criticism not only from the New Left of the 1960s, but also in later years from the Marxists and the far Left. Alexander Cockburn, for instance, wrote a memorial of Howe in *The Nation* blasting him as a reactionary engaged in a rearguard campaign against what Cockburn considered the authentic radical Left.[2] Some observers regard it as one of Howe's achievements, however, that he was maligned by both the far Left and the neoconservatives. They value the moderate Howe of the last decade who was able to weather the ideological storms of a conservative era with greater serenity than he did when the New Left derided him. And the elder Howe did so under even greater stresses than during the 1960s, for in the 1980s and 1990s, he had to fight on two fronts. By contrast, the middle-aged Howe had faced assaults on his left flank alone; he continued to publish in *Commentary* and only began to oppose the neoconservatives in the early 1970s, as they shifted rightward decisively.

## Whither Socialism?

In 1969, Irving Kristol criticized Howe's stubborn "utopian faith," a jibe that prefigured later attacks by prominent neoconservative intellectuals such as Midge Decter and Joseph Epstein, all of whom argued that Howe lacked the insight and courage to revise his views in light of Socialism's failures.[3] In a 1982 essay, Decter claimed that, following the obvious failures of the world Communist movement, "the 'animating ethic' of Socialism that Howe and *Dissent* were left with, and the cutting edge of Marxist theory and Marxist ideology, was no more than a will to remain utopian: utopianism, as it were, without utopia."[4] In a 1990 article, Hilton Kramer extended this critique of Howe's career: "For Howe, it seems, the Socialist idea was far too precious to be subjected to anything as vulgar as the judgment of history."[5]

Yet the differences between Howe and the neoconservatives always had practical political and economic consequences contingent on stances of programmatic action and organizational strategy. Responding in 1969 to Kristol's critique, Howe identifies the burgeoning gulf between himself and the emerging neoconservatives: "I really want to see the major segments of the American economy socially controlled and democratically operated, and I really want a major redistribution of power and wealth."[6]

This reply sums up Howe's core beliefs, which date back to his Bronx youth. His pained Depression memories of his parents' long working hours and low wages never dimmed, nor did his gratitude for the benefits brought by the unionization of his mother's job: "We could now have meat more often, my parents started to squirrel away a few dollars, and once my birthday came around, my mother bought me a few grown up shirts." Socialism would become, for Howe, a crucible of emotion and empowerment. In the words of Howe's biographer, Edward Alexander, a vocal neoconservative, Howe transformed Socialism "into a myth of considerable power as an ethical instrument of social and political criticism."[7] Within a radically changing landscape, the core ideal remained. Gerald Sorin, Howe's second biographer and a committed Left-liberal, defends Howe's continuing commitment to radicalism more forcefully:

> Howe's "gift of stubbornness" was neither a sentimental attachment to outworn traditions, cultural or literary, nor a blind devotion to a depleted and degraded political dogma. It was a principled commitment to the ideal of democratic radicalism, to a true egalitarianism, and to the never-ending struggle for decency and fairness in the face of social injustice.[8]

Howe strongly defends these ideals in a 1984 interview with the *New York Times Magazine* echoing his riposte to Kristol in *Commentary* fifteen years earlier: "I think it's outrageous that America should have the extreme inequalities of income and wealth (hence, also power) that in fact exist. . . . We want a society in which economic life has been transformed in the direction of greater democratic participation, so that workers may have some control over their workplace and their work life."[9]

As these comments suggest, at the heart of Howe's ethos was a more egalitarian society in which working people have a voice in employment conditions, in business decisions, and in profit distribution. Is this "democratic Socialism"? Is it a "social democracy"? Or is it a version of liberalism?

Wrangling about the precise terminology is jesuitical and here of little value. One's answer depends on one's view of human nature and indeed of human possibility. For instance, do you believe that the Scandinavian countries are the best societies that can exist? Or are they merely the best that have so far emerged? At all events, *pace* Kristol, the divergence between the positions of Howe and the neoconservatives is very real. Howe always insisted that some better alternative to American capitalism was both necessary and viable; the neoconservatives hold that the American system is the best available choice and that striving for "utopia" is misconceived and indeed dangerous.

For Howe, the ideal of a more egalitarian society remained fundamental to his moral compass, but in an increasingly qualified way. Indeed, he often referred to himself by the 1970s as a "radical humanist"; he had dropped "Socialism" from the *Dissent* masthead more than a decade earlier. By the 1980s, Howe began employing such terms as "democratic Socialism" and "market Socialism" to characterize his politics, seeking via the qualifying adjectives to offset the noun's negative associations. Still, he affirmed a communitarian, radical humanist impulse that balanced individual rights and social justice. Yet any speculative blueprint of the ideal society seemed to Howe vague at best and ominous at worst, a dilemma still fresh and immediate for Socialists of his generation, given the historical disaster of the Soviet Union. The practical alternative, as represented by the social democracies of Western Europe, also seemed lackluster, leading Howe to explain: "Social democracy today has become a decent and honorable party that . . . does not really aspire to move beyond the status quo."[10]

Howe's relationship to utopianism, therefore, was ultimately ambiguous. Although he wished to move beyond the conditions of limited social justice afforded by social democracy, he never elaborated in detail what the new society would look like. At times he became more the skeptical anti-utopian Jeremiah, the "American Orwell."[11] The main purpose of what he called "the radical imagination" (in his 1967 *Dissent* collection of that title) was the need for something beyond the here and now.[12] By 1993, Howe explained that "we *Dissenters,* the handful of us, try to hold fast to the vision of social transformation, even as we have dropped many of the traditional proposals for how to reach it."[13]

Howe's comments about the failures of Eastern European Socialism reflected his multiplying doubts about the compatibility between democracy and any form of economic and political collectivism. By the early 1960s, a commitment to "Socialism" no longer occupied his political center. During his last decade, he distanced himself from political activism and usually referred to himself as a "radical humanist" rather than a "Socialist." (At a 1988 *Tikkun* conference, he used that self-characterization, not "Socialist," and interviews with his friends and colleagues confirm this shift.)[14] That is partly why the collection that he assembled to sum up his career, *Selected Writings* (1990), contained only a couple of political pieces except for his most recent work. The volume is largely restricted to his literary and cultural reflections; his political essays had come to seem dated to him. At his funeral, practically nobody from his old life as a Trotskyist showed up; virtually all the attendees belonged to the *Dissent* crowd or were colleagues in the New York literary scene.

None of this gainsays the fact that Howe's ethical and ideological commitment remained radical and egalitarian. Irving Howe was not just a utopian, but a pragmatist who acknowledged that the historical moment for actualizing his most cherished political aspirations had passed—and he did not expect it to return again in his lifetime.

## *Dissent's* Early Days

The road to Howe's evolving political moderation had already begun in the early postwar period, when he started to withdraw from Trotskyist activism and voice sharp reservations about the politics of his Shachtmanite sect. The watershed moment can be dated as the founding of *Dissent* in January 1954. Along with fellow radical Stanley Plastrik, Howe had previously striven to remain connected with Trotskyism and the International Socialist League (ISL). Immediately after Dwight Macdonald's independent, contrarian journal *politics* folded in 1949, Howe vigorously pursued the idea of launching a magazine of radical intellectual thought. An erstwhile editorial board member of *politics* and Macdonald's onetime editorial assistant, Howe first proposed publishing such a magazine within the confines of the ISL Trotskyists, whom he and Plastrik hoped would be willing to work with them.[15] Not surprisingly, Howe's insistence on intellectual independence within a Marxist sect expecting party discipline proved difficult to implement. And yet he persisted. It was only in November 1952, when the ISL definitively refused to sponsor their magazine and officially censured Howe and Plastrik that they sallied off on their own.

From the beginning, the new journal faced the intricate task of navigating between radicalism gone astray and conservative reaction. Fortunately, the *Dissenters* of the mid-1950s did have a clear sense of one immediate duty: denouncing McCarthyism, the anti-Communism that suppressed free speech in favor of patriotic jingoism. Howe explains, "You didn't have to be a Socialist, you just had to be a consistent liberal. You didn't even have to be a liberal, just a defender of democratic rights. Since we felt that many of our friends and former allies were not doing that, because of the Cold War, this became one of the main centers of our attack. So on that front we were on the offensive" (Isserman 1982). Faced with the specter of McCarthyism, *Dissent* had a palpable enemy, as well as an unmistakable, if inconsistent, ally in mainstream American liberalism. Regarding Stalinism, though it emerged from the same Marxist tradition as *Dissent* itself, opposition was also unhesitating: Stalin's tyrannical regime represented a brutal totalitarianism that destroyed the very ideals it professed to embody.

The case of Trotskyism was more ambiguous. Howe's mature reflections on Trotskyism betray a nostalgia for having been part of both a movement passionately dedicated to a noble ideal and a group wherein he learned the skills of rigorous argument for a cause. Still, whatever polemical and organizational talents this sectarianism might have fostered, it was also quite confining, both intellectually and politically. Howe acknowledged these limits, along with the fact that his affection for his Trotskyist past was a form of nostalgic retrospection. (He titled the chapter in his autobiography about his years as a Trotskysist pamphleteer and activist "Life in a Sect.") In fact, once he had broken with the ISL, Howe's fondness was much stronger for Trotsky himself than for Trotskyism, as his 1978 study of Trotsky evinces.[16] He continued in later years to see Trotsky in rather heroic terms, as a "great man" of history, a problematic position for some of Howe's otherwise admiring critics.[17] Perhaps surprisingly, despite their contrasting political stances, Howe's two biographers share a high opinion of Howe's mature stance on Trotsky, arguing that the elder Howe redeemed his youthful lionizing of Trotsky, utterly rejecting his erstwhile hero's core ideas even if retaining an element of personal affection and esteem for the man himself.[18] Howe judged Leninism as problematic at the source, a conclusion that undermined any residual feeling of allegiance to Trotsky's politics.

Founded in the aftermath of Howe's long struggle to cast off the intellectual shackles of Trotskyism, *Dissent* inevitably reflected Howe's attempt to wrest free from sectarianism. "The negative side," Howe explains of Trotskyism, "was that, as regarding American politics, it led us into a dead end from which some of us extracted ourselves only after a certain number of years. And indeed the formation of *Dissent* began as part of that process of pulling out of that sectarianism" (Lewis). If Trotskyism represented a reconsideration of Communism, *Dissent* signified for Howe a reconsideration of Socialism itself, one that attempted to remain faithful to its egalitarian ethos yet unbound by the Shachtmanite straightjacket of narrow sectarianism and ideology.

*Dissent*, however, was not only about recasting the path of a wayward sect. The journal reflected different agendas among the members of the founding group—Howe, Plastrik, Lewis Coser, and others. For instance, *Dissent* was not just a reconsideration of American radicalism, but also an effort to introduce European democratic/libertarian Socialism to the American scene, which is why Coser, a refugee from Hitler's Germany, played a big role in the early years and why *Dissent* modeled its political position on Macdonald's *politics*. (Macdonald's circle of contributors included an extensive list of European democratic Socialists, including Orwell and Camus. Some *politics* board members, such as George Woodcock and C. Wright Mills, immediately joined the *Dissent* editorial board, while Coser brought in a number of European refugee intellectuals as readers and even contributors.) *Dissent* was also a radical experiment that coincided with the launching of a private Jewish college in New England, Brandeis University, and both it and the magazine grew together during their radical founding years in the 1950s. (Both Howe and Coser were early members of the faculty.) Coser remained an active co-editor throughout the 1950s, but gave way to Michael Walzer in the 1960s and largely bowed out thereafter, except as an occasional contributor. Instead, Howe turned to a younger generation, represented by the participation of Walzer, and later Brian Morton and Mitchell Cohen, as co-editors.

The origins, impetus, and evolution of the magazine are largely beside the point even for many of *Dissent's* critics on the Left. They believe that, however much Howe claimed to reconsider the radical tradition, *Dissent* soon became a boring, tame organ that repeated the sectarian mistakes of 1930s Socialism, notably when it refused to join hands with the New Left in a common program.

Instead it maintained its lonely Third Way course, which vouchsafed it a degree of self-righteous independence at the expense of public influence. *Dissent's* critics at *The Nation,* for instance, hold that it drifted towards liberalism and accommodated itself to the Democratic Party, thereby allowing its edges to be tapered to the extent of losing all the force of its professed critiques.

Howe maneuvered between extremes to maintain both an authentically progressive vision and a plausibly pragmatic editorial policy. Doing it well became an enduring, vexed dilemma for *Dissent.* For Howe, part of *Dissent*'s purpose was to move away from the sectarian past while safeguarding those elements of Socialism consistent with democratic practice. Breaking from a group with which one has deep historical and visceral emotional relations is difficult. Howe's long and multifaceted evolution away from left-wing sectarianism meant repeated, ongoing episodes of disaffiliation, a tugging and tearing at old loyalties. If *Dissent*'s commitment to defend free speech from right-wing assault was easy to reaffirm, its reckoning with the checkered history of Socialist tradition was not. Howe explains: "If you take the magazine in the fifties from another angle, in its reconsideration of Marxism, of Socialism, we were far from being on the offensive. We were querulous, uncertain, we keep stressing the 'problematic'" (Isserman 1982). Nonetheless, Howe fought to distinguish and rescue a Socialism that combined democracy, equality, and human rights from the crimes committed under the banner of state Socialism.

Howe and Coser jointly penned the magazine's manifesto in *Dissent*'s second issue, turning a Tolstoy remark ("God is the name of my desire") into the magazine's credo: "Socialism is the name of our desire."[19] Idealism is, by its nature, misty and abstract, yet without it political discourse ultimately becomes a game of positioning rather than a matter of principle. Indeed, Howe was ultimately less a "political" thinker, let alone a policy wonk or pork-barrel tactician, than a "metapolitical" thinker: largely uninterested in policy (which he associated with Washington bureaucrats, business-as-usual Democratic Party operatives and technocratic liberals), he sought to promote "images" of a better world. In this respect, he was a true literary-political intellectual rather than the figure already coming by the Kennedy-Johnson era to dominate the Washington scene: the policy wonk.[20] Even as *Dissent* became more policy-oriented, Howe kept his eye steadily on the big picture, as the editorials that he wrote for the magazine evince.

In its early years, the primary issue for *Dissent* was to show how the term "Socialism" had been savagely exploited—and to defend the tradition's honor. "We were seeking," Howe recollects, "to rescue the idea or image of Socialism from the horrors of the Gulag, from the lies of the Moscow trials, from the cultural barbarism of 'Socialist realism.' . . . It was the Gulag that discredited the Left, not those of us who told the truth about it" (Cain). To Howe, the moral and political atrocities of the Soviet Union did not reveal the truth about Socialism, but rather functioned as a disastrous disruption misdirecting liberalism and the progressive course of twentieth-century history. With enemies on the left and right, and little support from the center, Howe's mission was a solitary one. Still, the course of independent radicalism that the magazine charted, though difficult, was determined: "We felt beleagured, but we felt good . . . In the fifties we were proud, happy, pleased about it" (Isserman 1982).

Howe avers repeatedly in these interviews that the balancing act performed by *Dissent* was aerobatic, a dance between dissenting from American society and acknowledging the superiority of Western democracy over Stalinist collectivism: "We couldn't say it didn't make any difference who won. The West for all its faults represented democracy, the Russian camp was totalitarian. We were not indifferent to the struggle" (Isserman 1982). If *Dissent* in its early years saw American society as the lesser of two evils, the balance had decisively altered by the outset of the Reagan years. America had become subverted by unconstrained capitalism at home and by expansionist misadventures abroad, though it generally still remained an advocate and ally of freedom. Working from both a Trostkyist sectarianism and from the European Socialist tradition, Howe founded the magazine partly to furnish a hospitable setting for clamorous debate on the left; though he continued to mistrust American individualism, he had begun to step away from the kind of left-wing Eurocentrism that maintained a Marxist orientation. He continued to criticize inequality and social injustice in the U.S. while settling uneasily into a willful, agonized schizophrenia regarding the United States—a divided stance that invited the vituperations fired at him from the Left from the 1960s until his death. Howe remonstrated: "We distinguish sharply between the democratic political structure of America, which is precious, and the socioeconomic arrangements of American capitalism, which we criticize fundamentally" (*NYT* ).

*Dissent*'s attempt to maintain a tradition of Socialism was conducted in somewhat of a vacuum, bereft of a major movement though not in the total absence of political organization. The period's great Socialist organizer, Michael Harrington, was a close colleague of Howe's and a regular contributor to *Dissent.* Howe lauds Harrington's presence in the pantheon of American Socialists: "All of the great leaders of American Socialism have been tribunes. [Eugene] Debs was a tribune, [Norman] Thomas was a tribune, Harrington was a tribune. They were great public spokesmen in that almost Emersonian tradition" (Isserman 1991). The ongoing failure of American Socialism, however, left Harrington, who was both a brilliant organizer and a serious thinker, without an actual movement. Indeed, Howe and Harrington stand in historical hindsight as the last major beacons of social democracy, with Harrington its most important leader and Howe its intellectual voice and cultural eminence. Howe explains that Harrington "believed that in order for the Socialist idea to survive or to grow and prosper there had to be an organization" (Isserman 1991). Similarly, Howe felt the need to found a journal that upheld the tradition in straitened circumstances. Yet Harrington's and Howe's steady, workaday expectation of a leftward resurgence proved illusory. In fact, it continually frustrated them and consumed their energies, ultimately lending their lives something of a "Waiting for Godot" character.

Howe and Harrington did learn from past mistakes, particularly from the failure of orthodox Marxists to formulate detailed plans as to how a Socialist society would actually engage and function. *Dissent* in general, and Harrington in particular, became notable for sophisticated theoretical discussion of economic and policy issues, typically presented in carefully crafted, programmatic documents. Yet most of these statements never had a realistic chance of being implemented. Harrington's *The Other America* (1962) did exert substantial political impact; it is often credited with launching the War on Poverty. Whether and how much influence *Dissent* wielded is unclear; certainly it was read by left-wing policy experts and shaped their decisions, but since the *Dissent* Left represented by the Democratic Socialist Organizing Committee (DSOC) and Democratic Socialists of America (DSA) never attained much prominence in the Democratic Party—let alone came to power—the magazine's ultimate influence on policy matters is difficult to determine.

A political vacuum tempers radical boldness and invites searching reflection. One might say that the Howe of these interviews exemplifies the maturation of the American Left: no longer to let "the best" represent the enemy of "the good;" the latter could be a decent society which, despite its flaws, promised to widen the margin of hope. Here emerges Howe's ambivalence toward "utopia," his wariness that an excessive idealism, as had happened with state Socialism, can easily be perverted. If a limited good mixed with what Howe considered an unsavory side compromised too much, if greater virtue or nobility were demanded, the precise nature of that "more" was murky. Even as he became more politically savvy, however, Howe remained committed to high-minded principles. Although Howe eventually sided with the anti-utopians, insofar as he opposed any collectivist vision that concentrated political and economic power in one center, his temperament was that of a utopian, one who dreams of a better world and seeks to articulate the journey toward that future place.

The quest for "a better world" entailed for Howe a critique of the here-and-now. From the start, *Dissent*'s thrust was not to emphasize the elements of America that worked, but to point out the shortcomings of American society, primarily economic inequality. If the Right harbors a fundamental disdain of social initiatives and organizations, Howe possessed a comparable skepticism toward corporate institutions. Of course, *Dissent* was more than willing to criticize the U.S. government, but the magazine characteristically contrasted it with an idealized polity. In practice, *Dissent* usually acted more to deter liberal democracy from its worst impulses than to advance a thoroughgoing radical critique of advanced capitalism.

Unwilling to let institutional corruption prevail uncontested, whether of the public or private sector, the magazine in effect functioned as part of the

American system of checks and balances: "dissent" was the responsibility of the public intellectual. When the ship of state veers off course, as it inevitably does, oppositional culture provides a rudder to rechart a path toward the social good. Paradoxically, the philosophy of opposition that magazines such as *Dissent* represent, which might appear to undermine a society, actually makes it stronger, enabling its citizenry to expose and root out corrupt practices borne of the arrogance that increasingly infects the powerful. The culture of opposition, then, becomes a crucial part of the institutional balance that the United States Constitution fosters. On this view, the more a magazine such as *Commentary* eschewed criticism of America as it actually functioned, and the closer it moved to accepting (or even celebrating) the United States as it existed, the less it upheld the traditional obligation of a free press: to speak as a critical voice and public conscience.

To be fair, most neoconservatives, at least during Howe's lifetime, regarded themselves both as hard-headed pragmatists ("mugged by reality," in Irving Kristol's phrase) acquiescing to an imperfect world, and as skeptics inoculated by historical experience against an unworkable utopianism exalted by American radicalism. Kristol was an Aristotelian in his conviction that democracy is the worst form of government—except for all the other kinds that have been tried and found wanting. The neoconservatives thus consider themselves eminently pragmatic and willing to honor the evidence of experience and history, which show that American capitalism and political democracy have never succumbed to the evils of Fascism or state Socialism. Kristol and the neoconservatives have never claimed that American capitalism or American democracy are "utopian" in the sense of being the best possible society or economic system. Indeed, the essence of their critique maintains that the striving itself for "the best possible" system invites an unworldly idealism exceeding the capacities of the normal human being, inevitably curdling when the attempt fails, and thereby souring and poisoning the starry-eyed visionaries. Yet the anti-utopianism of the neoconservatives has also tended in practice to slip toward an image of a utopian America. Aware of this irony, Howe argued that his neoconservative contemporaries had become complacent about social inequality, if not actual defenders of such inequality.

During the 1960s, however, *Dissent* adopted not only the role of public critic, but also an additional one: critic of counterculture. It was a thorny job to oppose the culture of opposition, especially in its most fashionable and dangerous guises. Ever since *Dissent*'s founding, the Soviet Union had received this treatment: the magazine frequently editorialized about how the USSR had succumbed to the lures of utopian abstraction, pointing out that one can go back to the French Revolution and witness how a movement that begins by declaiming the rights of man descends into a bloodbath. With the rise of the New Left, Howe saw the risk of still another chapter gone awry in the tortuous history of political radicalism.

Ironically, the turbulence of the 1960s inspired the mass movement that Howe had long been awaiting, a left-wing uprising promising real change of the kind that Howe and his little circle of intellectuals had dreamed. Socialism represented the name of *Dissent*'s desire, but extremism and demagoguery bore the name of its fear. The magazine thus often argued for a measured program akin to those in the social democracies that had emerged in Western Europe. Howe's preference for gradualism stemmed from his view that it was ultimately wiser to build safeguards into a left-wing vision and patiently allow a step-by-step native radicalism to develop. This "steady work" was soon to be challenged.

## Radical Resurgence: Howe and the New Left

Gradualism rarely leads to radical change, which seems to require challenges posed by severe crises or great historical events. Along with fellow social democrat Michael Harrington, Howe had spent years hoping for a new movement. When the mass movement—the New Left—finally arrived, Howe saw it as fraught with danger. Once the blizzard of change had died down, he would spend his last decades wishing for a return of its possibilities. The potential for change in the mid-to-late1960s never issued forth in the systemic, ordered transformation that Howe would have preferred. In a 1984 *New York Times* interview, Howe reiterated the need for change amid a politically quiescent atmosphere reminiscent of the 1950s: "Now we're in an interesting stage where the left has begun to do programmatic work in preparation for what we expect, or hope, will be the next surge forward of American liberalism" (*NYT*). "Programmatic" is a revealing word here. Howe conceived left-wing activism as a matter of promoting a "program," which is the focus of that interview. By sharp contrast, the New Left represented a movement dominated by idealistic youth who had no time whatsoever for what they regarded as the dreary prose of *Dissent* and its boring gradualism.

Howe's belief in a version of parliamentary gradualist Socialism, which owed to his evolution away from radical Socialism and toward social democracy, was out of step with the 1960s. Massive, transformational, social—indeed revolutionary—change is generally accompanied by blood and terror. Yet in bourgeois America of the early 1950s and 1960s, Howe believed, there reigned a spirit of smug conformity, self-righteous apathy, and overbearing self-satisfaction. If it takes crisis to disturb this torpid pleasure, crisis inevitably provikes extremism; the genie released from the bottle is not easy to control, and one's wish may not yield what one expected.

So it happened in the 1960s, when a younger generation lacking much historical awareness gained unexpected influence. Demographics drove the movement: the 1960s witnessed the largest generation of youth ever to enter American society at one time. So too did issues of real social justice inspire it, primarily civil rights. Yet opposition to the Vietnam War—from fear or anxiety or indignation about being sent against one's wishes to fight in a distant, alien country for a cause that one does not necessarily understand or believe in—inflamed revolutionary passions above all.

In July 1963, Howe and members of the *Dissent* editorial board met with leaders of the Students for a Democratic Society (SDS), seeking to find common cause with the New Left. In a charged climate, Howe and the *Dissenters* hoped to furnish a dose of tactical caution and historical perspective. They expected the students to come with a certain degree of humility and even deference, willing to listen to their intellectual and radical elders—such as Howe had done with figures such as Norman Thomas and Max Shachtman, and in later years with Phillip Rahv and Lionel Trilling. Instead a confrontation prevailed. "Apart from the intrinsic political and intellectual differences," Howe recalled about the meeting, "which were serious enough, there was also a clash of generations, and styles, which made it almost inevitable that we wouldn't be able to get along. I wouldn't push the comparison too far, but there are some elements of comparison between the young militants in the SP [Socialist Party] vis a vis the Old Guard in the early thirties. And I suppose we were cast in the role of the Old Guard (although we weren't quite so old, we were in our forties) vis a vis the SDS" (Isserman 1982).

What upset Howe more than anything else was the presumptuous arrogance—in Howe's estimate—of Tom Hayden, whom Howe described as a "commissar." Howe was indignant that Hayden had such little respect for history generally and for the historical experience of Socialists like Howe himself in particular. Instead, Hayden and his colleagues were setting about to reinvent the wheel, rather than draw on the wisdom and experience of the "world of their fathers." Howe himself always had revered that world, both in its Jewish and radical guises; he was aggrieved that the youth of the 1960s could ignore it so blithely.

As the New Left grew more doctrinaire and dogmatic, Howe feared the emergence of populist demagoguery. Memories of Huey Long frightened Howe and reminded him of European Fascism; on the Left, he recalled that shrewd Stalinist rhetoric about "Mother Russia" had galvanized the Russian people to defend the state Communist system during World War II, even though that system had become a nightmare. Howe saw populism, both in its American and European forms, as inevitably vulgar and demagogic in its appeal—and he discerned the same tendencies at work in the rhetoric about "participatory democracy" within the New Left, with its naïve enthusiasm for Castro, Mao, and other third-world revolutionaries. Howe regarded much of this as a replay of the 1930s.

This fear lurks in the background of Howe's controversial essay "New Styles of Leftism" (1965), which castigated the New Left as shallow, individualistic, and lacking in historical perspective. The essay outraged and offended Tom Hayden, Todd Gitlin, and other New Left leaders for decades. These SDS spokesmen lacked the perspective of the *Dissent* crowd, for whom the memory of the USSR's hijacking of "Socialism" burned deep as a traumatic, visceral experience. It was an event that festered in the bones of an older generation who sought to pass on the lessons of history to the young radicals. By the time of the interviews in this collection, Howe was able to discuss his failure to communicate with the New Left, albeit in a sardonic, self-deprecating way: "They felt they were involved in a real mass movement, this tremendous thing sweeping the country, and here's this group of sour, aging old social democratic intellectuals, rigid anti-Communists, etc., etc. What did they need us for?" (Isserman 1982). Howe, of course, felt that they had needed the *Dissent* writers for a proper rearing in the history of American radicalism and the perils of Left sectarianism and extremism. Yet his statement also discloses an ongoing anxiety about his own ineffectual politics. He recognized, uneasily, that the New Left was already a social movement; it didn't need the *Dissenters*' political support or even its paternal blessing.

Not surprisingly, Howe attributed his break with this young generation of leftists to a lack of historical continuity, the very function that *Dissent* had undertaken to perform. "Part of the problem was that there was a missing generation on the non-Communist left," Howe observed. "There was a distance of some twenty years between us. The generation between should have been Harrington's age. The rupture in tradition was something we were paying for very heavily" (Isserman 1982). Ultimately, to the extent that Howe was a "radical intellectual," the emphasis belonged on the noun rather than the adjective. He was a writer passionately interested in history, having already co-authored (with Lewis Coser) a compelling and substantive history of the Communist Party (*The American Communist Party*, 1957). Much of his criticism of the New Left was that they were ill-read and had no knowledge of or even interest in the history of the Left. Conversely, from the viewpoint of the young activists, Howe and his magazine represented the irrelevance of Howe's armchair intellectuality.

Lacking historical perspective, the activists of the 1960s accelerated through a series of ideological stances and developmental stages precipitously. As Howe explains it, "Everything in some way happens too fast. No phase of it can go through a reasonably organic development. The participatory democracy stage lasts two or three years and then it is over with. Now that isn't enough time for people to think it through" (Gitlin). Worse, as the 1960s wore on, a weary, battle-scarred Howe felt himself possessing less energy to remedy this, to engage in the institution-building that might create historical continuity and effective public action. In their wake, Michael Harrington strove valiantly to maintain the radical tradition. In 1973 he formed the Democratic Socialist Organizing Committee (DSOC), which in 1982 became the Democratic Socialists of America (DSA). Harrington remained the leader of the DSA which, since his death in 1989, has exerted slight impact. Rather, the neoconservative renegades from Howe's own group of New York Intellectuals around *Partisan Review*, accumulated abundant resources to found institutions and develop a historical memory of their own.[21]

## Europe or America?

As American neoconservatives, rather than Socialists, became socially respectable and started to influence mainstream American politics, Howe re-examined a distinctly American phenomenon: the individual as social rebel. In 1986, in another long step away from the Eurocentrism shared by his erstwhile fellow Trotskyists among the New York Intellectuals, Howe reconsidered Emerson on the occasion of Harvard's prestigious William E. Massey lecture. Howe had voiced low opinions of Emerson and Thoreau in the 1950s and 1960s, dismissing them as writers representing an individualistic American tradition at odds with an internationalist and Socialist vision. By 1986, however, Howe had begun to revise his judgment, as part of a wider revaluation of American individualism and the protest tradition.

Subsequently published as *The American Newness: Culture and Politics in the Age of Emerson,* Howe's lectures describe an eccentric coterie of fringe Americans: "Emerson surrounded himself with intellectuals—free-lance writers, stray and erratic thinkers, heterodox ministers—who created a fragile avant-garde, probably the first this country has ever had."[22] This motley crew resembles in some aspects the ragtag group of intellectuals who made up *Dissent;* Howe's description also suggests that, by the mid-1980s, he bore a grudging respect even for the freewheeling New Left. By this time, despite *Dissent*'s roots in European Socialism, Howe could also claim a certain kinship with America's more individualist tradition of independent radical thought, as represented by Thoreau and Emerson. In his interview with Susanne Klingenstein, he points out that "the Emersonian tradition has been the basis for the strongest voice of internal criticism and dissent in American culture, that the Emersonian tradition at its best, especially that of the early Emerson—as it has gone through a whole line of American literary and social critics—that this tradition is the fundamental basis for the creation of what we call an adversary culture, a culture which is in opposition to the wrongs of society."

Howe had come to see American transcendentalism as representing something much larger than "individualism" in its early postwar guise. It formed the essential liberal element within his preferred Socialist vision, an element defending the sacrosanct freedom and dignity of the individual in opposition to state collectivism. He came to grant the responsible individual voice in society as an indispensable feature of the "dissenting" tradition, exemplified by essays such as Thoreau's "Civil Disobedience." By the 1980s, Howe realized the inadequacy of relying too heavily on European imports as the basis of a revived American radical thought, particularly in a country with its own vibrant protest tradition. Howe now recognized that Emerson and Thoreau are arguably more useful for understanding the New Left than Marx. Moreover, a deep and long American tradition could also serve as a powerful counterweight to the impressive institution-building of the neoconservatives.

Nevertheless, Howe remained adamantly opposed to America's almost willful ignorance of history, literature, and political and social thought. Emerson was in fact a link to old Europe, he noted, as well as a philosophic exemplar of Americanness. It is, after all, unlikely that many of the New Left leaders whom Howe scorned had much more knowledge of Emerson than they did, say, of Bacon, Locke, or even Orwell. All this reflects the fact that Howe was not primarily opposed to the traditionalist conservatism associated with Edmund Burke, but rather to the ideological neoconservatism that gained power with Ronald Reagan's election. In fact, some cultural conservatives waxed enthusiastic about "Uncle Irving," whom they adopted (with his approval) because they broadly shared a stance of cultural conservatism and a respect for literary and political traditions. Edward Alexander traces Howe's defense of the Western canon to his disgust with 1960s radicalism. "For the sake of radicalism itself," Alexander argues, Howe believed that "the accumulated wisdom of the past has to be treated with respect, even reverence."[23] Howe's respect for history, and his conviction about the need for radicals to understand history, leads him, in Alexander's estimation, to "speak in a markedly conservative manner. The past, he insists, is the very matter upon which the life of the mind subsists."[24] Even though Howe's views on most political and social questions were far to the left of the conservatives, they occupied common ground on many literary and cultural matters.[25]

Howe possessed a notable conservative streak within his radical and liberal temperament. Interestingly, the neoconservatives endorsed Howe's position on the hot-button cultural and literary controversies of the 1980s, such as the debates about the Western canon and related issues in the culture wars. For instance, Alexander lauds Howe's stand against those on the academic Left who saw him as an old fogey. Likewise, Howe made common cause with the emerging neoconservatives in the late 1960s and early 1970s against New Left excesses (at the very time he was distinguishing his positions, especially on economic matters, from former allies such as Irving Kristol). At the same time, Howe also made common cause on cultural matters with the cultural conservatives, such as Russell Kirk and his journal *Modern Age*, founded in 1957 to uphold a traditional conservatism.

All this reflects Howe's strategic flexibility and willingness to join hands with people who otherwise scorned him. The cultural conservatives affiliated with *Modern Age* were also vocal critics of corporate life and numerous features of American capitalism, and in these respects, they sided with Irving Howe rather than the neoconservatives. Howe's accomplishment in the 1980s and 1990s was to withstand a two-front war waged against him, from both the Marxist Left and from the neoconservatives, and he carried off the struggle with aplomb and restraint. This helps account for Howe's broad appeal during his last decade, when his following widened to encompass conservatives, centrists, liberals, and independent radicals. Along with his enduring commitment to a better life for the poor and working class, this broad appeal explains his posthumous reputation in some quarters as "the American Orwell."

Yet this cultural conservatism, together with a central interest in class differences and economics, relegated Howe and *Dissent* once again to a spectator position on the sidelines of a major American left-wing movement, albeit one largely limited to academia: the multicultural ferment in American education during the 1990s. Howe explains: "There are constituencies, different groupings, and especially in the DSA as it went along, one of the things that became boring was you had a feminist constituency and you had the Hispanic, black and the environmentalist, etc., etc. and regional constituencies, and those that felt that New York was getting too much attention, etc. This has been going on since 1903 and it's not over yet" (Isserman 1991). The roots of 1990s multiculturalism and its attendant identity politics are deep and, to Howe, they were annoying and obfuscating.

Certainly Howe's observation here inveighs against that side of ethnic identity politics which tends toward fragmentation and self-indulgent victimization. As his critics on the Left like to point out, however, it also slights very real social grievances and overlooks the multi-layered, hybrid nature of both American and international culture, particularly in the current era of postcolonial and global literature. Howe had similarly derided the orthodoxies of radical feminism from its onset in the 1960s—especially its rigidity and tendency to fragment into purist coalitions. On this score, too, he has been accused of failing to value the progressive possibilities offered by an array of voices and perspectives, or, in the eyes of his harshest critics, of turning his back upon the disenfranchised.

On economic matters, however, Howe refused to compromise his stance to accommodate the new climate, defending in particular the interests of workers and of the poor. Indeed, he saw his defense of education in general, and the canon in particular, as undergirding an authentic radicalism—a thoughtful, well-rooted radicalism that understood the past, and how, where, and why to break from it. As Gerald Sorin observes: "Ignorance of literature and history, Howe insisted, allowed his students to assume that they, and everyone else, were totally free, that through mere exertion of will and intelligence people could make anything they wished of their lives."[26] If such Panglossian rosiness colored much of the thinking of the New Left, it also possessed affinities with Reaganism's blithe optimism, which replaced one kind of naiveté with another. Howe's reflections on America at the height of Reaganism remind one of how much the 1980s changed things, how much they set the tone and agenda for what followed in the Clinton years—the modulated, balanced neoliberalism of the 1990s, with its loss of faith in government and its collusions with corporate power. "One of the things that's happened in this country over the last six or seven years," Howe argued in 1984, "is a loss of social sympathy and a decline of social solidarity, the rise of a very ugly form of 'possessive individualism' which can be summed up by the slogan,

'I've got mine, Jack'" (*NYT*). The "possessive individualism" that Howe abhorred was something that he directly associated with the neoconservatives and their emphasis on capitalism.

Reaganism, then, came to represent for Howe a ruggedly individualistic, capitalistic version of America. Yet Howe's treatment of individualism was quintessentially idiosyncratic. Conceding a partial respect for the New Left, he is flattering about what he regards as "individualism" within the tradition of Emerson and Thoreau. But he uses the same word in his severe critiques of the neoconservatives, never distinguishing which elements in these two traditions provoke his admiration and contempt. Such a distinction is pertinent insofar as the Emersonian tradition prized a social individualism that allowed one to be unconventional and dissenting, whereas the economic individualism of the neoconservatives affirms a market-oriented capitalism that appalled Howe as nothing more than a dressed-up form of greed. Howe had scant esteem for Emerson until late in his career—he associated "Emersonian individualism" with contemporary economic issues, holding that it necessarily ran counter to communitarianism. But with the ascendancy of the neoconservatives, Howe saw that Emerson was quite different both from them and from Howe's stereotype of him: the distinction between social and economic individualism seems to have become apparent to Howe, and he highly valued the former.

Still, Howe's tempered Socialism evolved by the 1980s more in response to the Right than to the Left. Partly chafing against the neoconservatives, partly acknowledging the shortcomings of Lyndon Johnson's Great Society programs that had attacked poverty and racism, and partly aspiring to a wider audience in a conservative decade, Howe adopted the oxymoronic phrase "market Socialism." Ironically, Eastern European Communist governments were also bandying this phrase by the 1980s. For instance, the East Germans felt that they had to introduce many elements of the market because planned government was simply an economic failure. And so, both in the American capitalist context and in the Eastern European Communist context, the phrase was embraced for reasons of expediency and with an eye toward gaining broader support. Howe explains: "In a market-Socialist society, you would have an increasing tendency toward economic egalitarianism. This doesn't mean everyone would receive exactly the same pay or have exactly the same amount of money. But the gross and growing inequalities of income and wealth that characterize capitalist society today would be gradually leveled down" (Holt). While acknowledging the individualist ethic deep within America's history and the robust economy generated by mixed capitalism, Howe insists also on investing it with a communitarian accent and a utopian impulse: "And there would be evolution toward a social ethic of cooperation rather than the mad greediness and destructiveness that we have witnessed in America in the last decade" (Holt).

## Howe's Past and America's Future

The direction in the new millennium both in America and globally has been away from such a cooperative ethic and instead toward a corporate ethic advanced under the banner of neoliberalism and "globalization." This trend is interpreted as a movement toward fair competition in the eyes of those who support it, while its critics regard it as a form of corporate self-enrichment for a tiny minority of the world's population. On this view, globalization reflects not the social individualism of the Emersonian or Thoreauvian rebel, but the economic individualism of CEOs and international bankers (combined, in the United States, with a strangely discordant Christian fundamentalism). This ethos has come to dominate today's political discourse, though the government safety net introduced by the New Deal and Great Society has been only partially dismantled. From today's standpoint, Howe's critique of the political and social culture of the 1980s rings prescient: "And conventional politicians are beginning to feel uneasy about the disintegration of political life, the ascendancy of money in campaigns, and the reduction of political discourse to these crude and empty thirty second 'sound bites'" (Holt). Of course, what was an emerging current three decades ago has today become a way of life. "Conventional politicians" are no longer "beginning to feel uneasy" about all those things—rather, they acquiesce to them all as the norm of political life.

American society today springs in manifold respects from the Reaganism against which Howe bristled. True, George W. Bush unexpectedly emerged as a radical activist of the Right who became anathema to many conservative admirers of Reagan. Yet the world today is also a quite different place than in Reagan's time. Corporate globalization is far more advanced, having rushed in to fill the vacuum left by the death of Communism. This is a very different kind of internationalism than Socialism had once predicted, and it was well under way by the end of Howe's life. Already in 1989, as Howe points out, "in the Dominican Republic, a Socialist government recently faced riots because the I.M.F. forced it to accept a bankers' 'discipline' and raise the price of food and other necessities. In this setup, money is more sovereign than independent governments" (*NYT*). Ten years later, this form of globalization was to spark a new, albeit brief, activist eruption in the 1999 Seattle protests and subsequent picketing of the World Trade Organization ministerial meeting. By 2003, the movement had morphed into widespread protests against the imminent Iraq invasion.

Ironically, Todd Gitlin, one of the SDS activists with whom Howe had clashed in 1963, advocated moderation in his 2003 response to the radical elements among the antiwar protesters. Warning that even a few violent extremists can sabotage a nascent protest movement, Gitlin argues in *Letters to a Young Activist:* "You will probably do more good if you accept that history is a Mobius strip—that the topside turns into the underside, that the romance of the revolution to end all revolutions is as dangerous as it is delusional."[27] Chastened by the long reaction against the 1960s, Gitlin here takes on Howe's earlier role, remembering that when "*our* elders lectured us on the virtues of moderation we didn't listen to them. We thought they were tired, stuck, timid and reconciled."[28]

A movement is only as powerful, however, as the mass media and the general public will grant. While extremist activists undercut themselves with an anti-Americanism that forestalls a wider appeal, more important is the circus-like media that effectively disperses or defangs all opposition, as in the repeated playing of Howard Dean's infamous scream. At a moment when the Left has been showing signs of life, it has been undermined by a broad consensus between the mainstream press and the Right, often orchestrated by its well-organized, disciplined institutions. Since the unrest of the 1960s and 1970s, the conservatives did the necessary organizational work, the often humdrum, laborious tasks of forging a movement rather than simply coasting on popular dissatisfaction. For the Left, the predictable result recurred: once the external causes of mass unrest such as anti-Vietnam War sentiment disappear, so too does public dissatisfaction—and the movement riding it thus also dissolves. By contrast, today's Right, spurred on by the neoconservatives, has rejected classic conservative views of limited government and instead employed government in a concerted project to remake history, all of which upsets old-fashioned, traditionalist conservatives.

America today is a land of extremes far from even Ronald Reagan's conception (via Norman Rockwell) of "Morning in America," let alone Howe's radical ideal of a "united" States sharing a common vision. As the protests in the spring of 2003 during the start of the Iraq war made clear, little sign of Howe's sort of melioristic politics exists nowadays. Instead a timid, centrist Democratic Party and a tiny, yet loud, radical Left prevail. Like the New Left, the latter may be capable, in a crisis, of stirring crowds of thousands for mass protests, but it is unable to guide a social movement toward achievable political goals.

Gone is the era of Norman Thomas—Howe's hero and the leader of the Socialist Party in the 1930s and 1940s.[29] "Socialism" remains a thoroughly discredited term today in mainstream America, and even "liberal" has acquired a widespread stigma. Most old-time liberals, now often calling themselves progressives, have become somber. They turn out dutifully when necessary, but the old fire is gone. Perhaps this signifies a maturing awareness of what is actually possible. Or perhaps it reflects a spirit of despair. Howe himself had trouble getting excited about *Dissent's* latter-day platform. "The welfare state doesn't stir the imagination of apocalypse or violent extremism," he explains in an interview with himself, "but it is part of that steady process of social transition, a sort of 'long march' in and through democracy that is central to the Socialist project" (Howe). This is what Howe referred to as his "steady work," and it comprised the essence of his gradualist, parliamentary Socialism—or what was in practice a form of social democracy. He fully admitted that his magazine was sometimes lackluster, and here emerged the tension between utopian idealism and pragmatic policymaking. Howe realized that a vision of utopia could generate impassioned support. But it could not last or build institutions. He distrusted populism. He remained a utopian by temperament and in literary-cultural matters, but his explicitly political vision turned anti-utopian: he warned against abstract systems that invested power in one set of hands. And he ultimately embraced an Emersonian style of social individualism counter to the populist collectivism that had aroused his fervor in the 1930s. He supported instead a politics that promoted social peace, productivity, egalitarianism, and stability.

Such a vision demanded an organizational politics for its realization. *Dissent* was Howe's attempt across the decades to combine principled idealism with practical politics, and it is a tribute to his endurance and energy that he managed it so well. *Dissent* is distinguished as being the oldest radical magazine in continuous publication in the English-speaking world, now in its sixth decade. That extraordinary feat has been achieved on a shoestring budget. And for its first forty years, this accomplishment was largely due to the efforts of Irving Howe.

Still, in today's West, commitments to a radically egalitarian society are relegated to small corners. In actual politics, such arrangements remain institutionalized in a few social democratic societies that command relatively little attention. For instance, Chile's centrist version of democratic Socialism has led to the most dynamic economy in South America, a continent where uninhibited free trade agreements have proved disastrous. Yet media attention mainly goes to the roar and thunder of leaders such as Hugo Chavez, during his presidency of Venezuela, much as it did to the extremes of the New Left. Elsewhere on the globe, the heritage of democratic Socialism remains checkered, as it was at the end of Howe's life. And a still deeper, idealistic version of a Socialism that would transform human nature, in which individuals temper their acquisitiveness to build a more just world, is nowhere on the horizon.

Speaking about the death of Michael Harrington, Howe grew pensive: "I'm even wondering about the [survival of the very] idea of Socialism. Namely that [Harrington] began to see Socialism as increasingly problematic. As a possible historical option but further and further off, not as an immediate possibility" (Isserman 1991). Howe also worried about Harrington's historical legacy: "If there is any kind of continuing Socialist tradition, which is problematic, yes, he will be remembered" (Isserman 1991).

Howe was likely thinking also of himself here. He lived a life of enormous productivity and notable accomplishment, winning a degree of recognition that most would judge a huge success. But history's verdict might be that it all comes to naught. As Joseph Epstein once expressed it, sternly yet perhaps accurately: "Almost everything he did of a political nature will be forgotten."[30] Not only Howe's conservative critics express this conviction about the leading *Dissenters*. When Maurice Isserman's biography of Michael Harrington appeared in 2000, the liberal social critic Alan Wolfe wrote that Harrington would most likely be "forgotten," indeed that his prodigious energies invested in a marginalized American Socialism were spent in vain.[31] Nonetheless, if they would read him, Howe has much to teach young activists and intellectuals today. They could benefit from his example across a half-century of brilliant criticism and durable engagement in organizational politics.

With the strong reaction against the Iraq war and the Reagan coalition of the 1980s fragmenting, the intellectual energy that has long fueled the Right seems to have dissipated. The opportunity seems ripe for the first mass movement on the Left since the 1960s, and it is just conceivable that the Left might learn from its past mistakes. Might a widening margin of hope render Howe's vision compelling and fresh once again? Could his work help to launch a "New New Left" more historically aware than its predecessor? It will not happen without patience and effort, for it depends on enough people believing in an "image of Socialism" and in the practice of "steady work." Yet perhaps reading Howe might begin to help young radicals in a nascent movement adopt the best features of both the Old and New Lefts.

For that to happen, Howe's "steady work" must not only be perused but also practiced. And yet, perhaps tomorrow's activists may be even less inclined than the SDS leaders to engage in thoughtful historical study. Chastened by experience, much of the current progressive movement seems more pragmatic, but it is still short on political perseverance and historical knowledge. Howe believed that unless the Left learns that those who refuse to learn from the past repeat its mistakes, all the work of *Dissent* will collapse into dust and ashes. Here again, for any kind of wiser, balanced radicalism to emerge, the emphasis must fall equally on both "radical" and "intellectual." And that means that history must also be emphasized, including the dissident history in which Irving Howe played such a central role for much of the twentieth century.

## Notes

1. Irving Howe, *A Margin of Hope* (San Diego: Harcourt Brace Jovanovich, 1982), 344.
2. See Alexander Cockburn, "Irving Howe RIP, A Few Tasteless Words," in *Irving Howe and the Critics: Celebrations and Attacks*, ed. John Rodden (Lincoln: University of Nebraska Press, 2005), 62-63.
3. See Kristol's *Commentary* letter, collected in *The Worlds of Irving Howe: The Critical Legacy*, ed. John Rodden (Boulder: Paradigm, 2005), 188-91.
4. Midge Decter, "Socialism and Its Irresponsibilities: The Case of Irving Howe," *Commentary* (December 1982): 30.
5. Hilton Kramer, "Irving Howe: 'Socialism is the Name of Our Desire,'" *The Twilight of the Intellectuals: Culture and Politics in the Era of the Cold War* (Chicago: Ivan R. Dee, 1999), 151. The essay is from the *New Criterion* and is reprinted in *The Worlds of Irving Howe*, 307-11.
6. Irving Howe and Kristol, "The New York Intellectuals," *The Worlds of Irving Howe*, ed. John Rodden, 193.
7. Edward Alexander, *Irving Howe: Socialist, Critic, Jew* (Bloomington: Indiana University Press, 1998), 244.

8. Gerald Sorin, *Irving Howe: A Life of Passionate Dissent* (New York: New York University Press, 2002), xiv.
9. Personal motivation is, of course, only a small part of a much larger Socialist vision. Speaking of the early *Partisan Review,* and its attempt to wed modernist culture to Socialism, James Gilbert writes: "To H. G. Wells, who influenced many early Socialist writers, the advance of Socialism included in the widest sense 'all science, literature and invention.' The reconstruction of society would usher in a new culture, a new literature and art, but there was no certainty at first about the nature of this culture except that it should be modern." *Writers and Partisans: A History of Literary Radicalism in America* (1968; repr., New York: Columbia University Press, 1992), 9.
10. Irving Howe, "Two Cheers for Utopia," *Fifty Years of Dissent,* Nicolaus Mills and Michael Walzer, eds. (New York: Foundation for the Study of Independent Social Ideas, 2004), 249.
11. See John Rodden, "Irving Howe: Triple Thinker," in *Irving Howe and the Critics,* 10-11.
12. See *The Radical Imagination*, ed. Irving Howe (New York: Harcourt, 1967).
13. Irving Howe, "Two Cheers for Utopia," *Fifty Years of Dissent,* Nicolaus Mills & Michael Walzer, Eds. (New York: Foundation for the Study of Independent Social Ideas, 2004), 250.
14. See John Rodden, "Irving Howe: Triple Thinker," in *Irving Howe and the Critics,* 1-26.
15. Forged in the setting of small ideological sects, Howe's political and administrative stance was impossible to reconcile with Macdonald's. Macdonald never contributed even a single piece to *Dissent.* He criticized Howe on many occasions for editing what Macdonald considered a tepid and tedious policy-oriented magazine utterly different in spirit from the freewheeling *politics.*
16. See Irving Howe, *Leon Trotsky* (New York: Fontana, 1978).
17. See John Rodden, "Irving Howe: Triple Thinker," *Irving Howe and the Critics,* 1-26. For instance, Ian Williams castigates Howe for his "romance" with Trotsky and views it as a major weakness in Howe's later work that inhibited his capacity to fully appreciate the tragedy of Socialism in the late 1980s, because he conflated it with Communism—even though he explicitly condemned Stalinism throughout his career. See "An Ex-Maoist Looks at an Ex-Trotskyist: On Irving Howe's *Leon Trotsky*" in Rodden, *Irving Howe and the Critics,* 37-47.
18. Edward Alexander praises Howe's *Leon Trotsky* as achieving "a rare balance between praise and detraction, admiration and tough-minded criticism of the man who became Lenin's accomplice and Stalin's foe." *Irving Howe: Socialist, Critic, Jew.* (Bloomington: Indiana University Press, 1998), 193. While not entirely satisfied, Alexander believes that the book largely redeems the "hubris [that] had once been Irving Howe's" in his youthful support of Trotsky and justification of his brutality (194). Gerald Sorin makes a similar argument regarding *Leon Trotsky*: "But Trotsky was a political failure, Howe said, who refused to rethink revolutionary Marxist-Leninism even in the face of its ugly realities." Trotsky's orthodoxy and ultimate rigidity caused him to remain blind to "the most precious values of modern society—individual liberties and freedom from coercion." *Irving Howe: A Life of Passionate Dissent.* (New York: New York University Press, 2002), 271.
19. Lewis Coser and Howe, Irving Howe, "Images of Socialism," *Dissent* 1 (1954): 122.

20. Although Howe served with distinction as vice chairman on the Democratic Socialist Organizing Committee (DSOC), and along with Michael Harrington formulated some concrete policy proposals for introducing certain Socialist mechanisms into American capitalism, his basic role in the DSOC was to promote a vision of a better, a.k.a. Socialist, society. Even his most programmatic essays in *Steady Work* (1967) and in his uncollected *Dissent* essays were journalistic pieces that he seldom reprinted.
21. Russell Jacoby attributes much of this conservative intellectual success to a willingness to address a broad audience relatively straightforwardly and in plain-spoken language: "Unlike left academics, more easily seduced by professional journals, jargon, and life, the conservatives are committed to lucid prose; for this reason they are readable and are read." *The Last Intellectuals: American Culture in the Age of Academe* (1987; New York: Basic Books 2000), 198.
22. Irving Howe, *The American Newness: Culture and Politics in the Age of Emerson* (Cambridge, Harvard University Press, 1986), 15.
23. Edward Alexander, *Irving Howe: Socialist, Critic, Jew* (Bloomington: Indiana University Press, 1998), 145.
24. Ibid.
25. See Samuel Hux, "Uncle Irving," in Rodden, *Irving Howe and the Critics*, 48-56.
26. Gerald Sorin, *Irving Howe: A Life of Passionate Dissent* (New York: New York University Press, 2002), 184.
27. Todd Gitlin, *Letters to a Young Activist* (New York: Basic Books, 2003), 40.
28. Ibid., 64.
29. See John Rodden, "Irving Howe: Triple Thinker," *Irving Howe and the Critics*, 1-26.

    Many cultural critics believe that the capacity to study and learn from the past, and certainly to read and follow the arguments of longer works, is diminishing in our video age. Ilan Stavens, for instance, argues: "Truth is, the age in which ideas matter is long gone, and with it the responsibility of intellectuals to verbalize, to ponder, to force upon people's consciousness those ideas. Science and technology advance at such speed today that the arts and social sciences seem to have a difficult time keeping up." "On Lionel Trilling" in *The Essential Ilan Stavans* (New York: Routledge, 2000), 113. Alan Wolfe connects the phenomenon of the shrinking public sphere to an increasing international consumerism: "The global triumph of capitalism is good for people who want to share the joys of consumption, but not for nurturing the questions of intellectuals, who thrive on opposition to what everyone else takes for granted." *An Intellectual in Public* (Ann Arbor: University of Michigan Press, 2003), 378.
30. Personal conversation between Epstein and John Rodden, Evanston, IL, November 2006.
31. Alan Wolfe,"Sects in the City," *The New Republic*, 3 April 2000: 34-38.

# Chapter 1

**William Novak, "The Lost Worlds of Our Fathers and of Yiddish Literature," *Moment*, March 1976, 24-27.**

## Introduction

*World of Our Fathers* (1976) marked the culmination of a long evolution in Howe's career, from a Trotskyist who fervently supported an international Socialism that eclipsed his own Jewish background to a literary intellectual and pioneering scholar of *Yiddishkeit*, the culture of Yiddish-speaking East European Jews, whose upbringing and history were integral to Howe's identity. Although Howe's early stance as a Marxist revolutionary had been extreme enough for him to describe World War II as a capitalist, imperialist struggle, he was to look back years later aghast at the ideological rigidity of his youthful writings.

Yet even as early as 1946, with his first published book review in the *Partisan Review*, Howe's treatment of Yiddish author Sholom Aleichem furnished a glimpse of another Irving Howe, the young man whose childhood in New York's distinctly Jewish Lower East Side was animated by a verbal pathos and brave fatalism characteristic of the East European *shtetl*. The young Howe privileged his political life over his Jewish roots and his personal life, a bifurcation then apparent in much of Jewish intellectual life. As Howe matured, he would become a champion of Yiddish literature, most notably in co-editing (with Eliezer Greenberg) *A Treasury of Yiddish Stories* (1954), a landmark collection that introduced a hitherto unexplored literary world to an American audience. As Howe points out in this interview, Jewish intellectual life in the 1950s had been moving toward "a confrontation with the fact of being Jewish which for various reasons—chiefly our aspirations to worldliness—we had suppressed." *World of Our Fathers* moved from this literary genre to a more direct grappling with Howe's heritage. In doing so it struck a nerve in a Jewish community struggling to keep some kind of connection to its past, becoming Howe's first and only best seller and transforming him—for his allotted (in late 1976 and early 1977) fifteen minutes—into a minor celebrity.

Yet as some critics, particularly neoconservative ones, have pointed out, *World of Our Fathers* paints a picture of the Jewish immigrant community slanted toward Howe's humanism and Socialism. Alvin Rosenfeld takes this critique one step further, arguing that Howe neglects both Judaism as a religion and identification with Israel, "the two most encompassing cultural forces in American Jewish life in the post-Holocaust years."[1] Rather, Howe is a proponent of a fading secular Jewish culture. In this interview, Howe acknowledges his biases, admitting that he left much out, that "histories tend to be written by people like myself who are secularists." Of course, any work must have its emphasis, and *World of Our Fathers* reflects Howe's own first-generation experience in New York, his family's debt to the union movement, and his impassioned involvement with Socialist politics.

If Howe explains here that his interest in Jewish Socialism was one antecedent for the book, he also discusses how his earlier anti-Zionist radicalism had given way by the 1970s to a deep concern for Israel's welfare and survival. This trend may be traced backward to Jean-Paul Sartre's *Anti-Semite and Jew,* published in English in 1948, which provoked a controversy regarding anti-Semitism as a shaping influence in Jewish identity. According to Edward Alexander, "'Jewishness' was now at least recognized as a subject of serious inquiry. Howe was forced to admit to himself that his earlier failure to face Jewish problems candidly had made him one of Sartre's 'inauthentic' Jews."[2] In Howe's case, as with many secular Jews, such negative prods may have been just as important as cultural and religious feelings in leading to rethinking Jewish identity. For Howe, another catalyst was the controversy over Hannah Arendt's *Eichmann in Jerusalem* (1963), which its critics charged with partly blaming the Jews for their fate in the Holocaust. Howe explains that the debate "forc[ed] us into a confrontation with the fact of being Jewish which for various reasons—chiefly our aspirations to worldliness—we had suppressed."

Important as the Arendt controversy was in American (and indeed international) cultural politics, we should not attribute excessive social significance to it; the founding and precarious existence of the state of Israel demanded by the 1960s such a rethinking. Still, Howe would never become a Zionist, and he continued to criticize Israeli policies with which he disagreed. Not Israel and its fate or promise, but rather the deepening Jewish-American nostalgia for a fading world, along with a childhood and youth that Howe and his generation of Jews could not escape, constitute the recurring themes of *World of Our Fathers.* Minus Judaism, however, Jewish culture is an indistinct, protean, sometimes amorphous phenomenon. Both the secular Yiddish world generally, and a fragile Yiddish language caught between cultures in particular, form poignant examples. Howe acknowledges this fragility in this interview: "It's clear that the last remnants of that experience, and of Yiddish, the language of that experience, are coming to an end."

This interview first appeared in *Moment*, an independent, eclectic, secular magazine of Jewish affairs founded in 1975 by Elie Wiesel and Leonard Fein. Covering a wide spectrum of viewpoints, *Moment* is still in publication and remains culturally influential. It is significant that it featured Irving Howe as it was emerging as a prominent voice of secular Jewishness. William Novak, who conducted this interview, was *Moment*'s executive editor during 1975-77, which implied the quasi-official editorial approval of Howe's work by the magazine.[3]

Both in its timing and subject matter, this interview is distinctive. Of Irving Howe's great loves—politics, literature, and Jewish culture—it exclusively addresses the last. In the immediate aftermath of the success of *World of Our Fathers*, Howe's Jewish voice becomes predominant here. The interview reflects Howe's brief celebrity and his status before the Jewish-American public as a widely acknowledged spokesman of American Jewry and the Yiddish tradition.

## The Interview

*Irving Howe's new book,* World of Our Fathers *(which is reviewed elsewhere in this issue) has just been published to critical acclaim. The book is a broad and sweeping account of the lives of those European Jews who emigrated to America and settled in New York's Lower East Side around the turn of the century. Irving Howe, who has been editor of* Dissent *during the two decades of that magazine's existence, has published countless books, articles, and anthologies on politics, culture, and literature. Still,* World of Our Fathers *is likely to stand as one of Howe's two or three most significant contributions to American and Jewish culture. The conversation took place in November at Mr. Howe's home in New York.*

**Q:** *How did you come to write this book?*

**A:** It was the culmination of a great many different interests and experiences. It brought together my interest in Yiddish literature, in Socialism in America, which to a large extent also means Jewish Socialism, and my interest in the whole nature of the life that I've lived, the past out of which I've come—the experience of the East European immigrant Jews. The older I become, the more it is clear to me that things which have previously seemed disparate or unconnected are very deeply connected. For example, the particular milieu with which I've been associated in American literary-intellectual life, the New York Intellectual community, is something that one cannot understand apart from a grasp of the East European immigrant Jewish experience. You cannot understand it only in those terms, but you have to understand the world out of which these people came in order to gain some sense of what happened to them later on.

So the book was a kind of summa for me, a bringing together of a whole range of interests and experiences. And it was something else. I began to feel that more and more I was dealing with a lost world. When I say this, my friends in the Yiddish movement, including Yiddish writers, become angry, and I suspect this is not because they think I'm telling a lie, but because they fear that it's the truth, which is a painful thing. But it's clear that the last remnants of that experience, and of Yiddish, the language of that experience, are coming to an end.

**Q:** *I don't think you answered the question. You told me, in retrospect, how the book came to be written. But I want to know how this book came out of the Irving Howe whose primary interests seem to be literary criticism and American politics. Except for your translations from the Yiddish, this is your first Jewish book. Why?*

**A:** That's a good question, but it isn't easy to answer. You're asking me to be in touch with the deepest motives of my life, and there's no reason to suppose that I'm any more successful at that than other people are. I'll put it this way: my interest in Jewish things on a cultural level has steadily increased. I've now been working with Eliezer Greenberg for more than twenty years on various anthologies of Yiddish literature in translation. Currently, we're doing still another one on Soviet Yiddish writers. And I've willy-nilly become a kind of Yiddish writer myself—a Yiddish writer who writes in English. I really can't write in Yiddish and Yiddish writers would vouch for that. But I've become a sort of cousin to them and a friend to a number of them. I feel a very strong kinship with them, mostly through Greenberg, but also with others, such as the late Jacob Glatstein.

Another reason, of course, for my increased sense of Jewishness is through my increasing interest in Israel. I've never been a Zionist in any ideological sense, and I'm not one now, but it's perfectly clear that for me and many other people, the sense of concern for Israel has increased very sharply over the past decade. And this necessarily forced a confrontation with some of my earlier assumptions. I had to gradually reject some of the ideas from the Socialism of my youth with regard to Zionism; many of those ideas were quite wrong. For me Socialism meant Marxism, and it was in direct opposition—or so I thought—to Zionism.

After the establishment of the state of Israel, though, my anti-Zionism became moderated into non-Zionism. People like me were impressed by Israel's democratic nature. People could speak freely there. And that's another way I was moved toward the book.

But I think there's something else, too. As one gets older, one is more and more drawn to ask oneself about sources, about the basis of one's life, to search for "roots," if you'll pardon my use of that cant expression. One wants to know what makes one different from, say, other American intellectuals who are gentiles, professors of English. And yet at every moment one is aware that one is different.

I think for many of us a crucial turning point was the furious debates that occurred in New York intellectual life over Hannah Arendt's book on the Eichmann trial (*Eichmann in Jerusalem*, 1963). You'll remember that the debate over that book had a ferocity, an intensity, that I can't remember experiencing since the late thirties in the debates over Stalinism. My sense of it is that, for many of us on both sides of that debate, what was really at stake was that the book, for good or bad, was forcing us into a confrontation with the fact of being Jewish, which for various reasons—chiefly our aspirations to worldliness—we had suppressed. The issues raised by the Arendt book were so explosive that it turned us back to the Holocaust and from there to the basic facts of Jewish identity.

The debate over the book was among American intellectuals; the interesting thing is that the Jewish community barely reacted to the debate. It was intellectually helpless. It was the so-called alienated intellectuals, those whom rabbis find convenient to scorn, who really launched a major attack on this book. They had the equipment to attack it.

So I suppose from all of that my book emerged, from some kind of effort at self-discovery.

**Q:** *Still, yours was no ordinary book, and you bit off quite a mouthful in starting to work on it.*

**A:** The original scheme was that the book would be half its present size; but my editor was willing to accept it when it came in at 1,300 manuscript pages. He didn't flinch and the cutting was infinitesimal. If I had known then what I know now I would never have undertaken it, because of its size. It took about seven years to write, although during most of that time I was doing other things.

**Q:** *What were the major sources for your research?*

**A:** We used a number of sources, and the most important of these was the Yiddish press, which was enormously helpful but not always entirely accurate. The *Jewish Daily Forward* was an absolute gold mine. There were many people writing for the *Forward* in its early years who were really sociologists, although they wouldn't have used that word. They had an eye for provided sociological generalizations, and the book could easily have been three or four times longer.

**Q:** *So the problem was that you had too much source material.*

**A:** Well, on some items there was no end to source material, although on others we weren't able to find enough. On economic matters, for instance, there was never enough. The Yiddish press and the Yiddish world in general had only a very rudimentary sense of statistics and economics.

**Q:** *Even with their strong Socialist tradition?*

**A:** You have to remember that their Socialism was pretty elementary, and it usually sufficed to say that the workers were suffering. The idea of gathering statistics on wages, or housing conditions [never occurred to them]. The economic part of the book is, accordingly, one of its weaker sides.

**Q:** *Many people have a picture of the Lower East Side as a warm, colorful, and happy place. Is this a true image?*

**A:** I hadn't assumed that it was such a warm, carefree place to begin with. The images that you get from people like Harry Golden are, well, pretty golden. One of the things that upset me was the discovery of how bad things were in the 1880s and 1890s. Most writing about the Lower East Side tends to blur the distinction, which I think is very important, if perhaps exaggerated a little in the book, between the early period, 1880-1904, and the later period, starting in 1905. The eighties and nineties were like the opening years of the pioneer period in American life, years of terrible suffering, cultural deprivation. . . . The people who came over at first were not among the most cultured Jews; the intelligentsia did not come until later, after the turn of the century. The Bundists, for instance, who became the leadership of the Jewish trade unions, did not come until later. I draw a pretty sharp line of difference in the book between the two periods.

As other scholars have pointed out, the Jews who came in the 1880s and nineties had lost touch with their culture, and there was a serious rupture between the immigrant life of the end of the last century and life back in Eastern Europe—and what happens in the early years of the twentieth century is a partial re-integration of East European Jewish culture and American culture.

**Q:** *How Jewish were the Jews of the Lower East Side?*

**A:** We have to remember that a good many of these people were observant, and that the histories tend to be written by people like myself who are secularists. There's always the temptation to ignore the extent to which many of them were religious. But the distinction which we're inclined to make between observant and nonobservant is probably overdrawn. Many of the immigrants who came over, in both periods, were a little observant and also a little radical, or half-religious and half-Socialist. Only minorities were totally religious or totally radical. A great many were in-between.

**Q:** *One of the delightful sections of your book is the part about the lives of children.*

**A:** One of the things that struck me as interesting was the tension between home and street. The street was really the great Americanizing agency. We must never underestimate the shrewdness of our not terribly well-educated parents and grandparents. They understood, even if they couldn't put it into words, that the street was the agency that would take their kids away from them, and so they resisted the street. The schools offered the same threat, of course, but there the parents were willing to pay the price. But they were trapped. If they gave their kids to the schools, they couldn't also keep them off the streets.

**Q:** *But how did they fight the street if the parents were working?*

**A:** Well, mother is home. The image of women working applies mostly to younger women, most often before they were married. Mother would say, "Don't go down and become a bum." Sometimes the kids would listen. Music lessons, reading, Hebrew school all helped. These things, in my opinion, existed not only for their own sake, but also to fight the street. It's hard to say if this was consciously expressed or understood. Resistance to the street means staying away from vulgarity and danger—the famous joke: "You'll go downstairs, catch cold, and I'll die."

Although the other kids on the street were mostly Jewish, they were thought to be less refined. Sex would rear its head, and that's something Jewish parents found very hard to cope with, often ignoring it. Immigrant parents were shy, even puritanical, on this whole subject; they didn't know how to cope with it. Necking on the roof or in the park—parents didn't know how to handle this. The street really was the enemy of the home.

**Q:** *And were there also Jewish street gangs?*

**A:** Yes, although they tended to be less violent than their gentile counterparts. One of the better sources for this subject, by the way, is Eddie Cantor's autobiography. Eddie Cantor in his youth was very close to being a juvenile delinquent. And there are some things about street gangs in the Yiddish press.

**Q:** *I'd like to turn the discussion to the Jewish community of New York in our own time. In 1973 you wrote an article for* New York Magazine *entitled "Thinking the Unthinkable About Israel." It was widely quoted and commented upon, and I get the impression that at that moment you entered into the discussion with and on behalf of the American Jewish community in a way that represented a new direction for you.*

**A:** Yes, that was important. My expression of concern for Israel was not new personally, although this was the time I chose to make it public. I think the article's effectiveness depended upon the sense of horror that many people had that a second act of the Holocaust might take place in Israel.

**Q:** *I don't think it was a new position for you, but it was one that you hadn't made publicly before, and I believe that it liberated many Jews, especially intellectuals, to talk about this subject more openly.*

**A:** Yes, and here, whatever strong disagreements I've had with Norman Podhoretz, I do share with him a very strong sentiment against what might be called Jewish repressiveness, or Jewish gentility. If you want to scream and yell, you should feel free to scream and yell. Even if the gentiles don't like it.

**Q:** *There seems to be a general consensus that American Jewry has veered dramatically to the right in recent years. Do you agree that it has?*

**A:** There's no question about it. I tried to understand the phenomenon a couple of years ago in an article I wrote for *Dissent* with Bernard Rosenberg. We tried to discover whether the Jewish connections with liberalism were coming to an end. And the conclusions we reached were that the identification itself was not coming to an end, but that the content of that identification is changing. The sense of what the Jewish community means by liberalism is becoming a little more conservative, a little more cautious. But it is difficult to see how a secular Jewish community could abandon its commitment to liberalism.

**Q:** *But now we are developing a more articulate and more sophisticated understanding of self-interest. And sometimes it seems to conflict with the basic principles of liberalism.*

**A:** Then you've got a problem, and you've got to use your brains. You decide at which point one or the other is more important. All of life is full of conflicts of values.

**Q:** *Has there ever been a time for American Jewry when liberalism and self-interest were so sharply in conflict?*

**A:** I don't think they are so sharply in conflict. By and large the tradition of liberalism is in harmony with the general positions of Jews. I use the word "liberalism" pretty loosely to include my sense of Socialist politics as well.

**Q:** *And how does that liberalism affect the issues that face Jews today?*

**A:** One example is affirmative action. I agree with Leonard Fein's article in *Midstream,* a few years back, which argued that it's possible to support affirmative action in a way that does not conflict with Jewish self-interest. I don't think, as some people do, that it runs directly against the Jewish interest.

But support for Israel is a much more crucial matter. If there were a political candidate with whom I agreed on most domestic political issues but who was weak on Israel, then I would not find it possible to support him. And I should mention that although I supported McGovern[4] last time, it turned out that his record on Israel was nothing to boast about.

**Q:** *During the 1960s, liberals worked to reduce the power of the American Empire, and sought to reduce adventurism in foreign policy. It was not always easy to make the case that Israel was an exception. Do you have a way of synthesizing a liberal outlook on foreign affairs with strong American support of Israel?*

**A:** I don't think it's so difficult. The liberal position on foreign policy states that America should be devoted to the support of democracy and democratic norms wherever possible. This is one of the strongest reasons for American support of Israel, and in that sense there is a harmony between liberalism and Jewish self-interest. I think that the argument from democracy is much more effective than some argument about strategic interests, than arguing in terms of geopolitical considerations in so-called sophisticated terms.

## Notes

1. Alvin Rosenfeld, "Irving Howe: Yiddish Culture and Secular Jewishness," *Irving Howe and the Critics: Celebrations and Attacks,* ed. John Rodden (Lincoln: University of Nebraska Press, 2005), 170.
2. Edward Alexander, *Irving Howe: Socialist, Critic, Jew* (Bloomington: Indiana University Press, 1998), 62-63.
3. Novak's career took a sharp turn after his editorial stint at *Moment.* He put his literary and editorial talents to work in more remunerative activities. The publication in 1984 of Novak's "ghostwritten" autobiography of then-Chrysler president Lee Iacocca led to a second career as a "super ghostwriter," putting together autobiographies of figures such as Soviet dissident (and later Israeli right-winger) Natan Sharansky, Magic Johnson, Nancy Reagan, and Oliver North, among others. He is also co-author of *The Big Book of Jewish Humor,* which has achieved a coffee-table success that might be compared to *World of Our Fathers,* albeit in a far lighter vein.
4. George McGovern, U.S. Senator from South Dakota, made a brief run for the Democratic presidential nomination in 1968. McGovern won the nomination in 1972 yet lost the presidential election in a landslide to Richard Nixon.

# Chapter 2

**Sol Stern, "Israel, American Jews, and the Peace Now Camp," *Jerusalem Post Weekly*, 24 August 1976.**

## Introduction

Of all the interviews in this volume, this one most prominently addresses Howe's relationship to the Jewish community. It occurred at the pinnacle of Howe's popularity, due to the success of *World of Our Fathers*. The book had actually reached number seven on *The New York Times* bestseller list and earned Howe a 1977 National Book Award. Yet Howe's support for the Israeli Left, particularly the peace movement, led to attacks from Jewish leaders who saw him as disloyal, as unwittingly giving aid and comfort to those bent on Israel's destruction. This interview is largely Howe's defense against such charges.

Sol Stern, who conducts the interview, was born in Tel Aviv. His family immigrated to the United States when he was three years old, and he was raised in the Bronx. Like Irving Howe, he was a graduate of City College of New York. In the early 1960s, he attended graduate school at the University of California at Berkeley, where he became a student activist and met many of the leading figures both in the Free Speech Movement and in Berkeley's chapter of Students for a Democratic Society, probably the most important activist organization at the time. By the mid-1960s, he was writing for the radical Left magazine *Ramparts* on whose editorial board he also served (1966-72). The young Stern was a prominent advocate for reconsidering the case of Julius and Ethel Rosenberg, who were executed in 1953 as Communist spies after what leftists generally considered a show-trial.

Spurred largely by his commitment to Israel, as well as by his anti-Communism, Stern had broken with the New Left by the mid-1970s, shortly before the time of this interview. He would continue an extensive freelance career writing on Israel and related issues. By the 1990s, Stern sided with conservatives on a variety of issues, notably on school reform, arguing that unions protect inferior teachers and that private school vouchers should be adopted.

In this interview Stern voices a concern that recurred in numerous reviews of *World of Our Fathers*, namely that Howe's work overemphasized the Yiddish, secular, and Socialist aspects of Jewish life in the United States and neglected the religious dimension. Furthermore, this is the only interview that mentions Howe's relationship with the American Jewish Committee, the organization that sponsors *Commentary* and was similarly critical of Howe. Nevertheless, as in his later relationships with former New Left figures such as Todd Gitlin and Morris Berman (both of whom eventually joined *Dissent's* editorial board), Howe and Stern got along well; as Stern turned away from his radical past in the 1970s, he extended an olive branch to Irving Howe, who might be said to have served—as in the cases of Gitlin and Berman—as a midwife in Stern's migration away from the far Left. Although both Howe and Stern had long shared a contempt for Soviet Communism, Stern shifted much further toward the right than did Howe, moving into alignment with such journals as *Commentary* and *National Review*.

The interview opens with a discussion of the success, quite unusual for an author associated with academia and with a small group of intellectuals, of *World of Our Fathers*. Delighted though he is about the book's reception, Howe worries that the cause for its popularity is superficial, indeed just a romantic, fleeting nostalgia: the book's sales may signify "a kind of emotional 'last hurrah' [for] many middle-class suburban Jews . . . [that] gives them an opportunity to have one last emotional wobble and then continue with their lives." The book may represent only a last glance back on the road to assimilation, an observation that Howe makes also in *A Margin of Hope*. For Howe, of course, *World of Our Fathers* meant far more; in this interview he even goes so far as to refer to it as "a disguised autobiography." In its concern with the Jewish milieu that incubated Howe, *World of Our Fathers* may be seen as a kind of subterranean story of his youth some six years before the explicit autobiography, *A Margin of Hope*.[1]

As a secular Jew who had as a young man denied the relevance of his Jewishness, Howe had special reasons to ponder his Jewish heritage. "It becomes harder and harder," he says, "to know what the content of being Jewish means." Reviewing the motives for maintaining a secular Jewish identity, Howe concludes that all the reasons, with the possible exception of identification with Israel, risk fading away. Indeed, many Israelis have shared with Howe a secular, often Socialist, Jewishness linked to a traditional milieu fast disappearing. Like so many Israelis, Howe struggles with wanting to maintain his Jewishness without religion, although the meaning of the word "Jew" outside of religion is indefinite and unstable. Since 1948, Israeli Jews, unlike Americans, have lived with a recurring threat to their very survival that keeps them sharply aware of their historical identity—but this too may (hopefully soon) pass.

Howe's status as author of *World of Our Fathers* and as a key figure in the revival of Yiddish literature might have given him some intellectual cover when it came to criticizing Israel. Howe even became friends with leading left-wing politicians in Israel between the 1970s and 1990s. They perceived him to be criticizing not Israel, but rather the conservative and right-wing policies of the Likud. A few liberal and radical supporters in the American Jewish community shared the Israeli Left's view of Howe as a spokesman for an authentic Israeli politics that renounced brutal counterterrorist tactics.

Yet discussion of Israel has long been circumscribed within the American Jewish community, far more so than in the freewheeling Israeli press. Howe faced sharp criticism from various Jewish-American sources. Indeed, Howe's disavowal of Zionism during the 1940s made his position even more embattled, even though many of his critics might not have known this earlier version of Howe. Certainly, the wider public was not aware of his earlier stance on Israel, which was expressed in small Trotskyist publications in the 1940s. Still, from at least the time of the Six Day War, Howe remained a firm supporter of Israel's right to exist, even when he criticized specific policies.[2]

The Israeli peace movement, referred to as *Breira* in this article, would crystallize with the founding of "Peace Now" (*Shalom Acshav* in Hebrew) in 1978. Howe actually published a short book under the imprint *Breira*.[3] For Israeli peace activists, the key issue, not mentioned directly in this interview, was—as it remains today—the settlement of religious Jews on outposts in the West Bank and to a lesser extent the Gaza Strip, areas that the international community has long intended to be part of an eventual Palestinian state. The settlers, by contrast, believed (and continue to believe) that all these lands are divinely ordained to be part of a greater, biblical Israel. And they hoped (and still hope) eventually to drive the Palestinians across the Jordan River.

Many Jewish organizations in the United States regard the Israeli peace organizations, or at least their American defenders, as a danger to the future of the Jewish state, which, they hold, dares not make itself look weak. The belief that Jews outside Israel do not have a right to criticize Israel was also pervasive. Howe, by contrast, considered the West Bank settlements an incendiary obstacle to an ultimate peace and so chose to speak out. He remained a bit hesitant on the issue, however, as this interview evinces when he poses both sides of the dilemma: "Would I say Israel has the right of self-determination even if it is mistaken? Or would I say, if Israel continues along on this course, it's going to back itself into a position where there might be a disastrous war . . . ?" Although he felt compelled to speak up, Howe admits his anxious uncertainty about Israel's future prospects.

Yet Israelis are not Howe's primary audience in the conversation with Stern. Howe sought to defend his controversial stance toward Israel by granting this interview to the international edition of the *Jerusalem Post*, noted for its extremely pro-Israel stand and large American audience. The newspaper was (and still is) oriented towards Howe's kind of Jewishness—mainly a secular Jewishness quite sympathetic to cultural and intellectual life, one that had enthusiastically greeted *World of Our Fathers*. Speaking in a publication that will also be read by American Jews, Howe defends his support of Israel's peace organizations and reaffirms his secular Jewishness, both of which the newspaper's main readership overwhelmingly also supports.

## The Interview

For Irving Howe, the writing of *World Of Our Fathers* was also a personal journey back to a living community that had shaped him. His own parents arrived in New York City in 1912 at the tail end of that tidal wave of East European Jewish immigration that is so dramatically depicted in the opening chapters of the book.

Born in 1920 in the Bronx, speaking Yiddish as a first language, Howe grew up in a milieu of secular *Yiddishkeit* and trade unionism. As a teenager he was organizing for the Young People's Socialist League on the streets of the east Bronx. Then it was on to City College of New York and from there into the avant-garde world of the New York Jewish literary scene.

A career followed quickly as one of America's most distinguished literary and social critics, editor of the Socialist magazine *Dissent*, author of critically acclaimed books.

Now comes a kind of collective *recherche du temps perdu*, a massive work that occupied the past six years of Howe's life. "It would be grandiose to say it was a disguised autobiography, but it is my sense of things," he says.

"In a sense, it is my story, the experience of the secular, Socialist segment of the immigrant community as the sons and daughters moved into the intellectual world."

It was an unusually fortuitous matching of author and subject; the result is perhaps the most striking of this year's publishing season in America.

Other books about American Jews by authors such as Harry Golden and Leo Rosten have made it big before, but Howe has turned out an 800-page work of scholarship and history that reaped the critical acclaim of *The New York Times Book Review* and the *New York Review of Books* among others. So it would be safe to say that this is the most commercially successful *serious* book ever written about American Jews.

For Irving Howe it has all been somewhat overwhelming. None of his previous books ever sold more than 12,000 copies and his reputation has been limited to a restricted literary and academic circle. Now he suddenly finds himself besieged by requests for appearances—at synagogues and before countless Jewish organizations—and he is the recipient of hundreds of letters by concerned young Jews. A professor of English literature, a secularist, and a Socialist, he is being asked to provide guidance for the most perplexing problems of Jewish identity and the Jewish future in America.

When I spoke to Howe recently in his office at the City University of New York in a huge building near Times Square, he was still puzzling over the extraordinary response the book has evoked in the Jewish community.

"I was completely surprised," he says. "If I want to flatter myself I say it's a good book which people recognize as such and the *New York Times* review—which is nowadays crucial for any book—was very positive and very flattering."

But Howe recognizes there is something deeper at work: "I'm not very sure what the explanation is. The most negative and caustic interpretation would be that this is a kind of emotional 'last hurrah.' That going back on the part of many middle-class suburban Jews, going back and reading this stuff, encountering it, gives them an opportunity to have one last emotional wallow and then continue with their lives. They remember their Socialist grandfathers and they vote for 'Scoop' Jackson—or something like that.

"I wouldn't doubt that there is that side. On the other hand, to be fair and to have some sense of the complexities . . . I have had a great deal of mail. A lot of people say: 'I feel that I have discovered my roots.' 'I found out where I am.' 'I found out who my grandparents were. . . .' So there is a stratum, not a very large one, a thin stratum of young Jews in America who are deeply pensive. They are struggling very hard and they are very serious. They want to give what they call 'positive content' to their Jewishness.

"The essential problem for Jews in America, though, is that if you're not religious, it becomes harder and harder to know what the content of being Jewish means. The very phrase 'Jewishness' is revealing. It already has a certain looseness and ambiguity to it. In the old days no one used to talk about 'Jewishness.' They said: 'I am a Jew' or 'I believe in Judaism.' But Jewishness—the word—reveals the difficulty, the ambiguity of the situation.

"And so, in that sense, it may be that the book came along at the right time, striking many people on that nerve—that they want to have some feeling of being Jewish or that they do have it and they want it to mean more than contributing money to Israel, or even political liberalism."

One criticism that has been made of Howe's book, particularly in some Jewish publications, is that, in depicting the immigrant experience, he overemphasizes the Yiddish, secular, Socialist aspect to the neglect of other factors, particularly the role of religion. Howe readily acknowledges the complaint: "I knew that criticism was going to come. I think there is some truth to it."

Nevertheless, whatever aspect one chooses to emphasize, one is led to an ultimate identity crisis in American Jewish life. It is the very success of the Jewish immigrant experience in the U.S. that now poses the most serious questions about the future of American Jewish life. In his public appearances after the publication of his book, Howe has tried to address himself to that paradox. In a recent speech to the American Jewish Committee, he identified four strategies by which a sense of identity had been historically maintained for nonreligious Jews in America. There was the immigrant experience with its distinctive Yiddish culture; the belief in the ethical (i.e., liberal) values stemming from the Jewish tradition; the need to keep alive the memory of the Holocaust; and finally, the rise of Israel as a state and a centre of Jewish concern. The problem, Howe argued, is that "except for Israel, all of these pressures of Jewish experience have been losing some of their force."

Even concerning Israel, Howe sees difficulties looming: "For if one could, in practice, establish oneself as a Jew by 'working for Israel' then one might put aside those irksome spiritual problems that life was now imposing especially on nonreligious Jews. This is neither an unworthy nor a dishonourable evasion—first comes survival and then definition. But it has left a growing mound of intellectual debts which sooner or later must be paid."

Howe himself has been wrestling with some of the difficulties of working for Israel. Long a passionate supporter of Israel, particularly in debates with its New Left critics, Howe of late has associated himself with "Breira," the dovish American Jewish organization which has publicly criticized Israel Government policy on the administered territories and the Palestinians.

The result has been that he is having to respond to attacks from both American Zionists and Israeli officials in the U.S. It is a position that has left him troubled by what he sees as a fundamental conflict. "I have no easy answer because there are two different principles in conflict. One principle is wanting very urgently to help Israel. The other principle is opposing American arm-twisting. But suppose the American pressures take a direction which is essentially O.K. or desirable? I have put this question to my friends in 'Breira' and it doesn't really get to them. It doesn't touch their imagination.

"It bothers me a lot because in principle I feel it's bad for large powers to shape the policies of smaller ones. But suppose America is pushing toward a proper kind of settlement? It would be foolish and self-deceiving to deny there could be a conflict, and what I would do then I honestly don't know. Would I say: Israel has the right of self-determination even if it is mistaken? Or, would I say, if Israel continues along on this course, it's going to back itself into a position where there might be a disastrous war which it might even lose because America wouldn't support it?"

It was, said Howe, a very painful dilemma for himself and ultimately one that might touch many American Jews. Finally he turned to me and asked: "Do you have an answer?"

It was perhaps the most appropriate note on which to end an interview with Irving Howe. For as he had said in this speech to the American Jewish Committee: "I think it is fair to say that being Jewish remains an experience of weight, significance and value. We are left with questions. And that too is the very essence of Jewish experience. For how does a Jew answer a question if not with another question?"

## Notes

1. On this point, see *The Worlds of Irving Howe: The Critical Legacy,* ed. John Rodden (Boulder: Paradigm, 2005).
2. Howe's stance on Israel (and the barrage of criticism that he encountered from numerous official Jewish spokesmen and organs) resembled Woody Allen's similar critique of Israel's settlement policies in the late 1980s. Likewise, their treatment by the American Jewish community was often harsh, met by a similar storm of disapproval from Jewish-American commentators.
3. See *The Worlds of Irving Howe: The Critical Legacy,* ed. John Rodden (Boulder: Paradigm, 2005).

# Chapter 3

### Sandra Greenberg, "Fiction, Society, and the Literary Critic," *Book Forum: An International Transdisciplinary Quarterly*, 1981, 534-40.

## Introduction

The interviews in this volume showcase Irving Howe as a "triple thinker" devoted to the three "loves" of his intellectual life—Socialism, literary criticism, and Yiddish culture—a triad captured in the title of Edward Alexander's biography, *Irving Howe: Socialist, Critic, Jew* (1998).[1] Unlike the political bent of the first two interviews in this book, this interview with Sandra Greenberg, at the time a writer living in Creve Coeur, Missouri, showcases the middle of these three terms: Howe as literary critic. This is unsurprising, given that it appeared between the publication years of Howe's best seller and his autobiography, when he was much in demand as a speaker about literary life and Jewish issues. This contrasted with the 1960s and 1970s, when he primarily visited American campuses to discuss political questions. In the literary realm, Howe's central and ongoing interest was the modernist movement that began in the early decades of the twentieth century and largely ended in the years following World War II. Beginning in the 1970s, his interest in Yiddish literature and secular Judaism as a cultural phenomenon also became apparent.

This conversation witnesses Howe engaging in a serious, even grim, discussion of modernist literature that bears on issues of tradition and society. Crucial here are the horrors of World War I, which led to a bitter cynicism about the ultimate advance of civilization and provided a historical backdrop to modernist and avant-garde literature. Howe mentions this cavernous subtext only indirectly: "The whole modernist idea is associated with historical crisis, with the sense of living through a time which is qualitatively different and more difficult, a time when all the premises of human existence . . . are called into question." Accompanying the disillusionment with European society was a questioning of the European colonial project, a digging up of its arrogant and often brutal side, exemplified by much of the work of Joseph Conrad and George Orwell. It is this critical spirit that Howe finds integral to modernism, and to art in general, creating an implicit link between political upheaval and distinguished literature: "the best writing comes from calling into question one's own beliefs, one's own views, one's own premises." Howe himself practiced this kind of Keatsian "negative capability." Or to cite F. Scott Fitzgerald: "the mark of a first-rate mind is to hold two opposing ideas together and not crack up." Howe was a master at holding together and even synthesizing opposing ideas, or in showing why they might not be as opposite as was conventionally assumed. That was how he could be politically radical and culturally conservative.

The literary tradition that Howe upheld was one that valued independent thinking and critical intelligence. These values have animated the trajectory of the history of the novel. Although the modernism that Howe favored is often seen as a break from that tradition, it may be insofar as it expresses a political despair and social rootlessness, but not in its exploration of consciousness and sympathy with all facets of human life. So in "The Idea of the Modern," Howe's seminal 1967 essay, he praises Joyce for avoiding easy political solutions, unlike the case of Ezra Pound regarding Fascism. Rather, Joyce remains in the quotidian, in the humane, aesthetic world of "the streets of the city and its ongoing commonplace life."[2] In this strange way Joyce, argues Howe, stays true to the modernist avant-garde impulse to remain outside the boundaries of political ideology.

Howe contrasts the brilliance of the modernist era with a contemporary American literature that adopts some aspects of the sensibility and style of modernism, a mode that in 1981 was only starting to be called "postmodernism." For Howe, this development was part of the flashy shallowness of a consumer society that appropriated art that had once been culturally oppositional. If upheaval and questioning had spurred great art in early twentieth-century Europe, a more affluent, complacent postwar era had generated a tamer art.

Unlike many commentators, who applauded the postmodern spirit of play, Howe was severe in his judgment of the postmodern sensibility: "The United States, with its endless capacity for absorption, found that it could not take the essential spirit of modernism, but only many of its decorative elements, and defang them, make them unthreatening, domesticate them." This critique seems also to spring from Howe's experience with the superficialities of the New Left, which had treated him harshly in the late 1960s when he warned about the dangers of extremism, sectarianism, and superficial radicalism. "New Styles in Leftism" was the dismissive title of Howe's most famous and controversial critique of the New Left, which appeared in *Dissent* in 1965. (His stern assessment of literary postmodernism could well have echoed it: "New Styles in (Post-)Modernism.") Howe had based his polemic against the New Left on his knowledge—partly from bitter experience—of the history of the Old Left, which had repeatedly overreached and fragmented into hostile sects. Determined not to learn from history, the New Left repeated this pattern, radiating a brief, hopeful luminosity in the early 1960s that was followed by a quick burnout by the end of the decade, a topic Howe takes up in this interview and later in this book.

For Howe, a scrutiny of history always necessitated an awareness of literature, and to him the plague of cultural faddishness and trendiness during the 1960s was rooted in cultural currents much deeper than simply the New Left movement, reaching to American society's far corners: a glib distrust of traditional knowledge. As he explains, "An educated person has some awareness of the kinds of issues, problems, and questions that have plagued humanity over the centuries, but that have also enlivened human thought. . . . The mark of the uneducated person is his behaving as if he is the first person in the world and has to discover everything for himself." Beyond the New Left, beyond the youthful students, these words illuminate Howe's increasingly caustic attitude toward an educational establishment and a cultural elite too willing to jettison the lessons of history for glitzy intellectual fashions such as deconstruction and multiculturalism. Not that Howe necessarily opposed the study of new and different voices; his advocacy of Yiddish literature attests to that, as does his early championing of Richard Wright and his spirited engagement with Ralph Ellison (though some critics have derided Howe's work on Ellison as skewed and reductive). Whatever Howe's limitations, he considered ethnic diversity in literary studies that is not also grounded in a rich appreciation of the Western tradition shallow, since the latter's liberal values encourage an openness and indeed provide a foundation for multicultural literature as it is actually practiced.

This stance exposed Howe to attacks from the left and at times allied him with conservatives. Edward Alexander, for instance, writes in his biography of Howe that aesthetic sensibility "was an essential part of the democratic idea. It arose from within Western traditions spanning the period from the Renaissance to the Enlightenment."[3] The debates about the established literary canon, the tradition of Great Books, and indeed the value of Western civilization itself were just beginning at the time of this interview. They were soon to catch fire and become the "culture wars," and Howe considered those professors willing to throw out the canon arrogant and intellectually immature. Samuel Hux's 1995 essay "Our 'Uncle Irving': Howe's Conservative Strain," argues that Howe considered the Western tradition a gift for all, including those "minority and working-class students the radicalized professors professed to be so concerned about."[4] Among the cultural warriors whose conservatism appealed to Howe were E. D. Hirsch, William Bennett, and John Silber. But Howe was not completely alone as a figure on the left who castigated the literary academy for lacking artistic standards: a few voices (e.g., historian Eugene Genovese and William Phillips at *Partisan Review*) joined him. Howe was accused of stodginess and intellectual elitism, but he maintained that his highbrow tastes were legitimate and indeed a commitment to literary integrity. So the battle was not merely between conservatives and radicals; rather the culture wars divided the Old Left and the New Left too. The permissiveness that swept the 1960s led conservatives to make similar criticisms of American youth and education, and also to a similar defense of Western culture.

Howe's defense of Western tradition, nevertheless, differs from that of at least some conservatives in his emphasis on the dissenting nature of that tradition, on how it often speaks for the poor and marginalized, and on how it strives, at least implicitly, for a better society. Hux summarizes Howe's critique of the neoconservatives as "frantic ideologues with their own version of P.C., the classics as safeguard for the status quo."[5] Howe always maintained his concerns about inequality, about the need for not only democracy but economic egalitarianism. In the 1980s, after the failure of the New Left and the election of Ronald Reagan, his continuing embrace of Socialism might have seemed stubborn, a refusal to face reality. Indeed, by 1982, Midge Decter had delivered precisely this judgment, as discussed in the Introduction. Decter was only one of several neoconservatives who portrayed Howe as a blind utopian ignorant of the practical realities of political life who had remained an ideologue despite his explicit shedding of his Marxist views. In this interview, Howe sidesteps the question of "how we go about getting" a Socialist society. His refusal to elaborate on such a question has led to the charge that he is indeed little more than a utopian. Here, however, his evasion seems driven by despair about the many failed movements toward Socialism and about the conservative zeitgeist of the early 1980s. Howe himself had become ambivalent about "Socialism" at this stage of his life. In many respects he did not at all insist that he was a "Socialist." Rather he referred to himself numerous times in the 1980s and 1990s as a "radical humanist," a term that acknowledges the historical passing of a Socialist vision even as it continues to affirm its cultural significance and the hope of greater egalitarianism and justice in the future.[6]

Still, Howe continued until the end of his days to give "two cheers for utopia."[7] For him, the tradition of the West, together with a deep knowledge of history, meant a march toward a better society; for many who call themselves conservative, it has meant that a flawed human nature is always liable to overreaching ambition and susceptible to self-rationalization and the lures of ideological abstraction, so that striving for a utopian ideal invariably ends in failure. On one related point, Howe would have agreed: past progressive success contributed to the thinness of recent American culture. In an affluent society, the need for deep historical knowledge seems less than pressing, a lamentation that Howe voices at various points in this interview in connection with his critique of the commercialization of American society and our lack of a substantial literature. Those contemporary American authors whose works Howe praises are an omnibus group, generally with historical and intellectual connections to an ethnic or regional subgroup: Bellow, Malamud, Welty, Olsen, Porter, and O'Connor. What this sundry sextet has in common is a concern with local color, with nuanced accents on time, inflection, and dialect; little explicit attention is directed to the suburban middle-class crisis of affluent emptiness. Howe's best criticism engaged a broad variety of contemporary voices, illuminating them with informed understanding of the rich Western tradition. For him it was never a question of either/or.[8]

This interview was conducted at Washington University in St. Louis while Irving Howe was serving as Visiting Hurst Professor in the English Department in the winter of 1980.

## The Interview

**Q:** *Mr. Howe, you recently described current novels as thin, lacking in substance and morality. Do you believe the novel as a form is exhausted?*

**A:** I think it is presumptuous for critics or anyone else to speak of the exhaustion of a form that has been so rich and fruitful as the novel has been. All literary forms go through high and low points, plateaus and planes, and right now we seem to be experiencing what I take to be a plane. This is a judgment that other critics would probably call into question or deny, and it is possible that what we are confronting here is a generational difference, namely, that people of my age find it difficult to adapt to some of the new voices and tones and sensibilities that have since appeared. That is always a possibility, and it is foolish to deny it. I, of course, stand by my own judgments; other people have a right to call those into question.

**Q:** *What, more precisely, are your reasons for believing that we are on a "plane" right now?*

A: Much of the fiction that is published these days, though I can't pretend to read it in great quantities, strikes me as willful, lacking in imaginative density, deficient in the sense of the richness and complexity of society, sometimes even deliberately narrow in its moral scope. For one thing, we are living after a very great cultural period, the period of modernism, and as a result of this, it is very difficult, understandably, for newer writers to find their own way, and to not be overwhelmed by the masters who have preceded them. A lot of the things that are around these days seem to me very contrived, in the bad sense of the word, sometimes almost adolescent in their tone and voice, as if the complex burdens of modernism have proven to be too much to bear.

**Q:** *You have said that you connect the rise of relativism and skepticism with the prevalence of disintegrated characters in modern fiction. You contrasted Tolstoy,* *who wrote with an abundance of self-confidence and certainty, with such modern writers as Ford Madox Ford and Joseph Conrad, who create fragmented, disintegrated characters. Since relativism is clearly flourishing rather than diminishing, do you believe characters in future fiction will disintegrate even further, almost to the point of dissolving?*

**A:** I don't think characters in future fiction can very likely disintegrate any further, because one of the things that marks contemporary fiction is virtually a dismissal of the idea of character in its traditional sense, as well as a lack of interest in the dynamics and the pleasures of storytelling. There are younger writers who have deliberately, they say, given up the whole idea of storytelling, of narrative, and this seems to me, really, to be a kind of disaster. It is giving up the heart of the novel, and perhaps also the heart of literature in general.

**Q:** *What do you believe are some distinctive themes and ideas of modern literature?*

**A:** That's a big subject . . . but if I were to try to put it into a few phrases, I would say that the essential element of the modernist impulse is to see the whole of human existence as problematical. There are no longer any certainties; the various transcendent sanctions of the past have been lost. Everything has been called into question. There is a large tendency toward subjectivity, toward skepticism, toward relativism, toward restlessness; restlessness is seen as having a value in and of itself. Experimentation is not a necessary component of modernist literature, but it is frequently an accompaniment of it.

**Q:** *How do you feel about this?*

**A:** It doesn't make any difference how I feel about it because, in a way, there it is; it is one of the greatest achievements of the last century and a half, and extraordinarily brilliant and profound works have been created out of the modernist impulse. The whole modernist idea is associated with historical crisis, with the sense of living through a time which is qualitatively different and more difficult, a time when all the premises of human existence that have sustained people in the past, are called into question. And out of this has arisen the great work of Eliot and Joyce and Brecht and Babel and Borges and Beckett and many others, as well as great work in painting and in music. One of the impulses has also been the calling into question of all accepted genres, forms, decorums, and sensibilities, which were inherited from the past. I think it has been the decisive shaping influence upon the sensibility of literate and educated people. There are elements of it now, in retrospect, which seem to need reexamination, especially on the political side. One of the unhappy aspects of modernism was the tendency of some, not all, but of some of the modernist writers to be impatient, and indeed, snarlingly hostile, toward liberal values, and this I find increasingly disturbing.

**Q:** *Do you believe there is a connection between neurosis and literary genius, between brilliance and pessimism?*

**A:** I don't know; I really don't know. I wouldn't pretend to say. I would say this: there is something about the kind of work that writers do, the fact that they are constantly drawing from within themselves, which would seem to suggest that the psychological cost for that sort of work is very high. I believe very strongly in Yeats's remark that out of the quarrels with others one makes rhetoric and out of the quarrels with oneself one makes poetry. Though I myself don't do creative writing as it is called (I don't write novels or poetry), even the kind of thing that I do, which is expository writing, I find that the sense of strain drawn from oneself, in some sense, of almost attacking oneself, is enormous. And the best writing comes from calling into question one's own beliefs, one's own views, one's own premises. And this, of course, is no easy thing to do. There's a high price to pay for this. I would advise people looking for tranquil lives not to marry writers.

**Q:** *Or not to be writers.*

**A:** Or not to be them.

**Q:** *Who, of the writers currently publishing, do you believe will create fiction that will survive, that will conquer and defy the limits of time?*

**A:** It's very, very hard to say, because one doesn't have any clear idea of what survival means these days, or whether civilization itself will survive. There are a few writers who seem to . . . have a fair chance of surviving. A couple, not many, but a couple of the novels of Saul Bellow, especially the beautiful fiction, *Seize the Day*, a few stories by Bernard Malamud, a few stories by Eudora Welty, one story by Tillie Olsen, a few stories by Katherine Anne Porter, quite a few by Flannery O'Connor (though she is dead, she is really contemporary). . . . Not a vast amount.

**Q:** *What do you believe these writers are doing or saying that is going to enable them to survive while others will not?*

**A:** They have very great talent, they are honest, they find forms which are appropriate to what they have to say, and they succeed in creating, even if only sometimes on a small scale, a self-sufficient, imaginative place or world.

**Q:** *In your introduction to* Modern Literary Criticism, *you said that one of the distinguishing marks of The New Critics*[9] *was their belief that content and form are inseparable. Do you believe this is true?*

**A:** That's terribly hard to answer. . . . I believe there is a separation between form and content, otherwise the two words wouldn't have arisen. The fact that the two terms have been with us for a very long time in one way or another indicates that people saw something in the way of difference, that they saw the difference, crudely put, between how a thing is being said and what is being said. The New Critics came along with the perfectly sound, corrective suggestion that in literature we could not separate what was being said from how it was being said—that indeed, how a thing is said in literature determines what is being said. And yet we know, for example, that while the short story as written by Rudyard Kipling and the short story as written by Isaac Babel, or the ballad as transposed by Kipling and the ballad as transposed by Brecht, have many points of similarity, nevertheless, what the two writers in each pair are saying, the vision of life, the vision of the world that they communicate, are very different.

**Q:** *In your introduction to* Modern Literary Criticism *you also said: "If criticism now finds itself in a state of uncertainty and perhaps even exhaustion, one reason must surely be that it has lost the buoying sense of purpose that had come from the avant-garde experience." What do you think caused the dissolution of the avant-garde?*

**A:** All world views, all new modes of sensibilities and styles, such as Romanticism in the early nineteenth century and modernism in the late twentieth century, have a life of their own; they don't last forever. They satisfy certain historical and emotional needs, and then with the change of conditions, they tend to exhaust themselves. By the avant-garde, we mean here something pertaining to modernism. The avant-garde, let's say, is the grouping of writers who are the bearers of the modernist spirit. By its very nature an avant-garde has to be a grouping which is not accepted by the dominant forces of society. But something happened in the middle of the twentieth century which had not been anticipated: namely, the absorption of a good deal of avant-garde tradition, avant-garde literature, into the dominant culture. Writers like Eliot, Brecht, Joyce, Proust, and Kafka, and many others, who had been strongly resisted beforehand in the academic world, suddenly became the favored texts in the universities. The dominant mass culture of the United States, with its endless capacity for absorption, found that it could take not the essential spirit of modernism, but many of its decorative elements and defang them, make them unthreatening, domesticate them. Also, there is something about the whole modernist spirit which creates so much tension, so much internal turmoil, that it may be that there is some kind of internal dynamism in the modernist spirit which has led to exhaustion. The historical crisis which had given rise to modernism, or which at least had been its matrix, continued to exist, in some ways to get worse, but it would be committing a genetic fallacy to assume that because "a" is the cause or the matrix of "b," the persistence of "a" necessarily means the persistence of "b." My impression is, and one cannot be entirely certain of these matters, but my impression is that modernism has come to an end—has been exhausting itself—though there are still a few heroic survivors like Beckett, but essentially, what we have had is the slick imitation of its externals and the shaking off of its essential spirit.

**Q:** *How do you believe the death of the avant-garde affected literary criticism?*

**A:** At one point, in the twenties and thirties, literary critics had a sense of commitment, a burning purpose and urgency, a great need to become the spokesmen of, the expositors of, the defenders of, the explainers of, modernist literature. After all, literary criticism is a secondary procedure, and it thrives, most of all, when there is a body of fresh literary work which is not always clearly understood, which is perhaps seen as an affront to the dominant ways of feeling and thinking. Critics find their fulfillment in being the spokesmen, in being the articulators, for that new body of literature. In more recent years, not many critics have felt there was anything like that to set them into motion, to stir them, to inspire them, and this, I think, is one reason for the decline of interest in criticism.

**Q:** *In your article entitled: "What's the Trouble: Social Crisis, Crisis of Civilization, or Both,"*[10] *you said that one of the strongest symptoms indicating that America is experiencing a crisis of civilization rather than simply a social or political crisis is that "the enterprise of education is in grave trouble" because "there seems barely any consensus among educators as to what they are supposed to profess, barely any agreement among educators as to what they believe education to be or do." What is your image of an educated person, and what do you regard as the moral and cultural values that you would like to pass on from generation to generation?*

**A:** I would say that an educated person is someone who has some acquaintance with the great works of the mind that have been written in the past. If one wants to reduce this to a few simple examples, I would say someone who has read a couple of Plato's dialogues, and a couple of Shakespeare's plays, and an essay or two by Montaigne, who has looked into Homer and Virgil—and who perhaps has even gone so far as to read a few passages from the Bible. Yet, it is not merely a question of this name or of the other, but of having some sense of the continuity and the depth of Western civilization. An educated person has some awareness of the kinds of issues, problems, and questions that have plagued humanity over the centuries, but that have also enlivened human thought. This way one does not live as if he is just beginning from scratch; there is a sense of a living, vital tradition behind him that sustains him, and sometimes disciplines him. The mark of the uneducated person is his behaving as if he is the first person in the world and has to discover everything for himself—which of course is impossible—so therefore he never discovers very much. One great problem with American education is the lack, or the breakdown, of this connection with the past, of the sense of a living tradition. . . . It is a question of having certain attitudes and receptivities—a feeling for, a sense of the possibilities of, the life of the mind. I think it would be utopian or foolish to claim that the majority of our graduates from American colleges have anything of the sort.

**Q:** *What has enabled you to remain exceedingly devoted to Socialism for the past forty-five years?*

**A:** I have remained a Socialist because I believe in the idea of a society in which the values and processes of democracy are extended from the relatively narrow limits in which they function today (as much as I value what we do have in the way of democracy) to other areas of life: socioeconomic life, life of the corporation, life of the factory, where presently democracy barely exists, or doesn't exist at all. I became a Socialist because I thought that the values of capitalist society—its competitiveness, its exaltation of brute success, its tendency to put down those at the bottom—were in conflict with humane values. And I remain a Socialist because I believe in the idea, whether or not it can be fully achieved, of something to aspire to, a goal, a vision of society where we will not have the shameful contrasts that we have in this society between rich and poor, between those who have too much and those who do not have enough, and between those who have an excess of power and those who have none. So my sense of a Socialist society is one of an indefinite extension of democracy and democratic values, and tendency toward greater egalitarianism, though not a literal egalitarianism, but a move in that direction, and a society which would encourage more fraternal, friendly, cooperative values.

**Q:** *Do you have any idea of how we go about getting this society?*

**A:** I'll skip that one . . . that's too much.

**Q:** *When reading from your as-yet unfinished autobiography at a recent lecture, you said that you spent very little time in class during college because, "Who could go to class when the world was going to blow up?" Do you often have this same fear today?*

**A:** Sure, I have that fear every day; it seems to me a constant possibility, a constant shadow upon our existence, and I don't see that any sensitive person can avoid living with that fear. At the same time, if we are going to live, we cannot allow that fear to overwhelm us; first, because there is still value and pleasure in the time that is given us and we have no other; secondly, because if we are to act politically or socially in some constructive way to perhaps control the forces that move toward atomic warfare, then we simply cannot give in to our fears and our anxieties and our depressions, though I certainly share them. There are days when one wakes up in the morning and it seems as if the world is too terrible to contemplate, and those are just the days one has to prod oneself into working and responding.

## Notes

1. See Edward Alexander, *Irving Howe: Socialist, Critic, Jew* (Bloomington: Indiana University Press, 1998); and John Rodden, "Irving Howe: Triple Thinker" in *Irving Howe and the Critics* (Lincoln: Nebraska University Press, 2005), 1-24.
2. Irving Howe, "The Idea of the Modern," *Irving Howe: Selected Writings 1950-1990* (San Diego: Harcfourt Brace Jovanovich, 1990), 158.
3. Edward Alexander, *Irving Howe: Socialist, Critic, Jew* (Bloomington: Indiana University Press, 1998), 238.
4. Samuel Hux, "Uncle Irving," in Rodden, *Irving Howe and the Critics*, 54.
5. Ibid.
6. On this point, see John Rodden, "Irving Howe's 'Partisan' Orwell," *Irving Howe and the Critics*, 117-31.
7. See Irving Howe, "Two Cheers for Utopia," *Dissent* (May 1993): 131-33.
8. On this point, see Irving Howe, ed. *Modern Literary Criticism* (Boston: Little, Brown, 1959). This anthology, intended both for the general public and for students, collected three dozen widely ranging American and British critical essays from 1917 through the 1950s.
9. John Crowe Ransom, Allen Tate, Robert Penn Warren, and R. P. Blackmur. For a more in-depth examination of the New Critics, see Irving Howe's introduction titled "Modern Criticism: Privileges and Perils," in *Modern Literary Criticism* (New York: Grove Press, 1961).
10. "What's the Trouble: Social Crisis, Crisis of Civilization, or Both?" *The Seventies*, ed. Irving Howe and Michael Harrington (New York: Harper & Rowe, 1972), 52-72.

# Chapter 4

**Maurice Isserman. "*Dissent* in the Fifties and Sixties," 24 January 1982; 21 October 1982.**

## Introduction

Maurice Isserman, noted for his revisionist views of the Communist Party, conducted this pair of unpublished interviews to collect material for an intellectual history of twentieth-century American radicalism, *If I Had a Hammer . . . The Death of the Old Left and the Birth of the New Left* (1987). Born in 1951, Isserman's formative years coincided with the radicalism of the Civil Rights Movement and Vietnam protests. During his time at Reed College, he lived in a revolutionary collective. He earned his Ph.D. from the University of Rochester in 1979 as a student of Eugene Genovese, the eminent scholar of slavery and the American South and a long-time Marxist (who would later move to the right). Isserman's dissertation on American Communism had put him at odds with Howe; indeed he criticized Howe and Lewis Coser's *The American Communist Party* (1957) as too severe on the far Left and for giving ammunition to the Right. At that time Isserman was far more sympathetic than Howe to the positions of people such as Communist leader Earl Browder, who defended the Soviet Union. Isserman also corresponded with Dorothy Healey, onetime head of the American Communist Party's Southern California branch. The two would later work together on *Dorothy Healey Remembers: A Life in the American Communist Party* (1990).

Although Isserman's revised dissertation, *Which Side Were You On? The American Communist Party during the Second World War*, came out the same year as this interview, Isserman's own politics at the time were already altering toward a more moderate path in the Left-liberal direction of Irving Howe. Like the 1950s, the 1980s were a time when the Left felt itself in limbo; this interview reviews important elements of its history in a search for continuity and for a possible path to the future. Indeed, the interview reveals the idea of revolutionary change as illusory given the history and culture of the United States, which tends toward long periods of relatively conservative quiescence punctuated with bursts of upheaval. It is during these bursts that the Left has had a chance to see some of its ideas enacted, albeit in a piecemeal fashion, as in the New Deal reforms of Franklin D. Roosevelt.

From its start, a primary raison d'être of *Dissent* was to serve as a platform to promoting left-wing ideals during the conservative 1950s, a role it found itself repeating at the time of this interview, at the outset of Ronald Reagan's presidency. Significantly, the interview occurred at the very moment when *A Margin of Hope* was being published, a time during which Howe looked back nostalgically on the first two postwar decades. He explains: "We were learning to work piecemeal, treating Socialist thought as inherently problematic, quite as every other mode of political thought must be treated in our time."[1] This "piecemeal" approach sometimes meant that *Dissent* gave way to an almost postmodern political fragmentation, though Howe himself would never put it that way. He was no postmodernist. Desperately wanting to revive the Left but realizing he could not, he nonetheless hoped to leave a historical record, perhaps for future generations to complete this task.

In looking back on the 1950s and 1960s, the years of birth and coming to maturity of *Dissent,* Howe speaks with a touch of defiant pride that his magazine had survived, that it had even achieved an honorable reputation. Indeed, the history of *Dissent* is a crucial part of the story of Irving Howe; his life and the biography of the magazine are interwoven far more than is the case with any other person associated with it. Coser and Brian Morton moved on to focus on other interests, whether scholarly or literary, and Michael Walzer and Mitchell Cohen, the current editors, have never been so fully identified with the magazine as was Howe. This interview is part of the backward-looking stance characteristic of Howe's work since the mid-1970s, when he began work on *World of Our Fathers.* It continued throughout his last two decades—hence the span of this collection is characterized by a backward glance that eyes a possible future: the search for a legacy for Howe, *Dissent,* and the utopian ideals of Socialism.

*Dissent* aspired in the 1960s to renew the Left, somehow to bridge the Old Left and the emerging New Left. But in actuality the magazine encountered an incommensurable chasm. Pondering this failure to connect two generations, Howe discusses here the history of *Dissent,* its internal struggles, and its evolving and often embattled political stances. At a time when the radical spark of the 1960s had run its course and the Reagan counterrevolution reigned triumphant, Howe is skeptical and self-critical about *Dissent*'s impact. As he explains, "When we began we thought we were going to have large reconsiderations of Socialist theory, that we would put Humpty Dumpty together again. But this was a foolish expectation." Despite the nadir of influence that radicals were experiencing at the time, it had not been so evident in the 1950s that Socialism's death would be sounded by the late 1980s. And the coming collapse of Communism would deal the final deathblow to the term "Socialism" too, though many conservative critics had long pronounced it already dead.

In this interview, Howe delineates the interplay between a wish to keep alive a democratic version of the Socialist tradition and the difficulty of defining just what that tradition is, both in its relationship to Marxism and its relationship to those parts of Europe that come closest to enacting some version of a democratic Socialism. On the American political and intellectual scene, *Dissent* became a platform less for sweeping statements of vision than for pragmatic policy proposals. Howe explains why the editors believed that this was the only path available: "Even if the idea of Socialism was a) unreal, b) mistaken, or c) very far off, that there was still a tremendous moral and social value in participating in day-to-day struggles that seemed worthwhile and even noble: higher wages, civil rights, the whole spectrum of things that people were concerned with."

Beyond *Dissent*'s role as a mouthpiece for this revised, gradualist version of democratic Socialism, the interview discusses how *Dissent* was also a place, albeit a brief and uncertain home, for independent thinkers, many of them with an anarchist bent and little concern for the details of policy, such as C. Wright Mills, Paul Goodman, and Norman Mailer. Mailer's notorious "The White Negro," published in 1957, was an abortive attempt to include the creative, individualist, beatnik fringe (some might say posers) in a forum for which it was essentially alien. Although gadfly individualists such as Mailer did not remain within the confines of a magazine devoted to measured analysis and gradualist solutions, they nevertheless did exemplify *Dissent*'s anti-ideological bent, its reaction against Communist orthodoxy.

In a strange way, such heterodox writers may have belonged in a magazine that lacked a social movement or even a coherent guiding ideology and the possibility of real political power. For these ostensible weaknesses opened up space for sustained and thoroughgoing intellectual questioning. In a word: for "dissent." In its refusal to take a party line, *Dissent* diverged ideologically from the assumptions of the Old Left and the Trotskyist pieties of the young Howe. The magazine remained staid enough, however, given its ultimate rejection of anarchism and radical individualism, to be always deemed adamantly unsuitable by all sides to serve as a trumpet for the revolutionary New Left of the 1960s. The second interview here furnishes insight into Howe's relationship with the 1960s, a time of burgeoning hopefulness in the Civil Rights Movement and the renewed activism that it birthed, of confusion over Vietnam, and of struggle and frustration in its ambivalent relationship to the New Left. Regarding Vietnam, *Dissent* and Howe felt often caught between a fierce anti-Communism and an awareness of the region's imperialist history and how the United States was implicated in it. The magazine had trouble coming to a firm position, vainly hoping for a "third way" between Communism and capitalism that, in Vietnam at least, had virtually no chance of arriving. Still, *Dissent* never really gave up its dream of a "third way," an aspiration that was part of Howe's own "margin of hope." This was why he always insisted on "two cheers for utopia" (as he titled his final, posthumously published *Dissent* essay), and it was partly why his neoconservative critics castigated him as a naïve utopian and Socialist ideologue who ignored political realities.

It is possible that the activist spirit of the New Left may have buoyed Howe in its infancy, but he quickly found that he could not endorse its leadership and harbored all-too-sound premonitions of the disaster toward which it was hurtling. To Howe, the movement's immature leadership, blissfully unaware of history, saw a grand revolution as imminent. He explains: "Part of the problem was that there was a missing generation on the non-Communist Left. There was a distance of some twenty years between us." The generational critique of the Left played itself out in microcosm in the confrontation several years earlier between Howe and Tom Hayden during a now historic meeting of *Dissent's* editors and SDS leaders that left them permanently divided, and with them the Old and New Left too. Although Howe had intended *Dissent* to fill any such generational gap and to facilitate a historical continuity of Left thinking and Left activism, such hopes were crushed. Indeed, Howe considered the New Left to be obsessed with style at the expense of substance. With his knowledge of left-wing sectarianism and repeated disappointment in the prophesied arrival of Socialism, Howe had grown older and wiser, yet still little able to affect the larger political arena. With bitter 20/20 hindsight, he explains the perspective of the young radicals: "They felt they were involved in a real mass movement, this tremendous thing sweeping the country, and here's this group of sour, aging old social democratic intellectuals, rigid anti-Communists, etc., etc." Given this divergence, *Dissent* never had much of a chance to shape the radicalism of the 1960s. Howe's *Steady Work: Essays in Radicalism, 1954-1966* was published in 1966. Its title alone indicates his aspirations toward political continuity, but it is significant that the book ends at the very moment when the possibilities for the Old and New Left to join hands had evaporated.

Nonetheless it bears noting that the young radicals of the 1960s had moved far closer to Irving Howe by 1982 than the reverse—voices such as Todd Gitlin and Marshall Berman, who had expressed major differences with Howe, even began to write for *Dissent* and ultimately joined its editorial board. He became the Grand Old Man of the Left by the mid-1980s, after the publication of his autobiography, and one can even say that *Dissent* became a big (or at least medium-sized) tent for the liberal-Left, housing both former New Left radicals and Old Left stalwarts. (Isserman himself is an occasional contributor to *Dissent.*)

One can ponder the what-ifs: What if such a development had occurred in the early 1960s? What might have happened then? Howe's leadership of a mass radical movement consisting of the Old Left and the New Left working together would have been at least conceivable. By the time of the Reagan years in the

1980s, it was impossible. Indeed the situation was something of a throwback to the 1950s, when a beleaguered Left had shrunken to a faithful remnant, and its members held together in loyal opposition against a much more powerful shared enemy.

By 1982, Howe seems soberly aware of the realities of history. As he says of *Dissent* and the New Left, "Now it seems to me there was an element of doom in the differences between us." In these reflections Howe's personal mistakes, especially his overreaction to the young New Left leadership, come to seem fated, and the break between the *Dissenters* and the New Left virtually inevitable.

The interview below influenced Isserman's *If I Had a Hammer*, which largely follows Howe's narrative regarding the tragic character of relations between *Dissent* and the New Left. His study does, however, criticize the inflexible nature of Howe's anti-Communism in his dealings with the New Left, as well as the latter's intermittent infatuation with the Cuban Revolution.

## The Interview

### "Success Was Survival."

**Q:** *It seems to me that there was an ambiguity in* Dissent's *outlook—or more basically in its mood—in the 1950s. On the one hand you have a defiant note, best expressed in Harold Rosenberg's article on "Couch Liberalism" where he's responding to Fiedler who says "we're all guilty" and replies, "What do you mean? I'm not guilty. We were right, and we're still right." On the other hand, there's the mood expressed best by [Ignazio] Silone*[2] *in "Choice of Comrades" where he says, "We are all refugees from the International," which I think means that we've all been implicated in some crimes, or at least, we've all paid allegiance to political movements that have not lived up to their promise. You wrote that Silone represented "tired heroism"—there was some criticism in what you wrote, but also admiration and the implication that if you can't have a real political movement at least you can have a strong personal ethic to see you through. Were you aware in the fifties that there was this kind of conflict in mood within* Dissent*?*

**A:** Well, Silone wrote as an ex-Communist and that gave his thing a special slant. But those of us who had not been in the Communist movement didn't especially feel that sense of past sin, so we didn't share that confessional impulse. As Rosenberg said in his piece, we don't want to confess to things we didn't do. But the deeper division you're suggesting there is a real one. In relationship to the intellectuals then moving right, to the [American] Committee for Cultural Freedom, we felt very combative, we felt self-confident, we felt secure. From the very first issue and for several years we were constantly attacking them, sniping at them (after awhile they got quite irritated at this—they felt we showed bad manners. Maybe we did.) But that was on a nonideological basis, in terms of such issues as defending civil liberties against McCarthyism. But to say that you didn't have to be a Socialist, you just had to be a consistent liberal. You didn't even have to be a liberal, just a defender of democratic rights. Since we felt that many of our friends and former allies were not doing that, because of the Cold War, this became one of the main centers of our attack. So on that front we were on the offensive. But if you take the magazine in the fifties from another angle, in its reconsideration of Marxism, of Socialism, we were far from being on the offensive. We were querulous, uncertain, we kept stressing the "problematic" (people who were less friendly would say there was a lot of ideological nail-biting). This is one of the reasons that the magazine never achieved great popularity, and why some of it must seem dull to non-Socialists. Those kinds of articles as a rule are not as lively as the first kind. Obviously Rosenberg's piece attacking Fiedler (which I had a hand in stimulating him to do) attracted a lot of attention, a lot of people were delighted with it. But that really didn't have anything to do with Socialism. We were caught here in a conflict, which has always been present in the magazine, but was especially acute then—the conflict between the journalistic impulse, and on the other side, what I thought of as our fundamental purpose, the reinvestigation of the Socialist possibility. I wasn't going to knock myself out, work without pay, for the first purpose. Because that first purpose, what you might call "intellectual hygiene", fighting against current abuses, I could have done in other places, I could have written some of these things in *Partisan Review*, etc. The major function of *Dissent*, as I saw it, was the more ingrown, "family" considerations of reconsidering Socialism, insofar as we were ever able to do that. There was always this conflict. Sometimes one purpose would predominate, sometimes the other. Our first issue was quite lively, quite polemical, but after it came out some people asked me what was particularly Socialist about it. So then Lew Coser and I sat down and wrote an article called "Images of Socialism," which was rather influential (in a limited way), for the second issue, to face in the other direction.

**Q:** *How about the question of mood? It seemed to me there was almost a kind of sadness informing a lot of the writing. I remember one article where Coser said something to the effect of "what we've gained in humility, we may have lost in persuasiveness."*

**A:** That's true. We were leaving behind a lot of the Socialist tradition, at least its Bolshevik aspects, and this led to a kind of reflectiveness, your word "sadness" is not inappropriate, maybe weariness. It became all the more enjoyable to go on the offensive, to be confident, in the other task.

**Q:** *Silone was a hero of the early* Dissent. *What made him attractive to you?*

**A:** I don't know if the other people around *Dissent* felt this way, but to me he was a hero. See the section in *Politics and the Novel* on Silone: it really answers your question. That essay, "Choice of Comrades," was personally very important to me, more than to the other *Dissent* people, who felt that, later on, Silone got a little soft and there's something to that. In that essay it seems to me he really embodied in human terms the essential crisis of Socialism. The essay suggests that what it finally comes down to is what kind of people do you want to be, what values should they have. That of course is never enough in a political movement, we always knew that, and so did Silone, by the way, who in later years was briefly active in the Italian Socialist Party. Also here was something about the conflict he experienced in his life between being in politics and being a writer, which in a somewhat different way I had also experienced. I felt a kinship with him.

**Q:** *Who were other* Dissent *heroes in the fifties?*

**A:** Well, for a time, C. Wright Mills. I don't know if he was a "hero", but he was certainly a very valiant ally. He wasn't part of our group—I have a sketch of my experiences with him in *The Decline of the New*, a piece that I wrote after his death. When we came out we were attacked very harshly—Nathan Glazer did an attack on *Dissent* in *Commentary*—and Mills, who was not part of our group and never would be, came to our defense. (Mills never had any "movement" in him. Most people who have been in movements, good ones or bad ones, are different from people who have not been. They have certain kinds of training and habits, good habits and bad habits. Mills was not the kind to get involved in movements. Later on he wanted to be a guru for the New Left but you couldn't see him sitting down and raising money for a magazine, putting it out, going to the printer, etc.) But he did come to our defense writing a very sharp reply to Glazer in *Commentary*. And at that time *Commentary* was a very influential magazine—it was turning to the right, but what that meant then was very different from it meant under Podhoretz. It was by comparison much more liberal and open. His letter gave us an important sense of having friends who were supporting us. We were a lot younger then, most of us in our thirties. I was thirty-three, Coser thirty-eight or thirty-nine, and it made a great difference in tone. We had a lot more energy, zip. We found other allies in the intellectual world. Harold Rosenberg, who was some kind of estranged freelance Marxist, Luxemburgist, I don't know exactly how to describe him. He had been in a state of withdrawal for some years, not writing in the usual intellectual magazines, and we prodded him to come out of semi-retirement, and he wrote a couple of very powerful pieces which were important for the magazine. The magazine has never had enough resources of its own, enough writers, we were like a baseball team which could field nine good players, but if somebody got injured there were no substitutes. So characteristically if we put out a strong issue, you could be pretty damn sure the next one would be weaker. Meyer Schapiro and Norman Mailer were others who were close to us and helpful allies. But if you ask who were our "heroes," I don't know if I can answer your question.

**Q:** *What about Trotsky? I'm thinking of the publication of his diaries in exile, which were reviewed and excerpted in* Dissent *in the fifties.*

**A:** We were moved by the personal element in Trotsky then, we were moved by the image of a man holding to his views at all costs. The excerpt we ran from his diaries had very little explicit political matter. But we had moved away from Trotskyism. Starting *Dissent* marked the culmination of this move, not the beginning. When we started, we considered printing articles reconsidering Bolshevism, but we didn't because we had lost interest in that. We more or less decided that that was finished as far as we were concerned. So Trotsky was just a figure we admired for his moral courage. We certainly didn't look to him for political guidance. We had become Left social democrats. As for our identification with Trotsky in exile, we didn't think of ourselves as great heroes. In some things people have written, like Victor Navasky's book with its praise for *Dissent,* it strikes me as slightly comic. It makes it seem as if we were being harassed or we were fighting with our backs to the wall. Maybe psychologically, or intellectually.

But nobody was bothering us, we weren't important enough. But I suppose to some extent the image of Trotsky as a moral hero in the late thirties was a reinforcement for some of us, for people like Geltman and Plastrik and I who had come out of that milieu. Then there were others who had nothing to do with it: Bernie Rosenberg, Coser.

**Q:** *This was not a very hospitable time for Left intellectuals, even if nobody was knocking on your door at midnight. Did you have a sense of being beleaguered?*

**A:** I remember when I got an offer to come and teach at Brandeis in 1953, just before the magazine started. Until then I had been freelancing. The offer was attractive, but I was a little scared. I wrote to Coser, who was then at Brandeis, and asked if it was the kind of place that would protect us from McCarthyism. He answered, very cogently, that if it was a mild attack it would be all right, but if it was a major thrust we shouldn't count on it. Actually Brandeis was OK. We had a sense of being intellectually beleaguered. Let me put it this way. I had been, in a marginal way, a member of the New York Intellectual *Partisan Review* milieu. And now there was a kind of [breach] between us and them. And they of course were more numerous and powerful. So we were beleaguered in that way, within the intellectual world. But then we were beleaguered in another way, within the anti-Stalinist left-wing world, [where] we were also looked upon with some hostility because we were anti-organizational, anti-ideological. The Shachtman group understandably felt bitter about us, and they felt in some way that *Dissent* was directed against them. There are different ways of feeling beleaguered. We felt beleaguered, but we felt good. In the late sixties I felt beleaguered, but I didn't feel good. In the fifties we were proud, happy, pleased about it.

**Q:** *In* Dissent's *first issue you wrote that in America today there's no significant Socialist movement, and in all likelihood no such movement will appear in the immediate future.*

**A:** We were sure right about that.

**Q:** *And yet, throughout the decade there are articles saying this or that event marks a turning point, or is the harbinger of better things to come. You wrote an article about the Montgomery bus boycott in which you compared its significance to the sit-down strikes in the thirties.*

**A:** But we weren't talking about a Socialist movement. You're right. Towards the end of the decade there's a real feeling of breaking out of the constrictedness of the cold war business, we feel the conservative mood is coming to an end, and there's tremendous sense of release, hope; the Kennedy election confirms that, at least symbolically. Some of our friends were involved, like Bayard Rustin with the Freedom Riders.[3] Michael Walzer went down to North Carolina in 1960 or 1961 and interviewed black students. There we are talking about an American social movement, but it had nothing to do with Socialist movements.

**Q:** *Well, did you see yourself as a center for some sort of reborn Socialist movement?*

**A:** Here I think there would be differences of opinion. Probably Coser and some of the others were less oriented toward that possibility. My guess would be that he really began to feel there wasn't much hope for an American Socialist movement. What was necessary was to "stand fast," so to speak, a moral obligation. I still had more interest in the idea of an organizational resurgence. So that when DSOC was formed many years later, I became moderately active in it. Or take Joe Clark, who came out of the CP. Joe has always been by nature more responsive to organizational things than some of our other people, like Bernie Rosenberg, who was never in an organization and doesn't think in those terms. In the early sixties we weren't thinking of *Dissent* as the "center" of a new Socialist movement; we were so interested, so stirred up by the birth of the Civil Rights Movement, and then the beginnings of the new student movement to which in its early days we were quite sympathetic, that this was enough.

**Q:** *There were* Dissent *conferences and* Dissent *study groups on a number of campuses, which suggests to me at least an attempt to be an intellectual center in an organized movement.*

**A:** Yeah, that's fair enough. Those groups didn't survive. We dropped that. But in the late fifties and early sixties we did have such groupings, and I suppose the logic of such groupings is the hope of reforming an organization.

**Q:** *Who was the force behind those? Who was most interested, who did the work?*

**A:** Well, in New York it would always be Stanley [Plastrik]. I was in Boston, and behind it there, along with Milton Sachs, who was close to us then. And Lew came. We had a group at Brandeis. The faculty was pretty wild by the standards of the time, and we had six or seven people involved there. I don't think you should overestimate the importance of those groups. We thought of them partly as support groups for the magazine, more than the basis for any movement.

**Q:** *There are a lot of articles in* Dissent *in the fifties on the British Labour Party. You're reprinting stuff by Cole,*[4] *and Stanley is writing articles analyzing the British situation. In a way you're acting as if you're a ginger group for the Labour Party, except there's this ocean in the way. Did you hope for the possibility of some similar party developing in America?*

**A:** No. The further along we went, the more skeptical we became about the possibility of a mass Socialist party, or even something like the British Labour Party. We began to move in two directions. First, toward using the category of "welfare state" as an analytical apparatus and concern, which we hadn't quite done before, at least not in a coherent way; and second, to the idea that though there would not be a Socialist movement of any consequence, there would be a series of autonomous movements of different kinds, trade union, black, things of that sort. So that the idea of Socialism began to seem more distant, more abstract. And though we still thought it was our obligation to think and talk about it, there began to grow a gap between the concerns of the immediate historical moment and the idea of Socialism. We felt we wanted to bring Socialist values to bear upon contemporary politics, but we didn't see much likelihood that there was going to be a new organizational focus. As for the British Labour Party, we felt they were going through intellectual experiences parallel to our own, and also because various times over the past thirty years the magazine would turn towards different social democratic movements where it seemed there was some intellectual life. So, for example, in recent years we became interested in discussions of Sweden. In the late fifties there was a lot of intellectual life in the British Labour Party. We felt they were articulating some of our concerns. We learned from them. I was in touch to some extent with Cole, not with [Richard] Crossman,[5] and not with [Anthony] Crosland (at that time he was a little too far to the right for us, though I think he was the brightest of the bunch).[6]

**Q:** *Do you think* Dissent's *tendency to look overseas for, if not models, then inspiration was a habit left over from your days in the Trotskyist and Shachtmanite movements?*

**A:** Possibly, though that's something that's been there since the beginning in American radicalism, in all groups. I don't want to be quoted on this because it sounds self-serving, but I think at points *Dissent* has been of a higher intellectual caliber than most similar journals in Europe because we weren't encumbered by organization; we didn't have to worry about what this branch would say, what that group would think. In some ways, though we looked to them, we were also ahead of them. We were ahead of them, for example, in considering what Socialism could mean for a relatively prosperous and stable industrial society. Now if you have a mass movement of hundreds of thousands of people you don't have to face this question, you're busy electing people, doing this and that. In some ways we were ahead because of our situation. But in the fifties, in the [Clement] Attlee and post-Attlee periods in the British Labour Party, there had been real achievement and real difficulties, and some of these people were doing serious thinking.[7]

**Q:** *There were several articles in the early* Dissent *that presented critiques of left-wing sectarianism, Coser's being the most notable. You prided yourselves on your break with the sectarian, dogmatic mold of Socialist politics, but were there habits of thought, "souvenirs" of your time in the Trotskyist and Shachtmanite movement that you carried with you in these years.*

**A:** Before I answer that, let me say one thing about Coser's article. I felt it was very cogent and sharp, but I thought there was a vindictive edge to it and wasn't entirely happy with it. One of the things you have to get clear is that it is not as if every piece reflects a collective purpose or intent. Manny Geltman and Stanley were unhappy with Coser's piece. But we printed it, because we believed in free exchange. I felt there was an element of excess to that piece beyond what was necessary. What habits did we bring over? That's a very interesting question. Look at yesterday's [*Dissent* editorial board] meeting. I think it wouldn't be hard to say to yourself which of the people who spoke had been in an organized movement and which had not. The people who were in organized movements may be as shallow, as wrong-headed, as superficial as anyone could be and yet they develop a certain style, you learn how to talk. I didn't think George Eckstein had much to say, and he said it very poorly. [Bogdan] Denitch, I don't know if he had more to say than George, but he said it coherently, assertively.[8] I didn't think Joe Clark had much to say, but again he said it well, aggressively, loudly, etc. What we brought was a certain style, and in the case of Plastrik, Geltman, and I, we learned it from Shachtman. You took pride when you spoke; there should be a beginning, a middle, and an end. You took pride in giving a coherent presentation, even without notes. When I give a political speech, I notice I still make the notes in the same way that Shachtman did. I learned it as a kid, imitating him. He had habit of cutting a sheet of paper in half, lengthwise. It's very clever, because when you're speaking if you have a very wide line it's hard for the eye to follow. If it's narrow, you can move more quickly with it. That's a trivial detail. But there was the whole pride in coherence, in theory, and sometimes of course the result was and is glibness. Certain references, certain terms, certain comparisons. Let's say we're talking about Poland in the last thirteen months, and you make a reference to "dual power" and your listener thinks of Trotsky's very brilliant discussion of dual power and the Russian Revolution. Someone else can be just as intelligent and thoughtful, and not have that particular reference. So I think we brought that over. Also I think we made a deliberate effort to break with some of those efforts. To break with the habits of high theorizing, and pompous world situation reviews.

**Q:** *Well, of course, the problem with a habit is that you're not aware of it being a habit, naturally [assuming] everyone reasons the way I do. How did you become aware of these habits?*

**A:** We began to make fun of ourselves a little bit, and when one of us would go off on one of these elaborate constructions, somebody would make an ironic remark. We tried to learn to converse rather than to speechify. The tradition of the Left has always been that you sit around and make speeches at each other. And then there were people who came from other backgrounds, who spoke in very different styles. A guy like Bernie Rosenberg always speaks ironically, amusingly, chaotically, never tries to build up a big theoretical system. Later on, someone like Dennis Wrong, he would speak more empirically. Coser, who came out of the European Left movement, after a time was very much influenced by American sociology, so some of that would creep into his language. That affected us. And as our general theoretical structures began to collapse, what had indeed been a habit became available for self-scrutiny.

**Q:** *And how did this affect what went into the magazine, as well as what was said in meetings?*

**A:** When we began, we thought we were going to have large reconsiderations of Socialist theory, that we would put Humpty Dumpty together again. But this was a foolish expectation. But after Coser and I wrote our "Images of Socialism" piece, we came to realize that the project was beyond our capacities, probably beyond anyone's capacities, that if the historical crisis was indeed as deep as we thought it was, it wasn't going to be solved by writing an article or a thesis. One habit we got rid of damn fast, thank God, was having numbered theses. Very pedantic. There's a lot of scholasticism in left-wing writing. We began to think there was no point in trying that big reconstruction. It would take a very long time and maybe it wasn't necessary to have theory embracing every aspect of human experience. So we didn't know whether we believed in the labor theory of value, but we found it quite possible to live without that. In the beginning we were close to Karl Korsch,[9] and it was clear that [such a theory] was the sort of thing he wanted, and we didn't, so we just sort of parted. He didn't know what we were up to. At the beginning we had the idea we should look for big theoretical articles, like in the beginning we had an article on Russia by Adam Kaufman, refurbishing Shachtman on bureaucratic collectivism, but then we lost interest in that kind of thing. We moved from high theory to middle-level intellectual work, not just empirical, not just what happened last week, but somewhere between abstraction and empiricism.

**Q:** *Clearly one of* Dissent's *major interests, which never wavered, was in the nature of Soviet society. People like Deutscher*[10] *would come into* Dissent's *pages, and then be shown the door when they disagreed on that issue. If the magazine was not polemical on some issues, if it lacked that harsh edge, it certainly had it on that one issue.*

**A:** Absolutely. We felt that the question of Stalinism was the key crucial political and moral question for the Left, and on this there could be no ambiguity. We drew the line. On many other issues there could be disagreement and tolerance, but on that question, we didn't feel that people couldn't express other kinds of views but they'd have to find someplace else to do it. With Deutscher, I myself wrote to him and invited him to participate. He was an old polemicist. He didn't feel offended. He was angry, but not offended, if you know the distinction. He replied quite strongly with his own point of view. We thought it was important to confront Deutscher's views because he was a man of some substance. He wasn't exactly "shown the door," because he was never, as it were, invited in. He was a guest.

**Q:** *There were a couple of articles that raised the possibility of a new analysis of Stalinism, of the possibilities of forms of national Communism emerging in Eastern Europe.*

**A:** You mean after 1956? Sure. The question of what is now called Eurocommunism was then called national Communism, not exactly the same, but some similarities. On that we were ready to be open. We saw the possibility of some trend towards democratization arising from within the ranks of the party, but we were skeptical of Deutscher's view that something could develop organically out of the society itself. We were very stirred and excited by Hungary. Coser and I wrote a sort of longish article and put it out as a pamphlet for our subscribers.

**Q:** *What did the revolts within the Communist system mean to you? Did you see it as a rebirth of the possibility for Socialism?*

**A:** In a totalitarian society every revolt is going to have a spectrum of different opinions. Up at Brandeis I had a violent debate with Herbert Marcuse. Marcuse's view was that the Hungarian revolution had a strong fascist potential; he didn't exactly come out against it, but he wasn't going to be for it. I and Lew and the others were very much for the Hungarian revolt, though we recognized that there was always the danger of people we didn't like taking over. That was the risk of democracy. The same thing's true of Poland now. The argument is inverted when applied to right-wing authoritarian countries. Some people say if you have a revolt against the military government in Chile, the Communists will take over, but I think that is a risk you have to take.

**Q:** *You used the word "totalitarianism" to describe Communist countries, but you don't seem to use it in the same way that Hannah Arendt did, since she would have denied the possibility of there being any base for revolt, the nature of totalitarian societies being such that this was simply eliminated.*

**A:** As I remember it, in that little thing that Coser and I did, we took a poke at Hannah and at Deutscher, arguing against both theories. She had to revise her views after Hungary, in fact she issued a new edition of her book on totalitarianism, where she spoke about the role of the workers' councils. I think you're right, that if you took her theory of totalitarianism without qualification, then it posits the idea of a historical dead-end. Orwell's *Nineteen Eighty-Four* in fictional form ratifies this idea in an admonitory, fearful way. This was very much part of the atmosphere of the 1950s. I've written about this in my own book. I think it would be hard for someone who didn't live through that to understand the power of that feeling, the sense that totalitarianism was virtually unbudgeable, short of war. Hungary, East Germany, later Czechoslovakia, shook that, and yet in another way confirmed it, because we felt a terrible frustration in regard to Hungary. Either you are for peace, or you are for freedom, and in some ways there is a conflict between the two. And while we might rant and rave about Hungary, we were not in favor of starting a world war to save Hungary.

**Q:** *It seems to me that that sense of history coming to a dead end was rejected, to some extent, in* Dissent *in the discussion of mass society. At the very end of the 1950s, you wrote an article about the possibilities for political change and said one of the things we have to do is get rid of this stupid idea that Americans are just automatons tied to their TVs. But one of the places that "stupid idea" had appeared repeatedly was in* Dissent. *Were you always uncomfortable with that idea?*

**A:** That's a complicated thing. We had a lot of stuff about mass culture and mass society. It was a theme we virtually dropped after the fifties. Some of the stuff on mass culture was good analytically and critically. My own personal opinion is that the theory of mass society had some validity, and still has some validity; there are elements of experience in modern capitalist societies that class analysis will not explain. But some writers pushed it too far. Coser had the inclination to do that in those years. Possibly I did. I didn't write about it that much. No one escapes the pressure of an historical moment. Marxism wasn't working very well, class analysis wasn't that effective. I published a piece in those days, it's in one of my collections, it's called "Mass Society and Post-Modernist Fiction," which takes up some of this in literary terms, and offers a description of the theory of mass society, the atomization of publics, etc. I think there is a certain truth to that, but how much? So we moved toward an eclectic view, trying to combine elements of Marxism, the mass society approach, Danny Bell's pluralist theory, whatever seemed to work. I wouldn't doubt that a kind of *fin du monde* was there at some points in the fifties.

**Q:** *Of course those ideas would continue and become very influential in the sixties. I encountered them through Marcuse. The New Left's conclusions about all this were voluntarist. You have a mass society, so you have to break out of it, become an outlaw, whatever. In the fifties the conclusions were determinist. You can't challenge this, you can't move.*

**A:** That's true. Marcuse took some of this and gave it a voluntarist, and I would add, elitist bias or turn. We printed a very brilliant article later on by a young man named Allen Graubard attacking Marcuse on just this point. There was a sense in the fifties of "no exit." All doors closed. And that's why when things began to move in the south with the blacks, and Kennedy came along, we had a sense of "my God, oxygen!"

**Q:** *There is a certain historical irony in all this, that ideas devised in one period to describe a particular sense of reality will turn into their opposite in the next.*

**A:** To be very dialectical about it, the final irony is that there was an element of continuity here.

**Q:** *In the sense that . . . ?*

**A:** In the sense that Marcuse didn't believe there was any possibility of shaking ordinary people. Finally he just wanted to shock society, through a kind of salutary terror. In both the fifties version of mass culture theory and the sixties version, there was a disdain, or a lack of interest in the possibilities for ordinary democratic, small or big "d" participation in the system, reform, etc. There was a kind of apocalyptic view behind it. All or nothing. If you can't make a revolution, you can't do anything.

**Q:** *In 1959 you wrote that the Democratic victories in the recent elections represented an opportunity for another liberal advance in American society, perhaps* *even of the dimensions that we had in the 1930s. To which several other editors responded quite critically, Plastrik, Mailer, Rosenberg among them. Coser described the elections as the victory of "sophisticated experts at mass manipulation."*

**A:** Yeah. I think, for once, I was right. Things did open up. Not so much for what Kennedy did as for what he made possible. The early sixties were a very hopeful, constructive moment in American political life. There were internal tensions among us. There were people like Rosenberg, who wouldn't agree with Marcuse, but his position was always essentially an old-fashioned Debsian Socialist position. You stick by gospel, and if you can't run candidates you still don't vote for old party candidates. I don't think the magazine showed this, but by this time we were, or some of us were, learning that if you pull down the lever for an old party candidate it wasn't the sure road to hell. It took us a long time to make that adaptation.

**Q:** *You certainly wrote scathingly about Stevenson, Humphrey, and other Democrats in the fifties.*

**A:** I think I was right. I don't think there was a contradiction between saying those things, on the one hand, and saying we had to vote for Stevenson. There was a division then among us, as there has been in every election since. The people who would go along with me, by and large, would be Geltman, Plastrik, Coser sometimes. Rosenberg would always take a kind of Debsian position. Sid Lens,[11] when he was near us, would have that kind of Socialist fundamentalist position. The three of us, Manny, Stanley and I, got to this position pretty early. I think I voted for Stevenson in 1952, and said something about it in the first issue, in a sort of embarrassed or evasive way.

**Q:** *At the risk of repeating myself, do you think there is some validity to this idea of* Dissent *creating ideas in the fifties that would, in a later incarnation in the sixties, horrify you?*

**A:** This is a question you should really put to Coser. Those people around us who spoke about mass society in the fifties, they were really saying that they thought there was no politics left for Socialists. And that's one reason they turned so much to themes of mass culture. This was a point of criticism that some people made of the *Dissent* group as a whole. That we had given up on the idea of politics. Some liberal intellectuals around *Commentary* said that. We were making the analysis of mass culture into a substitute for political activity or analysis. I think there was something to that in retrospect. Since I and Stanley and Manny didn't find that a comfortable place to be, one of the reasons we turned to what is now the DSOC position is that we wanted to get out of that cul de sac. I think there were important differences between that position and the position that Marcuse took. I don't think that the contempt for liberalism, for day-to-day politics, for trade unions, which was present in Marcuse's views, was also present in those *Dissent* people in the fifties who held to the mass society view. I think you could argue that the mass society theory, at least a little bit, led to that position, [or] was inherent in the mass society approach. Behind the leftist theory of mass society (there is also an aristocratic version associated with Ortega y Gasset), there is a feeling that the Marxist theory of the revolutionary role of the proletariat is mistaken, that the working class had been assimilated or absorbed, or whatever. Some of that was present later in Marcuse, but it took a much milder, less arrogant form in the fifties. Some of us were moving away from that. We couldn't believe that when things began breaking in the South that this was merely epiphenomenal, it wasn't revolutionary, etc. The mass society approach carried within itself strong resemblances to, or residues of, the old left-wing sectarianism. Either you got our full program from dialectics to anthropology, or it's nothing. We felt it was something. In his very interesting article in 1939 on the USSR and war, Trotsky wrote that if there wasn't to be a world proletarian revolution, then it would be the task of Socialists to defend the interests of the slaves, since he thought everyone would be enslaved. Well, everyone was not enslaved, democratic society persisted; it's foolish to call workers slaves. But we had another version of that. And I still feel this. Even if the idea of Socialism was a) unreal, b) mistaken, or c) very far off, there was still a tremendous moral, political, social value in participating in every day-to-day struggle that seemed desirable, [such as] higher wages, civil rights, the whole spectrum of things that people were concerned with. And there was a tendency among the subscribers to the mass society theory to say, well, it's all one flat, boring plain of affluence, etc.

**Q:** *There was one* Dissent *editor who certainly gave voice to themes that would later come to dominate the sixties, and that was Norman Mailer. I'm thinking of his article on "The White Negro." His articles of the late fifties had a very apocalyptic strain. You had to be like blacks, you had to live on the edge, sexual politics. What is he doing in* Dissent? *He's kind of the wild card in the deck.*

**A:** He's the wild card in the deck. He's the price we have to pay for saying we're ready to be open to a variety of views. Mailer had come in, we looked upon him as an acquisition, he was interesting, he was lively, he was friendly. I later felt, and I've written this, that I made a moral slip in accepting "The White Negro" without at least challenging him, arguing with him about that sentence about the candy-store keeper. On the other hand, you know, the magazine never had enough good material, certainly never had enough lively material. After you've edited twenty-five pieces by sociologists who can't write English and you get in a piece like "The White Negro," full of bounce and brilliance, and I was probably the first person to read it, this sensational piece which he contributes for nothing, for which he could have gotten thousands of bucks even then, and it helps liven and sell the magazine and get it around, it would have taken a lot of strength of character to get fussy with him. I probably was afraid he'd say, well, screw you, I'll sell it to *Esquire* or something. Which he could have done in a minute. I must say for Norman, he's a very nice guy, and after all the years of disagreements, he's been very nice to us. He has a certain gallantry, there's nothing nasty or bitter or sour about him. I should have challenged him on that sentence, and I might have been doing him a favor if I had, since he's taken a lot of flak over it since, and may well regret it.

**Q:** *Apart from that one objectionable sentence, the whole style and message of the article is so un-*Dissent.

**A:** Right. Well, he was the wild card. Soon after that he went his own way. He's kept his name on the masthead, but has no real connection with the magazine . . . He would come to meetings and express those ideas, and we'd sort of stare, and didn't know what to make of him. But he was always so nice, and he'd laugh, and we'd laugh.

**Q:** *What was the response to "The White Negro"?*

**A:** A lot of attention. There were some objections. Ned Polsky had a very cogent criticism of it in a subsequent issue.[12] People didn't say, why'd you print this, because they understood we didn't have a party line. Mailer came out of the Wallace movement, he had certainly been a fellow-traveler. The first time I met him was at the Waldorf Conference in 1949, when he made a speech that shocked its sponsors. We met at that point, I came up to him afterwards and introduced myself. We made an appointment. He was involved in the founding of *Dissent.* We weren't so rich in allies that we could afford to turn people like that away.

**Q:** *Do you think he showed a better insight as to what was coming down the road than other writers in* Dissent? *A lot of "The White Negro" is a brilliant prediction of the late 1950s.*

**A:** In some sense, of course. In some sense we were limited by our rationalism. That's one of the handicaps of the Marxist tradition, I suppose. We didn't see the potential for violent outburst. In some sense he anticipated it, in some sense he helped create it, too. He was the father of some pretty miserable stuff. He was prescient. I don't know if there was ever an actual living person you could call a hipster, but as an archetype that [idea] was very brilliant.

**Q:** *Was C. Wright Mills ever an editor of* Dissent?

**A:** No. Mills once said to me, "I can understand equality and liberty, but I don't know what they were talking about when they said fraternity." It was one of the most self-perceptive things he ever said. He had no feeling for fraternity. He really was a cowboy radical. He had no gift for cooperative relationships. There were tensions in our group, naturally, but still it's remarkable that we kept working together for twenty-seven, twenty-eight years with only a few defections. He was not part of our group, but he was an ally and a friend in the fifties.

**Q:** *In 1958 or 1959 he writes a "dear Irving" letter complaining about the "futilitarians of the Old Left," and focusing on the Third World War thing. And he asks, "in foreign policy, from what do you dissent?" and suggests that in its assumptions* Dissent *resembles Dulles.*

**A:** I remember. He knew better than that.

**Q:** *Of course. In your very first issue you say that America has to learn it's living in a revolutionary age. And after Dien Bien Phu, you said we regret that the Stalinists have taken over, but if the U.S. gets involved in Vietnam it would only lead to a long, futile war—a very prescient comment.*[13] *However, there are certain articles that go the other way. You wouldn't disagree with, let's say, George Kennan's argument that the Soviet Union has to be contained. And it must have been hard to know where to draw the line sometimes: we have to contain the Soviet Union, but we don't support American foreign policy. That becomes most glaringly obvious in a long article by Joseph Buttinger, a critique of* The Ugly American, *which turns into a defense of American policy in Vietnam. "Vietnam is the first country in Asia where the West, by replacing imperialism with policies of aid, has stopped the Russians without firing a shot. Our aid can give life and prosperity to a war-ravaged country."*

**A:** Which turned out to be nonsense. We were not happy with that article. We might as well go into the whole Buttinger story. Without the Buttingers we never could have started the magazine. Here we'd better make some distinctions about what I want you to quote, and what has to be off the record. Buttinger was an Austrian Socialist. After the Dollfuss repression in 1934 he led the underground Socialist youth.[14] Apparently he was very good. He came from a poor family, and was a self-educated Socialist. His wife came from a very wealthy American family, the Gardiners, from Chicago I think, involved in the stockyards, or something like that. She was a medical student. In some ways her story parallels the story in Lillian Hellman.[15] I suspect Julia[16] may in part be based on Muriel [Gardiner]. She helped the Socialists, helped rescue people. She's now eighty years old, and a terrific woman. She writes on psychological themes, she's an analyst.

When we started the magazine we made up our mind we would not fall into the trap that a lot of left-wing little magazines have: you start, you get subscriptions, and you collapse after two issues. We wanted to be sure that at least we could deliver one year's worth of subscriptions. We raised among ourselves and friends about a thousand dollars. That wasn't as little as it may seem today.

But it wasn't enough. I was then at Princeton and I gave a seminar which became my book *Politics and the Novel*. The Buttingers came to hear me. They were living nearby. They were not involved in Socialist politics, but Lew Coser knew them, or knew of them, and got in touch with them. They were friendly, and they contributed a thousand dollars. And that enabled us to get started. They have been regular contributors to the magazine ever since. This is no secret. This is all still on the record. They've never tried to influence editorial policy. Joe would participate as an editor and express his opinions, but they never tried to do what angels so often try to do, to influence policy by their control of the money. In those days he became very much involved in the Vietnam thing. At that point he had a pro-Diem line. We weren't that aware of the whole question of Vietnam except we were dubious. Buttinger was not a very skillful writer, and he handed this thing in. And it was a problem. But we printed it.

Now we're off the record. We weren't very happy with it. But this happens in all magazines. You start with the intention of printing only the best ever written, but it doesn't work out that way. What would have happened if we hadn't printed it, I don't know. It might have led to a rupture. We felt in some sense morally obliged to print it. It wasn't yet clear to us in 1959 what the political implications of Vietnam were. Very soon afterwards he made a big switch, and became a severe critic of his own earlier views on U.S. policy in Vietnam. If you don't have a party line, then it becomes very hard to make determinations as to what won't go in. There are tacit boundaries. Here we can go back on the record. We all disagreed with what Buttinger wrote there. We were not tremendously happy with it. It all got lost in the shuffle anyway.

But to come back to the major question of foreign policy. This has always been a major source of difficulty for us. I think we worked out over the years a pretty consistent line on domestic policy. Whether it's right or wrong is another question. On foreign policy there is still some remnants in our people of the old Third Camp position, "a plague on both your houses." The form of that among people like Geltman and Plastrik, and here to some extent Coser too, was that we couldn't say it didn't make any difference who won, the West for all its faults represented democracy, the Russian camp was totalitarian. We were not indifferent to the struggle. For example on the question of the Berlin crisis, we were for the West (leaving aside the question of what our "support" means). At the same time we recognized that there were counter-impulses in the West, imperialist, reactionary impulses, and that especially in regard to the third world, this made for severe difficulties, and things were being done which we were opposed to. In the fifties the third-world thing hadn't yet become as important as it would later on. Then it was the question of Europe. And there we felt very strongly that Europe had to be protected, and only American military might was sufficient to do that. At that point the fear of Communist victory in France or Italy was a genuine one. So the formula we developed was one of "critical support." That was the position which Geltman, Plastrik,` and I took when we quit the ISL. It's a difficult formula, with all kinds of ambiguities. You can push it more towards support one time, towards criticism another. If you go through the magazine very carefully, it may be that by an excessively close textual analysis you'll get an unfaithful picture. There's a shift in emphasis here and there. In any given issue I disagree with a third of what's printed.

**Q:** *That's an interesting point, that you were more interested in Europe than the rest of the world. In your review of a Mills pamphlet you asked what would be the practical results of the U.S. dismantling its overseas military bases. Which means one thing if you're talking about Frankfurt, and something quite different if you were talking about Saigon.*

**A:** Take a look at the piece I wrote about Mills that reviews the whole conflict. To me that was a very painful experience. Mills was a gifted man. That was the first major loss the journal experienced. And it was a personal loss.

**Q:** *I don't want to second-guess your editorial judgment [of] twenty years ago, but I came across several articles in* Dissent *that just didn't seem to belong there. One was Richard Hofstadter's chapter on populism.*[17]

**A:** Why did we print that? Well, first because Dick was a personal friend of mine. And secondly he's very good. And there were times when I would feel that quality counts for more than opinion. I would get tired of Sidney Lens's prose and would want something very accomplished instead. We drew upon a group of intellectuals, people like George Lichtheim,[18] Nick [Nicola] Chiaromonte, Harold Rosenberg, Lionel Abel and some others, and we would print things that were of varying viewpoints. One of the problems the journal now has is that most of them are gone.

**Q:** *Well, whatever the problems of its interpretation, "The Age of Reform" is a wonderful piece of history, so maybe that's not the best example. But let me give you another example. Hannah Arendt's article on Little Rock.*

**A:** Oh, that. That we printed in order to start a fight. Occasionally you've got to be a journalist. You print a dumb article by a famous person because it will attract attention, and then you arrange to have it attacked. We all disagreed with it. If you don't print some anomalous things in the magazine then it becomes terribly predictable and boring.

**Q:** *Who did you have in mind as a readership when you started the journal?*

**A:** We weren't entirely sure. There were quite a few people who had dropped out of the various radical groups but maintained an interest in these ideas. Some of them were friends of ours. Then there was a generation of young academics who were leaning toward the left. Say people of your age today, who are close to DSOC. That was a group we had in mind. There was also a handful of people around the trade union movement. That would be about it.

[We were looking for] not so much an academic audience, as one of leftish, intellectually inclined people. *Dissent* isn't a magazine that lends itself to easy subway reading. We didn't attract so much of the older radicals, people who had been in the SP, the ISL, some from the CP, who were either uninterested in that "junk," as they would regard it after they left, or who looked for something that would keep more of the old Marxist language, something like *New Politics,* when it later appeared. We wouldn't find many of our old friends' names on our subscription list. Mostly they were new names.

**Q:** *When you were starting the journal in 1953 how would you have defined success?*

**A:** Survival. At that point just to be able to keep going was a success. The organizational core of the magazine was composed of people who had come out of the ISL. One of the things we couldn't bear was the prospect of being heavily in debt, and having printers' bills facing us. We couldn't practice Keynesian economics. Under Stanley's management I think there was only one year when the magazine was in debt. We needed the psychological reassurance, not of having money, but at least of balancing the books. Beyond that, success would mean getting a whole new generation of people around us. We got some. Walzer was a tremendous acquisition. He was my student at Brandeis. And there were some others. But in honesty I'd have to say that essentially the magazine has been the voice of a particular generation. If we've had influence, if there will be continuity, it will take different forms.

## 21 October 1982

### On SDS, Vietnam, and the New Left

**Q:** *In reading through* Dissent *in the later 1960s, the years when I was in college and a member of SDS, it struck me that I had no memory at all of ever reading or hearing of* Dissent *in those days, even though by the standards of the time I suppose I was a reasonably well-read young radical. Do you think that people in the New Left, perhaps better-read than I, were exposed to any of the arguments you made in the 1960s about the dangers you saw in the direction the New Left was headed?*

**A:** My sense is that there wasn't the kind of connection that there ideally should have been. The New Left was a movement of activism, focused around a couple of specific issues. Probably some of the SDS kids read *Dissent.* As I described it in my book [*A Margin of Hope*], at the beginning there was a meeting with some SDS leaders. It didn't work out very successfully. The SDS people had a whole entanglement with the LID,[19] which I personally was not involved with. Harrington was involved in that. He feels he made mistakes. I think he's overstating it. Possibly he made tactical mistakes. But now it seems to me there was an element of doom in the differences between us. Apart from the intrinsic political and intellectual differences, which were serious enough, there was also a clash of generations, and styles, which made it almost inevitable that we wouldn't be able to get along. I wouldn't push the comparison too far, but there are some elements of comparison between the young militants in the SP vis-à-vis the Old Guard in the early thirties. And I suppose we were cast in the role of the Old Guard (although we weren't quite so old, we were in our forties) vis-à-vis the SDS. Differences of feeling and style and attitude, which to an unmeasurable extent aggravated the division. The funny thing was that in the beginning they probably felt we were too ideological. Then later on, once the Maoists got in, we felt they were too ideological. By the late sixties I was, or felt I was, the subject of a great deal of attack by SDS and its adult fellow-travelers, but it wasn't over anything I wrote. That's an important fact. The written word didn't count for much with them. It counted perhaps excessively with us. I recall reading some crazy thing that SDS put out about "liberal Fascism," which to me raised echoes of "social Fascism," and then I wrote something about it and found I had to remind myself they probably didn't know what social Fascism was.

**Q:** *Let me float a counterfactual proposition. Suppose that the early sixties meeting with SDS leaders had gone differently, that Tom Hayden became the new Michael Harrington. Would it have made any difference in the long run in the development of the New Left?*

**A:** Not if that was the only thing different. I think if the war issue hadn't heated up so fast that the division might not have become so severe, and that at least part of the SDS leadership might have been more amiably inclined towards us. There was something about Hayden, that although he was clearly the most intellectually gifted of the group, there was something really hard and rigid and fierce about him. The others were just very nice kids, they were open. If we hadn't been allies, we might have at least had more cordial relations. Part of the problem was that there was a missing generation on the non-Communist left. There was a distance of some twenty years between us. The generation between should have been Harrington's age. The rupture in tradition was something we were paying for very heavily. If the Vietnam War hadn't heated up, if the New Left had had a slower, more organic development, which would have meant not nearly so spectacular a rise in membership and not so extreme a plunge into Marxism-Leninism, then it's entirely possible that we could have done better. We had pretty friendly relations with Al Haber.[20] My relations with [Carl]

Oglesby[21] were always pretty good. Relations with Paul Booth were never as exacerbated. But with some it became absolutely hopeless.

**Q:** *Have you read Todd Gitlin's book?*

**A:** Yes. It's not the whole story, but it's a thoughtful book. We've established more amiable relations since. With Hayden, he's now I suppose to our right; Hayden never stops to make a public accounting of where he's been, why he's changed. I can understand if not appreciate their response. They felt they were involved in a real mass movement, this tremendous thing sweeping the country, and here's this group of sour, aging old social democratic intellectuals, rigid anti-Communists, etc., etc. What did they need us for? Why should they pay attention? In terms of the actual mass movement, there was no particular reason why they should. Something else happened, which I think proved very important. They acquired a whole phalanx of adult fellow-travelers who did them no good. A lot of old would-be Leninists, and half-Leninists, and once-Leninists, who thought, "Oh my God, maybe the old ideas weren't so wrong after all. The revolution is coming. Here's the future cadre." I remember a fight I had, which you should look up, with Philip Rahv, and with a lot of other people. You had people with no politics, or at most milky liberals, and suddenly they're revolutionaries, burning draft cards, etc. They were swept up. It was very hard emotionally to cope with this. Young people want total faith. I think I will see it again, if I live long enough. By 1990 or so there will be a new left wing, and they'll do it too. Maybe this is something that has to be in America. We always talk about how the movement, whatever movement, has to Americanize itself. I must have made a thousand speeches about that. There's always the possibility that part of the sectarianism we don't live, and part of the fanaticism has its roots in the American experience. The Wobblies and the whole Emersonian tradition. This is a problem which no reformist movement has ever been able to cope with.

**Q:** *I have one problem with that Emersonian interpretation. I'm not sure, if you looked at other countries' left-wing movements, you wouldn't find a similar dynamic, which might just be part of the internal dynamics of radical movements instead of the product of a particular national heritage.*

**A:** In England, sure, with the Protestant tradition.

**Q:** *Well, even elsewhere in Europe. Among young people there might be a need for an initial period of total belief.*

**A:** That's true. The only difference here is that it takes the form of personal testimony, which in Catholic countries might not be as important. Even in DSA we see it today. One of the reasons for the crisis in the organization is that the leadership whipped up a lot of excessive expectations for the merger, and the kids got very enthusiastic. Now they see we're still at the stage of recruiting one, two, three people here and there, it's not going to be a big mass upsurge, and they are understandably impatient, and they become quickly disenchanted. Now just think what it was like in 1968 or so when they were surging ahead, they had a mass movement. One of the most fascinating things about the New Left was the rapidity with which it collapsed.

**Q:** *One of the things I liked about Murray Hausknecht's article on Columbia in* Dissent *is the idea that a lot of New Left themes were raised in the pages of* Dissent *in the fifties. What he's suggesting is that there was a political socialization, of sorts, going on in the fifties, that people were imbued with certain radical values, but without the structure of an organized Left, without the example of adults actually practicing left-wing politics. Later on the* Dissent *parents (literal and figurative) were outraged when their children lived out the values which they had gotten from their parents.*

**A:** There's something to that.

**Q:** *I guess that wasn't a question. Another thing that struck me in reading through back issues of* Dissent *from the sixties was that there was never a moment when you say, "OK, that's it, that's the final straw, we're giving up completely on these people in the New Left." You start complaining about the New Left very early, certainly by the time "New Styles of Leftism" came out you were identified as a critic of the movement . . . .*

**A:** That was taken to be a declaration of war.

**Q:** *But even after that you can find articles in* Dissent *favorable to this or that New Left activity or demonstration.*

**A:** That's true. And some *Dissent* people like Walzer felt that I was too harsh on the New Left. Again it was generational thing, because he was younger.

**Q:** *You must have had an enormous sense of disappointment in the sixties when the movement you had spent the whole of the fifties waiting for finally appears, and it's not one you can live comfortably with.*

**A:** Terrible. I would say that in my own political life, though there were other times when I was objectively in more difficulties and more isolated, I never felt more beleaguered than in the late sixties. Because finally in politics it's always the people who are relatively close to you that matter. I mean fighting with Norman Podhoretz, who cares? It's almost fun. In the late sixties it was fratricidal violence. . . . It's interesting that Harrington didn't get the same flak I did; I guess his style is less polemical. He didn't get attacked as much as I did, but didn't get any farther politically with the New Left than I did either. He was honest and said what had to be said, perhaps in more temperate way, but it was the same result.

**Q:** *What relation was there between* Dissent *and LID in this period?*

**A:** It wasn't much. More of a formality than anything else. A number of *Dissent* people had no interest in organizational matters. People like Coser, Plastrik, and Geltman were very skeptical. I was a little more involved partly because of my friendship with Harrington. For a time I was on the LID board. Then there were disagreements on the war. They were just concerned with getting trade union leaders and money. In an interesting way that group repeated the history of the Lovestone group[22] [by] assimilating themselves into the labor bureaucracy. Tom Kahn.[23] So it wasn't an important thing for us.

**Q:** Dissent *seems to have been on the upswing in the early sixties, going bimonthly with a slicker appearance.*

**A:** That didn't work out. A bimonthly has neither the advantages of a quarterly or a monthly. You can't really stay on top of topical events in a bimonthly, but you're more tempted to than in a quarterly. To go to a monthly would have meant a tremendous change, to have a full-time staff, and we could have never afforded it. It was undertaken because we felt life was getting exciting, we wanted to get into the act, but it didn't work. Circulation may have gone up a little bit, but not dramatically.

**Q:** *Very early on* Dissent *began "dissenting" about Vietnam. We talked last time about the Buttinger piece as the one exception to that. There is a continuing search for a "third camp" position on Vietnam: you don't want to support the Communists, you don't want to support the American war effort, but for about three or four years you express a hope that out of negotiations some kind of third camp in Vietnam will emerge. Various readers wrote in and challenged you on this, "Who are you talking about?" That seems to me like some baggage from the Shachtmanite movement you still were carrying around.*

**A:** It may have been. There were in South Vietnam small groups of independent leftists, but they never had much influence, mostly intellectuals. Buttinger was in touch with them. He reported on their existence. It was clear to me even then that this was pretty much a longshot. It was a hopeless situation from our point of view, but if there were any hope it could only be in such a solution. There was period of time, or so we thought, [when] there were a lot of refugees from the north in the south, [when] there was a trade union movement in the south, . . . a period of time when it seemed like there as a slender possibility of some independent force emerging there. If the U.S. had played a different role, perhaps encouraging land reform in the countryside, civil liberties in the cities, it might have made a difference. This was of course before the large-scale American military involvement. Do you just wash your hands, and say let the Communists take over? In the long run that was probably inevitable. I spoke at one of the first antiwar demonstrations in 1965 in Washington, the one organized by SANE.[24] At that point we still felt it was possible to participate.

**Q:** *There was an article in 1964 called "Last Chance in Vietnam" by* "Dissenter." *Who was* "Dissenter"*?*

**A:** *Dissenter* was me. I wrote that after some of our friends came back from Vietnam. Milton Sachs came back from a trip. He was not much of a writer, so we just put it together for him.

**Q:** *In 1963 Walzer and Rosenberg wrote an article calling for a King-Reuther third-party ticket in 1964. Was there a debate within* Dissent *over endorsing Johnson in 1964?*

**A:** No. There wasn't much of a debate. That was just something they wanted to say. When you run a little magazine, you're sometimes tempted to say things just because you have the opportunity, even if you know there isn't much chance of anything coming out of it.

**Q:** *One of the weaknesses of* Dissent's *domestic politics in 1966-67 is that it was talking about a vision of politics that didn't really exist: the kind of Negro-labor coalition that showed up in a lot of hopeful* Dissent *articles.*

**A:** Well, it was splitting. We were right, at least in a negative sense, that if that coalition split, that would ensure a victory for reaction. That enabled Nixon to win. The margin in California, which was the crucial state, was very narrow. If a few thousand more people voted for Humphrey who sat on their hands, he might have won the election.

**Q:** *One of the things that* Dissent *does during the Vietnam war is to talk about American foreign policy in a systematic fashion. That's something I felt was missing from it in the fifties. The word "imperialism" began to be used by people like Mike Harrington. Was this a conscious decision on the part of* Dissent *editors?*

**A:** I think you may be overstating the extent to which there was a coherent *Dissent* policy. Individual writers went off on their own. If Mike wrote that way, he wrote it on his own. [Henry] Pachter, I recall, had a long article on imperialism, attacking the Leninist version.[25] Mike still felt himself to be a little bit more of a Marxist than the rest of us. We put out a collection on foreign policy around that time. In the fifties the focus was very much on domestic affairs, McCarthyism and all that.

**Q:** *I'm not yet at the point in my research where I have drawn many conclusions about the Shachtmanite movement, but it's striking how many people came out of that movement asking fundamental questions about their own previous illusions.*

**A:** Shachtman was a very remarkable man. He was the most brilliant person I've met on the left in America. It doesn't come through in his writing at all. Most of his writing sounds like speeches because he didn't care to write, and he would dictate them. But he was also dreadfully flawed. He had very bad habits as a result of leading a sect. He was always thinking in advance of his colleagues and afraid to reveal his heresies. He was trapped in trying to keep a small group together, which is a hell of a lot harder than being the leader of a mass party. And at the same time trying to think, to move ahead. At the end of his life he wasn't in any strict sense a Socialist at all. Which is okay with me. But he was always a few steps behind in articulating where he was intellectually. He didn't trust the people around him very much, and he was right. He was so much smarter and more gifted than most of the people around him. There were two people around him who were very gifted. One was [James] Burnham,[26] and the other was an extraordinarily interesting man named Joseph Carter.[27] Talk to Manny Geltman about him. We were all really shaped by that experience and sometimes when I hear Mike Harrington speaking, or hear myself speaking, I can hear the intonations and the rhythms of Shachtman's voice; he was very quick, but very narrow. He really did struggle and think, but he never found an adequate mode for expressing it.

## Notes

1. Irving Howe, *A Margin of Hope* (San Diego: Harcourt Brace Jovanovich, 1982), 238.
2. Ignazio Silone was a Communist who broke with Stalin in the late 1920s and supported Leon Trotsky. He thereafter became a democratic Socialist and an acclaimed fiction writer, whose novels include *Fontamara* (1933), *Bread and Wine* (1937), and *The Seed Beneath the Snow* (1942).
3. Bayard Rustin was an important leader in the U.S. civil rights movement during the 1950s and early 1960s. He was the chief organizer of the March on Washington in 1963, at which Dr. Martin Luther King, Jr. delivered his "I Have a Dream" speech.
4. G. D. H. Cole was a British libertarian Socialist and leading Fabian Society thinker. He was a political theorist and economist who taught at Oxford University and exerted influence within Labour Party circles.

5. A prominent Socialist intellectual, Richard Crossman was one of the Labour Party's leading Zionists and anti-Communists. He was a long-time contributor to the *New Statesman and Nation*, serving as its editor during 1970-72. Crossman also edited a famous collection of anti-Communist essays, *The God That Failed* (1950). He held a number of his ministerial positions in the Labour government of Harold Wilson.
6. Anthony Crosland was one of the British Labour Party's leading intellectuals between the 1950s and 1970s. In *The Future of Socialism* (1956), he argued against further nationalization of the British economy, maintaining that the Socialist commitment to greater equality and higher living standards was in the process of attainment through steady growth in a mixed economy. Crosland later served as Secretary of State for Education (1965-67) and Secretary of State for the Environment (1974-76).
7. Clement Attlee, a long-time leader of the British Labour Party, was Britain's first postwar prime minister (1945-51).
8. Bogdan Denitch, a long-time contributor to Dissent and member of its editorial board, was a close associate of Michael Harrington and a cofounder of the DSA. He was also a political sociologist and a colleague of Howe at the City University of New York.
9. Karl Korsch was a Communist theoretician from Germany, who fled to the United States in 1936. His attempt to update Marxism for contemporaneous conditions was rejected by official Communist parties.
10. Isaac Deutscher was a left-wing British historian who wrote biographies of Stalin and Tolstoy and coined the term "non-Jewish Jew."
11. Sidney Lens was an American labor leader and political activist. Formerly a Trotskyist, he became an editor of *The Progressive* and later a candidate for the U.S. Senate from the Citizens Party.
12. Ned Polsky was a radical sociologist who specialized in the sociology of deviance. He was the author of Hustlers, Beats, and Others (1969) and taught at the State University of New York, Stony Brook.
13. Dien Bien Phu was the decisive battle in French Indochina (March-May 1954) between the French army and Vietnamese Communist revolutionaries. The confrontation culminated in a comprehensive French defeat, which led to the end of the war and the agreement by France at the 1954 Geneva Accords to withdraw from its Indochinese colonies.
14. Engelbert Dollfuss was the Austrian chancellor (1932-34) and a close ally of Benito Mussolini. Opposed to the Nazis, Dollfuss nonetheless abolished the Austrian parliament in 1933 and established an authoritarian regime grounded in conservative Roman Catholic and Italian Fascist principles.
15. Lillian Hellman was a popular playwright and a vocal, sympathetic voice for Communism during the postwar era. She was author not only of acclaimed dramas such as *Little Foxes* (1939) but also of three controversial personal memoirs in the 1970s and 1980s that defended her Communist allegiances and castigated numerous American intellectual critics of Communism.
16. Julia was the the title character of a 1977 movie about a heroic Socialist who fights the Nazis, based on *Pentimento*, a 1973 memoir by Lillian Hellman.
17. Richard Hofstadter was a leading American political historian and a long-time member of the history department of Columbia University (1946-70).
18. George Lichtheim was a German-born intellectual whose writing concentrated on Marxist theory and the history of Socialism. He was an influential European Social

Democrat in the early postwar era who wrote for a number of publications on the European continent and in the U.S.

19. The League for Industrial Democracy was a Michael Harrington-led group that split with the SDS.
20. Al Haber was a founding member and the first president of SDS.
21. Carl Oglesby served as the president of SDS in 1965 and was radicalized by the Vietnam War. In the 1970s and 1980s, he repudiated much of his former left-wing activity and turned rightward into a centrist politics.
22. The Lovestone group, also known as the Lovestonites, led by Jay Lovestone, formed a faction within the American Communist Party in the late 1920s and early 1930s. Known as the "right opposition," the Lovestonites supported Nicolai Bukharin in his unsuccessful showdown with Stalin. The purge of Bukharin induced the right oppositionists in the U.S. to split from the American Communist Party.
23. Tom Kahn was a labor activist and an aide to civil rights advocate Bayard Rustin and drafted the plan for the 1963 March on Washington. In the mid-1980s he became international affairs director of the AFL-CIO and channeled aid to leaders of both the Polish trade union, Solidarity, and other free unions in Eastern Europe.
24. The peace group SANE was founded in 1957.
25. Henry Pachter was an émigré from Nazi Germany who became a scholar of Socialism and a member of the editorial board of *Dissent*. He also taught history for many years at the New School for Social Research and City College of the City University of New York.
26. James Burnham was a radical leftist and Trotskyist during the 1930s. He was briefly a member of the SWP, allying himself with Max Shachtman against the SWP's majority faction led by James P. Cannon. In the wake of the Nazi-Soviet pact of August 1939 and the USSR invasions of Poland and the Baltic Republics, Burnham and Shachtman viewed Stalin's regime as a new form of imperialism unworthy of any support from Socialists. In May 1940, Burnham withdrew from the SWP. In later years, he repudiated Marxism utterly and became a prominent intellectual within the newly emergent conservative movement, including service as an editor of *National Review*.
27. Joseph Carter, the pseudonym of Joseph Friedman, was an early leader in the American Trotskyist movement and the first editor of *Labor Action*, the official organ of the Workers Party. Irving Howe was a colleague of Friedman and succeeded him as editor of *Labor Action*.

# Chapter 5

## Grace Schulman "A Margin of Hope at the 92nd Street Y," 7 November 1983.

### Introduction

In this sprawling, previously unpublished interview, conducted by the poet Grace Schulman at New York's 92nd Street YMCA, Howe gets to play before a home-court crowd, for whom he is reading and commenting on his intellectual autobiography, *A Margin of Hope,* published in November 1982. In 1983, although still riding the wave of bestseller success with *World of Our Fathers*, Howe was more concerned with this political and intellectual memoir. Facing a literature-oriented interviewer, yet dwelling on politics and the failure of Socialism, Howe is in a pensive, backward-looking mood. Grace Schulman, born in 1935, was by the time of this interview an established poet and critic, as well as the poetry editor for *The Nation,* a position she held from 1971 to 2006. As long-time head of the 92nd Street Y Poetry Center, she invited Howe for this occasion. She had already published literary criticism on the work of Ezra Pound and would go on to write and edit volumes on Marianne Moore. Beginning with *Burn Down the Icons* (1976), she had published several volumes of her own poetry, continuing to this day. Schulman's vocation is obvious in her choice of questions. Indeed the inflections in her own poetry may have been influenced by Howe's role in bringing Yiddish literature to a position of some visibility.

At this time Howe was prominent in a number of areas, which overlap in this reading from his autobiography. He had emerged as the leading Left-liberal Jewish intellectual in America and, with the deaths of Edmund Wilson in 1972 and Lionel Trilling in 1975, had also arguably become the leading literary-political intellectual. Given this new status and the marvelous reception accorded *World of Our Fathers*, he felt that it was time for an autobiography.

Much of this transcript consists of a reading from a manuscript of his memoir, which Howe explicitly referred to as "an intellectual autobiography"; it contains very few details about his personal and family life. Instead *A Margin of Hope* paints a vivid picture of the context and background of Howe's young life as a Socialist on the streets of the Lower East Side and in City College. In a more distanced, detached way, it subsequently covers both his own political evolution and the development of *Dissent* magazine. *A Margin of Hope* then discusses the turbulent and paradoxical 1960s, a period of early promise for the Left that ended in violence and dashed dreams, and closes with a brief discussion of the even more disappointing and dismaying 1970s.

Howe during this reading plays the role of the intellectual celebrity. Pronouncing on literature, culture, criticism, and to an extent the Jewish condition—at a time when it was very good to be a Jew in America—he addresses how the immigrant experience led to an intellectual ferment for his generational cohort of Jewish intellectuals. Howe admits that his own ideological motivation has come to a dead end: "It's been my fate to experience the defeat of the Socialist idea." All that remains, he says, is a vague idealism: "I cling to a vision of a society beyond the manifest inequities of the given." As subsequent interviews in this volume show, Howe and his *Dissent* colleagues continued to propose concrete policies to promote elements of that vision, though he acknowledged that an organic social transformation seemed unrealistic.

Schulman's questions prompt Howe to discuss the literary and political culture of his time as both an onlooker and a participant. He describes *Partisan Review* as "based upon a wonderful and brilliant misunderstanding. The misunderstanding was that it was possible to combine anti-Stalinist leftism with highbrow literary life," a paradox that explains much about the early postwar New York Intellectuals who simultaneously claimed to speak for the proletariat and for the artistic elite. This is a contradiction that, it could be argued, Howe spent the rest of his life trying to resolve, even as some conservative members of his intellectual circle would drift further into elite territory, particularly on matters of economic and political policy.

In answering Schulman's questions, Howe's view of writers and intellectuals who grew up in the 1960s and beyond contrasts revealingly with the memories of his youthful deprivations in the Depression-era Bronx. Some of Howe's observations about the differences between the generations specifically target the younger portion of the audience. Indeed Schulman, fifteen years younger than Howe, serves here implicitly as a generational bridge. Howe seems to wish to preserve for a new generation a life time has eroded, a life memorialized in *World of Our Fathers*. For Jewish writers, he explains, "The exhaustion of this experience, how it is fading away, leaves them with terrible problems of theme and subject." He extends this analysis to American authors more broadly, to a generation growing up affluent and safe within the confines of academia; such "writers are lonely and they haven't come to grips with many of the basic experiences of the present historical moment." If there is a grand historical struggle, well-to-do Americans in the late twentieth century are aware of it only in a hazy way, in contrast to Howe's experience as a young boy. Despite an overall deprivation, there was a struggle, a movement, and even brief victories. For young Howe, the central victory occurred when a successful unionization effort in 1932 brought his family new clothes and better food. By contrast, for the generation of writers emerging in the 1980s, Howe notes, a word such as "Socialism," even if they embraced it, could only have an oddly abstract ring.

Midway through the interview, Howe detours to a discussion of Emerson, an author who sheds light upon the personalities and interests of those young Americans who had baffled Howe. Committed to communitarian solutions, Howe as a youthful Trotskyist had looked upon Emerson with contempt as a bourgeois individualist. Such a view did not stand the test of Socialism's continuing failure to gain a foothold in America or explain the individualism of the New Leftists—what Howe would come to call their "moral rectitude." Howe's distaste for maverick individualism remained, but he came to see it as part of the American character and as a source of political dissent. Furthermore, as the attraction of Socialism receded, as centralized decision-making seemed less workable, and as the concept of a mixed economy and terms such as "market Socialism" came to the fore, Emerson's individuality was no longer anathema to Howe's principles. By the time of this interview, Howe admired Emerson (albeit in a tempered, qualified way) as an exemplar of America's distinctively revolutionary nature.

As the interviews with Todd Gitlin and Susanne Klingenstein will later show, these convictions anticipate Howe's full-blown argument about Emerson in *The American Newness* (1986), which he began writing in the early 1980s upon receiving an invitation to deliver the distinguished Massey Lectures at Harvard University in 1984. These lectures, and their subsequent publication as a book, extended Howe's reputation as an American literary critic with a strong social and political bent.[1] This interview provides a preliminary glimpse of Howe's complex and evolving thought on what might be termed "social individualism." By the 1980s, Howe had come to admire Emerson's social nonconformity.

But Howe maintained his adamant opposition to any form of individualism that could slide into a neglectful, conservative disdain for the welfare of all. If Emersonian individualism is double-edged, it also defines the hope that has driven America forward. Howe here introduces a leitmotif that is amplified throughout this volume, notably in the interviews with Gitlin, Klingenstein, and Cain: his ambivalent relationship with Emersonian thought and what that says about his relationship to America. The Gitlin interview is particularly significant for the way it relates Emersonianism to the New Left, revealing Howe's dislike of individualism and the moral self-righteousness it can import, but also his esteem for the activism it can stimulate.

Worried that America might be losing its activist spirit, and instead hurtling past a turbulent to an isolated—and commercialized—individualism, Howe contrasts contempory American literature with that of selected other national cultures—Japan, Latin America, and Eastern Europe. In these diverse settings, Howe suggests, the political situations have stimulated literatures with an ideological edge, literary art that may signify the possibility of new social progress.

Despite all the good feeling during this evening at the 92nd Street YMCA, this interview reflects a sense of hesitant political engagement, an uncertainty as to how to remain true to the Socialist ideal of fighting for the disenfranchised while enjoying the upper-class benefits of a distinguished professor and best-selling author. Schulman and others would return to honor Irving Howe at the 92nd Street YMCA in May 1993—alas, without Irving's live presence, since the occasion was his memorial service.

## The Interview

*Irving Howe is surely one of the most distinguished men of letters in America today. For years he has been a literary commentator of profound insight. His inquiries into the writing of our time extend beyond fiction and nonfiction, to poetry, which is one of his deepest concerns. He founded the magazine* Dissent *in 1954, an important intellectual publication that will celebrate the three decades of its life next year. As a writer for* Partisan Review, *as author of such volumes of critical essays as* The Decline of the New *and* Politics and the Novel, *as editor of many anthologies, he has contributed a great deal to the literary criticism of the past three decades.*

*He was in fact one of the New York Intellectuals that he himself wrote about in a meaningful essay that was published about ten years ago. His criticism abounds with human insights and elevates literature by his careful, witty, and penetrating concern with a moral vision and the larger social implications of the men and women who have written the books we read today. And his sensitive editing of anthologies of Yiddish poetry has done and will do much to keep that literature alive. One volume, edited in collaboration with Eliezer Greenberg, has been published, dedicated to Yiddish writers destroyed by Hitler and Stalin. Another is being prepared now.*

*In addition to these vast accomplishments, he has written the moving and important book* World of Our Fathers: The Journey of the East European Jews to America and The Life They Found and Made, *a comprehensive study of one of our most important cultural groups, the immigrants who created our intellectual and cultural values.*

*Perhaps his greatest contribution, though, has been his memoirs, and especially* A Margin of Hope, *an intellectual biography. That, I believe, is among the most important books of our time. After writing of the people as well as the literary trends and movements that have shaped our culture, he reveals a prose style of amazing intensity as well as a remarkable aesthetic stance toward reality. For example, his passages about death. He writes: "A serious person who has spent a lifetime without religious faith must accept the idea of eternal nonbeing. Having taken pride in skepticism, I must have the courage of its consequences. That doesn't, however, keep me from a bemused interest in notions of reincarnation, since no one would mind a thousand years of sleep if at the end, knuckle to one's eye, there were a prospect to waking."*

*Quoting from Virginia Woolf, he writes: "I like the way she uses the word 'shrunk'; learning to savor the time that remains, I recognize it not at all as an invitation to sublimity. I do not merge with Godhead. I do not become enlarged. I am not a transparent eyeball. I seek no transcendence. No, I shrink pleasantly. A quiet hour, an ease of minutes, as if nestling in the hand of being. It doesn't happen very often. It goes against the grain of restlessness, but I am in training."*

*Passages such as these have great power. To my mind, the tone is reminiscent of Dante in the* Commedia, *portraying the self always with humility as an ordinary person, somehow privileged to see extraordinary events, to experience the physical world, and to contemplate a remote unseen universe.*

*The work of Irving Howe is urgent for our time. If he is known today as a political and literary writer, those genres having a public immediacy and impact, he will be known also, for he is, as a creative writer of compelling force, with a vision of truth about the century, about the nature of time passing, and about modern man in relation to a world of complex social and political pressures and conflicting demands. It is a great honor to present Irving Howe, who will read to you tonight.*

**IH:** Thank you. These readings are usually and rightly reserved for poets. But here I am, a writer of prose, not even of fiction. At least not deliberately. What I will do tonight will be to offer fragments of autobiography, taken from a number of books and essays in the hope of forming a mosaic of remembrance. It starts, as it must, with the immigrant Jewish milieu of half a century ago.

## *Reading aloud from* A Margin of Hope[2]

**IH:** To be poor is something that happens to you. To experience poverty is to gain an idea of what is happening. When my father's grocery store in the West Bronx went bankrupt in 1930, and he became a customer peddler, trudging from door to door to offer modest credit to Italian and Irish housewives, we were really poor. Crowded into a small apartment with aunts, uncles, grandmother, in order to save rent. We were dropping from the lower middle class to the proletarian, that most painful of all social descents. This unsettled my sense of things. I was driven inward, toward book and dream. My parents became workers in the dress trade, my mother an operator, my father a presser. It was my mother, strong, humorless, and cloying, who held us together, through energies out of her depths. At first she would come home with a paycheck of twelve dollars a week, tired and troubled, yet gripping in her hands the life of everyone near her.

Helping my father overcome his shame at having failed at business, helping me adjust a little to the roughnecks of the East Bronx, helping my grandmother keep house. After my father found work, he often came home, especially in the summers, with blisters on his body, the result of hours spent over a steaming press iron. And my mother would apply a soothing mixture of baking soda and water to his skin. They held together, the two of them, through good times and bad. But how hard they had to work, how desperately hard everything was for them, and the thousands of others like them in our immigrant streets. Then came the great strike. In 1933, the International Ladies' Garment Workers' Union, which all through the twenties had been reduced to feebleness, took the risk of calling out the entire dress trade. Immediately, though they had never before shown any class militancy, my folks joined the picket lines. For a Jew to scab was as unthinkable as for a Jew to convert to Christianity. Once the strike was won life became easier. We could now have meat more often, my parents started to squirrel away a few dollars, and once my birthday came around, my mother bought me a few grown-up shirts. When it comes to a passion for shirts, I stand side by side with Jay Gatsby. And for quite as good a reason. The garment unions were an essential part of immigrant life, helping to ease its hardships, and give our people a fragment of dignity. In later years, whenever I heard intellectuals of the Right, or Left, attack unionism, I would be seized by an uncontrollable rage that then gave way to frustration. How to explain to young people what the strike of 1933 had meant. How to find words to tell of the small comforts the union had brought, meat on the table and grown-up shirts. Only after starting high school, did the idea of poverty come to me with any force. I began to read a magazine that printed Sherwood Anderson's quavering reports about North Carolina textile workers who had been on strike for months. And these articles brought tears of indignation to my eyes. Was I aware that I might also have been feeling sorry for myself? Probably not. It was easier to feel sorry for others. I might add that in the years that I was reading these pieces by Sherwood Anderson, I would also sit in my little room in the East Bronx, consuming scores of novels about farm life in the American Midwest. Books by Willa Cather, Ruth Suckow and other by-now-forgotten writers. Sitting there in the tenements, I would wait desperately for the rains to come.

The realization of what it meant to be poor, I had first to discover from reading about poverty. The sense of my own deprivation grew keen after I learned about the troubles of people I didn't know. And this was typical of many other boys and girls of my generation, in whom family trouble and intellectual stirring joined to create a political consciousness. From the confusion and waste of immigrant Jewish experience, there arose its most notable human type, the self-educated worker. What he or she learned from the Yiddish lectures, classes, newspapers, was incomplete, hazy, half-baked, but whatever remained was earned. With a passionate stoicism, these men and women struggled against the thickening of their capacities. They sensed that if once they gave way to circumstance, they would be lost. They worked to open themselves to the world's beauties. Stumbling into simple aesthetic experiences to recreate themselves according into an ideal image. This image had come to them from a confusion of sources, from the old Jewish respect for learning, from the heightened morale brought by the renaissance of Yiddish culture, from the Socialist vision of a humane existence. The self-educated worker seemed a peculiarly intense figure, indeed a peculiarly Jewish figure, who brought with him yearnings and capacities that had been honed to sharpness by the pressures of ghetto life. His transformation was from a narrow but coherent religious culture to a quasi-secular culture at once vibrant and amorphous. And not only was he a proletarian searching for articulation, he was also a Jew who hoped that by approaching Western thought, he would satisfy his own blossoming needs and remedy the disadvantages of the Jews as a people.

Through the late-nineteenth and early-twentieth centuries, learning came to seem an almost magical solution for the Jews, a people that had always placed its faith in the sheer power of words. Learning in its own right, learning for the sake of future generations, learning for the social revolution, learning in behalf of Jewish renewal. On the East side, the Yiddish editor and writer, Abraham Cahn kept prodding the immigrants: "In America, a worker can even go to college and get an education. It takes a long time. But you must try to be an intellectual, not just a doctor or a lawyer." One of Cahn's colleagues wrote: "We know workers have little time or strength to read after a hard day in the shop. But a half hour of serious reading every day, for several years, can provide an excellent education." A persuasion of restlessness moved these men. You must try to be an intellectual. In behalf of a freedom they associated with the life of mind. All gone now, but the glory of the immigrant world. This world left us with a rich bequest of strength, but there were also handicaps, a storage of fears. In 1903, Abraham Cahn printed an editorial in the *Forward* about baseball, a subject that until then had eluded his public scrutiny. A father had written bemoaning his son's fondness for baseball. What is the point of this crazy game? It makes sense to teach children to play chess, but baseball? The children could get crippled. I want my boy to grow up a mensch, not a wild American runner. Poor Cahn, trying to cope with problems beyond the wisdom of our Solomon, replied that Jewish boys should be allowed to play baseball. As if anybody could stop them. "Chess was good," he wrote, "but the body needs to develop also. Baseball is played in the fresh air. The really wild game is football. The aristocratic game in the colleges. Accidents occur in football, but baseball is not dangerous." Even for Cahn, there had to be a limit, his Jewish fright and Socialist rectitude drawing the line at aristocratic football. Suspicion of the physical, fear of hurt, anxiety over the sheer pointlessness of play. All this went deep into the Jewish psyche. It was a price, hardly the largest, that Jews paid for the conviction of specialness. They could no more suppress their true feelings about the frivolities of street or gymnasium, than they could deny the shudder that passed through them on walking past a church. Decades would have to go by before the sons and daughters of the immigrants could shake off, if we ever could, this heritage of discomfort before the pleasures of the body. What they were struggling for was nothing less than the persuasion that they had as much right as anyone else to feel at home on earth. But their parents were saying, No, Jews could not feel at home on this earth. Seemingly comic disputes over matters like baseball released profound clashes of worldview. Perhaps nothing less than whether Jewish messianism still mattered in this world.

In the Jewish streets of the early thirties, radicalism seemed not at all an exotic import. The Socialist movement flourished a bit. Sentiments of rebellion, fantasies of revolution seemed natural, spontaneous. I became a Yipsel, a young Socialist. Some of my critics say I remain that to this very day. There could be worse. In the streets then, there never seemed any place to go. The thought of bringing my friends home was inconceivable. For I would have been as ashamed to show them to my parents as to show my parents to them. I had enough imagination to suppose that each could see through the shams of the other, but not enough courage to defend one against the other. Besides, where would people sit in those cramped apartments? My self-consciousness, which led myself into a maze of superfluous lies, in relation to my parents, made it difficult to believe in the possibility of a life grounded in good faith. I could not imagine bringing together the life that was given, with its sweet poignancy and embittered conflicts, and the political life I had chosen, with its secret fellowship and sectarian vocabulary. So we walk the streets. . . .

In the winter, when the Bronx is grey and icy, there were cafeterias in which the older comrades, those who had jobs, or were on WPA, bought coffee while the rest of us filled chairs. In the summer we would parade around the middle bulge of the Bronx from the tenements on Wilkins Avenue in the East, to the forbidding apartment houses of the Grand Concourse on the West. I remember these night walks as carefree, relaxed, away from the pressures of family and politics, though always with some secret anxiety that I would get home too late. For my parents, with their sweet blind innocence, were more distressed by my irregular hours than my irregular opinions. The streets would be empty, the summer nights cool, a kind of expansiveness would come over us. Our enemies slept. The world was ours. We would glide away in our Melvillian freedom, away from the frustration of the movement, and dreary thoughts of the next morning, when with momma's quarter in my pocket for coffee and lunch, I would be taking the subway to City College, prepared once again to cut the classes that had, I was entirely confident, nothing to teach me.

We lived by politics, but not by politics alone. The impulses that had led us to political radicalism also made us responsive to avant-garde culture. At the age of 16, I was lent a copy of Edmund Wilson's *Axel's Castle*. This was probably the first book of literary criticism that I read from start to finish. Even though I had only a skimpy acquaintance with the writers that Wilson discussed, something about Wilson's moral gravity moved me. It always would. Passing through the Trotskyist movement a year or two later, I began to hear about literary topics the Socialists had seldom noticed. We were now reading the great modernist writers, Joyce, Proust, Mann, Yeats, with almost the same attention we gave to Marx and Trotsky. Modernist writers we admired on principle. It seemed only right that we of one vanguard should tip our hats to the giants of another. Still, these writers were not easy to approach. They had not yet been domesticated by the academy. They still bristled with difficulties. With T. S. Eliot, however, I fell crazily in love. More with the music of his verse than its meanings. I knew he was a reactionary, but I didn't care. The opening lines of "Prufrock," the first stanzas of *The Wasteland*, the haunting melody of "The Hollow Men," "this is the dead land, this is the cactus land," made me dizzy with excitement. Here is poetry of the bareness of our time, the loneliness of our cities. Eliot had meant his poems mainly as reflections on the sterility of a faithless age. I read them mainly as reflections on the decay of bourgeois civilization. A liberal, a Stalinist, so I thought, and not with complete foolishness, could never appreciate Eliot, never respond to his despair as we did. He was our poet, just as he was the poet of those mad southerners in Nashville, about whom we were starting to hear. No doubt, people like ourselves misunderstood him. But it seems just possible that our misunderstanding brought us closer to one strand of his work than could the understanding of his disciples. In any case, I loved his poetry with all the ardor of youth. May he, in the heaven that must now be his, forgive my misapprehensions?

In those days, the transitions of life were abrupt. One day I'd be reading Eliot, and the next day orating from a soapbox. The institution of the street meeting is now almost forgotten. But in earlier decades it formed a vivid part of the city's life. A mode of agitation, a form of entertainment, a training school for young speakers. Six or seven of us would set up at a busy intersection of the East Bronx. Inept speakers could shout themselves horse in ten minutes. A skillful soapboxer could keep on for three quarters of an hour, gathering a crowd of a hundred and fifty people, and bringing it all to a climax with an exciting question period. It was in the question period that you could tell the difference between mere ranters and real speakers. A candidate for debate would rise up in the audience, sometimes a rugged individualist, brandishing the one idea he remembered from high school economics, who would ask on what grounds we proposed to deny John D. Rockefeller and Henry Ford the right to pass on his wealth to his descendents. There followed from the platform a cascade of refutation. From sarcasm about the extent to which Rockefeller's or Ford's descendents ever did a day's work, to impassioned descriptions of how terrible were the labor conditions in the mines of Rockefeller and the plants of Ford. And they were terrible. More ambitious speakers would take a crack at simplifications of the theory of surplus value. To be able to popularize Marxist economics was a source of pride. Questions might come from the Stalinists, who in those days were pretty thick in the Bronx. If they asked about left-wing united fronts we were prepared with devastating replies about Stalinist duplicity in pre-Hitler Germany and the insane Stalinist theory of social Fascism. If they asked if we were naïve enough to suppose the bourgeoisie would be the first ruling class in history to surrender power without armed resistance, we found that harder to answer, since we weren't so sure ourselves. As a street orator I was a total failure. Within a few minutes I could disperse a crowd that another speaker had taken an hour to bring together. If I spoke first to warm things up, I would start shouting at the top of my lungs and then look around with bewilderment. Why was the street so empty? We had a comrade named Irving Panken, who in a few minutes could achieve a magical rapport with a street audience. This other Irving had a high, reedy voice that cut through street noises like a blade. He seemed to pour into his oratory all the passion of his soul. A feeling for the sheer outrageousness of life, the pain that gripped the years of the workers, broke through his rhetoric. The grief and anger that floated along with his spittle would shake people. A hush would come over the street, and a collective recognition that this boy was touching some tissue of experience that all of them knew to be tender. Some of these listeners were expert at judging street speakers, quite as their fathers had been at judging cantors. And when the other Irving finished you could hear a murmur, "That's what I call a speaker." A speaker like the other Irving gave himself up to the inner flow of his passions, and the result was trancelike. Other speakers were more calculating. Once when there was a strike of bakers in the East Bronx, my YPSL circle rushed to the scene, eager to help the working class. It was a chilly fall night, the street dark, the bakery shut. Getting up on the platform I felt overcome by a sense of desolation. A handful of comrades, a blackened bakery, not a soul in sight. I started to shout but soon stopped, my voice dwindling to a whisper. Then an old-time Socialist, Claessens, got up to speak, and as if out of nowhere people started to gather. With an endless fund of amusing stories, all adapted to a simple political message, Claessens conversed rather than orated. The other Irving drew people through the ferocity of his emotions; Claessens relied on skills of intimacy.

About a week later one night at dinner my father turned to me with his velvety sarcasm and asked, "What do you have against that poor baker? A poor man tries to make a living and you tell people not to buy his bread?" Speech-maker that I now fancied myself, I found myself without a word to say. How had he learned about that meeting a good 15 blocks away? It turned out that a *landsman* of his had been passing by, and had hurried to report to my father the carryings on of his errant son. As for the question itself, I answered it about as well as I would answer all his other questions. . . .

Immigrant streets, Socialist politics, City College: all swept aside by the war. Military fate sent me to Alaska for years of freezing, daydreaming, and the job of deciding which records of disbanded army units to keep or destroy in the fire I tended in the middle of an abandoned mess hall. Boxes of records would keep pouring in day after day, as I sat there trancelike, throwing them into the fire. Leafing through the records I noticed that one kind kept appearing most frequently: psychiatric reports. I soon came to read these with fanatical attentiveness. Up there in Alaska, I got my first intimate sense of psychiatric practice, something very different from psychiatric theory. One army psychiatrist, a Major Z from Brooklyn, wrote reports at once passionate and dry. He made each one into a tense, sometimes tragic narrative, so that a listing of symptoms grew into an exposure of suffering. As he concluded his stories of crackup, Major Z would almost always recommend that his soldier patients be sent back to the States, a sign of professional rigor, of personal kindness. Each account ended with an admission of limits, more we do not know or cannot say, as if to dramatize the helplessness of our knowledge. It was from this Chekhov of the Aleutians that I first learned about the magnitude of human disorder. Then one day, while thumbing through a batch of records, I saw something that made me jump from my chair. It was a report, this time by another psychiatrist, describing "psychoneurotic symptoms of Major Z," and urging that he be sent home. Why at that moment didn't Thomas Mann miraculously appear to whisper his knowledge that the true doctor must be the secret sharer of his patients' sickness? Those reports of Major Z had had their source in a communion of weakness. I never heard what became of him after the war. A theorist of sickness, a mere routine success, a lost practitioner in some obscure upstate town? For me Major Z remains intact in memory, the unmet teacher and healer of the papers I saved from fire. . . .

How do you become a literary critic? That was the question I set myself after the war when I grew somewhat alienated from my Socialist group and thought of turning to the freelance intellectual life. There were then no schools for critics, no certificates of qualification, no examinations. You declared yourself a critic, if you had enough brazenness and a little talent. I soon found myself a fellow-traveler, half-in, half-out, of the *Partisan Review* milieu, the group later called the New York Intellectuals. Coming into this world, I had the good sense to listen. I listened to Delmore Schwartz entangle himself in his own wit as he declared T. S. Eliot a culture hero, yet ripped apart his Christian snobbism. I listened to Lionel Trilling slide through categories, the will, the moral imagination, the exact meaning of which remained elusive. I listened to Philip Rahv chart American literary relations through lurid diagrams of power, in my impatient scrappy way pocketing a phrase here or a thought there. I listened hard. And imitated. How else does one learn?

Becoming a literary critic seemed fairly easy. It was something you might pick up in a few months. Becoming a writer seemed very hard. It would take several decades. My notion about criticism was a piece of foolishness, half jokingly indulged. But my idea about writing was serious. All you needed to be called a literary critic, it seemed, was a determination to read with charged attention and a pencil in the clutch of your fingers. Marking passages up and writing things down, you quickly discovered that reading had become spoiled with purpose.

Then you tried to chart the articulated patterns of a novel or poem, its narrative line or theme, its interplay of event and character, quite as a specialist might study x-rays. You might also pick up a few semi-technical terms, like structure, vision, sensibility, without inquiring too closely into their meanings. Finally you tried to locate whatever in a text seemed distinctive, some nuance or perception or tone of voice. But here the hopeful fantasy about the easiness of writing criticism came tumbling down, and you had to stare at the blinding hardness, perhaps the sheer helplessness, of the whole enterprise, before which only fools and pedants thought method a protective shield. I remember how hard it was when I had to review a book by a new and gifted writer, Bernard Malamud's first collection of stories. And all, all I wanted to do was describe whatever seemed distinctive in his style. Not once did I hear anyone in New York talk about critical method. It would have been regarded as bad form. Most New York writers didn't think of themselves as critics primarily. They thought of themselves as writers who did criticism. The difference seemed essential. Decidedly more interesting than theories of criticism was the act of writing. I supposed that my prose had a certain vigor, but I knew it was deficient in nuance, ease, modulations of tone and pace. So I decided to imitate, not the style of one or the other critic, which would have been disastrous, but the common style of a *Partisan* essay. By imitating a common style, I might develop a personal style. I studied the way these writers negotiated rapid thrusts, extreme condensations, the rhetoric of antirhetoric. I played with mixtures of high seriousness and street colloquialism, a style John Hollander has called New York baroque. I learned that this charged, burning style would not work for anything longer than an essay. Wondering if I could ever match the fluent wit of Elizabeth Hardwick or the rhetorical plentitude of Alfred Kazin, I narrowed my homework to simple effects.

**Q:** *How do you begin a literary piece so as to hold attention?*

**A:** George Orwell was masterful at this. Take the opening of his Dickens essay: "Dickens is one of those writers who is well worth stealing." Who but a brute or a hopeless academic would not keep reading after a sentence like that?

Edmund Wilson, by contrast, did not strive for striking leads, perhaps assuming that the majesty of his presence would be enough to hold his readers. Philip Rahv came on like a slow thunder of manifestos. Lionel Trilling would begin with a simulated hesitation but would soon plant a hint that a surprise lay ahead, some revelation about the ways in which we, the educated classes, were misconstruing the cultural situation. The New York writers developed a style of brilliance, and a style of brilliance is often hard to bear. At its best, the style represented a certain view of the intellectual life: freelance, peacock-strut, knock-out synthesis. It celebrated the idea of the intellectual as antispecialist. It celebrated the writer as roamer among theories, as dilettante connoisseur, as *luftmensch* of the mind. It could be wonderful. It could turn rancid. Our partial assimilation, roots loose in Jewish soil but still not torn out, roots lowered into American soil but still not fixed, gave us a seemingly endless range of possibilities.

Well or poorly, we tried to live by that vision of Ishmaelite pride and independence that Melville had called "the way of the loose-fish." It was a vision that could not last very long, since need and caution, realism and loss of nerve, erosion and complication would finally do it in. Decades later, though, I still ask myself: "What better than to be a loosefish?"

### *Reading aloud from* A Margin of Hope

**IH:** In those days, the early fifties, there were some other loose fish around. No one yet thought of biting an academic hook. I came to know such young writers as John Berryman, whom I admired and Delmore Schwartz, whom I loved. Once Berryman and I had a brief exchange that settled forever the limits of our acquaintance. "Don't you feel," he asked me, "that Rimbaud's chaos is central to your life?" I was guileless enough to say, No. And that for Berryman was the end of me. I might be a nice fellow, but I was not one of the haloed victims. Not like the Delmore he adored as the suffering poet of the modern city. But I don't want to suggest that persuasions of superiority were wholly his. Berryman might have Rimbaud and Chaos, but I had Marx and history. And for a time, they provided equally substantial if illusory comforts.

I had a similar exchange with Delmore Schwartz. In a quiet moment he once said to me, "Do you sometimes get up in the morning and feel that you can't even bring yourself to tie your shoelaces?" He spoke without pride and extremity for he knew that his psychic illness was an affliction that might destroy him.

Still there was I, cast by these brilliant young writers as a fellow with perhaps a spot of talent but deplorably, even amusingly, sane. If they wrestled with chaos, I surrendered to coherence. Nor did it help to protest that I too had my bouts of depression. I resented being categorized as rational. It seemed to foreclose possibilities of glamour. We were all too young then to grasp the deadly meaning of that difference in psyche and temperament that Berryman and Schwartz were pointing to.

Moving in or near these literary circles made it likely sooner or later to meet the great American critic Edmund Wilson. In 1952 I went to Cape Cod to talk with him about a book I was writing on Sherwood Anderson. He was now in late middle age, portly, red faced, looking like a cross between Henry James and W. C. Fields. He stammered yet seemed utterly self-confident. This wasn't really true. No writer of any distinction is utterly self-confident. And Wilson's notebooks published later betray recurrent anxieties about his work.

My interview with him yielded little about Anderson. Partly because he scoffed at my inability to keep up with his consumption of scotch and partly because, upon hearing that I had spent the war years in Alaska, he started grilling me on Eskimos and Arctic weather. That was his way. Wilson had a tremendous curiosity about the experiences of other people. Once when studying Hebrew, he showed up with copy of a Yiddish paper, cross as a bear because he couldn't make out the words, as though the alphabet was the same as that of Hebrew. When I tried to explain the difficulty, he just glared at me accusingly. At parties Wilson would float from person to person like a bumblebee from flower to flower, interrogating them about their work, extracting bits of knowledge that he put away in some inner compartment of his mind. He was able to listen to ideas he didn't like, but then would erupt into a crescendo of grunts, rumbles, sputters all on the way to assertion. It sometimes seemed there were several areas of space between what went on in his mind and the speech that came tumbling out of his mouth, as if his thought reached him in relays. But when aroused he could be very quick. Once at a seminar that Paul Tillich was giving at Princeton in 1952, where the theologian, charming as the devil and at least as slippery, spun out his notions about faith, those of us listening felt that the idea of a personal god, the god we had rejected, the only god we knew, kept fading farther and farther into the distance.

I asked Tillich, "You say religion rests upon a sense of awe before the fundament of being. Does that mean that if on a starry night, perhaps out at sea, I find myself overwhelmed by the beauty of the scene and become aware of my own transience before the immensity of things, I am having a religious experience." My intent, of course, was to distinguish between cultivated sensibility and religious belief. But Tillich, suave dialectician that he was, seized upon my question and said "Yes." Even though I called myself a skeptic, I had provided admirably, he grinned, a description of a religious experience. He had turned the tables on us, and we sat there uncomfortably, until from the back of the room there came the Wilsonian rumble, "Mr. Tillich, you're taking away our rights."

Along with Socialist politics and literary criticism went for me Yiddish literature, as if to round out my quota of lost causes. With the Yiddish poet Eliezer Greenberg, I started editing collections of Yiddish literature in translation, and through him I met other Yiddish writers, most notably the great poet Jacob Glatstein. Once I asked Glatstein what it felt like to be a major poet in a minor culture, and he answered me with flashing eyes, "I have to know about Auden, but Auden doesn't have to know about me."

I used to wonder, What could be the unspoken feeling of these literary friends? How did they cope with the certainty that the literature to which they had devoted their lives was approaching its end? They refused as a gesture of honor to acknowledge the bleakness of their future. Undeluded, they still felt an obligation to confront the world with firmness of posture. One of the arts of life is to know how to end. Meanwhile, where did they really live? Live, I mean, in their imaginations. About some Yiddish writers there could be no doubt. The strong poet Chaim Grade resided in the North Bronx, his apartment overflowing with books he had arranged in stacks as if he were attending a library. But in the deepest part of his self, he was still back in the shadowy brilliance of Vilna during the twenties, still absorbed with the ethical severities of the Musser movement.

Isaac Bashevis Singer seemed really to live nowhere at all, though everyone had his address. Glatstein knew that he was a distinguished poet, who if he wrote in any other language would be famous. It was hard for me to explain. They seldom brought it up but I felt obliged to bring it up once in awhile, with the utter indifference of American literary circles to the presence of a vibrant literary culture that could be found, literally and symbolically, a few blocks away. After the Holocaust, even the Yiddish modernists felt compelled to pull back, to reaffirm the tragic grandeur of their own tradition and erect barriers of distrust against gentile culture. Glatstein wrote some poems, he was a master of rage, declaring his contempt for the goyim and their American Jewish friends.

Only once was my friendship with these men strained. In 1969, when Cynthia Ozick published her story "Envy," at once brilliant and malicious. The story depicts two wretched Yiddish writers overcome with envy of another Yiddish writer, whom they call their Chazer. The pig, transparently Isaac Bashevis Singer, a great success among Americans. One of the two was given a powerful speech: "I'm finished. We're already dead. Whoever uses Yiddish to keep himself alive is already dead." But the total effect of the story is reductive and, as the Yiddish writers felt it, demeaning. When the Ozick story came out I argued in partial defense of it, but Greenberg, though usually prepared to separate personal feelings from literary judgments, grew inflamed. He turned on me in anger and said, "Some things are more important than writing a good story." Too late, I agree.

In his last years Greenberg became the editor of a once mighty Yiddish monthly, *Die Tsukunft*, the future. He would tell me about his struggle to get enough decent material. But later on he spoke less and less about this. One day he announced that he had resigned, and with a grimace sad and ironic, added, "*Die Tsukunft* iz un a tsukunft," the future has no future.

I attached myself to these writers, I found strength in joining their moment of weakness, I loved them, I loved their words. . . .

Politics continued to absorb me in the fifties as it always had and would. Directly after the war there had been a moment of euphoria, when we thought the world was rid of the totalitarian blight. But now into the fifties we came to see that the totalitarian curse would survive for at least the span of our lives. It was as if a sentence of history had been extended without limit. This meant we had to put aside the leftist notion that on a world scale capitalism was the sole enemy. There was now a greater enemy, the totalitarian state, sometimes of the Right, sometimes of the Left. In 1952 totalitarianism of the Left seemed the harder to cope with. How often have I cursed the fate that impelled me and my friends to spend so much time struggling against illusory leftist forms of the totalitarian idea. Even if we can claim a speck of credit for having undertaken this task, it's depressing to think of the waste of spirit it entailed. For even those of us never enticed by Stalinism had to suffer damage from the length and intensity of our opposition. The waste of spirit I've spoken of may seem puny when compared with the loss of years or life itself within the Soviet Union. Nevertheless in a milder way we did pay a price. Too many enervating polemics, too great a politicizing of our thought, and too little of the composure needed for serious intellectual work. A writer who devotes himself exclusively to politics courts the danger of dryness, the mental undernourishment of journalism. To be sure, even the most politically conscious writers of our time have found themselves another place, gaining distance from the intolerableness of the world through memory and imagination. Silone found this place in his humorous idylls about the Abruzzi peasants, Orwell in the decency of ordinary Englishmen, Octavio Paz in the labyrinths of Mexican solitude. In my own way, I found another place in literary criticism and translations of Yiddish literature. But was this really enough? Isn't there always a shrinkage of imaginative power when an engaged writer submits to the political moment? "The heart's grown brutal from the fare," Yeats had written. "More substance in our enmities than in our love."

I must move very fast now, about a decade a minute. And stop very briefly, superficially, to glance at scenes of turbulence in the mid-sixties. Professors who the day before yesterday were the milkiest of liberals now take avidly to revolutionary rhetoric. Confrontations with spongy university administrations become training sessions for revolution. Enthused academics, recharged intellectuals (I called them uncharitably guerrillas with tenure) keep telling me the kids are turning the country around. Turning it where, to what end? A polite young man dressed in elegant jeans challenges my mild defense of trade unions at a meeting on the Ohio State campus. Unions, he says, block the path of revolutions, give the workers a mere pittance, induce false consciousness. Be patient, I tell myself, be patient, you're not effective when you lose your temper. The angel dispensing patience with a heavenly eye-dropper skipped right past me. I try to explain why small gains can lead to class confidence, and in any case why it's inhumane to dismiss the daily needs of workers. Talk to the wall. The polite young man in elegant jeans stares at me with a cool contempt, as if seeing before his eyes a candidate for reeducation on one of Chairman Mao's manure piles.

The American Jewish Committee sponsors a conference on Jewish intellectuals and the New Left. Twenty-five people show up. The intellectuals reading from right to left include Seymour Martin Lipset, Irving Howe, and Paul Goodman. The spokesman for the New Left contingent is an old acquaintance, Paul Jacobs, who attacks the sponsoring organization as part of the Establishment, wondering out loud whether he and his friends should even deign to talk with its representatives. Rising to the bait, one of my gifts, I answer that Jacobs was not obliged to come, unless of course he has come simply to announce his departure. A rustle of tension. Paul Goodman, sitting next to me, pats my arm and says quietly to Jacobs, "You know, when people come together and sit around the table, the only thing they can do is talk to one another."

It's 1969 and I am at a think tank near Stanford. Each afternoon I drive to the campus to eat my lunch with my wife. One day a group of SDS students led by a fellow named Cohen forms a semicircle behind us chanting hostile slogans. They mean to carry the battle against decadent liberalism to the heart of the enemy. This continues day after day. Go elsewhere for lunch? My pride won't allow it. So each afternoon we are followed across the campus, object of a kindergarten confrontation. Then one day I wheel about and shout at the insufferable Cohen, "You know what you're going to end up as?" The question startles him, and before he can resume his chanting I cry out, "You're going to end up as a dentist." [*laughter, cheers*] Cohen blanches. The insult is simply too dreadful. And I march off, in miniature triumph.

Ah Cohen, Cohen, wherever you may be, are you really pulling teeth? And to this there's a footnote. After *A Margin of Hope* was published, I received a letter from someone I knew slightly at Cornell University, saying that Cohen was now teaching Comparative Literature there. A few weeks later, I got a letter from someone in Los Angeles saying that Cohen had become a corporate lawyer. I have visions of Cohen becoming a mythical figure, something like Kilroy. . . .

It's been my fate to experience the defeat of the Socialist idea, and to wrestle with the crisis of Socialist thought. This is not the place for an extended discussion of this theme. Yet let me say that I cling to a vision of a society beyond the manifest inequities of the given. To the problem of Socialism there is no answer, only a continuing effort to confront it. And so at the end of my recent book I came back to it, as I am tonight, with an imaginary but not wholly unimaginable meeting of four writers. They sit in my apartment, Octavio Paz the Mexican, Milan Kundera the Czech, V. S. Naipaul the Trinidadian, George Konrad the Hungarian. We talk about the fate of literary generations. Why with the utmost good will is it so hard for writers of one generation to connect with those of another. I read aloud two passages. One is from the ending of Ignatius Silone's *Fontamara*, where the peasants of the Abruzzi defeated by the Fascists and landlords keep asking, What are we to do, What are we to do? The other is from Andre Malraux's[3] novel about the 1927 Chinese revolution, *Man's Fate,* in which Kyo, a militant of fine consciousness, confronts the Shanghai police chief. "Do you want to live," the police chief asks. "It depends how," answers Kyo. "What do you call dignity," asks the police chief. "The opposite of humiliation," answers Kyo.

When I first read these books decades ago, I already knew that Stalinism was a blight. Yet it was still possible to feel that Silone and Malraux were evoking the pathos of authentic revolt. But today, can you still be stirred, I ask the assembled writers, by the passages I have just read? They respond wearily, with suppressed irritation and excitement. Paz, the oldest, grasps most readily what I am struggling to ask, perhaps just because he is the oldest. He fought on the Republican side in Spain, and there, as he writes in *The Labyrinth of Solitude,* found "a desperate hopefulness. The memory will never leave me. Anyone who has looked hope in the face will never forget it. He will search for it everywhere he goes." Yet Paz now suggests quietly, the passage of time cannot be undone. The books from which I have read are embedded in their historical moment, and the most one can feel toward them is a kind of fraternal distance.

Konrad, a writer who lives in Budapest, tolerated there but deeply distrusted, is too young to have looked hope in the face. What he has seen is the face of that god everyone knows to have failed. Nonetheless he wonders whether some residue of Kyo's hope may yet survive in the ashes of its destruction.

Naipaul speaks next, his voice caustic and his sentences brilliant. Aren't you trying, he says, to keep alive a last spark of illusion that might better be snuffed out? And then Kundera, the Czech refugee, talks in his wonderfully complicated way, laughing, mocking, plunging into sudden gloom, for he knows how strongly men can yearn for what he calls the unity of their circle. In the ensuing conversation someone rescues a sentence from Kundera's *Book of Laughter and Forgetting:* "Totalitarianism is not only hell, but also the dream of paradise." Everyone nods. We know what he is saying. And is that all? The writers gathered here have sung the dirge of utopia. Their voices ring with skepticism, doubt, weariness. But could their skepticism weigh so heavily upon them, had there not been an earlier enchantment with utopia, that of the generation of Silone and Malraux? Well, there is utopia and utopia. The kind imposed by an elite in the name of a historical imperative, that utopia is hell. But there is another. It exists at no point in time and space. It is never merely given. It cannot be willed either into existence or out of sight. It speaks for our sense of what may yet be, or may not. But whether a real option or a mere fantasy, this utopia is as needed by mankind as bread and shelter. "A golden age," Dostoevsky once wrote, "is the most unlikely of the dreams that have been, yet for it men have given up their lives." A utopia for the sober? A utopia for skeptics? A utopia for unyielding democrats who still want to say, Dignity is the opposite of humiliation? I put the question to my four writers. They stare, they smile, they shrug, and they start to answer. Thank you. [*clapping*]

**Q:** *When I heard you read tonight and thought about your earlier work, I became more convinced than I was before that your work seems to have gone from the impersonal to the personal over the years, culminating in the memoir* A Margin of Hope. *Do you see that as a trend in your work?*

**A:** I guess that is a trend. Partly insofar as egoism reveals itself more openly with the passing of the decades. [*laughter*] But there is another explanation for it. When I began to write literary criticism—I would leave aside the political things in which of course the first person singular was used with horror—but when I began to write literary criticism under the influence of the *Partisan Review* group, again the first person singular was looked down upon.

Now, in fact, the writing of this group was highly personal but it took the form of grammatical phrases, brilliant sentences and fierce polemics. It was personal in an impersonal way. So that I suppose, you could say that, beginning with the personal in an impersonal way, I moved on to the personal in a personal way.

**Q:** *Speaking of the* Partisan Review, *is there any magazine today like the* Partisan Review *in the late thirties and early forties that combines literary, political and cultural excitement?*

**A:** No there isn't and there really can't be. The *Partisan Review* was based upon a wonderful and brilliant misunderstanding. The misunderstanding was that it was possible to combine anti-Stalinist leftism with highbrow literary life. We didn't yet see that an important element of cultural literary modernism was reactionary, or rather we saw it but we just pushed it aside. We didn't want to recognize the full weight and meaning of that. That particular conjuncture was possible only in the United States; it didn't occur with the same force in any other country. It was possible only in the United States because the anti-Stalinist leftist intelligentsia was very powerful in the intellectual world and very powerless in the rest of the world. And so thereby it could have, within limited precincts, an enormous self-confidence. The magazine in those days had no more than a circulation of nine thousand, but it had enormous influence. Today, you have journals with circulations with ten or twenty times as much which don't have any equivalent influence.

**Q:** *Does good writing today still gather around left-wing ideology as it did in the thirties and forties?*

**A:** No. In the first place, good writers would have a bit of a time trying to find left-wing ideology. [*laughter*] No, at the moment good writing doesn't seem to gather around any ideology. And indeed, the most interesting thing about good writing at the moment is its dispersion.

The current literary moment—this is just my impression—in which there is an enormous amount of talent—no great writers, but that's all right; the great writers were getting old when we were young and we can still remember them. But an enormous amount of very talented people, and yet—to me at least and this might just be the sourness of someone getting old—to me at least the literary situation as a whole is not terribly interesting. I read this writer or that writer. I admire the stories of Raymond Carver, etc., etc. But the writers are dispersed, there is no center; there isn't a Chicago Renaissance; there isn't a Village.

And partly this is due to the fact that they have jobs in the academy, which is very attractive in some ways since it is desirable to eat. But which has bad effects upon literary life since it disperses them one roughly every ten square miles. And the effect of that is that writers are lonely and they haven't come to grips with many of the basic experiences of the present historical moment. So that as far as I can see—and all of this could change and maybe it is already changing and I haven't seen it—what you have is many people of great seriousness and good will struggling by themselves in loneliness or relative isolation or in small provincial groups. What you don't have is that strong commanding center such as New York was, for example, in the twenties and once again in the late thirties.

**Q:** *That's very interesting about New York. Do you find that it is no longer the cultural center of America?*

**A:** Well, it's the cultural center of the country insofar as we have cultural vitality. But that vitality in recent years has not been, I think, in literature, it's been in some other arts. The great art in recent years, in America, has been dance, and especially ballet and especially Balanchine, and we have been all privileged to live in the era of a very great genius. The way other people lived in the age of Picasso or Stravinsky, we have lived in the age of Balanchine.

What will come after that nobody knows. But this became the real center of energy in American cultural life, plus something else. Many of the kinds of young people who, thirty or forty years ago, would have wanted to write a first novel, are now what they call making films. You might not always see the films themselves, but they are making them. [*laughter*] And in some instances, no doubt, there will be films. So that—I didn't mean this in any nasty way at all—so that there is a transmission of energies from one art to another.

Yet there is of course still a lot of writing. It doesn't seem to me to have at the moment, to have a central commanding, unquenchable, irresistible impulse such as modernism represented at one point and social radicalism at another point or Emersonianism at a third point. There is a not only a dispersion of writers and a dispersion of energies, but also a dispersion of sensibilities.

**Q:** *Does Emerson still have a stamp on American writing as Emerson did at one time?*

**A:** Emerson will have a stamp on American writing as long as there is American writing. I myself have a certain ambivalence toward this; I regard him as the wicked angel of our culture, but after a while you have to reconcile yourself to the facts. And the fact is that the power of Emerson, both as an individual and even more as a symbolic figure, is absolutely enormous. The whole idea of transcendence that he represents, of the individual possibility for transcendence and sublimity, it is no accident that the efforts of the neoconservative cultural people, with the corporations which support them behind that, is directed very strongly against that whole tradition. They are very hostile to what they see as the broad enemy. Namely the tradition of Emerson, Thoreau, Whitman, Melville, and later into the twentieth century—Van Wyck Brooks, Randolph Bourne, and on to the *Partisan Review* people. This doesn't form one continuous tradition, of course; there are all kinds of inner conflicts and deviations. But this is where I think the strength of the American cultural impulse resides. If Emersonianism—I don't mean it as a doctrine, I mean it as something in the air, the sensibility and era—if that were to come to an end, then I think the country—the culture—would be in desperate circumstances. Maybe it is.

**Q:** *What about writing outside America? Are there any countries that you feel particularly are in a renaissance right now?*

**A:** Oh yeah, sure. Three places. Japan. Maybe that is already coming to an end. You know, we discover the literature of other countries thirty years after that work has been done. But that is inevitable. And I myself have in the last year or two been reading a great deal of Japanese fiction, Kenazake, Mishima, Kawabata. To a Japanese this is like saying I have been reading Faulkner, Hemingway and Fitzgerald. But for them it may be that those writers are also discoveries.

There is, I think, enormous cultural energy there. There's a more recent and still ongoing tremendous cultural energy coming from Latin America. And then the East European writers—most of whom now are in exile. The East European writers represent, I think, a peculiarly tragic case because they have enormous talent and great moral seriousness, yet because they are exiles they are going to face terribly severe problems, especially the writers of fiction, with finding themes, situations, subjects. The poets can write about the absence of things, subjects, situations, but the novelists need them.

**Q:** *Do you really feel that is true about poetry?* [*laughter*]

**A:** Well, a great deal of modern poetry deals with the absence of things. So it's possible.

**Q:** *What are the unique qualities of Yiddish writing, poetry particularly, that make it important to preserve?*

**A:** Well, for one thing, at least some of it is very good. [*laughter*] For another, it represents a special historical condition and circumstance—a special tradition.

Any tradition which is lost thereby represents a thinning out, a diminution, of the totality of culture. And for those of us who one way or another come out of the tradition, out of the Jewish past, and especially for us who don't have religious faith, the loss of that is enormously painful or would be. There are also certain special qualities in Yiddish poetry, a peculiar combination of wit and pathos, for example, a peculiar kind of playing with language that I don't see in other literatures.

*Q: When you wrote* World of Our Fathers, *did you have any preconceptions before you wrote and researched it that changed when you actually wrote it?*

A: Yes, and that is an interesting question. In two ways. I didn't know the extent to which the immigrant Jewish life of the 1880s and 1890s had suffered demoralization. The pathology which today in New York is attributed to other groups was then being attributed with about equal appropriateness to the Jews. The life of the immigrant Jews in the 1880s and 1890s was—I am convinced and I think I discovered—far worse than the tradition of Jewish historical memory has made out because later on there was an impulse to blot it out or to smear it over, to make it prettier.

On the other hand, I am glad to say, some of the notions about immigrant Jews, especially immigrant Jewish boys, all rushing off to the library to read Spinoza and Marx—turned out to be self-congratulatory illusions. It was wonderful when I worked on the book to find out that on Allen Street there were Jewish prostitutes, that there were Jewish barkeeps, that there were Jewish bookies, that there were Jewish gangsters. In other words, that Jewish life had that leaven of strength and toughness which all peoples need.

**Q:** *What will happen to the Jewish experience in American writing? Are there new writers today who are carrying on the tradition of Bellow, Schwartz, and Malamud?*

**A:** Well, there are writers who are trying to. And there are gifted writers. But I myself have a very colloquial, somewhat rigid view of this which most of these writers understandably wouldn't like to hear or to agree with. I think that so-called American Jewish writing has been primarily an immigrant writing. It hasn't been really so much about Jews as it has been about the immigrant experience.

Most of the best of what we called American Jewish writing is, I think, that. And it is possible to see for a number of writers how the exhaustion of this experience, how it is fading away, leaves them with terrible problems of theme and subject. It is hard to know, it is hard to imagine, what a kid, a Jewish boy and girl, say ten years from now, who wants to deal with Jewish experience will find manageable. Not all human experience lends itself to literature, only a small portion of it does. The experience of the slums was, by its nature, highly dramatic. Whether anyone supposes that the suburbs can do that, it seems to me very questionable. [*laughter*]

**Q:** *In the passages you read tonight, you mentioned Edmund Wilson and literary criticism. Is there any place today for the humanist literary critic in a climate of hermeneutics and phenomenology and such?*

**A:** That is a provocative question. The advantages to getting older are very few. But one of them is that you no longer feel obliged to keep up and you know that various trends and fashions which can seem very powerful are very likely to pass. In the late forties early fifties, there was something called the Chicago neo-Aristotelian school of criticism. And it really did have something, I think, significant to contribute, but it faded away. And no fashionable person in our English departments would be caught dead identifying him or herself as a follower of the Chicago School today. You would have to have a footnote explaining what it is.

Given the probability of recurrence in history, I think you can assume that certain phenomena of the present time will also fade. But the question you asked about a place for a humanist literary critic is a very painful and difficult question, and I ask myself that question several times a day and I don't know the answer, because behind it is an even more crucial question: whether, in the kind of world that we are beginning to have, there is a place for intellectuals at all. There's certainly a place for people who have skills along the lines of intellectuality, which can be bought or sold or misused. But whether there is a place for intellectuals becomes increasingly a question.

**Q:** *Have you ever found there to be a conflict between political ideology and literary judgment, that is, have you ever admired the work of a writer whose moral or social or political views you did not approve of?*

**A:** All the time. In fact to me it is rather astonishing how many writers I have admired on the wrong side of the fence, so to speak. In *Politics and the Novel,* I wrote admiringly of Dostoevsky, not that it takes any great skill or boldness to do that. But for example, one of my first great admirations was Céline, the French writer Louis Ferdinand Céline. In his case it was relatively simple, because there was a clear division between his two great novels, *Death on the Installment Plan* and *Journey to the End of the Night,* and his horrible fascist and anti-Semitic diatribes.

It is much more difficult with a writer like Ezra Pound. I was never a great admirer of Pound because I felt that in his case the literary and the appalling moral content were all but inseparable. I also have been aware of having certain feelings for writers who in historical terms are probably not of the first rank, but for whom I had a special sense of warmth, with whom I had a special sense of kinship. Silone would be such a writer. I think *Bread and Wine* is a beautiful book, and *Fontamara* also, but I don't believe myself that he is as good a writer as Proust or Joyce or Brecht or whomever. Nevertheless for me, Silone is terribly important. It's foolish to suppose that our real affections are always parallel to any effort at objective literary rankings. There are writers whom we love, just as there are people whom we love, even though we may know that they are not the best. [*laughter*]

**Q:** *Is there a place for Thomas Hardy's writing in the world today?*

**A:** There is always a place for Thomas Hardy's writings. A time in which there is no place for Thomas Hardy's writings would really be like the death of humanity. [*applause*]

**Q:** *In* Politics and the Novel, *you call Orwell's* 1984 *an antipolitical book, by which you mean hatred of the kind of world in which public claims destroy private life. Do you see this to be a kind of trend in writing?*

**A:** Of course, of course. The whole idea that public life consumes everything about us, seizes every part of us is a major trend. You have it in such a brilliant writer as [Milan] Kundera.

One of the most fascinating things about Kundera's fiction is that he shows how, in a country like Czechoslovakia, people try to establish enclaves of the private apart from public life, and that almost against their will and almost against their knowledge, all the poisons of public life seep into their private life. He shows that you cannot make that separation. That seems to me something very bitter as well as very poignant in his life. This is one of the great themes of writing, it's the central theme I suppose, of the East European writers.

**Q:** *Are there other themes of the East European writers that attract you especially?*

**A:** Yes, one of the things that I find very endearing about some of the living East European writers, someone like [Czeslaw] Milosz especially—whom I knew many years ago before anyone thought he would win the Nobel Prize and he was just as good a writer then—is the sense of trying to find pleasure in the dailyness of life even when the external circumstances are horrible.

This, I think, is a great theme in Milosz's autobiography and a central theme in his poetry as well. And I think you will find this, as you find it in George Konrad, in almost all East European writers.

**Q:** *Are there Israeli writers who interest you? Whom would you consider?*

**A:** All Israeli writers are wonderful. [*laughter*] Well, one of the Israeli writers with whom I feel closest is the poet Yehuda Amichai, who is in fact right now here in New York. And he is a great love poet. And love not only for women but also for a city. I don't know anyone who has written about a city, Jerusalem—Yehuda gets bored when people say this, I hope he isn't here—no one has written about a city with the eloquence and loveliness that he has written about Jerusalem. The prose writers, I am interested in all of them. I don't think that at the moment Israeli prose seems . . . well, let me not say, I don't really know. But there is one Israeli writer, Yakov Shabtai, whose work is not yet known in English, who died unfortunately about a year and a half ago. He has a novel which I read in manuscript, which the Jewish Publication Society is bringing out this spring and which I think is close to being a really great book.

**Q:** *What's the title?*

**A:** I don't know the title in English.

**Q:** *Is there any genre in America today that interests you particularly? The novel, the short story, or poetry?*

**A:** Well, one of the interesting things has been that there seems to be a renaissance of the short story in recent years. It is hard to explain this, since there seem to be fewer and fewer outlets for publishing short stories, fewer magazines. One could develop a fancy theory saying that American life has become so complex and problematic that it is difficult to encompass it in a full-scale novel, but that you can get glimpses of it, pieces of it, fragments of it on a tangent—and therefore short stories work. It is a lovely theory, but the trouble with such theories is that there is no way of either proving or disproving them. That, I think, is true of most literary theories.

**Q:** *You mentioned Raymond Carver and wrote about him. Are there others as well? Other short story writers?*

**A:** Yes. There are really quite a few others. I won't mention any by name. But there is a whole generation of younger writers at the present time who are doing short stories. There's a woman named Bobbi Ann Mason whom I think is very good, for example.

**Q:** *She will be here later this evening.*

**A:** Okay. That's a plug for Bobbi Ann Mason. [*laughter*]

**Q:** *Have you ever thought of writing a novel or short stories?*

**A:** I thought of it but quickly abandoned it, because I couldn't imagine writing dialogue. I thought at one point of trying to collaborate with someone who is good at dialogue. [*laughter*] But I thought I had enough trouble on my hands with various things that I had done. . . .

## Notes

1. See *The Worlds of Irving Howe: The Critical Legacy*, ed. John Rodden (Boulder: Paradigm, 2005), 296-98.
2. Note that this version is excerpted, abbreviated, and adapted from the published book.
3. André Malraux was a leading left-wing French intellectual and the author of *Man's Fate* (1933). He served in two DeGaulle administrations as Minister of Information (1945-46) and Minister of Cultural Affairs (1959-69).

# Chapter 6

**Stephen Lewis, "From the Thirties to the Rise of Neoconservatism: Politics and Intellectual Life Across a Half-Century," Radio Interview with the Canadian Broadcasting Company, December 1983.**

## Introduction

Conducted under the auspices of the Canadian Broadcasting Corporation, this previously unpublished interview evinces Howe's prominence outside the U.S., showing how the writing of a public intellectual exerts influence in unexpected places and ways. Howe might have seemed an unlikely subject for a lengthy broadcast in Toronto for an audience presumably unfamiliar with the Jewish intellectual scene in New York City. The interview therefore opens with a biographical introduction that illuminates how Howe's writings and work had guided the American Left during times of challenge and isolation. The interview itself showcases two knowledgeable observers of the political scene as they reflect on a history that, in its broad patterns, has repeated itself, albeit with new twists. The conversation addresses Howe's early autobiography, his critique of Reaganism and neoconservatism, and his long-standing defense of working people against both the ravages of grand political ideology and the interests of the wealthy.

Given that interviewer Stephen Lewis is interested in the history and trajectory of the Left, this conversation thematizes issues that also arose in the Isserman interview. Born in 1937 into a politically active family, Lewis became the leader of the Ontario-based New Democratic Party (NDP), a party oriented toward social democracy that had gained great influence in the previous decade. After Lewis' period of leadership began in 1970, he ousted the Waffle (also known as the Movement for an Independent Socialist Canada), the party's radical wing.

Lewis was an avid reader of *Dissent,* and the ouster fit Howe's anti-ideological prescription to choose pragmatism over dogmatism. The New Democrats' support soon surged. In 1975, the party became the official opposition and was instrumental in implementing workplace and rent policies—albeit on the smallish political stage of a Canadian province—similar in substance to those advocated by Howe in the magazine. Still, the party was never able to gain a majority of seats, and it suffered setbacks in 1977. In 1978, Lewis resigned to work in the Canadian media, among other activities. He was later to serve as ambassador to the United Nations, and subsequently also worked on African development issues.

This interview offers an account of the path of Socialism toward moderation, with a well-informed North American politician probing the thoughts of a like-minded intellectual counterpart. Lewis recounts what Howe's intellectual stewardship had meant for the Left in the 1950s, when Communism had discredited itself and conservatism held sway (politically if not intellectually). More than this, *Dissent* had provided during those years strong, practical policy guidance. Recalling his days at Harbord Collegiate Institute and the University of Toronto, Lewis exclaims that in "the late fifties and early sixties, *Dissent* to many of us on the Left was everything, it was a bible." With Reaganomics ascendant at the time of this interview, such leadership again seemed necessary for the moderate Left. That *A Margin of Hope* had just appeared invited the respectful treatment that Lewis accords Howe here. The interview covers the scope of Howe's life to the early 1980s, ranging from reminiscence about his early life—the focus of the autobiography's opening chapters—to a discussion of the Reagan administration, which closes *A Margin of Hope.*

The conversation opens with a discussion of the background of Howe's enduring attachment to Socialism, which had appealed to the youthful Trotskyist as a potential solution to the kinds of struggles suffered by his immigrant parents, small shop owners and later garment workers. The young and radical agitator was thunderstruck by the amazing turn in family fortunes brought about by unionization. The passions associated with that intimate experience of social justice remained with him throughout his life: "Whenever I hear somebody like a professor at a faculty occasion start ranting against trade unions, it immediately arouses in me an absolute uncontainable fury." Howe also exhibits a strong emotional attachment to the lost Jewish neighborhood of his childhood, again showing the roots of his later intellectual pursuits in Yiddish literature and in immigrant Jewish New York, as well as his early connection to a radical politics that promised a better life. Prompted by Lewis's questions, he offers telling thumbnail sketches that bring to life several intellectuals of his day.

The latter part of the interview addresses then-current events. Howe shows great dissatisfaction with the conservative ascendancy of the Reagan era and with the historical amnesia of mainstream America. He meditates bleakly on the possibility of a return to radicalism and on the impact that such a development might have, admitting that in recent years "the basic drive, the dominant energy in American intellectual life, has been that of the conservatives." This declaration shows how much the national mood had changed since 1950, when Lionel Trilling noted in *The Liberal Imagination* that there was no discernible conservative intellectual impulse in the U.S. Trilling's remark came at the tail end of Roosevelt's New Deal. Howe's observation, thirty-three years later, applies both to the decade of political quietude of the 1950s, interrupted briefly by the radical activism of the 1960s, and to the recent rise of the neoconservatives, who by 1983 were exerting significant influence through major intellectual publications (such as *Commentary* and *The Public Interest*) and also serving in the Reagan administration. Howe complains that "the big corporations have discovered the uses of ideology. And they are pouring a lot of money into the magazines, the institutions, and the think tanks of the neoconservatives."

Money, however, is only part of the story behind ideological change, according to Howe. Liberals had shifted to playing defense, to preserving changes that had already happened. And the sharp radical turn of the New Left toward extremism in the late 1960s had provoked a backlash. Still, Howe also identifies an extremist element in 1980s conservatism comparable to the radicalism exhibited by the New Left in its last years, a tendency largely absent in earlier waves of American conservatism. Howe's observations here foreshadow a critique by "traditional" or cultural conservatives two decades later against the administration of George W. Bush and his neoconservative advisors and supporters.

## The Interview

*Irving Howe is not just one of the leading intellectuals of the twentieth century; he is the complete eclectic. He is rooted in the East European Jewish tradition, which migrated to the United States, and in particular, to New York City at the end of the nineteenth century and which put its roots in scholarship and the trade union movement. The amalgam produced a tremendous literary and social culture of which Irving Howe became one of the chief exponents. His migration, the pattern of migration of his people, was mirrored in his wonderful book,* World of Our Fathers, *a cultural and social history of East European Jewry, which covers from the end of the nineteenth century to the mid-twentieth. It won the National Book Award in 1977.*

*The high points of his career, Howe's trade union experience, the Socialist experience, the Jewish experience, came together in active politics, anti-Stalinist, anti-Soviet, Trotskyite in nature particularly in the late 1930s and 1940s. He spent his life in passionate scholastic, dialectical debate. And then, as he developed his political arts, he became more and more academic, and more and more literary. And in the latter forties and early fifties he became part of that intellectual community that surrounded the journal* Partisan Review, *part of the most vibrant intellectual community that the United States produced in the postwar period, which has since largely disintegrated. When Socialism itself dismembered, he became founder and editor of a quarterly journal called* Dissent *in 1954.*

*Howe is better known as a literary critic and a political commentator. The two were inseparable for him. He is a great Yiddishist in the sense that he translates a lot of Yiddish into English that gives Socialist culture an almost folklore view of history. He is an apostle, in a way, of Trotsky and has published the* Selected Works *of Trotsky. He is a literary critic of extraordinary dimensions. He's written critical biographies of Thomas Hardy, Sherwood Anderson, William Faulkner. He brought together the literary and the political in a fashion that has rarely been achieved in the United States.*

*Howe is cherubic, gentle, and principled. He speaks with anecdotal passion and in the reverberation of the voice is a constant intellectual depth.*

**Q:** *Tell me about your strong early Jewish working class antecedents.*

**A:** I cannot walk by a small store in any city in America or Canada without asking myself, "How does he remain in business?" Because it reminds me of my own father's experiences. He ran a little grocery store and he lost it during the early years of the Depression. And to me a small store is immediately a focus of anxiety.

And this, I'm sure, is characteristic of many people who come out of a Jewish background. Whenever I hear somebody, a professor at a faculty occasion, start ranting against trade unions, it immediately arouses in me an absolute uncontainable fury. Because I remember that after my folks lost their little store, they both became garment workers in the New York garment district. My mother's first job was for $12 a week, my father became a presser, and in 1933 the International Ladies Garment Workers Union called a strike, which was then a very risky business, and suddenly my mother's wages, when the strike was successful, went up to $27 a week. Now that was a significant change. And suddenly there was meat on the table and I could have a shirt for a birthday present and things of that sort.

My parents were not political people. They were like the ordinary people, what we call in Yiddish the "folksmassen," they were neither religious nor political. They always voted for Franklin D. Roosevelt, but that was just part of being Jewish, and they were good trade unionists, but they never went to a meeting. They paid their dues. If there was a strike called, you went on strike. To scab was equivalent to apostasy, and the idea of the value of a trade union was sort of built into my life as a result of that.

**Q:** *In your own terms, the genesis of your Socialism was rooted in the Jewish community of New York and its internationalist background. It wasn't sectarian in that sense. It was almost universalist.*

**A:** Well, I grew up in the East Bronx, now called the South Bronx. And, at that time this was an entirely Jewish neighborhood. You could get by, almost completely, with Yiddish. And the Socialists at that point were the second party in local elections behind the Democrats. Radicalism of one or another sort was very pervasive in the immigrant Jewish community. The Communists were very strong, probably the best organized group, and so this was simply accepted as part of the secular inheritance of the immigrant Jewish community.

The trouble was we could never get beyond certain ethnic boundaries. We couldn't break into other kinds of communities. We couldn't break into, for example, the Irish neighborhoods. When I grew up, the Roman Catholic Church was looked upon as a bastion of reaction. And one of the most astonishing experiences of my life and from my point of view, very encouraging, has been to see the way the Catholic Church in America has opened itself up, has become much more liberal. In fact, at the moment, decidedly more liberal than the Jewish community. The milieu in which I grew up, the immigrant Jewish milieu, which was largely secular, leftist, etc., has almost entirely disappeared. There are only a few old-timers. You can imagine [how old] that is if I am still considered one of the young ones.

**Q:** *I can imagine. I am an expression of it myself, because although I understand a great deal of Yiddish, I don't speak it. And one of the things that almost brings tears to one's eyes is to go and speak to a meeting of the Workman's Circle, and there are loving remnants. There are fifteen or twenty people now, very old, who ask you questions in Yiddish, which you answer in English. In your own life, in the latter thirties, the inability to break into the broader community, to some extent I take it, resulted in the—retreat perhaps isn't a fair word, but I'll use it—an intense scholastic internal anti-Stalinist but post-Trotskyist debate.*

**A:** Yes. Well, you see, in the American intellectual community, and in the Left in general, Trotsky played a role, which he did not play, I think, in any other country. The intellectual world in America in the thirties was very heavily under Communist, or as we called it then Stalinist, domination. The majority of American leftist intellectuals, for example, supported the Moscow trials and believed that the trials were legitimate. Those of us who were anti-Stalinist and who were beginning to see the terrible things going on in the Soviet Union, tended to gravitate to the image of Trotsky because he was so eloquent and so forceful and so forthright, and unyielding, uncompromising in his opposition to Stalinism.

The negative side was that, as it regarded American politics, it led us into a dead end from which some of us extracted ourselves only after a certain number of years. And indeed the formation of *Dissent* began as part of that process of pulling out of that sectarianism. But the appeal that Trotsky had, for a little while, for a few years, has to be understood in terms of the special situation of American intellectual cultural life in the late thirties. He was the counterforce against the deceit and the mediocrity of Stalinist influence.

**Q:** *Before* Dissent *came, you had this minor and inconsequential aberration of writing briefly for* Time *magazine and then you went on to become part of that wonderful greatness of the* Partisan Review. *Can you nostalgically reflect on those days?*

**A:** Yes. In those days, *Partisan Review*, though it had a circulation of no more than six or seven thousand copies, was surely the most influential cultural magazine. You see, we won the intellectual war against the Stalinists and fellow travelers by the early forties. In France, presumably a much more advanced country, this took at least another thirty years. We won it because there was a greater spirit of independence, the tradition that goes back to Emerson and Thoreau of standing on your own feet among American intellectuals, and people like Edmund Wilson, James T. Farrell, Lionel Trilling, Meyer Schapiro, many others, broke away from the Stalinist influence during the thirties and they gravitated around this small magazine.

It was a magazine which tried—not I think with entire success but for the moment very interestingly—to combine two impulses, anti-Stalinist leftism and the defense of cultural and literary modernism. Two avant-gardes. As it turned out, the avant-gardes were moving in opposite or different directions. Nevertheless, for a short while, the union of these two things had a great impact. It also developed a style of its own. Freelance, polemical, aggressive, with a great concentration on bravura and brilliance. It perfected the essay as a literary mode. It didn't do so terribly much in regard to fiction [or] poetry, but for the combative brilliant display essay, it really was an extraordinary phenomenon.

Well, I came along in the late 1940s. I was born in 1920, so when I got out of the war in 1946, and I began looking around and to develop literary ambitions, and I decided that the revolution was not going to come in America, and I had no particular place in organizing it, since it wasn't going to come, I developed more literary interests and I made contact with the editors of *Partisan Review*. In typical leftist fashion, you'll surely appreciate this, my first overture to them was to send them an attack on their magazine. And Philip Rahv, who was the editor, also knowing something about the psychology of this, roared with laughter and said, "You don't think we're going to print this?" I guess I really didn't expect him to. But it began a friendship. You begin a friendship on the left by attacking somebody. It began a friendship and then it continued.

**Q:** *Are you good at thumbnail sketches? Let me throw some names at you. Edmund Wilson.*

**A:** I first met Wilson in 1951 or 1952. I was doing a book on Sherwood Anderson. Wilson had known Anderson when he was younger. I went up to Cape Cod to talk to him about Anderson. He was then younger than I am now, but I thought of him as great man, he was a great man in a way. He was fat. He looked like a mixture of Herbert Hoover and W. C. Fields, and little bit of Henry James thrown in physically. And we sat down to talk presumably about Anderson.

But Wilson had this omnivorous hunger for information. He found out that during the war I had been stationed in Alaska. Instead of my learning about Anderson, he learned about Alaska. I left him about one in the morning, and he was a tremendous drinker. And from the background that I come from, you don't really learn to drink. And he was terribly scornful. He was greatly amused at my inability to match him in scotch. Now the truth is, most of the gentile intellectuals couldn't match him either.

**Q:** *What about the essayist Dwight Macdonald?*

**A:** Dwight Macdonald was this gangling skinny chap who afterward developed a potbelly. When I first knew him he was a member of the small left-wing group that I belonged to for a time. A group led by a man named Max Shachtman, and then he [Macdonald] dropped out. And he started putting out a magazine called *politics*, a very brilliant left-wing magazine . . . very open, lively. I came out of the army and needed work, and Dwight hired me as a part-time assistant on *politics* for the munificent salary of $15 a week. I used to do a magazine chronicle for Macdonald and he gave me a pen name of Theodore Dryden, who he said raised ferrets on Staten Island! I suppose some future historian is going to be searching the population of Staten Island for this ferret breeder.

And afterwards we tended to drift apart, not so much because of political differences, but the notion that there was this intellectual community in New York was at one time true. But by the time word got out about it, it was no longer true. In general, I think that you can make that as a useful summary. When the word is out about something in *Newsweek*, it no longer is true.

**Q:** *When did you meet Saul Bellow and collaborate with him?*

**A:** Saul Bellow I met in the late forties at the house of a friend of his. By the time I met Bellow, he was an aspiring novelist, terribly thin-skinned, very handsome, and rather rude in manner. And then I knew him for a time when I was living in Princeton in the late forties and early fifties when he was part of a quite brilliant little group, [including] Delmore Schwartz, John Berryman, and some other young writers.

My first close relationship of a literary kind with Bellow came in the middle fifties, it must have been 1955, the year isn't exact in my mind. I was then working on a volume called *A Treasury of Yiddish Stories*, together with a Yiddish poet, Eliezer Greenberg, and we were doing translations, or editing translations of Yiddish fiction, the first such serious volume in the English language.

We came across an extraordinary story by a writer who was then totally unknown, Issac Bashevis Singer, called "Gimpel the Fool" and we tried to think—

you see, translation is like matchmaking, you try to find the translator who will fit the writer. And the one who seemed best to fit Singer was Bellow, and at that time he was not yet the great man that he'd become, and he was delighted with the opportunity to do this.

Bellow has a pretty good command of Yiddish. We sat him down in Greenberg's apartment on East 17th Street and he banged out this translation at enormous speed in a couple of hours. Greenberg would read the Yiddish to him; Saul would type it out in English. One in a while Bellow didn't know a word and Greenberg would translate it for him and I just sat watching the whole thing completely entranced. And then he took it and fixed it up a little bit. And that was it. And it turned out to really be a classical translation, and it was the beginning of Singer's career in the English language.

**Q:** *To hear you talk of this period, of the 1940s and 1950s, is to hear about a period of renaissance in intellectual and literary thought which one does not feel in the late 1970s, early 1980s.*

**A:** It may be that there are young people around who have groups and are doing exciting things and we don't know about them yet. I suspect that what you say is true in this sense. If you look at the cultural situation in America today, there is an enormous amount of talent. A lot of gifted younger writers, I could name some. Raymond Carver, Ann Beattie, a whole host of others. But somehow it doesn't add up to an interesting literary situation.

There is another reason for this. A lot of us have gotten into the academy, who never thought we would end up as professors. That is good from one point of view, because even intellectuals have to eat, and we eat more regularly when we have regular jobs. But for intellectual life there have been some disadvantages to this.

At that point, if you were a young writer, you naturally thought of coming to New York, getting a little place in the Village, and eking out a livelihood by doing book reviews and odd chores. Now, in a more affluent society, it is impossible to live the life of what Paul Goodman once called "respectable poverty." So writers have to get jobs, often in universities. There was a mass expansion of higher education in America after the war with largely good, some bad results, and as a consequence, the universities were willing to hire oddballs like us who didn't have Ph.D.s. The intellectual community is now scattered across the country.

This may be good for some regional culture, though it makes for a great deal of loneliness. But there no longer is that concentration, that focusing of energy, that makes for an intense creative life, so that you learn the situation today, where you can pick up a book of short stories—for some reason the short story is especially thriving in America—by this or that writer, and it really is very good writing. But you cannot say that you feel you are living in an intense and vivid and exciting cultural moment.

*It must seem quaint, strange, curious, surreal to some of the audience to hear all of these references to Stalinism and fellow travelerism and Trotskyism and these arcane ideological truths which possessed the lives of intellectual and literary figures in the thirties, forties, and early fifties. And yet it was tremendously real for them. And it honed an analytic skill, writing skills, argumentative skills, which served people like Irving Howe wondrously in the years that followed.*

*We also today think of the fifties as the era of McCarthyism. McCarthy was representative of two truths. One, the shift to the right in American society, which made a lot of these people uncomfortable, and the other, the gradual deterioration of those schizophrenic, left-wing commitments. What did Howe call it? "Extracting himself from the dead end." And so he established, as part of another community, of those who were creating something new, he established the magazine* Dissent.

*If I can be personal for a moment, in my day, in the university days of the late fifties and early sixties,* Dissent *to many of us on the Left was everything, it was a Bible. When we wanted to learn about NATO, we read* Dissent. *Or German re-armament, the civil rights movement, Vietnam, we read* Dissent. *It was central to the development of our own ideology on the Left both in Canada and in the U.S., and I suspect for a lot of British Socialists as well. And it was a growing counterpoint to the right-wing emphasis of* Commentary *and* Encounter, *and people like Irving Kristol and Norman Podhoretz, because* Dissent *had Richard Wright, C. Wright Mills, Erich Fromm, etc. It was developing psychoanalytic views of human behavior as well as Marxist views of human behavior.*

*So there was a whole Socialist framework on the one hand that Howe created and sustained against the gradual right-wing development. The Socialist group was partial, tentative, ever more modest in numbers. And that was very distressing for some of the literary figures whom Irving Howe enumerates. They simply lost their political commitment entirely and went off to pursue cultural and literary careers.*

**Q:** *We constantly hear right now comparisons with the fifties. I think that there are cyclical realities that keep repeating. And the beauty of your life is that it encompassed all of it and speaks strongly and feelingly with discernment, which is essentially that we have been moving steadily to the right for some time.*

**A:** I think that the dominant secular line in the postwar years has been toward the right. I don't like it but I must admit it to be a fact. But this was interrupted during the sixties by the early Kennedy period, then interrupted by the Vietnam War, which split the country right down the middle, and also split the intellectual community and some of my old friends were now new enemies or new opponents. And then of course there were certain unfortunate incidents during the administration of Mr. Nixon which caused a certain amount of shame on the right, something called Watergate and things like that. But the basic drive, the dominant energy in American intellectual life, has been that of the conservatives.

I don't think the best thinking—but there is a difference between the best thinking and the dominant energy.

**Q:** *Do you see a fairly straight line between the emergence of the Right in the fifties and the neoconservativism of today? I remember you saying at one point that what occurred in the fifties was as though it were a restoring of the balance, that for the first half of the century, certainly since 1917, that we had been preoccupied with left-wing analysis and thought, and that it was only natural that civilization would make that shift.*

**A:** I think that is largely true. Now this again may be nostalgia, it may be that I like old conservatives better than young ones, or dead ones better than living ones. The fifties, as it seems to me now, had a conservatism that was much more qualified. Much more reflective than the neoconservatism of people today. The conservatism of the fifties, for example, was not breathing fire to push the cold war. The conservatism of the fifties would have felt embarrassed at the thought of supporting someone like Ronald Reagan.

Today, neoconservatism is much more crude and blatant and ideological. One of the interesting things, and surely you've encountered this in your own experience, about ideological politics is the way it takes on a life and a rhythm of its own. In, for example, *Commentary* magazine, which is one of the centers of neoconservativism, it is as if each month that magazine has to take a more extreme position in order to justify itself to itself because it exists on its own excitation. Just the way the New Left did in the late sixties. And so Norman Podhoretz comes out for sending American troops to Central America, an utterly disastrous idea, which even the Reagan Administration hesitates to say in public.

I think that what is going to happen is that this is going to burn itself out. There is something about ideological politics which leads to self-immolation, to going up in smoke and flame. With one significant difference between this experience and that of the New Left, and that is, that in America today, I don't know if this is true in Canada, the big corporations have discovered the uses of ideology. And they are pouring a lot of money into the magazines, and the institutions, and the think tanks of the neoconservatives. Until about ten years ago, most American corporations thought all this intellectual talk was just nonsense and of no importance, and they simply went about their business of making money. But they discovered that in the welfare state, or the truncated version of the welfare state that we have in America, there is a conflict of ideas which is of crucial importance to them. It is just as important to Exxon as it is to the AFL-CIO.

So you have a new interpenetration between the corporate world and the intelligentsia. And you have this comic spectacle of someone like Irving Kristol, whom I recruited into the Young People's Socialist League in 1939, one of my biggest mistakes, who now sits on many corporate boards. He is a very nice and amiable fellow, but the thought of him now being a spokesman for Republicanism really raises whatever few hairs I have left. Therefore, it is possible that the neoconservatives, even if they burn themselves out intellectually, will have an institutional base that will enable them to persist.

**Q:** *You surely don't engage in self-flagellation over Kristol. One never knows in this world how quickly people will move from left to right, incorporating the new fanaticism.*

**A:** As a matter of fact I sometimes think that my own intellectual career consists of constantly turning my head from left to right, watching people who had attacked me from the left as they move toward the right.

**Q:** *About ten years ago on the left in Canada there was the emergence of something called the Waffle Group, which was intensely nationalistic and ideological and left-wing and given to all of the traditional nationalization and other programs. Now of course many of them are respectable junior executives for the equivalents of IBM, and one sees in a mere decade a most remarkable shift.*

**A:** If you can't nationalize the industries, you join them.

**Q:** *They would say, in a spasm of self-defense, that you bore from within. I take it that the description that you have of the current neoconservatives and their extremism was really the kind of feeling that you had of the excesses of the New Left in the 1960s. Fundamentally, that is, what divided the Old Left, if I may put it that way, and the New Left, were the terrible authoritarian touches.*

**A:** With an important emotional difference, when I see what is going on now with neoconservatives, it raises an impulse to combat. I want to go in and start fighting. But, with the New Left in the late sixties, I had feelings of sadness and frustration because I saw once again the waste of energy which has been characteristic of American left-wing experience. I felt at the time that once again there was a terrible waste on our side. Now, about some of the New Leftists, I no longer felt that there was any real connection between them and me. They had gone too far and become Maoists and terrorists, and I felt that some of them, the Weathermen, were semi-fascists. But there were a lot of people within the New Left, who, driven crazy by the madness and the evil of the Vietnam War, pushed themselves into sectarian positions from which they could not retreat. Some of them have since come around and become relatively friendly with the kind of politics that I espouse, but there was a terrible waste, so that emotionally—I don't know if you've felt this in your own experience—I still find it harder to argue with people to my left than people on the right.

**Q:** *That's really interesting. I must admit I don't. But then it isn't the same experience because we've had an active political party in Canada, and so [I] resent the people on the left and the impact they have in undermining what [I] think to be the legitimacy of social democracy.*

**A:** You know the story, the wonderful story, I think it is a wonderful story, about Cohen. I was at Stanford in California in 1969. I was not at the university, but I was near it. My wife at the time was teaching, was working on the campus, and I would come for lunch. And there was a gang of New Left kids who would follow me shouting slogans, harassing me in the most absurd way, a childish kind of thing. And I should have known better, and not let it get to me but of course it did get to me, since I am only human. For a number of days I kept quiet, and tried to pretend that I was above it all, but finally I lost my temper and I turned around to this very bright boy named Cohen, who was the leader of this gang.

And I said to him, "Cohen, you know what you are going to be when you grow up, when you get older, you are going to turn out to be a dentist." And he turned pale, because you know, for some reason that is not entirely clear to me, the idea of a dentist around the radical world has always been associated with philistinism and petit-bourgeois life. He felt that this was the most dreadful insult that I could have given him.

Well, I got two or three letters from various people claiming that they knew who this Cohen was and what had happened to him. One report had him as an assistant professor at Cornell, another report said he was a corporation lawyer in Los Angeles, none of them made him quite literally a dentist, but all of them suggested that he had found a very comfortable place in the world of the status quo. And so it was very hard because it was like seeing your own children going off the deep end and rebelling.

Now the point you made before is absolutely right. If there really were a structured, coherent social democratic party in America, such as the New Democratic Party here in Canada, then one could feel that these people were doing it terrible damage by destroying its possibilities to win an election or to rule a provincial government or whatever the case may be. But with us, where left-wing politics has a much more chaotic, abstract form, it was sort of like a free-for-all. It was very hard in the late sixties, very hard.

**Q:** *Your most recent publication is the editing of a collection of essays on Orwell. We are doing this interview in the latter part of 1983. 1984 is upon us. I take it that this is quite visceral with you. That for many, many years Orwell has been central for you. I even recall that at one point you attempted to model your literary writing on Orwell, some of your journalistic writing.*

**A:** Yes, Orwell has been for me a very important figure. *Nineteen Eighty-Four* is a work of admonition, a work of warning and as such, it has played an enormous role. I now think that the greatest contribution that it made was toward the cleansing of the English language. When, for example, I hear Ronald Reagan say, "We are going to go into Central America in order to defend democracy" and in none of the countries that he wishes to go into *is* there any democracy, then the first adjective that comes to mind is that this is an Orwellian expression. It is a version of Newspeak.

Now fortunately, when one lives in a democracy, one can criticize this, and I think that the people who say that we have reached a condition at all like that of *Nineteen Eighty-Four* are being very foolish. Because the mere fact that they can say it proves that it isn't true. The whole thing of Newspeak and doublethink—this was such an extraordinarily brilliant innovation. When you read for example that in the Soviet Union, subscribers to the official encyclopedia get sets of new pages from page 428-32 to replace the existing entry with another one which changes it entirely, and they are supposed to cut out the pages and paste in the new ones, you say to yourself, Orwell was simply describing common reality.

You know the famous essay, "Politics and the English Language," which every politician should be made to read at least once a year on a day of penance, I think on Yom Kippur. All the Jewish and the goyische intellectuals and politicians should be made to read "Politics and the English Language." Would you introduce a bill like that if you were in the provincial parliament again?

**Q:** *We will make it mandatory in 1984* [*laughter*]. *It seems to be appropriate.*

*Indeed, after 1984, I imagine we can expect from Irving Howe exactly what we've had until now. He'll be writing and fighting and arguing and believing, making a magnificent intellectual and literary contribution. I think one expects from him his own phrase, I noted it down: "Living the intense creative life."*

# Chapter 7

**Editorial Board of *The New York Times*, "Howe and Harrington on the Future of Democratic Socialism Beyond the Reagan Era," *New York Times Magazine*, 17 June 1984, 24.**

## Introduction

In this dialogue, America's two preeminent Socialists of what could be called the "post-Socialist era" discuss the prospects of a radical rebirth in the late twentieth century. Although Howe was the more prolific and visible public intellectual, Michael Harrington (1928-1989) was far more influential as an organizer and lecturer, doing the hands-on work of keeping American Socialism alive.[1]

Like Howe, Harrington veered between literature and politics, attaining an M.A. in English from the University of Chicago; unlike Howe, Harrington left literary criticism behind, becoming active in politics for the bulk of his career. Each achieved national prominence in distinct spheres, though their preoccupations overlapped. Harrington remained quite interested in American literature and culture; nevertheless, his greatest passion was for politics. Each of them achieved national standing in the area of his main focus, which exerted a kind of halo effect that imbued achievements in other spheres with distinction.

Believing that democracy and Marxism were compatible, Harrington chaired the Socialist Party from 1968-72, the Democratic Socialist Organizing Committee (DSOC) from 1973-82, and the Democratic Socialists of America (DSA) from 1982-89. Indeed, through his energy and the force of his personality, Harrington largely held together the latter two groups, which worked within the Democratic Party advocating democratic Socialism, a stance that led to attacks from both the Right and the radical Left. Besides being an active organizer and gifted speaker, Harrington published numerous books and articles on political topics. His best-known and most influential work, *The Other America* (1962), partly inspired the War on Poverty, which was launched by the Johnson administration in the mid-1960s (a war that was, of course, never won, no more than such later efforts as the War on Drugs).

Harrington's relationship with Howe and *Dissent* magazine was intense and enduring. He wrote for *Dissent* from the early 1950s and was a member of the editorial board until his death. By the mid-1980s, however, Harrington's role was reduced to that of a prophet in the political wilderness, decrying Reaganism and describing the possible circumstances in which a rejuvenated Left might again arise, as in *The Next Left: The History of a Future* (1986). Still, Harrington and Howe remained respected figures on the Left, more so than any comparable political or intellectual figure today, when ideological tides and polarizing rhetoric have tainted even the word "liberal," much less "Socialist."

The appearance of this exchange between Howe and Harrington in the *New York Times Magazine,* for which both occasionally wrote, was significant; it lent weight to the contention that the DSA's political outlook merited serious attention, implying an endorsement by the mainstream press that a radical critique of America deserved a wider hearing. This interview followed scores of contributions from Howe to *The New York Times.* His book reviews spanned from the early 1950s through the early 1990s; he also contributed essays as well as innumerable letters to the editor. His range was enormous, covering such cultural topics as Yiddish humor and American movies and such political topics as the history of unionism and the positions of American Jews toward Israel.[2] More than that, Howe's writings in the *Times* served as a platform for speaking to a general public otherwise unfamiliar with the outlook and style of a (semi)radical New York Intellectual. This interview embodies that tone and style, expressed in a moderate language that voices a fierce moral call for economic justice. Howe and Harrington alternate roles here as interviewer and interviewee. They admit that there is no longer an American Socialist Party, or even a unified American Left, but only a loose collection of sects and fledgling organizations. Early in the interview they seem diffident, if not defensive, as when Harrington states that his criticisms of current policy are "in the name of the national security of the United States," and Howe adds: "This is not just a rhetorical stratagem, it's a genuine position." They are pained by the rightward turn that the U.S. has taken, worried that this might reveal America's underlying nature, and eager to reassure the vast readership of the *New York Times Magazine* that they are innovative yet practical—and not *too* radical.

Still, Howe and Harrington adopt a political perspective at odds with Reagan's America in the 1980s, and their statements of principle grow correspondingly bolder as the interview progresses. Adopting a decentralized politics as much by necessity as by inclination, they envision a near-future in which democratic Socialism attracts voters again due to an economic crisis, a severe recession induced by Reaganism (recalling how American Socialism was energized by the Great Depression). As Howe puts it, "The Left has begun to do programmatic work in preparation for what we expect, or hope, will be the next surge forward of American liberalism." As subsequent events would prove, however, this was wishful thinking. Although the Reagan administration's budget deficits were indeed escalating due to massive increases in defense and military expenditures, and a recession did in fact occur in the early 1990s, these developments turned out to be hiccups on the road to the neoliberalism of that decade. The ideological background had so changed by then that a Democratic president, albeit often in conflict with a Republican-controlled Congress, would largely continue policies that promoted an unfettered capitalism.

Most prescient in the Howe-Harrington dialogue are the observations about long-term economic trends regarding inequality, particularly from an international perspective, as in Harrington's point that "in the Dominican Republic, a Socialist government recently faced riots because the IMF [International Monetary Fund] forced it to accept a bankers' 'discipline' and raise the price of food and other necessities. In this setup, money is more sovereign than independent governments." This remark anticipates the antiglobalization activism that arose in the late 1990s, which appeared to have great potential to spur change. In the long run, then, some of the Howe-Harrington/DSA predictions about the deleterious effects of an approach favoring strong corporations and weak governments came true. And a leftist resurgence did in fact occur, albeit far later than foreseen in this interview (though also more international in scope). Although the mainstream media's preoccupation with the events and aftermath of 9/11 have marginalized public attention given to these economic issues, they remain seething at a subterranean level, rising to the surface in bastardized form, as in today's anti-immigration movement.

Despite their far-sightedness, Howe and Harrington give only piecemeal suggestions for reform and not any comprehensive and transformative vision. Their program amounts to a grab-bag of policies, really a mixture of capitalism and Socialism rather than a coherent, compelling radical vision. By the interview's end, they even wonder whether the name "Socialism" is necessary any longer. Indeed by the early 1980s, Howe had dropped the motto "a Socialist quarterly" from *Dissent*'s masthead and began referring to himself as a "radical humanist" rather than a "Socialist." What has gone largely unremarked is that the phrase "radical humanist" places less emphasis on politics and much more on culture and society, reflecting perhaps Howe's own conviction that it was his cultural and literary work that was most significant, not his political work, the latter of which would not survive.[3] He came to see himself as a humanist first and foremost, which is why he invested such energy in his defense of the Western canon and attacked so vehemently the advocates of multiculturalism. It could be argued that his Socialist values were a subset of his humanism, contingent on humanitarian values that he had directly experienced in his quasi-Dickensian immigrant childhood. Whatever his self-description, however, he never lost his strong emotional ties to the idea—and ideals—of Socialism.[4]

By the conclusion of this interview, Howe is able to formulate a strong statement of his governing idealism, which he refused to disavow even in the worst of political circumstances:

> We want a society in which economic life has been transformed in the direction of greater democratic participation, so that workers may have some control over their workplace and their work life. We favor a dispersion and decentralization of the excessively concentrated corporate ownership, so that certain industries, especially those with a monopoly character, would be socially owned (cooperatives, worker ownership, regional T.V.A.-like agencies) and would coexist with a private sector. . . . We want a social order that stresses cooperative and communal values, even as it also encourages individual personality.

In the new millennium, such impassioned appeals for a more just society seem largely absent within the American intelligentsia, or at least inaudible amid the sound bites and talking heads dominating the national media.

Despite its overall reticence, this exchange in *The New York Times Magazine* certainly attained a wider audience than any other in this collection. And in hindsight, it stands—however much Howe and Harrington tempered their radicalism for tactical reasons here—as a historic statement by two radical intellectual giants.

## The Interview

*During the clamor of the presidential campaign, a familiar voice seems strangely muted. The more-or-less middle-of-the-road Democratic candidates can be heard loud and occasionally clear, as can the neoconservative thinkers and their president. But who and where are the thinkers of the Left? Why have they been so relatively silent? What ideas and programs do they stand for? How do they see the nation's future?*

*The editors of* The New York Times Magazine *put these questions to two spokesmen for the democratic Left: Irving Howe, editor of* Dissent, *and Michael Harrington, co-chairman of the Democratic Socialists of America.*

**Irving Howe:** Is there an American Left today? I mean, a more-or-less organized movement which plays a role in our national life?

**Michael Harrington:** Yes and no. There are thousands of activists in the unions, the black organizations, the women's movement, the community organizing groups who are inspired by a democratic-Left vision. They constitute a sort of network.

**IH:** Network?

**MH:** We don't have a coherent, unified party—like the Socialist Party of Norman Thomas in the 1930s. The effort to keep a left-wing *party* has pretty much collapsed. And for many reasons: The American electoral system severely handicaps third parties, but there is still an informal community—numbering, I'd guess, between 20,000 and 30,000 people—who work together. Some think of themselves as Socialists, and belong to the organization of which I'm co-chairman, Democratic Socialists of America—not a party but a sort of activist educational league. Others contribute to the magazine you edit, *Dissent*.

So when we use the term "democratic Left," we mean a spectrum of opinion to the left of conventional liberalism, including both Socialists and freelance radicals. We all believe in democracy, we all want social change.

**IH:** This "network" tries to put a little starch into traditional liberalism, does practical work in popular movements, and also keeps alive the ideas of democratic Socialism.

**MH:** All of this means, of course, that the Left has suffered defeats over the past decade or so—that's just a fact. But there've been some good results, too. We've had a healing of relationships, especially between older Socialists like you and me and part of the New Left of the 1960s. Time passed, tempers cooled, old disputes faded. And by now practically everyone on the left agrees that the Democratic Party, with all its flaws, must be our main political arena.

That would have been heresy at New Left gatherings in, say, 1969. Well, that's over with—there's a distinct realism now within the Left on what we can do in American political life.

**IH:** But we've changed, too. We're more ready to see the virtue of some of the venturesome ideas of the New Left, such as its stress on "participatory democracy." And while we're talking about intraleft matters, let me just mention the question of Stalinism. There was a time when the Communists were a major force, a terrible problem, within the American Left. That's over with—forever, I hope. So I'd say that whatever else, we of the democratic Left did win the intellectual battle against Stalinism these past several decades.

**MH:** At a heavy price.

**IH:** The exhaustion of generations, a lot of bitter polemics. But we had no choice: it was an obligation of moral hygiene.

**MH:** I'd add that now, in the democratic Socialist milieu, there's even a small but significant group of former Communist leaders. They've broken with their past, yet I'm sure they still feel a little uncomfortable with my visceral anti-Communism. So something has been salvaged from the collapse of the American Left in the postwar years.

**IH:** When you're speaking of activists functioning in the unions, Mike, and the black and women's movements, maybe we should describe what it is that these people do. This is not the old Marxist-Leninist "boring from within" strategy. There's a wholly different vision of our relationship to American society. There's a feeling now that while we are very critical of many of today's American socioeconomic arrangements, we are absolutely committed to democratic institutions. We work with one major goal, and that is the increasing democratization of socioeconomic life.

**MH:** An illustration of this shift is that when I criticize American foreign policy, our intervention in Central America, the MX, I do that in the name of the national security of the United States.

**IH:** And this is not just a rhetorical stratagem, it's a genuine position.

**MH:** If you think back to somebody in the late sixties at an anti-Vietnam War rally getting up and talking about the national security of the United States—well, it would have been difficult.

**IH:** And you speak of the national security because you recognize that there is a totalitarian enemy out there which needs to be met.

**MH:** Our critique is that President Reagan's policy with regard to Nicaragua does not promote the national security, it hurts it.

**IH:** All of which shows that people, even we, learn something from experience, though it takes an excessively long time. We've learned that we don't care whether people call themselves Socialists or liberals or liberal leftists—what we care about is the political direction in which they're going. So we work within all the liberal organizations—some of us have even been out in the field, campaigning for one or another of the Democratic candidates. We are loyal allies and sometimes friendly critics.

You know, you were talking as if the only people committed to the left view were intellectuals. I think it's worth mentioning, though, that there are some, not vast numbers, people in the unions and the black community who also. . . .

**MH:** Oh, absolutely. Just to drop a few names: Congressman Ron Dellums of California; William Winpisinger, president of the machinists union; leaders of the women's movement like Gloria Steinem and Barbara Ehrenreich—all are part of our democratic-Left community.

On our left boundary, things are somewhat hazier. We have some people who tolerate our tactical approach to American politics but who still prefer to stress fundamentalist Socialism.

If we look back on why Socialism failed in America, there are many reasons, but one of them is a sectarian attitude toward liberal reform. It is ironic that the Socialist Party of Norman Thomas was all but destroyed by the Great Depression. Here was the greatest collapse that capitalism has ever known, a moment when the argument for anticapitalism was right there before your eyes, and the Socialist Party falls apart because it cannot come to terms with Roosevelt.

Every criticism Norman Thomas made of Roosevelt tended to be true. What was wrong—I talked to Norman about this before his death and he agreed—was that even though there were profound limitations to the Roosevelt reforms, the New Deal drew upon and reinforced a mass movement for social change in the United States. The Socialists made a terrible mistake in counterposing themselves to it.

**IH:** But let's come back to liberalism today. We're saying that we see ourselves as part of a reformist impulse in American society, that we share many of the values of traditional liberalism (civil rights, political freedoms, tolerance), but that we wish to extend those values into areas of social and economic life traditional liberalism has shied away from.

**MH:** I would add that out there, in the real world, there still exists something called capitalism. For all of its changes, it still exists. What has to be put on the agenda is structural change. The value of having a Socialist analysis of capitalism is that it allows us to advance some very large ultimate goals while trying to realize what is possible now.

**IH:** What we're speaking of used to be called Fabianism or a social-democratic reformist policy of incremental changes which create a welfare state that modulates and humanizes capitalist society.

**MH:** One thing that distinguishes us from the English Fabians[5] is that we reject their bias of a top-down elitist permeation of society. We are Fabians in that we understand that reforms are going to come by stages.

But we depart from the Fabians—and this is a very American emphasis—in our insistence on popular participation.

**IH:** As I see it, what happened in the last fifty years was a major social and political change, the creation of a rudimentary welfare state ushered in by Roosevelt and continued by Truman and Lyndon Johnson. Under the Reagan Administration, there has been a partial retreat from the welfare state, as a result of planned government attacks. But from our point of view, it is necessary for the country to enter what I call the second phase of the welfare state, which is much more difficult and much more complicated, because now corporate power has to be challenged and at least some national economic planning, democratically executed, has to be undertaken. That's pretty rough stuff for many Americans.

Now it's not as if the welfare state in the thirties came out of thin air. We all know Franklin Roosevelt, when he campaigned for president, didn't really make any proposals for reform. But once in office, out of sheer desperation he picked up some of the ideas that had been developed for many years by thinkers of the Left.

Now we're in an interesting stage where the Left has begun to do programmatic work in preparation for what we expect, or hope, will be the next surge forward of American liberalism. That programmatic work, which we'll discuss in a moment, isn't by any means yet complete, but I think we are living through a phase something like that of the intellectual preparation before the New Deal.

**MH:** I am convinced—I'm not quite as radical as Wall Street on this count but I'm convinced—that the current economic recovery is temporary, an interlude between two crises.

The only question is when the breakdown of this recovery will occur—most likely after the 1984 election, which bodes well for Ronald Reagan and not for us. But if I am right, and there is a renewal of economic crisis—let us say more inflation and unemployment—in the 1985-86 period, a lot of our ideas could catch fire.

I think we are coming to the end of a conservative phase. There will at least be a liberal—radical, perhaps—possibility, because the crisis is a very difficult one to deal with.

**IH:** A lot depends on what happens in the 1984 election. If a Democratic candidate, let's say Mondale, wins, then certain possibilities are open. He will have to face crises not quite as severe as those of Franklin Roosevelt, but still of considerable magnitude. He has not been campaigning on any very bold, liberal programs and he's going to need something more than "what you see is what you get." He's going to need some substance and it's possible that he will have to turn toward the liberal-left thinkers.

Of course, if Reagan wins, then we're in for a difficult period.

One other point, Mike, before we come to our actual proposals, and that is, we talk as if the larger political coalition around the Democratic Party is as coherent today as it was at an earlier point. Obviously it's not. There's a lot of jockeying and uncertainty about internal relationships—for example, what place is there for the "Yuppies" in such a coalition? How much influence should the labor movement have?

**MH:** What has happened since the New Deal coalition of the thirties is that the class structure of American society has become much more complex. You now have, for example, a middle class not of professionals but of salaried people who work in large hierarchical institutions, but have a social outlook markedly different from that of a production worker.

I think that the generational differences Gary Hart is stressing are profound. Such factors make it difficult to put together an electoral coalition. We certainly saw that during the 1960s, where you had a college-educated movement which was right on the issue of the war but often needlessly angered patriotic working people.

We have a similar problem within the Left. The Marxist Left of the thirties had a vision of the proletariat as a single cohesive agent of social change. Everybody remotely aware of what is now going on has abandoned that perspective. Like American society itself, the Left has become much more fragmented.

**IH:** Let's come to the question people ask us: "What do you want, short of some distant Socialist goal? What do you want done in this country during the coming period?"

I could mention a few immediate concerns. For example, we are totally against the shameful interventionist policy that Reagan has introduced in Nicaragua. We favor sustained negotiations on nuclear arms with the Soviet Union.

These are points which are not unique to the democratic Left; most ordinary liberals would agree.

**MH:** Right. But on international issues I think there are distinctively Socialist analyses and emphases. For instance, there's the familiar idea that revolutions in the third world are usually more a result of poverty than of Soviet plots. Socialists would take that proposition to its conclusion. There is a world capitalist market which systematically transfers wealth from the poor to the rich. The terms of trade—the low prices the poor nations normally receive from us and the high prices they pay to us—lead to that result.

That pattern affects even a "middle-class" developing country like Brazil. It has successfully commercialized its agriculture and increased production in recent years, but one consequence is more hunger, particularly in the Northeast. In adapting to the world market, it destroyed the subsistence plots of land.

So there is a "new colonialism" which often sends in the International Monetary Fund rather than the Marines. In the Dominican Republic, a Socialist government recently faced riots because the I.M.F. forced it to accept a bankers' "discipline" and raise the price of food and other necessities. In this setup, money is more sovereign than independent governments.

**IH:** Are there Socialist solutions to these problems that go beyond liberalism?

**MH:** I'd be more modest and say, Socialist emphases. The so-called Brandt Commission, headed by Willy Brandt,[6] the former West German chancellor, was composed of liberals as well as Socialists, but it stressed the structural solution of transferring capital and technology from north to south, from rich to poor, with the proviso that these be used to help the people rather than dictators of either left or right. The argument is that such a policy would create jobs both in the advanced and developing countries. It wasn't an accident that such an idea came from a group led by a Socialist.

**IH:** Let's turn to the domestic economy. What's distinctive about the proposals of the democratic Left?

**MH:** Let's put the question in a broad context. You've got Reaganomics, which is a mishmash, but one of its characteristics is to try to roll back the welfare state. It has purchased at intolerable cost a temporary recovery; the mounting deficits and continued high unemployment make it highly probable that the crisis will resume.

Second, there is a neo-liberalism represented to some degree by Gary Hart, which is opposed to the cruelties of attacking the poor but which says, "Look, we did spend too much. Government has to retreat. What government really should do is, through tax and other policies, encourage enough private savings and then the financial markets will allocate those savings and allow us to adapt to a new international division of labor."

There's a third point of view, represented by Felix Rohatyn, which is for planning, but it does not look to the popular base. It has an elitist bias—economic planning from the top.

I think on that spectrum—Reaganomics, neo-liberalism, and a kind of sophisticated conservative planning—that where we come in is with the notion that, yes, there has to be planning. On this we agree with Rohatyn. But we want economic planning that, as much as possible, is democratic, participatory, bottom-up. Second, not only bottom-up in process and procedure, but also directed toward satisfying the needs of those at the bottom and the middle rather than those at the top.

**IH:** Mike, let's go through some of the proposals that we make and then you can elaborate. One of the criticisms we make, for example, of the Democratic candidates is that no one speaks anymore about full employment. What do we mean by full employment?

**MH:** I would define full employment not, as is usually done in this country, by an unemployment rate. I would define it in the way that the liberal theorist Lord Beveridge defined it in England during World War II. Full employment is when employers are looking for workers rather than workers looking for employers.

How many people are looking for a job is in part determined by what people think are the possibilities of finding a job. Full employment is not some abstract rate; it is a situation where everyone who wants a job feels that he or she can find one.

One precondition is to reduce the workweek so that more people will be working fewer hours. That involves all kinds of problems—it's much easier said than done, but it's essential.

**IH:** The workweek has been cut before. One of the things that's so irritating about conservative thought on these matters is the assumption that somehow we have reached a point in human development where no further progress is possible—the absolute dead end of human achievement—and we must, say the conservatives, accept these limitations on the welfare state. I see no reason for such a notion either in terms of history or the development of technology.

But when you speak of full employment in a capitalist economy, doesn't this mean all but continuous governmental intervention, government work programs of various kinds?

**MH:** I think so. It's hard to suppose that the private economy in the next period, particularly with the technological revolution now under way, will, on its own, produce jobs for everyone. In particular I don't think it will produce jobs for those now at the bottom third of the American social structure. Government intervention is critical.

Having said that, I think one has said rather little. After all, Ronald Reagan intervenes in the economy every day. The question is, How is it done?

**IH:** We have a situation in which the urban infrastructure is virtually collapsing. This would seem a natural for government intervention.

**MH:** One of the things that has changed on the left is that when I think of government intervention, I want, wherever possible, that it not be done centrally out of Washington, but through local agencies responsive to local needs and decisions. Federal money is essential because the federal income tax is the only progressive source of public money in the United States. So, yes, there has to be government intervention, but what the Left would emphasize now is the need to get these work programs as close to the grass roots as possible and to provide for input from the working people and communities involved.

**IH:** You're speaking of a fairly complex and delicate mixture of basic funding from the federal government with a good deal of autonomy by democratically chosen local agencies.

**MH:** Right. You're getting, as a result of the current crisis, a rather dramatic increase in various kinds of worker participation in industry—some good, some not so good. The contract signed by Eastern Airlines with the machinists, the flight attendants and the pilots is one of the most significant union contracts of the last forty or fifty years.

In return for significant concessions on the part of the unions—they had to give up wages and other claims on money—the workers now have 25 percent of the equity in the company and 25 percent of the seats on the board of directors.

**IH:** You have the beginnings there of the American equivalent of what the Germans call co-determination, which means that you also begin to move—a small but significant step—toward workers' control of their economic life.

Let's go back to full employment for a moment. Full employment was taken for granted; it became virtually a platitude during the Roosevelt and Truman years. Since then, there has been such an ideological shift to the right that many conservatives and business spokesmen would say, "Well, O.K., but if there were full employment, wouldn't this lead to high inflation and wouldn't you then be caught up in a vicious circle?"

**MH:** The policies we advocate do include a risk of rekindling inflation. So do Reagan's; but leave that aside. Everybody on the left believes that there have to be *some* controls. Wage, price, income, rent, dividend controls.

Reagan has his way of fighting inflation. It's supposedly "no-hands"—the government does nothing. That's utter nonsense. The Reagan method involved a heavy use of governmental powers, through monetarism and other policies, to disemploy about twelve million Americans. Their unemployment did buy us lower prices. That is one way. You can roast the pig by burning down the barn!

**IH:** The economist Bob Lekachman says that a policy of controls doesn't have to be all the way across the board; it doesn't have to include small businesses, since to include them would raise the specter of bureaucracy and black markets. He says that if you had controls over a significant portion of the major corporations and major financial institutions, that would be enough. The rest of the economy could continue on a more or less unregulated basis.

Lekachman also makes the point that there are enormous costs which are not customarily recognized when you try to cope with inflation by creating unemployment; not only the human and social cost but the government payments of vast sums of money in unemployment insurance and other social benefits.

**MH:** The Reagan Administration uses a figure that every 1 percent increase in unemployment loses the Federal Government $25 billion in the taxes it will not collect and in unemployment comp and welfare it has to pay out. The AFL-CIO figure is $30 billion. If you then say that unemployment under Reagan was allowed to increase in order to fight inflation—unemployment went up from 7 plus to almost 11—even if you use Reagan's figure, that gets you close to $100 billion of the current $180 billion deficit. That's quite a cost to pay for the right-wing method for bringing down inflation.

Put another way, if we could get the full employment that the Left talks about, that would entail an enormous saving to the federal government because employed workers pay taxes and don't collect food stamps.

**IH:** One of the things that's happened in this country over the last six or seven years is a loss of social sympathy and a decline of social solidarity, the rise of a very ugly form of "possessive individualism" which can be summed up by the slogan, "I've got mine, Jack." It's a tremendous change in social tone, from, say, the early 1960s when we had a moment of relatively good feeling in this country.

I suppose we have to give Reagan a sort of backhanded credit for this.

**MH:** Reagan has done practically everything he campaigned for; he has been more faithful to his ideology than any president in my lifetime. It's a tragedy that the innovator really willing to strike out in new ways has come from the right and not the left.

**IH:** Mike, let's talk about this mysterious thing called industrial policy. Maybe it would be best to focus on one industry, the steel industry, in very grave trouble. A lot of steelworkers are unemployed. The dominant corporations are tending to place their capital elsewhere. The competition from abroad is very fierce, one reason being lower wages over there, but another being the fact that some foreign governments subsidize their steel industries.

There is a kind of technocratic elitist view of this which I find distasteful: that the best thing to do is just let these industries, or good portions of them, go down the drain and turn to high-tech.

**MH:** There are obsolete plants that should be closed down. Or you can do what the Swedish Conservatives did. They kept open plants that, economically, were no longer viable because they had calculated how much it would cost in retraining, unemployment benefits, relocating those workers as compared to what it cost to subsidize them in a losing form of production. They decided, for the short run, to keep the plants open.

Part of the answer in America is to create other new industries. There has to be, as part of your response to steel, a government initiative to rebuild the railroads, for example.

What then do you do with an obsolete plant? I think you phase the workers out so it's not they who pay the cost of the transition. If the entire society is going to gain from the efficiency of closing down the plant, then the entire society should pay the cost, which includes the human cost as well. You phase some of the workers into new jobs, many of which have to be created by government planning.

Secondly, I think you offer certain subsidies to the private sector. I would be for federal tax subsidies to steel corporations to create jobs in those parts of the industry where the demand is going up—specialty steel, for instance. If a company was willing to go to McKeesport, Pennsylvania, and open up a profitable modern steel plant, then fine, I would be for giving them a big tax break for creating jobs.

Thirdly, there's been a proposal that a lot of people in both Pennsylvania and Ohio and the steel areas have talked about, of creating the equivalent of a Tennessee Valley Authority to try to cope with the problem on a regional basis.

Another idea is to take the advice of economists like Wassily Leontief and adopt the goal of a 35-hour week.

Nineteen eighty-six will mark the 100th anniversary of the struggle for the eight-hour day. I think it would be rather good if the AFL-CIO said, a hundred years after the eight-hour day, we are now ready to talk about the seven-hour day. Leontief says, and I think he's right, that if you tried overnight to go from the 40-hour week to the 35-hour week at 40 hours' pay, you would cause enormous harm since increasing the wage bill by that much could decrease profits too much. And as the profits decrease you're drying up a major source of new investment. Pretty soon workers would be laid off because the company couldn't make it on that basis.

Suppose, however, company A paid you 36 hours of pay for 35 hours of work, with tax credits and other governmental policies making up the other four hours of pay. You will wind up with a total package of 40 hours of pay for 35 hours of work; but the 40 hours of pay will not necessarily come simply from that one company. It will be borne by society as a whole.

**IH:** Let's turn to the question of taxation and paying for the things we propose.

**MH:** Clearly, after the 1984 election, tax reform is on the agenda. The Republicans obviously don't want to say it, but they have got to take back some of the money that Reagan gave away in the 1981 tax bill, mainly to the rich. Right now it looks as if most of the debate will center around the Bradley-Gephardt bill for tax simplification. The Internal Revenue Code is an absolute maze. Congress, when it wants to promote an activity—let's say home building, rather than sending an individual a check to go and buy a house—writes the tax law so that the interest on the mortgage payment is deductible. That's a marvelous example: The bigger the house, the higher the interest; the more income you have, the more of a subsidy you get from the government. If you rent, you get zero subsidy. So Bradley-Gephardt says we take away almost all of these deductions. And in return we lower the tax rates because your taxable income is going to go up as a result of your losing many of these deductions.

What worries me—and this is why I think that the mobilization of a Left is so important—is that this is the kind of debate that takes place behind closed doors, involving technical details and fine print. The ordinary person just cannot follow it.

**IH:** That's one of the real difficulties of politics in modern society, a difficulty felt especially by people like us. In the old days, before Roosevelt's New Deal, when we were fighting to get a rudimentary welfare state established, the issues seemed simple and dramatic. Everyone could respond: Should we have unemployment insurance or not? Should we encourage unions or not? But once you establish some sort of welfare state, social issues tend to become technical, a matter of increasing this social payment or decreasing that one. The experts take over, and while the results can be tremendously important to millions of people, it's hard to make the issues seem clear and dramatic.

**MH:** Pat Moynihan identified the problem years ago as "the professionalization of reform." People at the base are not well equipped to enter into a technical discussion of economic issues. That's why I think we have begun to propose the novel idea that public money be available for such debates, so that ordinary people—residents near a proposed nuclear plant or in a town threatened by a plant closing—can hire their own experts. The steelworkers I talked to in McKeesport, Pennsylvania, were absolutely right in their suspicions that the companies were going to sell them out once they made wage concessions. Those steelworkers should have had their own experts to come up with their own plans. Corporations add the cost of their expertise to the prices that we all pay.

**IH:** Let me raise one point that is likely to be made in criticism of what we're saying. Most of the proposals we suggest involve a far higher degree of governmental intervention—indeed, economic planning—than has been true in the past and this raises the specter of bureaucratism.

**MH:** The Left today makes all of its proposals with as much stress on decentralization and public visibility as possible. But bureaucracy is a problem in every kind of modern, industrial or postindustrial society—whether it's capitalist, Socialist, or a mixture of the two. The bureaucracy of the multinational corporation can be as unresponsive and self-serving as that of government—and since the corporations aren't subject to democratic check the way government is, they can sometimes be a lot more unresponsive and self-serving. What is needed is popular participation and wariness; review and, if necessary, dismissal of officials; and an interplay of opinions and powers among autonomous social units.

I think, for example, one of the most interesting developments in the world Socialist movement is the idea of wage-earner funds in Sweden, under which there would be a kind of decentralized social ownership. A tax on profits above a certain level would be paid by corporations to a fund controlled by workers in the industry and representatives of the communities in which the corporations function. The fund would be used to buy stock in Swedish industries, and then the representatives of this fund would actually sit on the board of directors of these industries. There would be elections for directors of the fund.

**IH:** But let's be candid about this. It really is a proposal which moves toward a democratic Socialist society. And the United States is by no means ready for that, simply because most people in America are opposed to Socialism. So that, we can't think of such an idea in this country. But the idea of local control certainly has a strong . . .

**MH:** Very strong . . .

**IH:** . . . basis in this country. For example, the idea of cooperative ownership. I think that the modest trend toward worker-owned and worker-controlled local factories and economic units is tremendously encouraging. It offers a strong active force locally checking the possible excesses of centralizing government. It's often a matter of consciousness and awareness. Government involvement in the economy is going to happen, whether from right or left. The question is, what will its social stress be, progressive or reactionary, democratic or authoritarian?

Well, let's conclude by talking just a minute or two about our conception of Socialism.

**MH:** First of all, there's something out there, in the real world of business and money, called late capitalism. And then there's an ideal, cherished by millions of people in the world, called democratic Socialism. Between these two views of how things ought to be run there's a clash, even though, as the world has changed, the terms of that clash have changed.

**IH:** Concretely, we distinguish sharply between the democratic political structure of America, which is precious, and the socioeconomic arrangements of American capitalism, which we criticize fundamentally. For instance, I think it's outrageous that America should have the extreme inequalities of income and wealth (hence, also power) that in fact exist. It's deplorable that multinational corporations, responsible to no one but themselves, should wield the kinds of power they do.

As for what we mean by Socialism, I can only give a few telegraphic clues. We want a society in which economic life has been transformed in the direction of greater democratic participation, so that workers may have some control over their workplace and their work life. We favor a dispersion and decentralization of the excessively concentrated corporate ownership, so that certain industries, especially those with a monopoly character, would be socially owned (cooperatives, worker ownership, regional T.V.A.-like agencies) and would coexist with a private sector. We want to see enacted tax legislation and other democratic devices making for a redistributive income and wealth policy, so as to move toward a more egalitarian society. We want a social order that stresses cooperative and communal values, even as it also encourages individual personality.

So we are working politically through a mixture of what I call the far and the near—the far, our ultimate vision of a transformed world, and the near, our steady effort for social reforms.

It's not, of course, an easy sort of politics; it doesn't offer the lure of quick success. But I think it's a good politics. Perhaps this country will gradually move in our direction while avoiding our vocabulary. That's O.K. with us. After all, what's in a name?

## Notes

1. Gerald Sorin offers a vivid thumbnail description of Harrington at the peak of the New Left:

   > "The oldest young Socialist alive," as he sometimes jokingly called himself, Harrington, thirty-four at the time, was a "one-man stand-in" for radicalism's "missing generation": men and women in their thirties who would have been engaged in systematic activism on the left had their actually been a viable Socialist movement in postwar America.

   Gerald Sorin, *Irving Howe: A Life of Passionate Dissent* (New York: New York University Press, 2002), 201.
2. Howe's 1968 *New York Times Magazine* essay, "The New 'Confrontation Politics' is a Dangerous Game," criticizing the excesses of the New Left, had an immediate impact. In 1970, he published a follow-up essay, "Political Terrorism: Hysteria on the Left," that reaffirmed his condemnation of the shallowness, overheated rhetoric, and turn to violence of the young radicals. His change from revolutionary polemicist of the 1940s to moderate, evolutionary intellectual was complete.
3. See Rodden, *The World of Irving Howe*, 321-22.
4. However, his son, Nicholas Howe, always insisted that his father was indeed a "Socialist" until the end. Whatever the truth, the senior Howe no longer explicitly referred to himself by that word—whether due to strategic political reasons, expediency, or a genuine change of mind is impossible to say. Of course, neoconservatives such as Midge Decter accused him of always wanting to "protect his left flank." They have also argued that his positions on cultural and intellectual life were often indistinguishable from their own. Irving Kristol often makes this point. After the demise of the New Left, however, Howe no longer had to fight against the Left, and he reverted to his position of the 1950s, in which he consistently assaulted the Right. For Decter's and Kristol's views of Howe, see Rodden, *The Worlds of Irving Howe*, 67-70, 336-41.
5. The Fabians were a British Socialist movement, most prominent in the nineteenth century, who believed in a gradual evolution to Socialism.
6. Willy Brandt was Chancellor of West Germany (1969-74), after having served many years as Mayor of West Berlin and as Foreign Minister (1966-69). Brandt was a leading Social Democrat who initiated peace talks with East Germany and other Eastern European countries. He was awarded the Nobel Peace prize in 1971, but he was forced to resign in May 1974 following revelations that a top aide in his administration was an East German spy.

# Chapter 8

**John Rodden, "A 'Partisan' View of Orwell," October 1983 and April 1987.**

## Introduction

This hitherto unpublished interview highlights Howe's relationship with the writer who probably meant most to him both as a literary model and a political guide, George Orwell (1903-1950). John Rodden, who has written extensively on both Orwell and Howe, conducted this interview in preparation for *The Politics of Literary Reputation: The Making and Claiming of "St. George" Orwell*, a chapter of which was devoted to Orwell's reputation among the *Partisan Review* writers generally and Howe's *Dissent* circle specifically. Howe was in his mid-twenties when he began to read Orwell, and he immediately identified with Orwell's prose style and literary personality; ultimately he embraced Orwell's political orientation too.

During his Trotskyist youth as a staunch Shachtmanite, Howe was an impassioned Leninist and a vocal critic of American participation in World War II. In 1941, the twenty-one-year-old editor of *Labor Action* castigated Orwell in that same journal for his "Letter from London," a *Partisan Review* contribution that defended the participation of the Allies and Churchill's policies in the war. Howe especially took issue with Orwell's contention that "you either support this war or you are a supporter of Hitler."

By 1947, Howe had largely shed his Trotksyism, and he dropped even his Marxist politics a decade later. Indeed, Howe's painful movement away from orthodox Socialism went through several phases. Before his break with the Trotskyists he grappled with the Kronstadt rebellion, a 1921 uprising of Soviet sailors that Trotsky helped to put down brutally. Although Howe initially defended these actions, the event was ultimately important in his break with Trotskyism. Howe biographer Gerald Sorin argued that such changes "exhibit the habits of the true intellectual: a readiness to question one's own political positions and ideas—which have been acquired at some cost; a readiness to undertake yet another revolution of the mind—a readiness Irving Howe would demonstrate more than once over the years."[1] Such jarring shifts, particularly for someone with a strong commitment to radical egalitarian change, exacted a strong emotional price. As *Partisan Review* editor William Phillips put it, discussing the difficulty of leaving the Communist Party, "When one broke away . . . , one had a terrible sense of loneliness and paralysis,"[2] an experience Howe suffered several times throughout his life.

Still, as Howe moved from system and ideology to more nuanced thought, he maintained a strong core of principle, rooted in a firm support for working people and organized labor. His political development was already following, slowly and indirectly, the course steered by Orwell, who was more clear-sighted than the young Howe regarding the dangers of both Stalinism and international Communism. While Howe had believed that Stalin was mainly responsible for the historical disaster that the Soviet Union soon became, Orwell voiced loud and unceasing criticism of Soviet Communism and of fellow-traveling in Britain and elsewhere, each of which damaged the credibility of "true" Socialism, which was rooted in a balanced defense of liberty and equality. To the end of his life, Orwell remained a committed "democratic Socialist." Here again, Howe's politics paced in Orwell's footsteps: by 1952, he had formally resigned from the Shachtmanite sect, abandoned Leninism, and adopted a democratic Socialist politics.

Already by the time of Orwell's premature death in 1950 at the age of forty-six, as Rodden's interview discloses, Howe was rapidly evolving in the direction of democratic Socialism. He distanced himself from his Trotskyist convictions and even expressed qualified admiration both for *Nineteen Eighty-Four* and for Orwell's early fiction and posthumously published essay collections. When *Dissent* was founded in 1954, Orwell stood before Howe as an exemplar of good prose and intellectual integrity.[3] As editor of *Dissent,* Howe embraced not just Orwell's critique of Stalinism, but also his ideological skepticism, especially toward a Communist vanguard theory that allowed a small minority to use violence while claiming to act for the masses. As Howe points out here, Orwell "makes clear in both *Animal Farm* and *Nineteen Eighty-Four* that he is not only quite hostile toward Stalinism, but also extremely skeptical of Bolshevism and the Russian Revolution, including Lenin and Trotsky."

Unlike the case of Orwell, Howe's turn toward democratic Socialism was gradual and painful. He says of Trotsky: "I have become less and less an admirer of him as the years have passed." Yet he admits even in this interview, "I do think that he was qualitatively different from Stalin." He does not elaborate here on this conviction. It would be fascinating to find out more regarding what Howe means by "qualitatively different"; perhaps he believes that the Leninist doctrine of a

Communist vanguard holding the keys to History culminated in a revolutionary terror that shifted from a means to an end.

Although Howe still strongly identified with Trotsky in the mid-1950s, he was already siding with Orwell's independent, democratic radical camp, outraged that a small group of ideologues could seize control of a nation's political apparatus and oppress its populace. By insisting that freedom needed to be maintained even as equality became more widely extended, and indeed that liberty was the non-negotiable prerequisite for all efforts to achieve greater equality, Orwell meant to underscore his conviction that the only form of acceptable Socialism was democratic Socialism. Orwell intended this emphasis to safeguard his democratic Socialism from overcentralization and degeneration into state collectivism, a process that he believed could easily happen in Great Britain and the other Western democracies, and indeed that in his view had already begun to occur in the 1940s—as he observed both in his anti-utopias, *Animal Farm* and *Nineteen Eighty-Four*, and in numerous essays. This overall political stance became a leitmotif of Orwell's work, which, from *Down and Out in Paris and London* through *Nineteen Eighty-Four*, affirmed solidarity with workers (though often with a touch of romanticism).

As a prose stylist, too, Orwell served as an inspiration to Howe. Both writers sought clarity above all else, valuing simply expressed ideas first and niceties of literary style second. Yet both were also capable of the memorable coinage: "Big Brother" and "doublethink" for Orwell, "age of conformity" and "New York Intellectuals" for Howe. For both men, a decent politics was invariably contingent on clarity of expression and a plain-spoken style. Orwell believed that thought follows language; for instance, fascist jargon leads to fascist action. He repeated this conviction unforgettably in his fiction.

Similarly, as a *Dissent* editor, Howe was notorious for his ruthless copyediting, for excising weak phrases and needless jargon in the spirit of Orwell's "Politics and the English Language." Howe's prose, too, is notable for its directness, its sober, firm tone often leavened with a pinch of dry irony.

Orwell's example continued to guide Howe through the decades as a model of how to navigate between the Scylla of bloody radicalism and the Charybdis of smug complacency. Howe, of course, survived for more than forty years beyond Orwell's death, living into an era in which the very word "Socialism" became tainted. For the rest of Howe's life, the posthumous Orwell was his greatest intellectual and moral hero, replacing Trotsky.[4] Indeed, Orwell's influence acted as an inoculation and corrective to Howe's youthful embrace of the ideological straightjacket of Trotskyism.[5]

Howe was not alone in his admiration of Orwell. As Rodden documents in *The Politics of Literary Reputation*, various camps claimed Orwell as their own, interpreting not just his politics, but also his temperament according to their predilections. Disagreeing with those liberals who labeled Orwell a "saint," Howe painted Orwell as an angry, activist, radical figure. Yet Howe's Orwell was able to perform the paradoxical act of balancing a radical's rage toward the world's cruelties with a tempered, pragmatic politics. This Orwell was the figure whom Howe himself aspired to become.

The neoconservatives, too, remade Orwell in their image, albeit an image very different from Howe's. For instance, Norman Podhoretz, in his controversial *Harper's* cover story "If Orwell Were Alive Today" (January 1983), maintained that Orwell's anti-Communism and other criticisms of the dogmatic Left prefigured the stance of the neoconservatives. Podhoretz also lauded Orwell's qualified defense of "bourgeois" democracy and patriotic feelings for England (particularly the "common people").

Toward the end of his life, Orwell himself repudiated attempts to claim him as a conservative. Of course, how he would have evolved, politically and otherwise, can only be a matter of speculation. Nevertheless, Howe was occasionally willing to speculate, believing that Orwell would have opposed the neoconservatives in the 1980s and certainly never have become one of them himself. Howe disagreed with those who saw Orwell primarily as a Cold Warrior of anti-Communism who eventually would have denounced Socialism, had he lived. Similarly, Howe retained his commitment to Socialism "as an animating vision" until his death in May 1993. Like himself, Howe believed that Orwell would have remained a radical and would have shared *Dissent's* stance on the major events of the latter half of the twentieth century. Like many intellectuals of his generation, Howe saw Orwell as a political model—but a model of a Socialist intellectual, not an anti-Communist Cold Warrior.

The following exchange with Howe is reconstructed from notes kept by John Rodden after both their October 1983 conversation (at the George Orwell in 1984 Conference held at West Chester University in Pennsylvania) and after Howe's April 1987 talk at the University of Virginia (on *The American Newness*, derived from his recently published Harvard lectures). They formed the basis for chapters in *The Politics of Literary Reputation: The Making and Claiming of "St. George" Orwell* (1989) and in *Every Intellectual's Big Brother: George Orwell's Literary Siblings* (2006), both of which examined Orwell's relationship to Howe and the New York Intellectuals, and also to the literary-political tradition represented by *Partisan Review* and *Dissent.*

## The Interview

**Q:** *I am most interested in what led you as a young Trotskyist editor still struggling with sectarian allegiances to the Shachtmanites to identify so strongly with Orwell in the pages of the main theoretical organ of the Trotskyists,* The New International. *In your lengthy review of* Nineteen Eighty-Four *in November-December 1950, you described Orwell as a writer gifted with many valuable insights yet too readily dismissing the ongoing importance of Leninism. What prompted that stance, which seems so divided?*

**A:** I was still working through my convictions about Trotsky and Lenin at that time. I hadn't yet completely severed my ties with the Shachtmanites. That was to come two years later. Orwell was an important influence around that time for me, because he had been writing for *Partisan Review*, which I had just recently begun doing reviews for. He not only served as the model of a writer, but of a writer who looked to a much wider world beyond sectarian politics and even beyond literary New York or London. He addressed world-historical issues such as totalitarianism, but I was still too enamored of Lenin, if not Trotsky himself, to fully honor the value of his work.

**Q:** *When did you break with the Shachtmanites?*

**A:** In November 1952 I resigned in a joint letter with my colleague Stanley Plastrik. Shortly after that we went on to found a new magazine, *Dissent*. We had the subscription lists from Dwight Macdonald's old magazine, *politics*, where I had worked for many months as an assistant to Macdonald. I wanted to launch a similar idiosyncratic magazine, but one that would represent not one man's anarchist politics, as in Macdonald's case, but rather democratic radicalism, broadly understood in the sense of Orwell's own democratic Socialism. It was really the only radical outlet in the mid-1950s in the U.S.

**Q:** *Do you think Orwell himself would have contributed to it, if he had lived?*

**A:** Yes, I do. Some of his colleagues joined our editorial board, such as George Woodcock who had contributed a piece on Orwell to Macdonald's *politics* in the mid-forties. We also had other people around the magazine who were strong admirers of Orwell and who broadly shared his Socialist and radical outlook.

**Q:** *Around the same time that you wrote this piece so critical of* Nineteen Eighty-Four *in* New International, *you wrote a much more positive assessment of Orwell's posthumous work in a short review in* The Nation, *in which you called the new edition of* Down and Out in Paris and London *"a pioneer work, the product of a fertile and original mind."*

**A:** When was that?

**Q:** *In February 1950—you must have written that just around the time that you heard that Orwell died. He died on January 21, 1950. The piece appeared on February 4.*

**A:** I may have known that he was sick. Probably I had to turn in the piece before the announcement of his death. But you are right that the date would have been fairly close. All I can say is that within those few months—I probably had to submit that *Nation* review well in advance of the news of his death—my thinking was evolving in the direction of Orwell's own critique of the Soviet Union and the Russian Revolution. Of course he makes clear in both *Animal Farm* and *Nineteen Eighty-Four* that he is not only quite hostile to Stalinism, but also extremely skeptical of Bolshevism and the Russian Revolution, including Lenin and Trotsky. Our Shachtmanite sect wanted to draw a very firm line separating Lenin and Stalin. Around this time I was seeing how that was more and more difficult to do.

**Q:** *But it would be another quarter century before you really made an intellectual break with Trotskyism in your critical study* Leon Trotsky *(1978).*

**A:** Yes, that is true.

**Q:** *In your collection of writings,* The Basic Trotsky, *published in 1964, you continued to call Trotsky your "personal hero." Even in 1978, you referred to him as "still a hero of sorts for me."*

**A:** Well, all I can say is that is how I felt then. I have become less and less an admirer of him as the years have passed. But I still think he was a great historical figure, a human being larger than life who commanded the army responsible for the Russian Revolution as well as had a brilliant mind and a powerful prose style. Those don't make up for some of his crimes promoting and defending terrorism, especially in his book *Terrorism and Communism*. But I do think that he was qualitatively different from Stalin.

**Q:** *You went on in a 1955 review titled "A Moderate Hero," which appeared in* Partisan Review, *to dispute the temperate image of Orwell popularized by Lionel Trilling and others and to present your own preferred truculent, defiant, radical rebel image of Orwell. The entire review seems to be virtually an extension of your controversial essay of the previous year, "This Age of Conformity," in which you first drew the battle lines between the moderate intellectuals who had gathered around* Partisan Review *and* Commentary *versus the liberal-Left and radical writers around* Dissent. *Actually, you had marked out the difference even previously to that in* Partisan Review *in the 1953 "Our Country and Our Culture" symposium in which you were one of the few intellectuals to reject what C. Wright Mills referred to as the "American Celebration." You looked upon the 1950s as "this age of conformity," whereas most of your intellectual peers heralded the decade in quite glowing terms as the fulfillment and triumph of American capitalism and democratic values.*

**A:** That's an interesting way of looking at it. I do suppose that it [the 1955 *PR* review] reflects Orwell's increasing significance for me at that time. It was also the period that coincided with my falling out with Trilling, Robert Warshow, and several others who had begun to drift rightward.

**Q:** *A later and heightened phase of your admiration for Orwell occurred with your editing of* Nineteen Eighty-Four: Sources, Text, Criticism *in 1963, in which you compared* Nineteen Eighty-Four *to the work of Hannah Arendt, as if it were a literary version of* The Origins of Totalitarianism, *which had been serialized in* Partisan Review *in the late 1940s around the time that* Nineteen Eighty-Four *itself was published in the U.S. I was struck by the way in which you considered* Nineteen Eighty-Four *a kind of blueprint for Arendt's theoretical treatise.*

**A:** Well, I had served as her assistant at Schocken Books and got to know her very well. We later had a falling out at the time of the Eichmann trial [1963] because of her book *Eichmann in Jerusalem*, to which we devoted a *Dissent* symposium that she misunderstood. But I did consider *Nineteen Eighty-Four* and *The Origins of Totalitarianism*, both which after all appeared at the same historical moment, to reflect a similar outlook and vision even if their sensibilities and textures were quite different. Orwell and Arendt were both European thinkers who were issuing similar kinds of warnings and had similar kinds of concerns about the dangers of totalitarian tendencies.

**Q:** *A final major statement of yours about Orwell occurs with your* Harper's *essay-review of* The Collected Essays, Journals, and Letters of George Orwell *in mid-1968. In that piece, you openly identified in a quite impassioned way with the vision and values that Orwell represented for you and your generation of intellectuals. You said: "For a whole generation—mine—Orwell was an international hero." Could you elaborate on that?*

**A:** Yes, but what did I go on to say?

**Q:** *You added: "He stood against every shibboleth of the age: all the smelly little orthodoxies to which intellectuals succumb." And then:*

> *He stormed against those English writers who were ready to yield to Hitler; he fought almost single-handed against those who blinded themselves to the evils of Stalin. More than any other English intellectual of our age, he embodied the values of personal independence and a fiercely democratic radicalism.*
>
> *The loss seems enormous. . . . He was one of the few heroes of our younger years who remains untarnished. Having to live in a rotten time was made just a little more bearable by his presence.*
>
> *He is the greatest moral force in English letters during the last several decades: craggy, fiercely polemical, sometimes mistaken, but an utterly free man. He saw the workers neither as potential revolutionaries nor savage innocents nor stupid clods. He saw them as ordinary suffering human beings; quite like you and me. . . .*

> *Orwell's deepest view of life 'was' his faith in the value and strength of common existence: "The fact to which we have got to cling, as to a life-belt, is that it is possible to be a normal decent person and yet to be fully alive." Let that be inscribed on every blackboard in the land!*

**A:** Well, that was around the peak of my battles with the New Left, when Orwell and I were being attacked quite viciously by certain segments of the student movement and the counterculture. I saw Orwell as the great example from the 1930s and forties of an intellectual figure from the so-called Old Left, and I very much wanted to defend both myself and the tradition that he represented. I felt that the New Left had made some of the same mistakes as the Trotskyists and Stalinists in the 1940s, and I was outraged—perhaps I lost my cool—that they had repeated the very same mistakes that we had 30 years earlier.

I saw Orwell as a fellow spirit—a radical and engaged writer. Later, I came to appreciate more deeply the side of Orwell that wanted and needed to get away from politics. That was the side of Orwell which resembled Trilling.

**Q:** *What about Orwell's long-standing value to you throughout this entire period from the 1940s through the 1980s as your literary model, which you call him in* A Margin of Hope*?*

**A:** Yes, I came to prize highly the literary qualities of his work: clarity, precision, simplicity. I realized that those are the very same qualities that I could aspire to in my prose. Orwell and Edmund Wilson stood before me as the two critics who embodied them best.

**Q:** *In 1983 you have returned again to Orwell by editing a book devoted to* Nineteen Eighty-Four *for the upcoming so-called "Year of Orwell."*

**A:** Yes, well, I decided to collect a few pieces by various writers whom I admire, most of whom I believe are broadly in the same tradition as Orwell on the democratic Left. The book is really a tribute to Orwell's ongoing influence today [*Nineteen Eighty-Four Revisited*, published by Signet in November 1983].

**Q:** *In your West Chester talk today, you spoke out against the neoconservative "hijacking" of Orwell. The neocons, of course, claim that your deliberate cultivation of a close association leaves you open to the same charge.*

**A:** No. Orwell remained a Socialist and a radical, as I have. But that's not the point. Podhoretz has recast Orwell in his own image. By contrast, neither Trilling nor I ever said that Orwell "is me" or "is like" me. My construction of Orwell is just that—a construction—and of an admittedly self-serving kind. But it is a clearer and more openly acknowledged image than Trilling's in the fifties, and I make no claims about a "posthumous" Orwell as Podhoretz does.

**Q:** *Some reviewers felt that your memoir,* A Margin of Hope, *was deficient because it omitted any mention of your personal life.*

**A:** That is ridiculous. It was subtitled *An Intellectual Autobiography*, and that is exactly what it was. It wasn't meant to be a full-scale autobiography, it was meant to be a chronicle of my thinking as it unfolded from the 1930s to the present, and that is exactly what it was.

## Notes

1. Gerald Sorin, *Irving Howe: A Life of Passionate Dissent* (New York: New York University Press, 2002), 22.
2. Quoted in Terry Cooney, *The Rise of the New York Intellectuals: Partisan Review and Its Circle, 1934-1945* (Madison: University of Wisconsin Press, 1986), 96.
3. See John Rodden, *Every Intellectual's Big Brother* (Austin: University of Texas Press, 2003), 122-26.
4. See John Rodden, *George Orwell, The Politics of Literary Reputation*, (Rutgers: Transaction, 2002), 338-44.
5. See Ian Williams, "An Ex-Maoist Looks at an Ex-Trotskyist: On Howe's *Leon Trotsky*," *Irving Howe and the Critics*, ed. John Rodden, 37-47.

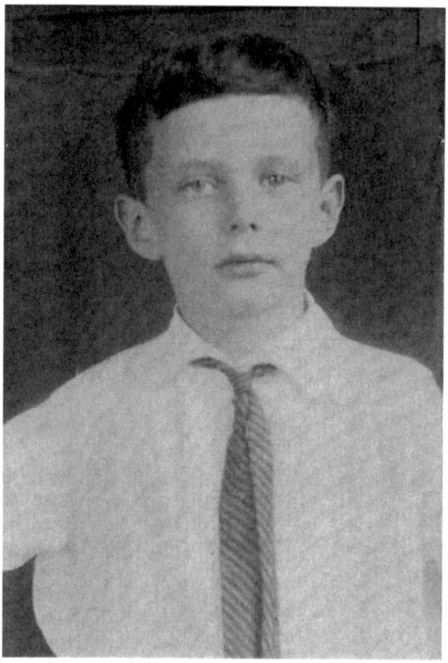

School boy, ca. age 12

Irving and Nina, Greece, ca. 1958

Irving, Nick, and Nina, New England seaport, ca. 1957

Irving and Nick playing baseball, Belmont, ca. 1959

Irving, Belmont, ca. 1959

Irving in his office in the English Department, Stanford University, ca. 1962.

Irving, lecturing in Japan, early 1980s

Irving, visiting the home of his daughter Nina and son-in-law Bill Bukowski, Montreal, 1986

Irving in Maine, 1987

Irving and granddaughter Anna Bukowski, 1991

Irving and granddaughter Anna, shortly before his death, spring 1993.

# Chapter 9

## Todd Gitlin, "Looking Back on the New Left and the Counterculture," 15 April 1985.

### Introduction

Todd Gitlin was one of the New Left leaders with whom Howe and the rest of the *Dissent* circle tangled in a contentious 1963 meeting with the leaders of Students for a Democratic Society (SDS). Intended to promote a dialogue between the Old Left and New Left, the meeting quickly degenerated into a confrontation. Warning them—in a paternalistic tone—of both the pitfalls of radical sectarianism and the dangers of self-righteous ideological purity, Howe and other *Dissenters* sharply criticized the SDS, and particularly the charismatic Tom Hayden, for taking extreme positions. For the rest of the 1960s, most of the New Left viewed Howe as a bourgeois liberal implicitly supporting the Establishment. But his criticisms of the movement were warranted. His vision proved all too prescient, and his prophesies bore terrible fruit, as the New Left fragmented into numerous fringe groups.

Howe's admonitions arose not only from his own experience with Stalinism in the 1930s and 1940s, but also through his scholarship about left-wing movements (such as *The American Communist Party* [1957], co-authored with Lewis Coser). He foresaw the New Left repeating the mistakes of the Old Left by adopting a radical, ends-justify-the-means politics. At the time of this interview, Howe had completed *Socialism and America,* which bemoaned the overreach of radical movements. Based on that work, he explains the collapse of the Socialist Party under Eugene Debs: "They took a revolutionary position without any expectation, without realizing that they would bring down the weight of the government upon them." Howe saw the New Left re-enacting this pattern of excess, thereby alienating a large part of the American public. But his warnings were to go unheeded.

As the New Left disintegrated into radical sects during 1969-72, Gitlin distanced himself from the movement. Such groups as the Weathermen, which went underground and instigated an ineffectual campaign of bombing government buildings, are only the most notorious (and criminal) examples of how Left sectarianism destroyed any chance of a radical mass movement. Reacting against this tragic missed opportunity, Gitlin evolved into a moderate, rather in the mold of Irving Howe, albeit as more of an activist and less of a polymath. Beyond these shared affinities, the warmth evident in the following conversation was made possible because the two men had patched up their differences and begun to work together: Howe had acknowledged his undue harshness toward "the kids"; Gitlin became a frequent contributor to *Dissent* (and former SDS president Paul Potter also wrote for the magazine). Indeed, by the time of this interview, as Gitlin points out in Joseph Dorman's *Arguing the World,* "I felt very much that the *Dissent* group was my crowd. This was basically the world in which I was having my political and cultural arguments. It was just a matter of time before they asked me [to join] the editorial board."[1] He did so in 1989.

So Gitlin softened his positions, and Howe in turn became more receptive to criticisms voiced from former SDS members. As he admits here about the 1963 meeting: "We were heavy-handed and didactic and no doubt patronizing, or so it must have seemed to you. We came on as know-it-alls." The two drew closer during the last eight years of Howe's life and came to see the Reagan era in similar terms. Indeed, after Howe's death, Gitlin wrote a laudatory memorial tribute to him in *Tikkun.*

In the interview below, Howe and Gitlin pore over the details, from their insider perspectives, of the fateful 1963 encounter and subsequent breakup. They discuss how the New Left's criticism of the United States' support of right-wing anti-Communist dictatorships, though largely justified in its own right, led to an intensifying, blanket anti-Americanism. Support grew for Communist regimes, such as Castro's Cuba and North Vietnam, on the view that the enemy of my enemy is my friend, that international Communism wasn't really so bad, and that some regimes were making notable gains toward equality (if at the price of restricting liberty). There is a grain of truth to these arguments that makes refuting them tricky; for instance, Castro supporters may be correct that his regime dissolved the rigid division between privilege and poverty.

Yet as Howe knew from bitter experience, an authoritarian regime will reinstitute lawless terror, changing merely the group targeted for victimization. Only an authentically democratic, postrevolutionary regime that scrupulously protects basic civil liberties has strong prospects of avoiding this outcome. As Howe predicted, the indulgent and self-congratulatory fantasy that an avant-garde is endowed with a special knowledge—that it can violate the rules of the democratic process yet nonetheless give birth to a just society—led to the failure of the New Left.

Howe remarks throughout the discussion on a peculiarly American absolutism, a position of "moral rectitude" that ignores political realities, which he associates with Henry David Thoreau and Ralph Waldo Emerson. Regarding Vietnam, Howe explains, "People said, 'I don't care if I'm the only one in the whole country, but I say get out immediately because it's an immoral war.'" This is, to Howe, a self-defeating position that belies the possibility of forming a political coalition.

Gitlin goes further, remembering the movement's gathering absolutism based upon the expectation of a final showdown: "In Chicago [at the Democratic National Convention in 1968], if you listen to the slogans and look at the signs, you realize half of the people thought they were on the verge of the revolution and half of them thought they were on the verge of Fascism. With both of them having in common apocalyptic fantasies." America is a land of extreme expectations that, unlike Europe, had in fact experienced a revolution that overturned everything, leading to the first modern democracy. Perhaps this is the reason for our strange optimism verging on moral certainty, the belief that radical change likely promises improved conditions.

Howe and Gitlin speak remarkably little about the resurgent conservatism under way in the mid-1980s. Beyond a shared nostalgic recollection, their meeting seems an attempt to explore and understand the mistakes of the past in order to learn from them—if ever the opportunity for real change should return. The meeting also focuses on the history of their relationship. Gitlin is extending an olive branch to Howe, and Howe accepts the offer of reconciliation. They both realize that they cannot move toward each other unreservedly unless they resolve their differences during the conflict-ridden years of the 1960s.

Today, in light of the mass protest movement occasioned by another war—the U.S.-led invasion and occupation of Iraq—this interview assumes new dimensions of significance. Again an unpopular conflict has spurred widespread demonstrations and public outrage, and again the chief decision-makers have refused to listen to the protesters. The new situation, however, has not led to the kind of broader movement that appeared in the 1960s, one that at least briefly seemed capable of leading to transformational social and political change. Rather, the major antiwar and antigovernment organizers, under the umbrella of the ANSWER coalition, have espoused a brand of radicalism unpalatable to most of America, while the Democratic Party has remained timid and centrist, although increasingly anti-occupation. The occupation's intensifying unpopularity has not led to any kind of nationwide progressive movement, though it has divided the Republican Party.

Writing in *Mother Jones* just before the invasion commenced in the spring of 2003, Gitlin employed arguments clearly derived both from the failures of the New Left and from his later involvement with Howe and *Dissent:*

> What a smart movement could do is put out the markers, create the organizational networks, and establish the foundation on which a more substantial antiwar movement might later be built. Alas, that is also unlikely.
>
> The leadership of the current antiwar movement is building a firebreak around itself, turning the movement toward the bitter-end orthodoxy of the Old Left and away from the millions of Americans whose honest concerns and ambivalence might fuel it.[2]

While Gitlin was clearly right about the alienating and self-destructive tendencies of the Left, he overestimated their potential destructive power currently, at least as events have unfolded thus far in the twenty-first century. The radical Left has remained too isolated to undermine any nascent movement. Whether Moveon.org and other Internet groups can bridge the gap between the radical Left and the democratic center remains to be seen. It must also be remembered that ANSWER grew out of an antiglobalization campaign largely owing to a widening gulf, both in the U.S. and internationally, between the wealthy and everyone else. Nevertheless, we have not yet seen antiwar activism translate into broader public concern about macroeconomic policy.

Meanwhile, Gitlin continues to argue, in such venues as *Mother Jones, TPMcafe, openDemocracy.net,* and *the Los Angeles Times,* for an antiwar movement that can appeal to mainstream America, to all those moderates disgusted with the war yet mistrustful of the radical Left. As Howe's position had been in the 1960s, Gitlin's work is often received with almost willful misunderstanding. This resemblance lends foreboding to Howe's comment, "My guess would be if the thing [the Vietnam era and counterculture] were to be replayed, then it would pretty much happen the same way. The same mistakes on our side and if there were any on your side." Indeed, if the 1960s replayed as farce the tragic mistakes of the Left in the 1930s, what ought we call our present-day re-replay?

## The Interview

**IH:** One of the most interesting questions [about the student movements of the 1960s] is, How can you keep a youth movement going? How can you keep a movement going which begins as an unattached group and remains in its essential quality a youth group, leaving aside politics, and then has no place to which to graduate its people. One consequence is that the leaders hang on too long probably. And they become a kind of bureaucratic . . .

**TG:** *That's not what happened on the Left.*

**IH:** No, that is not what happened. What happened?

**TG:** *Well, it happened to some people. See, this was a perpetual rumbling under-problem. Starting in 1962, Port Huron's*[3] *in late 1962. Starting already by late 1963 and with a flood by late 1964, the founding generation of SDS is trying to get out of it. They wanted to leave the campus. That's the genesis of ERAP and community organizers.*[4]

**IH:** I see.

**TG:** *And in effect it abandoned the SDS to a few, none of the original founding generation, a few cadres.*

**IH:** Were you an original?

**TG:** *No, I was picked up immediately thereafter. I wasn't in Port Huron.*

**IH:** No. And you weren't at that meeting that we had, that *Dissent* had. At that meeting there was Tom Hayden, Paul Potter[5]. . . .

**TG:** *The one you described in here? I was at that meeting, and it is one of the things I wanted to ask you about. The situation you have is that by the time membership starts cascading into SDS, at the time of the big antiwar march in April 1965, the original generation of SDS has almost entirely left the organization and professes no interests in students whatsoever. It's now the Narodnik phase.*[6]

**IH:** Going to the people.

**TG:** *At that point it absolutely intensifies the internal generational crisis. These people flood in, knowing nothing about the Left. Many people were no longer coming from elite campuses, they were coming from everywhere. Not educated. And there is nobody for them to talk to.*

**IH:** A mass movement developed too quickly.

**TG:** *It becomes radically a mass movement. And so that's a very important break point in the history. I think that's the pivotal period, 1964-65, of radicalization, but it's a very important part, this changeover.*

**IH:** This is before you get the Maoist phase?

**TG:** *Well, at the very end of that. It's in the summer 1965 that for the first time the PL*[7] *people start showing up and infiltrating SDS.*

**IH:** That's another thing that I think is terribly interesting about the development in retrospect of the New Left. Everything in some way happens too fast. No phase of it can go through a reasonably organic development. The whole participatory democracy thing lasts two or three years and then it is over with. Now that isn't enough time for people to think it through. To see what the strengths of it are, what the weaknesses are. And before you know it, you are swamped by a whole series of other concerns and developments. And the war takes on such ferocious intensity that it eats everything up. Of course, this is the reason for the success of the opposition group but it's also partly the reason for its crack up.

**TG:** *Absolutely right. I have some memories of that meeting at Joe Buttinger's. But actually I am more interested in yours. You have written about it twice now. You wrote about it recently [in* The New Republic*] and you wrote about it in* A Margin of Hope, *and I just reread that section.*

**IH:** We felt, or rather we anticipated, some of the fissures in the group of people who came from SDS. When you came, you barely had an organization. And the fissures were not so much in terms of ideology—though Hayden was already pushing the Cuba thing pretty hard and that's why we got into a fight at that meeting—we felt it in terms of different personality types, but political personality. There was something about Hayden already that I felt was hard, tremendously self-assured, at least externally, something of the charismatic leader speaking with certainty, holding something back. I am not saying that this was necessarily accurate but that was as I remember the impression that all of us had. And he unnerved us a little bit.

**TG:** *You met afterward and talked about this.*

**IH:** Sure. Not formally but we met and talked. And there was something about him that was disconcerting. We felt he was a Bolshevik type, so to say. The rest of you—there was Paul and you and one other guy . . .

**TG:** *Paul Booth was there and [SDS activist] Steve Max was there.*

**IH:** Yeah, I don't think that Steve spoke very much, if he was there. The rest of you we felt an easier relationship with because we didn't think that you were so precisely formed and we felt about some of you that you were essentially what in very crude terms I would call more social democrat personalities. Less rigid. Less ideological. You weren't casting yourself as heroes, and Tom already had this vision of himself. And by the way not without some justification because I think that he was tremendously talented. I think of the whole group in some ways he was the most talented in terms of being a public leader. And maybe what involved in our response was perhaps a certain a- or antipolitical response, in the sense that we had had our fill of leaders of that kind and were very intrinsically suspicious of them. He made a strong but essentially negative impression. All the rest of you we had liked. We didn't differentiate very much the rest of you, but there it was Tom and the rest.

**TG:** *My recollections are also that he did most of the talking.*

**IH:** And we felt that we mishandled the whole thing.

**TG:** *Do you remember any particulars in what you thought you mishandled or just the general climate?*

**IH:** Well, Manny Geltman lost his temper and went off on a long rant. What I think we mishandled was that we rose to Tom's bait in a way.

**TG:** *What was he ranting about?*

**IH:** Cuba. There was a big dispute immediately on Cuba. And I think this anticipated what, from our point of view, was the inevitable, practical incapacity that we had in comparison to what you had. Namely I think, and I still think, that we were essentially correct on most of the political issues that we were right about—Castro's authoritarianism and the North Vietnamese regime.

But we were heavy-handed and didactic and no doubt patronizing, or so it must have seemed to you. We came on as know-it-alls. One reason I think it happened, paradoxically, and that you couldn't have understood at that time, was that we were just so eager to make a connection. The thing was so important to us that we overloaded, so to say. We should have played it more calmly, more quietly. We should have expressed a difference with Tom, but we shouldn't have made it into an immediate ideological confrontation.

Because we should have seen that the rest of you didn't entirely or necessarily go along with him in that same strong way. But my guess would be if the thing were to be replayed, then it would pretty much happen the same way. The same mistakes on our side and if there were any on your side. And there again that absence of an intermediary generation is crucial.

**TG:** *Do you recall any argument about nonviolence?*

**IH:** At that meeting? No. That wouldn't have happened, I am sure. If any of you had raised that question, in favor of nonviolence, we wouldn't have balked at that. Do you?

**TG:** *I recall it.*

**IH:** In what way?

**TG:** *I recall Tom going through a kind of ultra-Gandhian appeal. Which was by the way not at all compatible with his political personality. And I remember your skepticism because Tom was taking the extreme Gandhian position of redeeming the enemy. Does that ring a bell? The effort is not simply to transform policy, it is through the soul force, it is to win the heart of the enemy. And you thought this was very naivé.*

**IH:** Oh yes, yes, yes, I begin to remember that. But I said I couldn't love Hitler or something like that. . . . Was Tom sincere about that?

**TG:** *Well, that was what I was going to ask you. You talk about your sense of something he was holding in reserve.*

**IH:** I think what he was holding in reserve was not so much ideas, but a sense of personal power, personal capacity.

**TG:** *No question about that.*

**IH:** A feeling that he was going to go somewhere. And consequently that he didn't need us. Well, in one sense of course he didn't, but in another sense he might have.

**TG:** *You ask whether he was sincere about that position. I think at that time he probably was. You have to recall that he comes out of the South.*

**IH:** Our people didn't understand how can you be in favor—I think that this is one of the things that Manny [Geltman] blew his top about—how can you be in favor of Castro, who speaks of exporting revolution to South America, and then also be in favor of nonviolence. Now, there is an obvious logical contradiction there, but the fact that you can hold both positions, that you can maintain contradictions, was a familiar experience. Sure.

**TG:** *It's a good question and I don't remember what he said. It is conceivable to me that he might have taken the position that it is for other people to decide how to do their revolutions. That was certainly a way of strategizing.*

**IH:** Now I remember something else and this is something that has bothered me for years and it's probably going to go on the rest of my life. I don't mind being attacked from the left and I don't mind being attacked from the right, but when somebody attacks me from both directions at the same time it gets on my nerves. I think that is one of things that we must have felt about Tom's speech. Namely, on the one hand there he was in favor of Castro-like revolution, and on the other hand he's talking about redeeming the souls of the enemy. And the two of these things together really would be bothersome. And yet I suppose that the two of them were together.

**TG:** *This is the way I would understand it now. Of course, I didn't think of it in these terms then. Tom is really emblematic of the New Left at that point in one particular respect. Though he had read a lot, he was not in any sense learned. What really drove him was, in a crude sense, maybe in a Norman Mailer sense, the existentialist proposition that people can change history, individuals can change it. There is a Leninist edge to that. There is a Gandhian edge. There's a SNCC [Student Nonviolent Coordinating Committee] edge. And all of this is glued together. Handfuls of people can take action and transform the situation. You can do it by sitting in at the lunch counter at Greensboro. You can take it, you can do it by storming the Moncada barracks in Cuba.*[8] *So in that sense, the salient issue is not for him violence or nonviolence; it is activity versus passivity.*

**IH:** Yes, and in your eyes we had given up the idea of activity.

**TG:** *Well, implicitly.*

**IH:** By talking so much about mass movements which weren't there, we didn't place any confidence in the possibility of individual reactivization.

**TG:** *In effect I suppose.*

**IH:** Yes. Well you see this is interesting for another reason. Later on when I tried to think about these things more calmly. . . .

**TG:** *By the way, maybe less important than a position on mass movements, which we were certainly in favor of, was a stance or a mood vis-à-vis intellectuality, which represented inactivity. Which was coded as inactivity.*

**IH:** In your eyes you saw intellectuality as inactivity.

**TG:** *To varying degrees, yes.*

**IH:** Some people became like us, professionals. And that is an amusing thing. I just got into a polemic about an article we printed in *Dissent* from Mike Fellow.

**TG:** *I knew him.*

**IH:** A bright guy. And he describes *Dissent* as a bourgeois Socialist journal. Okay, fair enough. And I said to him, "Look, you are doing the same thing I am doing through necessity—it may not be what you wanted to do—you are teaching to earn a living and I am teaching to earn a living, and then we write, which is what we wanted to do."

But to come back to the other thing. I thought about that a lot later. And I concluded that there were two traditions that came in opposition to the social democratic one. And one of them was what I'll call, short-hand, Thoreauvian. Strong stress upon the individual, pacifist in a way, above all the stand of rectitude. And the other was not yet, but soon would become, a sort of Marxist-Leninist one, or Leninist-Maoist, something like that. And one of the reasons we had difficulty coping with the whole phenomenon of the sixties is that at first we couldn't see the interweaving of these two.

Secondly, even if we could see it, we didn't know how to cope with this. You see I was active in SANE in those days, and Dick Flacks[9] was in there, and we clashed a couple of times. And there were people who would get up, very nice people, really good people, and I didn't yet know how to identify that, and all they cared about was their rectitude. All they cared about was just saying the right thing. And if you raised the question of political consequences or a possible maneuver to get support from a congressman, they would just blow their tops.

Now, there was a strong element of this high moralism in the early phase of the New Left.

**TG:** *I think that still describes the dominant mood in the peace movement.*

**IH:** That is correct. And there is something to be said for that, I think. It is desirable to have it around but it's not desirable that it should be dominant. It is desirable to have it around to try to keep people like me and others honest. But it is not desirable, I think, that it should run the show.

This was something, in retrospect, that we really had known it but we had known it under a different name. It had been present in the SP [Socialist Party] earlier. To a very considerable extent, in the Christian Socialists, the Midwestern types, and in Norman Thomas himself. And I think it had done a considerable amount of damage in the SP, and it was even present in the CP under a different guise. It masked itself in Marxist language but the fundamental impulse was directed to sticking to your guns. See I used to think that the sectarianism of the Left, which had been its great curse in America, came almost entirely from the Bolshevik tradition, and then I concluded that wasn't true at all. It did come from there, but it also had very strong native American roots, so that when we would be making the inevitable speeches which had been going on for fifty years about Americanizing radicalism we didn't understand that there could be some considerable disadvantages to this kind of thing.

**TG:** *Well, that's what was in Joe Buttinger's living room. SDS came out of the Midwest.*

**IH:** That was there. Well see this again was one of the things that irritated me about Tom Hayden. Not that he'd changed his mind and decided it was necessary to work in the Democratic Party. That's fine, because I agree with him about that. But that he never took the trouble, at least that I know of, publicly to say why he had changed his mind. I mean one of the things that he was attacking us on was just this question. To work in the Democratic Party was to sell out, to cooperate with the corporate liberals, etc., etc. And there was that posture of rectitude. Now as long as it was just that, I think we could have coped with it and we could have maintained some good relations as I see it. But once it became interwoven with, even though also in conflict with, the Leninist-Maoist-whatever thing inside the New Left, then we were lost in relation to it and I think that the Left was lost also.

**TG:** *Now that meeting took place in October of 1963. Sometime in the next two years, I don't know how to date it more precisely than that, I attended a debate between you and Tom.*

**IH:** In New York City, yes.

**TG:** *In one of those halls in Union Square. Do you remember what was the occasion?*

**IH:** It was just a discussion of the New Left and politics and sex.

**TG:** *Was this your next encounter with Tom?*

**IH:** I think that was the next encounter. I had published a piece in *Dissent* called "New Styles in Leftism."

**TG:** *Yes, I want to ask you about that too.*

**IH:** Which occasioned a lot of anger, etc. And I think that the debate was after that, though I'm not entirely sure. And one of the things that I remember about that debate was that Tom said he would not describe the Soviet Union as totalitarian.

**TG:** *That's what I remember.*

**IH:** And I pressed him very hard, [asking] how would you describe it.

**TG:** *What did he say?*

**IH:** He didn't answer. He didn't answer. That I remember very distinctly. And a number of people including Nat Hentoff[10] felt that I was unkind to this sweet young boy, who shouldn't be pressed so hard, although he was perfectly capable of taking care of himself. And the meeting ended on a very harsh note, and I even remember afterward [that] Mike Walzer, who was then very young, though he agreed with me, felt that I had been too harsh, and probably I was.

**TG:** *As a matter of tone, not necessarily a matter of. . . .*

**IH:** No, he didn't disagree with what I was saying, but instead of yelling, "What do you think, how would you describe it," I could have said "Look Tom . . . "

But you have to understand this also: if we have to understand the feelings of the other side, which we probably didn't, they have to understand ours. I mean to have this kind of thing at that date, after we had gone through the whole fight against Stalinism with what we thought was some conceptual clarity to have Tom talking this way, it was very hard to bear. Then there was another confrontation, which was later, between Tom and me. And, let me see—that would have been the year that I was in California. That was a fascinating experience. It was at the University of Kansas, no the University of—Kansas or Missouri? It was in Kansas City, which university?

**TG:** *The University of Missouri, Kansas City.*

**IH:** Right, exactly. Some kid called me up from there and said he wanted to have a symposium—it really should have been taken down [because] it would have been at least amusing—on foreign policy. They invited Brzezinski,[11] who was not yet a big government man, just a professor at Columbia, myself, and Tom Hayden. They offered me what was for the time a staggering amount of money, $1,200. Today that would be what, $4,000. And so I needed the money and I said yes. And I went under the assumption that, for that kind of money, you should sit down for a month and write a paper of some sort. And I said how long do you want me to speak, and the kid said oh, five or six minutes. And I was stunned by this. Now how the hell, what can you say about foreign policy in five or six minutes? You can't even rattle off the slogans. And I expressed this, and the kid with utter weariness and contempt said, Well if you need ten minutes, okay. I felt that we were living in a different universe. I guess we were. There was an enormous meeting in the gym, there must have been 1,500 people there. And Brzezinski saw the whole thing as a kind of amusing spectacle. He was friendly to me more than to Tom, and he put on his left face, which he's quite capable of doing, at least he was before Carter. And there was a gang of, kind of a New Left clique, a group which started heckling and booing me before I'd opened my mouth, and so it made for tension. Tom at that point was riding hard; it was after the invasion of Czechoslovakia which would have been what, 1968. So it was 1969. We didn't know yet that the whole thing was going to collapse. We were supremely confident. And there again was I think a very revealing confrontation. He didn't apologize for the Russian invasion of Czechoslovakia but he refused to condemn it. And to me this was the last straw, politically, morally, etc. And so I went after him pretty fiercely on this, and I'd say I had about a third of the audience and Tom had two thirds.

By then I thought this is hopeless, we're off on totally different paths, there is no possibility of any conciliation. And that any tactical mistakes we have made or mistakes of tone and approach finally don't matter for differences of such magnitude.

**TG:** *It must have crossed your mind that Tom on all these occasions was trying to get your goat.*

**IH:** Yes, and succeeded. [*laughter*] He was trying to get my goat but he was also doing something else. He obviously had a very keen sense of the audience, and he wouldn't have tried to get my goat if he had thought that that would lose him the audience.

**TG:** *What about in the New York event? Was the audience with him also? I don't remember?*

**IH:** No. I think that more my gang was there.

**TG:** *So when he refused to say that the Soviet Union is totalitarian. . . . See, I'm not sure, I honestly don't know whether he really meant that, or whether he was just refusing to play.*

**IH:** This was a smaller meeting, the one in New York, just about 150 people or something. And I think a good part of it was friends of mine, political friends. I think there was something else, I don't really know, but I think that part of it was he wanted to see himself as more open, politically, intellectually, as against people like myself who were fixed, judgmental, etc., etc. There were changes taking place in Europe which I wasn't willing to acknowledge, etc., etc.

**TG:** *I think there's also another interesting line of argument. If you look at the draft of the Port Huron statement, which was rather substantially changed, especially one part. There's a section called either Communism or Anti-Communism, and the most salient thing in it is a very long passage which basically argues that—it's a functionalist argument—anti-Communism has become the rationale for integrating into American society.*

**IH:** Yes. And for adventures abroad.

**TG:** *No, not even that. I mean the real animus is, subtext is, we shouldn't be anti-Communist because that's simply a way of selling you the contract. And so, we won't* *do that. There's very little in this about the Soviet Union at all, and most of what there is is very anti-Soviet, in fact.*

**IH:** Well, you know, we felt that the Port Huron thing was. . . .

**TG:** *But the emotional bite is this. . . .*

**IH:** There was also the idea of corporate liberalism which connected with that, the idea of, what was the phrase, cooptation.

**TG:** *So that it's conceivable to me that in 1965, not 1969 when he had gone way over to the Left, in 1969 which is right before he'd been to North Vietnam, that he didn't disagree with you that much about the Soviet Union. But it carried this whole bundle of other meanings that he didn't want going on.*

**IH:** Of course, there were the uses to which it was put domestically.

**TG:** *Well, of course, there was something to that.*

**IH:** Obviously.

**TG:** *But Mike, of course, argued there was another way to be anti-Communist.*

**IH:** So did I.

**TG:** *Actually, the final Port Huron statement, the revised one, has a passage [critical of the USSR], despite the LID, I mean I know there's disagreement on it, serious disagreement.*

**IH:** Well there's another thing. All through American history it seems to me, I'm just doing some work on it, there's a distinction between a movement and a party. And the movement takes an intransigent position, but once people of similar persuasion are in the party, then they have to make adjustments, compromises, and even concessions. And the abolitionists, those abolitionists who remained with [William Lloyd] Garrison,[12] who were nonpolitical, they were totally intransigent to the end. And then there were some who went inside and worked with the Republican Party. And I don't know which ones were more effective, I suppose it was good to have both. But there was terrible struggle, fierce disputes between them. Now if it had just been that issue, I think we could have lived with it, but I'm sure that after a certain time your relations to people like us weren't important to you because you had a mass movement and we didn't and you didn't give a damn.

**TG:** *But certainly up through 1965 it was important.*

**IH:** And after that we were in a different universe. We were at best a minor nuisance in your eyes.

**TG:** *Could you reconstruct what led up to "New Styles in Leftism"?*

**IH:** Yes. I read things, responses from various people and talking to people. I went to meetings, I attended SDS meetings, there were several national committee meetings that I went to, and the interminable style. . . . I mean on the one hand there's endless chatter which is part of participatory democracy and the price you pay for it. I was too impatient with that. I didn't see some of the virtues of that approach. But I also saw some of the disadvantages—you know, whoever had the most [chutzpah] hung on. And I could see a certain manipulative quality. See, when people told me the story about . . . Bob Moses, that he sat in the back of the room . . . I think that leaders should be up front so they can be attacked and held responsible. Sitting in the back was evading. He may not have meant to manipulate but I think he was manipulating. So that was a problem. And then I read some of the stuff by the blacks who were talking about violence, terrorism. Malcolm X, yes, I heard Malcolm X speak. And that was a pretty alarming experience. I mean, he was tremendously effective and a powerful speaker and very sanguine, very dangerous because I felt that—whatever the general limitations of nonviolence might be—that in the Southern situation nonviolence was absolutely right, morally, strategically, tactically, it was working, and that he was really a danger to that whole style, that whole outlook. And he never went South. He spoke to a movement in New York that was sponsored by the Trotskyists, and he was taunted about this. He said he'd go when the time is ready, well I've heard that kind of talk.

**TG:** *Did you think he was anti-Semitic also?*

**IH:** No. That issue didn't arise. Maybe he was, but that didn't strike me at that particular meeting. Maybe he was, but I don't know. Well, everything as I see it perhaps came too fast, it was too fast for our responses and too fast for yours. But the irony is if it hadn't come too fast, then you wouldn't have had a mass movement. But maybe in the long run it would have been better if SDS had had 20,000 people, slower organic development.

**TG:** *Oh absolutely. In retrospect it's very clear that what was decisive was the Vietnam War.*

**IH:** Right. And the Vietnam War forced such an intensity of response, and such polarization, that I don't know what could be done. And there, I think, we were right. I don't know if you saw it, but Mike Walzer and I did a piece about six years ago that we called a retrospective on Vietnam, justifying our opposition to the war but also [our] refusal to support [the Communists]. There was a lot I think of romanticizing North Vietnam.

**TG:** *I'm sure we agree on this matter. I often feel I'm in the same position vis-à-vis a lot of what's going on now as you were vis-à-vis us and I appreciate the culture too.*

**IH:** One of the things that surprised me was how little, at least in public, retrospection there was among the people of the New Left. After the fact. You people had something that people like us never had, you had a mass movement, you had it for a very brief period of time but it was a mass movement. One of the most remarkable things about it which I've never understood and have to have some explanation, was the sheer rapidity of how it seemed to explode, it was really an American phenomenon. Bang, as it were, overnight it was gone. Of the retrospectives that I'm aware of, I read one by Ellie Langer[13] which I thought was very sensitive.

It struck me as [unfathomable] why there were so few efforts, it's now what fifteen years, more than fifteen years. Why there were so few efforts of trying in a sustained way to say what went wrong, what happened, why did it all slip through our fingers?

**TG:** *That's a good question. One answer is that what had been the movement was in shock, and it was a protracted psychological trauma.*

**IH:** Well, I can understand that for three years, five years.

**TG:** *What went along with the shock and outlasted it I think was a sense of chagrin, I mean that's a very minor way of putting it, embarrassment, misery, all kinds of pain about it, accompanied by. . . . Well some people had found other gods to follow.*

**IH:** Rennie Davis.[14]

**TG:** *Or were honest enough or clear-headed enough not to do that but were in their own modest and shambling way trying to piece together sort of a countercultural style of life which was in effect opposed to that kind of reflection, I mean as a practice. You know Paul Potter would be an example of that. I mean he wrote a book, he did write. But he went basically refusing to think systematically.*

**IH:** What happened with [Carl] Oglesby?

**TG:** *Well, he was in a lot of pain at first. He did write an article which was an account, and actually in some ways a very astute one, from the vantage of 1969 about the crack-up of the movement.*

**IH:** And Hayden just kept barreling along.

**TG:** *Carl should be doing more, I mean he has a whole lot more to say. He's quoted at length in this new history of the antiwar movement.*

**IH:** Where is he now?

**TG:** *He's in Boston.*

**IH:** What is he doing?

**TG:** *Last I saw him about four years ago he was a staff writer for* Boston Magazine, *which is the city slick. He has moved quite far to the right in some ways. There's another answer also. Which is that a lot of people scrambled, the footing that they scrambled for was a footing for some sort of continued political work. And it was frightening to look back, looking back on the abyss.*

**IH:** The only basis upon which you could do the political work was to ask yourself what the hell went wrong.

**TG:** *Well, but many people concluded what went wrong was some sort of overweening national ambition, right, the idea of the revolution or something like that, so the proper response was to retrench to some sort of single-issue activity. Localism was the primary response.*

**IH:** Local organizing, but not very much came of that.

**TG:** *Not as much as the Right has done.*

**IH:** No. But something.

**TG:** *You know the alternative state and local public policy networks, local this and local that.*

**IH:** That was already reform politics.

**TG:** *Yes, that's what it is. Reform politics. Which is probably what they would have been doing all along had it not been for the Vietnam War.*

**IH:** See, it's not that I thought that what Tom was doing in the Democratic Party was wrong. But I felt that he owed it to himself and to his followers as a matter of honesty to say, not that he had to say Howe was right, that I know he'll never be able to say. I don't care about that, but he had to say, "I was wrong in my principled opposition to working inside the Democratic Party."

**TG:** *He's done that in interviews. Tom's also very evasive.*

**IH:** Yes, I know.

**TG:** *And I'm sure that has a lot to do with protecting his political position. I mean he. . . .*

**IH:** He wants to have it both ways.

**TG:** *Yes.*

**IH:** He wants to maintain himself as he was and as he is. With that kind of excuse, you can justify anything. But there's another very interesting question here. Let's say we see the SDS as a movement, using the distinction between movement and political party. But the question that you had to face was, What can you do with this movement after a certain point? And I guess people didn't think about that because you were so involved in. . . .

**TG:** *Not true.*

**IH:** No. You did think about it?

**TG:** *Starting in 1963, Dick Flacks, since he was always a little bit older . . . [began asking what happened] once you got outside the student framework. The people that we were already were so disparate, and since of course also the political style, the intellectual political style was a refusal of coherence, that is to say a refusal of coherent analysis and program, [Flacks noted and asked], So what was this? What did this amount to? Well [we] didn't know what it amounted to.*

**IH:** But I would put it another way though.

**TG:** *But I mean this was a nagging feeling.*

**IH:** I didn't know about that.

**TG:** *But it was clear. . . .*

**IH:** It was a feeling only among some of you.

**TG:** *Well, but among the. . . .*

**IH:** The activists?

**TG:** *Flacks, Paul Booth, Bob Ross, Richie Rothstein, and me. Basically. I mean we were. . . .*

**IH:** These were the more intellectual types. Roughly.

**TG:** *Yes. But we were representative of the early SDS group in many ways.*

**IH:** You mean there was probably more generational tension in that group?

**TG:** *Oh yes. By the way the SDS hated this, they were absolutely convinced that we were plotting to replace them, and to set up a counter to SDS. And they were very happy when it all fell apart.*

**IH:** You were already sort of graduates.

**TG:** *Oh yes. Worse, we were social democrats. We were the old farts, we were the Old Guard.*

**IH:** I see. You were replacing us as the enemy so to say.

**TG:** *Well, we didn't know about that.*

**IH:** But you see there's a more general question. You can run a movement as an oppositional force, a very powerful force. But at a certain point I don't think you can sustain the movement indefinitely. This was the experience of abolitionism, either it wins out on its great issue or it loses. And then Garrison said we quit, we won and that's it. [Abolitionist] Wendell Phillips said to hell with that, there are other issues, there are labor issues, and he started to get involved in politics. Then you would face the problem, it seems to me, of getting involved in politics, either the third party route, which I think is in America a disaster, or something to do with getting into the Democratic Party. That is to say you would have had to face the question of functioning, as the phrase used to be, within the system. Of course that whole counter-position, in the system, outside the system, is nonsense I think. It was a simplified idea because even a movement functions within [the system]. You were not a revolutionary sect trying to blow up, etc., you were functioning as a moral protest movement within the system. But you would have had to face the question of whether to become a political force of some kind.

**TG:** *How do political movements transfer themselves in American political life? How does a movement transpose itself, or shift, or transfigure itself into a political force or—can it without destroying itself? . . . Those of us who appreciated the prob-*

*lem were neither from the movement nor part of it really. We were from organizations that preceded the movement, or that in some way were originally organized to sing the praises of the movement and further the movement and make the movement more coherent and so on. The movement itself, as a mass movement, was limited in what it cared about.*

**IH:** I think I tell this story in my book [*A Margin of Hope*]. Going to one of these enormous demonstrations in Washington with Stanley Plastrik, listening to David Dellinger,[15] someone I always disliked. Even though he was on the same side as Muste,[16] I liked A. J. a lot and we got along well.

Dellinger, I thought, was a bad apple. There he was, speaking, and Stanley and I turned and we looked at each other and said, you know that we are the only two people here, in a crowd of three or four hundred thousand, listening to what he's saying, paying attention to the words. It was an eerie experience, uncanny.

**TG:** *I don't think there's such a thing as a generic movement. See, that was where the counterculture came in.*

**IH:** The counterculture played a role.

***TG:*** *Because the counterculture gives you a reason not to listen to speeches and not to read books.*

**IH:** Todd, do you see any reason to think that, if something were to occur again, that it would necessarily be different? That's a tough question.

**TG:** *No, certainly not necessarily different. Sometimes, when I am in a good mood, I think it could be different, but partly because there is some folk knowledge, very thin, of what mistakes were made in the sixties. It's very crude.*

*Already in 1975, I was teaching at Santa Cruz, and one day I am walking to class with the most sophisticated student in the class, and he says to me, "You were in SDS, right?" and I said "Yeah." And he said "That was the Weathermen, right?"*

**IH:** Oh jeez.

**TG:** *And that was in 1975! He became quite a good journalist. Well, that's ignorance. On the other hand, I think there is some knowledge that you don't want to end up like the Weathermen, but I worry about this.*

*Which is one reason why I have decided to go public with the sort of argument that I am making about the arms race. [And] talking about the need for political understanding about what is going on. And specifically, confronting the problem with the Russians, which I don't think necessarily undermines [one's] capacity to move politically. I think it actually shores it up. But I hear a lot of stuff that I cringe from.*

**IH:** What kind of stuff?

**TG:** *The Cold War, that the arms race is basically an American show.*

**IH:** And the Russians are really nice guys, that kind of thing?

**TG:** *Yeah, I mean nobody would quite come out and say, well not nobody, . . . [Instead they say], "Of course the Russians are there, but you shouldn't talk about that too loud." And [they say], "Are you really sure about Solidarity?" It shades off into that.*

*I feel for the first time in many years optimistic about the capacity to carry on the kind of arguments that I am making here within that world. I published this thing in* The Nation *which, first of all, I was amazed that they ran it, frankly. About a third or half of it is basically about the Russians. I expected to get pelted with shit from the Left and I didn't.*

**IH:** Of course, nobody was paying attention.

**TG:** *It is possible. Well, it got a fair amount of attention from those people. And I did some radio things based on it in the Bay area and I was almost disappointed, frankly.*

**IH:** What about the people who have gone? One of the things which I used to say, half as a joke, but alas it wasn't a joke, is that most of the people who would attack me from the left would end up attacking me from the right.

**TG:** *You know what happened to Freddy Cohen?*

**IH:** I heard different stories. I heard one story that he is teaching at Cornell, I heard another story that he is a lawyer in Los Angeles.

**TG:** *That is what I heard. Many years ago I heard that he was already a corporate lawyer.*

**IH**: Well, that is one version of it. Then, when I saw this piece, by David Horowitz[17] and Peter Collier,[18] as to why they voted for Reagan, that really made me sick. Because there was nothing about their argument which required you to vote for Reagan.

**TG:** *That is exactly what I have been saying. I agree with most of what they say.*

**IH:** There's no connection. You can vote for Mondale on the same premise.

**TG:** *Or you can have an entirely other politics.*

**IH:** Short of being a fellow-traveler.

**TG:** *It's so shoddy.*

**IH:** You know Horowitz?

**TG:** *I used to know him.*

**IH:** Where is he now?

**TG:** *LA. He's gone Hollywood. [Columnist Charles] Krauthammer wrote a piece on him.*[19]

**IH:** Ron Radosh[20] said to me, well, he's our Irving Kristol.

**TG:** *He's certainly not mine. It really disgusts me, the glee that yet another sixties hero, who of course is another media-anointed star, now reveals that he's [sold out] . . . [Black Panther activist] Bobby Seale was picked out by* Newsweek *in one of their "Where Are They Now?" columns. You know it's right out of central casting, just as Jerry Rubin was, and of course these people are capitalizing on it*[21] *. . . Most people—and this is where Flacks has done a lot of his research—most of the sixties activists, I'm not talking just about the pre-1965 core but here I would include the serious activists, they're not driving BMWs. They're not Jane Fonda or married to Jane Fonda. A lot of them are political activists, they didn't vote for Reagan. A lot of them are functionally like me in professions of various kinds.*

**IH:** In local groups.

**TG:** *Or in DSA, something like that. And one thing that sickens me is the mainstream culture celebration of the return, not just the return to the fold but the reinvention of the fold. What [*New Republic *owner] Marty [Peretz] is doing with this Krauthammer, there's something very sinister about the tone, I mean there's a real glee in this piece.*[22]

**IH:** Well, the *New Republic* is a sad, sad situation. It's sad. There is a role for a magazine which hangs on to liberalism.

**TG:** *Oh yeah.*

**IH:** Not radicalism, liberalism. They had good things. On domestic matters. And it's as if two different groups are editing. One week it's liberal and the next it's conservative. It's bizarre, schizo.

**TG:** *Go back to "New Styles in Leftism." I think it's an interesting, pivotal document. I was surprised you didn't write about it in your* [New Republic] *account.*

IH: No special reason.

**TG:** *I try to reconstruct my own mood on reading it, when I first read it. Which was I think the summer of 1965, does that sound right?*

**IH:** Yes. 1965.

**TG:** *I remember a double or triple reaction. First of all, a lot of this is right. It seems to me you talked about [Frantz] Fanon.*[23] *And independently, I was just going through my old correspondence, I discovered a letter I wrote to Jimmy Weinstein at* Studies on the Left *asking if I could review, and telling him what my argument would have been which was not so different from your argument.*[24] *And also, you probably talked about Che Guevara and so on, who I probably liked a lot better than you did then, but I could recognize that some of this is happening. And yet at the same time, I remember thinking, Well I can't agree with this, I forbid myself to. I mean there's a certain temptation and yet a certain feeling when I go looking, and this is right at the threshold of [being] conscious, when I go looking for reasons to distance myself from it, I can find them. Like tone, like it's much too savage, it's much too dismissive and it's much too sweeping. Okay, this is a tendency, it's not the only thing. In a way . . . it's like what Mike said to you after your thing with Tom, couldn't you say it nicer? Did you ever run into reactions like that? What kind of reactions from my generation?*

**IH:** Yes, for sure. But I had gotten myself in the position of being the polemicist. And partly it has a comic side and partly an irritating side. Harrington would be saying essentially the same things that I said at that time. Walzer was still too young. And yet Harrington didn't meet with as much opposition or hostility as I did. But people get boxed into roles. What you were just saying about yourself, and I suppose the same thing happened to me. You know this is the wisdom after the event. And that's why I ask you whether you thought things would be different. Because I suspect that people would again get boxed into roles. Probably I got a sort of strange gratification out of being the Socialist SDSers loved to hate the most. But I also had a sense of déjà vu. I remember once one of the SDS guys in 1968 came out with a theory of liberal Fascism, which was just too much because it brought up the whole business of social Fascism. And I had the feeling that people were reenacting parts and they didn't even know what they were doing. They were repeating historical roles.

**TG:** *First as tragedy, then as farce.*

**IH:** Right, exactly. They were repeating historical roles and there was a sense of not rage exactly, not really rage, but despair, which made for that savagery, a sense of helplessness almost, if you saw. I don't want to claim that I saw everything or that I was right about everything, but we saw a tremendous opportunity, a tremendous chance for the Left, and we felt it was going to go down the drain, a kind of thoughtlessness and excess, and it did.

**TG:** *I think one thing that fueled that, and I think this was also on my mind, is that by the summer of 1965 we were absolutely obsessed by the war.*

**IH:** You felt that to be against the war—at least most people did—you had to be for the North [Vietnam]?

**TG:** *No.*

**IH:** No?

**TG:** *I don't think I felt that.*

**IH:** No you didn't, personally.

**TG:** *Well, I don't think that many people [did]. I think there was much—even Tom, went through a lot of wrestling about what to say in criticism of the North. But, fearing, among other things, that they were now in a position to play a crucial role as would-be peacemakers, and feeling reluctant to burn their bridges to the North as diplomats, at that stage. I think later it became something else. It's very complicated, but, no, the "us" and "them" line was not "us" being on the side of North Vietnam, and you being on the side of America. It was: "What are you doing about the war? What are you doing to stop the war?" That's the mood. And the moral context is that.*

**IH:** Well we went to demonstrations. I spoke at the very first demonstration in Washington, and then after awhile we were, alas, on the sidelines, we were immobilized by our position.

**TG:** *I don't have a test for this. Nobody, by definition, inside movement circles was saying what you were saying, so it's not—you get back to the generational business.*

*One of the things that was said for example, that [Alan] Haber—the issue of exclusionism was still being debated up till 1965. And Haber wrote this long, very characteristically, very thorough and ponderous, but very interesting defense of the nonexclusionism policy, the most articulate defense, which is wrong—but—one of the things he says is, "We're tired of being lectured at from outside. We don't want to exclude that position either. Let them come in and make their case."*

*You talk about Emersonianism, there's a kind of sublime faith in the molecular one-to-one process in this position at this time.*

*So that your argument, your polemic, which is structural and categorical, seems to be coming from an entirely different universe.*

**IH:** I think that's true. Could the PL people have been excluded? I mean this is the problem in DSA, for example, on a smaller scale. DSA is relatively nothing, but it's more than the other nothings.

So you have the areas with semi-Maoist sects, etc., which look upon it as a place to reign. You have the same debate going on. The old-time politicals are horrified at the thought of these people coming in because they know what it means, and there are a lot of new people, very nice, democrats, who repeat the anti-exclusionists argument.

**TG:** *I've wrestled with that one a lot. It's probably not an either/or, maybe this is waffling, I don't know. The Haber position—there was something very interesting in the Haber position—"let us define our politics, and then [see] if people are willing to cooperate with other people on various projects in an ad-hoc way, . . . if [they] agree with our problems."*

*Now after a certain point, SDS refused to articulate its politics in a responsible way. It was Port Huron, and then the next year SDS issued a convention document and then never again after that, because there was partly a recognition that there was no consensus anymore. And DSA does organize itself around some political positions. So that gives you a base.*

**IH:** It's easier to handle with the DSA. On the other hand, I don't know what you could have done. Suppose some kid from the University of Iowa joins SDS and he's a PL person. I don't see what you can do to keep him out.

**TG:** *I don't think you can keep him out. But I think you can argue—when they act as a bloc and they do very effectively—against it. I reject the notion that to call it "that spade" is red-baiting.*

**IH:** You call it a spade? What do you do about a spade?

**TG:** *You defeat it. Then you're faced with, What if you can't defeat it?*

**IH:** That's the point. You're talking so very much like an intellectual now, which is not a criticism, but a description. And so do I. But what do you do when you have this organized bloc, just because it is an organized bloc? That maybe can't win but can paralyze. . . . That was one problem that the abolitionists such as [William Lloyd] Garrison didn't face. Organized Bolshevism. They had all kinds of nuts and opposition, but not that.

**TG:** *I guess at this point I feel if it gets to that point, you throw them out. I mean there are Spartacists, for example, or vultures, and I was hearing they were trying to colonize Columbia, where the kids are sitting to protest university investments in South Africa.*[25] *And I've seen them take over meetings, well you can't put up with them. You throw them out. I guess I would accept calling the cops on them if it comes to that.*

**IH:** But at that point in SDS, first you wouldn't have gotten the agreement of the leadership for doing it. See that was your dilemma probably. If you had raised that, you would have been isolated.

**TG:** *Of course. Everybody wanted to eliminate the membership criterion in 1965. Virtually no one except Tom Kahn, to his credit, wanted to keep it. And nobody [else in SDS] took this position. But it's not then. And, well of course, you could say, you knew [where it would lead].*

**IH:** [SDS] paid a heavy price for it.

**TG:** *I know.*

**IH:** I don't know that I knew how to handle it, but you're right. At least if [SDS] had come out candidly and spoken about what it meant you might have educated some of the people in your organization about what was going on; that this was not a disagreement like other disagreements. These were people who were out to either take it over or destroy it, it was a cannibalistic impulse.

**TG:** *They didn't want to destroy it. They were incredibly dumb. They fouled their own nest. They were just indelicate.*

**IH:** But it did a lot of damage.

**TG:** *Enormously. And it was also perfectly evident, already evident to me, that it* was *happening in concert, it happened in 1965.*

**IH:** A certain psychology was created, and I've seen this in other contexts, and once this psychology takes over, then it's cyclic, in which you have to keep raising the ante. That is to say, "To be more radical is to be more virtuous." So you come out for the revolution in three countries, I come out in five countries, and someone else, twenty countries. And pretty soon you have the tragedy of a girl like Judy Clark.[26]

**TG:** *I don't want to be accused of being too optimistic, but again, there is a more proximate history to draw on, and it is now pretty well understood, I think. Well of course, the young people don't know anything.*

**IH:** How could they?

**TG:** *But I think anyone who is over twenty-two knows there was a very live movement in the sixties that ended, and then something very bad happened [the Weathermen], and it ended. And something about it involved sectarianism.*

**IH:** See the question in my mind is—OK, let's say that the Bolshevik tradition is manageable by now in America because it's so weak and there are so few people involved. And whatever happens to this country I don't see any chance for the CP or the Spartacists . . . to amount to anything. They can make difficulties in local places. But the question is whether there is something in the very nature of the American tradition, the American experience, the American situation, which gives rise to this excess. I raise this in the piece that I gave you.

Something of the same sort happened within the SP in the early 1930s. It was a really promising party, a promising movement. And it was growing and had very good people, and much of the rhetoric and language—this I think has not been studied, but much of the language was similar to the participatory democracy of the SDS. It was really open, very broad, and it had a great leader in [Norman] Thomas who was all over the place, fighting on every issue—and some very talented, grown-up people, terrific trade union organizers. . . .

And it came up against the question, well there were several problems which it couldn't cope with one of them being the CP, but these guys came up against the New Deal. And by taking the intransigent position of total opposition to the New Deal and running Thomas, as a kind of political gesture in the 1936 and 1940 elections, it forced most of its trade unionists, and it had some damn good ones, to make a choice between the CIO and the SP.

See yourself in that situation. You are active and organizing tens of thousands, hundreds of thousands of workers, the greatest new mass movement in the country—organizing the industrial workers. You have a real place there, you see this as a great mass movement and then there's this new party, to which you are still emotionally and intellectually tied, which insists that you must not support Roosevelt, whereas the CIO was going to do that. So that the SP forces these people . . . to choose between itself and the CIO. Most of them are going to choose the CIO.

They were right in a way to do it. And in a way, you have the same kind of idea, much of the same. It would be very interesting for someone to do a study comparing those choices.

**TG:** *Actually a comparable thing today is, there are large networks of community organizers, local activists who are not in DSA or anything else, and they are sometimes very effective on utility issues. And they are, I think, they cringe at the thought of ideological politics. Because for them it represents the politics of the small meeting hall rather than the big movement. And there are the big movement people.*

*Unfortunately they're not opposed to the CIO, they're not that good. They are post-Nader.*

**IH:** They don't have those opportunities.

**TG:** *It's a different world.*

**IH:** I think there's this ingrained sectarianism, which comes out of the Protestant tradition, the Protestant sects. A whole tradition of dissent in this country. And it had great moral power, and one wants to have that moral power, without that moral power, we're lost. And yet, it's so profoundly apolitical or ineffectively political in its impulses.

Well, I'll send you a copy of my book [*Socialism and America*, (1985)] when it comes out. Because I try to talk about it in relation to the SP. There were three great faces of American radicalism in the twentieth century—Debs, the thirties, and SDS—and each of them collapsed. And the question in my mind is—Are there parallel courses which operate in each instance, and is there something about the American society which leaves those courses to manifest themselves? And if there are, it's a little scary.

**TG:** *See, this would be true if the norm is that this is a conservative country. And more than a conservative country—it's a country in which most people have committed to normal, private, everyday lives. There are not continuing political traditions, not just political traditions but traditions of realizing yourself in the public world, public life. Therefore, what makes it possible to be political in the first place is furious moralism.*

**IH:** The interesting thing is that it's thrived not during times of conservative upsurge but during times of liberal upsurge. [Moralism] thrived at the time of progressivism, the Socialist and Communist parties at the time of the New Deal, and the SDS at the time of Johnson, who domestically was [liberal] . . .

**TG:** *But the founding SDS generation, we are children of the fifties. And there's a sense of breaking out of the old ground too. Kennedy was doing the same thing too.*

**IH:** Kennedy was opening up the gates of freedom.

**TG:** *And that's a problem. You have to negotiate your relation to Kennedy. You appreciate something of the same style. . . . But those people were pretty savvy.*

**IH:** That posture of intransigence is so deeply ingrained in the American spirit. I see it all the time.

**TG:** *I think there's a lot to that, I'm not sure that movements in Catholic countries are any less sectarian. I mean I think there are also built-in problems for lefts in the West.*

**IH:** Maybe so, but there of course in the Catholic countries you have an anticlericalism, which serves an equivalent function, and you have the strong Marxism, a kind of more traditional, radical Marxism which counterposes itself to democracy movements, mostly rhetorical bullshit, but still there. But the anticlerical bias. Look at the incredible conundrum of the Nicaraguan government. They have all these economic and social problems and they have to go and take on the Church. An utterly suicidal venture. Why couldn't they waiver that? They couldn't somehow, emotionally.

**TG:** *But I don't think, if you look at what happened in Italy, in the late sixties or seventies, you could not find a more sectarian CP.*

**IH:** But in Italy there is something different. The CP [there] is really sui generis. There's nothing like the Italian CP.

**TG:** *Look at Spain during the Spanish Civil War. There is no absence of sectarianism.*

**IH:** It's a Marxist sectarianism. The question—I know about Marxism, oh do I know about Marxism. But the question really is whether there is, is there something in this country which makes for a distinctive—it's in England too, with this happening in the Labour Party which ought to be coasting into the next election with a great victory—which tears itself apart.

**TG:** *One of the few things I ever read about sectarianism which I thought was provocative, was this statement, in a book about France 1968, by Tom Nairn,*[27] *if you know that name, of the* New Left Review. *The way he put it is: "Sectarianism is a kind of a shadow war for the possession of a revolution, which is only an idea."*

**IH:** How do you combine these two?

**TG:** *That is a very interesting question which I have been trying to understand. How could so many people, who are not stupid, feel emotionally at least that there was some chance that what was happening was not simply a dissolution but a revolution.*

**IH:** I'll tell you a story, I think I have this in my book. I gave a talk at Wayne University in late 1969, and a nice guy got up. He wasn't a Maoist, he wasn't a Weatherman or anything. He wasn't even hostile. He said, "Do you really think there's not going to be a revolution in this country in the next couple of years?" And I said, "Yes, of course, I think so. There's not going to be one." He looked at me kind of astonished. I said how could anyone who's really intelligent hold such a stupid idea. But didn't you see among yourselves the enormous hostility which you encountered?

**TG:** *Well, yes, of course. Ellie Langer caught it beautifully in her memoir. In Chicago [at the Democratic Party Convention in 1968], if you listen to the slogans and look at the signs, you realize half of the people thought they were on the verge of the revolution and half of them thought they were on the verge of Fascism. With both of them having in common apocalyptic fantasies.*

*This gets back to your Christian theme. The millenarianism. This guy comes up to you, feeling something in the air, and that's the great American tradition of that, this Great Awakening.*

**IH:** And now you have the bomb reinforcing that.

**TG:** *Absolutely. And there's a war going on every day and there are lurid images, very powerful images.*

**IH:** Lenin once said very wisely, Lenin was very smart, "Capitalism always has a way out." That's something that the Left in America never understood.

**TG:** *[Joseph] Schumpeter was right about capitalism.*[28] *Capitalism turns problems into markets. It's a very shrewd system. This millenarianism, I would anticipate that there will be a lot more of it simply on the ground that we're entering the new millennium.*

**IH:** The only kinds of issues upon which there seem to be any possibility of opposition are black and white. South Africa, Iraq, Nicaragua. There seems to be, no domestic issue seems to stare anybody down.

**TG:** *I think I now believe that this is the rhythm of American politics, and that. . . .*

**IH:** Well, if it is, then we're in more trouble than . . . I remember something else; to me this was one of the most traumatic things, but useful maybe. You know the name George Kateb.[29]

**TG:** *Yes, I was amused by your story about him. I read one of his books one time too.*

**IH:** [He said to me] that social democracy is boring.

**TG:** *Well, it's true. Absolutely.*

**IH:** But so is any reform politics. Especially in the welfare state where it becomes [so tamed]. . . . The struggle to initiate social security, that was an exciting thing. But now the struggle to improve it, or to keep it from being abused, it's very important, but it doesn't have high drama.

**TG:** *One thing that was interesting in the early sixties was that . . . we were not the only people who had an apocalyptic vision of the domestic future. Through ordination. That ordination was the deus ex machina that was going to create [the revolution]. But Mike [Harrington] believed it also. Many people believed it in the early sixties.*

**IH:** In some sense it still is true.

**TG:** *There was going to be mass unemployment very soon. It wasn't just kooks who were saying that. Our little bible was a talk that had been given by Ray Brown. I don't know if you remember Ray Brown. He was an economist who worked for the Federal Reserve.*[30]

**IH:** He was a black fellow?

**TG:** *No.*

**IH:** Oh yes, I do remember.

**TG:** *He's the one that hung out with Stanley Aronowitz*[31] *and that crowd. And we reprinted this paper called "Our Priceless Economy."*

**IH:** He didn't consider the possibility of the creation of all kinds of new jobs.

**TG:** *Absolutely not. But once there was a millennial edge to domestic fantasies, that helped fuel the Iraq thing, because we believed we'd better go out there and be ready to catch the poor because otherwise the right wing will get them.*

**IH:** Do you still have an informal network, keep in touch?

**TG:** *More so over the last few years, yes, I see a few people and talk. Dick Flacks I see continuously. He is writing a book which I partly disagree with, but he's also wrestling with this same set of issues.*

*See, he's come out concluding that we should forget about left-wing organizations completely. Think of the Left as a culture, as a socialization world, as the embodiment of public values against the tendency toward private withdrawal, and leave it at that.*

*That's where he comes to.*

**IH:** But how can you have that culture without some organization?

**TG:** *Well, I think he'd say, "Let it be local." I disagree with that. But anyway he's very much alive to these issues.*

**IH:** Are you in touch with Hayden?

**TG:** *No. I am going to see him soon. I think he's in touch with almost no one I know of in the old network. He's a machine politician. He lives in a different world.*
*[The conversation now shifts to Howe's years of teaching at Brandeis University in the 1950s.]*

**TG:** *Let me ask you some questions about the fifties. Brandeis. The Brandeis scene is very interesting because it sounds like it was maybe one of two that I know of that had some continuity from the fifties and sixties. The only other one I know of is [the University of Wisconsin at] Madison.*

**IH:** Yes.

**TG:** *And you were very important—you played an important part, not only for people like Marty [Peretz] and Jeremy [Larner],*[32] *but for Barbara Haber. . . .*

*Certain incidents stand out in people's memories as critical points and prefigurations of later things. For example, the debate that you had with Howard Fast is very vivid in all of these memories.*[33] *What are your memories of that of that? First of all, how did it come about?*

**IH:** He agreed, to our astonishment, to debate with me.

**TG:** *Who invited him up?*

**IH:** I can't remember . . . I do remember that Jeremy [Larner] was the chairman and the sad thing about that story was that [Fast] was on the verge of breaking from the CP and he was stupid. Why did he agree to do it? Because he knew he would be put in the false position, and he was put in the false position, of defending Stalinism straight down the line.

**TG:** *This is early 1957? You think? Or late 1956.*

**IH:** Certainly after Hungary. And I'd been laying in wait for something like that, and I really went after him. I was pretty fierce in those days. And I think I beat the hell out of Fast. He wasn't much of a debater. I didn't realize until afterwards that he wasn't speaking with great conviction. But one of the things that stuck in the end was some of the kids felt sorry for him, not that they agreed with him. But they felt, "Why did I kick him around so much?"

**TG:** *Barbara was one of them.*

**IH:** Yeah. He was helpless. And again, there was a lack of a historical sense that Stalinism was kicking millions of people around. Not just verbally, but physically. He saw it in the terms of a larger context, and the way he lied for example, about the Jewish/Yiddish writers. And I knew he was lying and he knew he was lying.

**TG:** *He took the position that there was no problem.*

**IH:** No. Everything was going to be all right. And there were essentially two audiences, there were kids who were very bright screaming at the audience. And he was not quick on his feet to begin with, and secondly he already half-agreed with what I was saying, but that we didn't know at the time.

I remember afterward, I had a big class of marvelous kids, and I made it a principle not to talk about politics in the classroom, but to do my job. But every once in a while it happens. And they felt sorry for him, and I said it was like someone who kills his mother and father and then pleads mercy. I suppose Barbara might have told you that story!

**TG:** *No! But I know the joke.*

**IH:** Some joke. Ha! The kids were not hostile about this to me, but they didn't understand the passion with which I and the Cosers [Lewis and Rose] felt, and even Jeremy, who was chairman, didn't understand. . . . Well, he understood it but he couldn't share it. They hadn't gone through the pain that we had gone through of the Moscow trials and all the rest of that.

**TG:** *Did you already see the emergence in embryo of a counterculture, bohemia, marijuana?*

**IH:** No. Oh, there was a little bit of marijuana, I remember once Marty Peretz smoked. You see I didn't know what the hell it was all about. I still don't in a way. People in my generation were very innocent about this. Growing up in the thirties, coming from immigrant Jewish families where there was a lot of ingrained Puritanism, more by habit than ideology, for us the horizon of boldness was sex. Just to find a place to be alone with a girl, some space, was a great problem. We all lived in crowded apartments. I grew up with an aunt, an uncle, a grandmother, my parents, myself, in a four-room apartment. The first time I had a room to myself as a kid was a great event for me. We were just desperately poor, and then, if somebody's parents went away and we had an apartment, it was a great luxury. So we literally knew nothing about drugs. It wasn't an option. We didn't know anything about homosexuality either. I remember hearing in, say 1938 or 1939, that [a] writer, who was close to the Left at that time, was a homosexual, and I was ashamed to ask what that meant. I was seventeen, I was eighteen years old. And that may seem impossible for you but it was true. We just didn't know about such things. So [too] when I heard that Martin Peretz had taken some marijuana, once when Norman Mailer came up, and Norman then was very provocative, he embodied himself as a great radical hero. He was another one who always attacked me from the left, all through the sixties. And I heard that Marty had shared some marijuana with Norman Mailer. I had kind of, first a shudder of bewilderment, really. What the hell is this all about, this nice kid, what's he doing? I didn't know whether marijuana was harmless or would poison him or what. It was all very new. And the kind of kids we had at Brandeis, the ones who counted for us, were extremely intellectual, a whole gang of them. The counterculture didn't arise there at the time. These were kids who were in many ways reenacting almost consciously the experience of my generation of radical kids. They tended to romanticize the period and I remember making speeches telling them that the period wasn't so hot, it was nothing to look back on.

**TG:** *But there were people who described themselves as bohemians and felt in fact that the campus culture divided that way. There were the [straight] kids and the bohemians.*

**IH:** Abbie Hoffman was a student, but it's interesting, I don't remember him. He never came in, maybe he came in to a class of mine or something, but I never knew him.

**TG:** *He writes in this memoir of his that he was very much affected by Frank Manuel,*[34] *among others.*

**IH:** But Frank Manuel was highly intellectual in his approach. . . .

**TG:** *But I'm not sure there was a distinction then. I'm not talking about a beatnik culture but, I mean, arty.*

**IH:** There was a very great deal of avant-garde, yes. The intellectual wanted to read *Ulysses,* to talk about Picasso, that kind of thing, yes.

**TG:** *I think that atmosphere existed in a number of places in the late fifties and is one of the important seedbeds of the New Left.*

**IH:** Very likely.

**TG:** *Very much in Ann Arbor, Madison, and Berkeley.*

**IH:** See, the New Left never flourished at Brandeis. But in some sense, no left-wing groups flourished because the whole campus was left. So there was no need to distinguish yourself.

**TG:** *And do you know Vicky Bonnell?*[35] *Do you remember her?*

**IH:** I know the name.

**TG:** *She's my colleague.*

*[The conversation shifts to Herbert Marcuse, a German philosopher and member of the Frankfurt School who wrote about social and sexual liberation and was very influential with the New Left.]*

**IH:** . . . [I remember now the argument] that I had with her [about Marcuse].

**TG:** *Well, that's what I was just coming to. When was that?*

**IH:** Directly after the Hungarian revolution of 1956, maybe a week or two afterward. And the importance of that I couldn't yet have foreseen, I mean the symptomatic importance of it. And I had been quite friendly with her, but he [Marcuse]was a very charming guy, cultivated, amusing, clever, and he had written something for *Dissent* and he was quite friendly. The differences between us, the fact he asked me to read his manuscript, the one, the book about sexual liberation. . . .

**TG:** *Eros and Civilization.*

**IH:** Yes, *Eros and Civilization,* and I looked at a piece of it, and I thought it was a very interesting book. And I knew he was more of an orthodox Marxist than I was ready to call myself by then, but the magnitude of the differences hadn't yet become clear. And then it turned out that whereas I supported the Hungarian revolution, he took a much more ambiguous or ambivalent position. He didn't come out in support of the Stalinist government, the repression, but he talked about something equivalent to the way we described things now with the Soviet Union. He talked about the danger that there were fascists in the opposition and revolution, etc., etc. And I tried to say that there may very well have been reactionary elements, it would be inevitable in any situation of revolution, there would be a mixed bag, but there was no evidence that the revolution itself was bad. And this was a pretty fierce confrontation too. You see the temperature at Brandeis, political and intellectual temper, was higher than in most other places, because it was a very strange faculty, there can't have been another school in the country with that kind of faculty. There were a lot of European refugees, mostly people from the Left, and there were sort of freelance characters like myself who had never gotten degrees. So that it was a time, some people joked it was Alcove One at City College or Alcove One and Two, repeated. There were virtually no Stalinists, or if there were they kept quiet, but there were different shades of left. And that debate, while it didn't have as much impact upon the students, it's interesting the [Howard Fast debate] got to the kids more than the debate with Marcuse, because I guess the [Fast debate] was closer to home. And then there was another factor which at the time I didn't realize. A lot of these kids probably came from CP homes. Bright kids, you know, parents had been in or near the CP.

**TG:** *Well, that was true later, it might have been a little early for that.*

**IH:** Well, no.

**TG:** *1956, that early?*

**IH:** Sure. Parents who had been in the CP in the thirties and forties had dropped out, been near it, fellow-travelers. There was a big culture around the CP, and especially Jewish kids in New York. So this hit them hard. Whereas Hungary seemed to them somewhat more distant. But, to repeat, on the faculty, the Fast [debate] was just a diversion, almost an entertainment, or getting rid of some energy. Whereas the debate with Marcuse was seen by a small number of people as an extremely serious matter. He and I didn't talk to each other for about a year afterwards, and beyond that it was at best a polite relationship.

**TG:** *What about in say the early sixties. Did you have the sense that the political culture which was developing among students was in some sense available or feeling the need to choose sides between roughly you and roughly him? When did you leave there?*

**IH:** I left in 1962.

**TG:** *Well, let's say in 1960, 1961, 1962.*

**IH:** No, that didn't arise as a significant issue as far as I remember. What the big issue then was the Freedom Riders in the South. Because I remember that it was around then that we sent Michael Walzer . . . down to North Carolina to do his first big piece for the magazine, and he did a piece on the city of Greensboro . . . North Carolina. That was the big thing, the Freedom Riders. But I went to Stanford, and it was really very interesting because at Stanford I helped to organize, in fact it was Al Lowenstein and I who did it together, we organized the first political meeting they had on that campus in years, or maybe decades.[36] Around, remember when there was the bombing in the Birmingham Church in 1963. And we organized a protest meeting and relayed funds, and I made the financial pitch for money. We raised a couple of hundred dollars, in fact maybe even more, close to a thousand. And there was the beginning of a politicization. And Lowenstein, whom I didn't know very well, he was with the law school, he already had a gang of followers. But there was nothing yet. By the time I went back, when I was with this think tank in 1969, then of course it was absolutely at its peak.

**TG:** *I don't have any more specific questions, but what else is it I ought to be thinking about?*

**IH:** Well, I think if your book is to have value beyond a memoir, and of course a memoir has value, try to ask these really very difficult questions. There's no way of answering them precisely, [but] how much of what went wrong was avoidable? How much of it was due to being swept up by circumstances? See, we were caught, . . . if you want, try to imagine . . . the traditional difficulties of social democrats or Mensheviks. I've often thought about Martov's[37] difficulties in the Russian Revolution. I don't know to what extent you're familiar with this?

**TG:** *A little, I mean I've read about it but. . . .*

**IH:** Yes, well, Martov was really prophetic in what he said. He advocated the creation of an all-Socialist government rather than an exclusively Bolshevik one, of a coalition democracy. But it's also clear to me that, [given] the tremendous emotional sweep of the revolution, . . . it was a hopeless adventure. It's that kind of question that you are trying to struggle with.

**TG:** *I have been. I mean it's very difficult.*

**IH:** Exactly the questions that can't be answered are always the ones that you want to study. Of course, the questions that can be answered are not interesting, in a way. Well, say an exclusionary thing, you might answer. But whether the mistakes are somehow, whether the difficulties or mistakes are ingrained in the situation in a future generation if there is one, I don't know that there has to be one, if there is one which goes through a similar experience, repeatedly.

**TG:** *I cannot shake the sense that that a trained historian would be raising a lot of eyebrows at this point because you're not supposed to ask these questions.*

**IH:** The hell with that.

**TG:** *The hell with that. I cannot shake the feeling—well two feelings—that point in different directions. One is that the little, the microscopic problems of tone and voice and quickness to anger and so on are not central. In other words if you had been sweeter. . . .*

**IH:** No, it would not have made much difference. It might have made for better relations between you and me, but it wouldn't have made for better relations between SDS and me.

**TG:** *Right. That is correct. You know Michael Harrington, in his reflections on his mistakes at Port Huron, I think is basically right that there were tensions there that were exacerbated and yet down the pike you could see the collision course.*

**IH:** Let me add one small point. I think by then people like Harrington and myself really had a social democratic politics but we didn't yet have a social democratic style.

**TG:** *At what point?*

**IH:** In the middle sixties. Maybe into the sixties, our style still had elements of the Trotskyist background, of Shachtman's brilliant polemical style. It was brilliant, it was also very [divisive], it worked only in a certain special environment.

**TG:** *That's a good point.*

**IH:** . . . The whole Shachtman group went through quite a remarkable transition, namely, it was moving toward a social democratic position, from say 1941 forward, but it was doing so in an inalienable vocabulary, it was doing so still holding on to remnants of the postwar style.

**TG:** *Because of being unwilling to acknowledge . . . ?*

**IH:** I don't know if you know the economist David Gordon?[38]

**TG:** *I don't know him personally, but I read some of his stuff.*

**IH:** He's very bright. I've asked him any number of times, three or four times anyway, to write for *Dissent*. And what he writes seems to me entirely in harmony or largely in harmony with what he says, there's no very great difference. And he can't bring himself to associate himself with what he regards as a social democratic publication. Okay, that's his business. But the interesting thing about this is not that he doesn't write for us, but that it's the word [Socialism]. And I don't condemn him for it because I went through something like it, I understand it. But I think at a certain point you've got to be willing to say, well the hell with that. Because there really aren't any very great differences. I mean life is hard enough.

**TG:** *Yeah. I mean a lot of these things are a residual, absolutely. But the other side of my argument [is that I was historically aware of the dangers, which might have evaded the slide] toward inevitability. Generation, experience, politics. You know I was very well read for my crowd on this. I mean I read about thirties sectarianism, I read Orwell, I had read a lot of things. And my attitude was, that's never going to happen to us. We're not going to fall into that shit. But it's easy to make the move from that, relatively easy, to say that the way not to get into these terrible attractions to Stalinism and so on is to avoid the arguments altogether, to try to bracket them off and focus on what was manageable and sort of be agnostic in a principled way about, it's a strange position but you could see why it was an attempt to avoid this, I read [American historian] Daniel Aaron's history,* Writers and the Left, *I knew about all that.*[39]

**IH:** In some ways you [at SDS] were placed, I'm not trying to exonerate SDS because I think you all made a lot of terrible mistakes, but in some ways you were placed in an impossible position. Because history put too many burdens on you.

**TG:** *We shouldn't have been a Left, we were a bunch of Pishers.*[40] *And at some level we knew that.*

**IH:** Okay, a bunch of Pishers. But turn it around and see from where I sat. I felt that your kids were smarter, not smarter, but luckier and more effective than our kids. Tom Kahn is quite as smart as I, maybe smarter. And yet Tom Hayden had the opportunity to be the head of a mass movement and Kahn did not, and this did something not only to, but also for Hayden. It corrupted him in some ways, but it also enabled him to grow, develop.

**TG:** *Well, Tom Kahn, I think, had his moment in a mass movement. I mean of course he couldn't quite pull it off. I interviewed him about a month ago. Interesting, part of how he understands his venom at the time of Port Huron is that, he said that actually what upset him more than the Communist stuff was the attack on the liberal-labor establishment. And he says that what had been going on is that he had actually been tempted by that position.*

**IH:** Oh, sure.

**TG:** *In his civil rights phase. And now he's at the moment of retreat from it, so he's especially sensitive.*

**IH:** When I first heard of Tom Kahn he was attacking Bayard Rustin. And he was taking a very intransigent position.

**TG:** *Go to jail and let them throw away the key and don't get bail.*

**IH:** Yes, exactly.

**TG:** *The other side of it, well this is my hunch more than anything else, is that the war drove us nuts.*

**IH:** Yes. It drove the whole country nuts.

**TG:** *But I was already coming out in things I'm saying and people were saying to me in, even late 1963 and 1964, early 1965, I mean talk about moral passion, it was war, it gets to be an obsession.*

**IH:** That's very important, Todd.

**TG:** *Not to stand for this, it cannot be permitted to go on.*

**IH:** I remember those years as the years in which I felt the greatest pressure upon my life. Even 1938-39, the Hitler Stalin pact, well for one thing I was a kid, I was in my late teens. And for another, . . . we had a sense of fatality. We believed the world was going to blow up and we were right in a way, but not in the way we thought. And there was nothing you could do, it was the final great crisis of capitalism. And we yielded to it. There was no expectation of being able to do anything about it. Whereas there was an inexorability to Hitler and Stalin. Whereas in the late sixties . . . I think I went a bit crazy too in my own way. See, when you asked me about the savagery, that was part of it too. There was a sense that things could be done if they were done right. I don't know that what I proposed was always right, but I felt it to be that way. And everyone felt that the decisions being made were urgent. It's not like what position DSA should take now on something or other.

**TG:** *So that if your point of view about the war failed, by God we could actually affect the course of events.*

**IH:** Exactly. Maybe that is a delusion, but it's what we felt.

**TG:** *It's certainly what we felt and I don't think it was entirely delusionary.*

**IH:** Well, you see, I felt the same.

**TG:** *The sense of despair and, at the same time, a sense of getting the position right were fused.*

**IH:** Well, the big dispute in SANE, for example, [was] on whether to come out for unconditional withdrawal. Toward the end of the war I did favor that, but earlier I was against because I felt that if you did not say that you could mobilize a larger public against the war, against Johnson. And it's hard to know what was right because this was a tactical estimate. But that's when we met up with the intransigent rectitude. People said, "I don't care if I'm the only one in the whole country, but I say get out immediately because it's an immoral war." And I would say, well yes it is, but if you want to mobilize people who don't entirely agree with you, you know the arguments. And at that point it did seem as if what we said could have a real significant effect. And that's I feel one of the reasons for the desperation.

**TG:** *But it's curious, because underlying the desperation was also a sense that nothing we did mattered.*

**IH:** Did you really feel that way?

**TG:** *Often. Usually. I think that was the dominant mood in the New Left.*

**IH:** Very strange. Curious. I mean you were rocking the country.

**TG:** *I know, but the war was going on and seemingly getting worse.*

**IH:** You got Johnson to decide not to run.

**TG:** *I know. But then we got Nixon.*

**IH:** Well, that was another tragedy, people who refused to vote for Humphrey.

**TG:** *I agree now. But it was impossible to argue to vote for Humphrey, emotionally. I mean now I think that's also an important moment.*

**IH:** Yes, that was a. . . .

**TG:** *I think Humphrey [deserves] a large [share of] blame. I mean I don't feel that it was entirely our part. I mean Humphrey could have had it.*

**IH:** He was no hero, of course. But, you see, it took a long time to convince people on the left that when you vote for somebody in national politics you're not giving them a standard of virtue. You're just saying, we prefer him to the other side, that's all.

**TG:** *That meant lesser evils and nobody wanted to hear that then.*

**IH:** Nobody wanted to hear that then, but that's the way. . . .

**TG:** *That's what politics is. Now the sense of hopelessness, it's curious. I think, if you want to argue psychologically, which I think is irresistible at some moment, that a lot of the revolutionary passion and the rah rah stuff, which you caught as early as 1965, was compensation for the fact of utter helplessness. Specifically with relation to the war. You see even the transference of both virtue and power, on to the North Vietnamese and the Viet Cong was a way of saying, was a way of compensating for this terrible sense that they were getting crushed.*

**IH:** It's sad, especially if you see it as a sequence of mistakes, if you see it in relation to earlier events in the radical movement, that what happened is not just an isolated event.

**TG:** *How do you feel, I'm very eager to see this book of yours. What part does World War I play in your understanding of what happened to the Socialists?*

**IH:** Oh hell, it plays an enormous role, because there again I think that the Debsian SP analysis of the war was essentially right. That it was an imperialist war, etc., etc. But the position of utter intransigent opposition that it took, you see, there must be some parallel in this way. They took a revolutionary position without any expectation, without realizing that they would bring down the weight of the government upon them. They were still naïve Americans who thought, "We have the right to say any goddamn thing we want," you know. They had a revolutionary language without any preparation of being a revolutionary movement. It never occurred to them that if you are going to oppose a war head-on, that you might have to take precautions, to go a little underground, to hide a press or something else. And the government decimated the party. In some sense Socialism never recovered from that. It really destroyed, especially in the Midwest, destroyed most of the locals. And there was a real movement. And in some sense the same thing happened again. . . .

**TG:** *It wasn't the same.*

**IH:** I mean this impulse to big revolutionary talk without expecting consequences and without really being revolutionists. You see, when the CP in the old days and especially in Europe . . . talked this way, they were serious about it, and they were prepared for the results. And Americans are not.

**TG:** *So what you have is apocalyptic imagination without. . . .*

**IH:** You have naïve democratic behavior.

**TG:** *That is a very American combination.*

**IH:** You bet. That's the thing that I wonder, when I say "recur," that's what I wonder about.

**TG:** *Yes. Pushed to a comparable circumstance. That is to say, if the central activity, the central focus, is an insupportable war, is another war for something.*

**IH:** Whatever causes the crisis, yes. If it arouses strong moral passions. See, and I'm sure that for people like my old friend Julius Jacobson, when he sees this he'll look upon this as the ultimate heresy. That I don't even support the SP opposition, which on the left was always looked upon as a glorious element of the past. And maybe in some ways it was. But it also destroyed the movement.

**TG:** *There's still another irony because the strength in America, which is a memory hole etc., comes from having a past. But if the past is a past of error?*

**IH:** It's a past of great dedication, some wonderful people, two tremendous leaders in Debs and Thomas, though both of them made a vast number of mistakes, mistakes which were morally honorable. The paradox of it is, the irony of it is that, tactically speaking, the best model is the Popular Front, in my judgment now, but morally speaking, it's the shabbiest. Now how are you going to explain that in this country?

**TG:** *You explain that by saying that moral rectitude is one thing and politics is another.*

**IH:** Even that isn't quite enough.

**TG:** *Go to church on Sunday and do politics the rest of the week.*

**IH:** But you want some of that moral energy.

**TG:** *Well, you have to have the moral energy without moral exclusivity. That's the trick.*

**IH:** [*big sigh*] As soon as you work it out, I'll be with you.

**TG:** *There's no way of [evading it].*

**IH:** You have to have that awareness, you see. That's why the idea of the tradition is so important. You have to have that awareness. I'm absolutely sure, when my book comes out, I'll be attacked all over the place, from all quarters, by *In These Times,* by all kinds of people. It'll be seen as another index, another sign, of social democratic evasiveness.

**TG:** *Well, but then if the problem is not one's theoretical or moral stance, but of the relation between one's theoretical and moral stance and one's practical work, then this is yet another. . . .*

**IH:** See, the Debsian party was not yet a mass party, but it was a large party. It had . . . in some parts over a hundred thousand members. It had a big class [component], it had real institutions, it was something. But it was not strong enough to be able to withstand the government persecution. And it went headlong in and it took this noble, let's say even correct, heroic, admirable stance, without as far as I can tell having any awareness. The only one that seemed to have any awareness that it would create enormous trouble was Morris Hillquit.[41] And that's because he was a shrewder, less apocalyptic kind. And they marched right into the disaster.

**TG:** *What did they think was going to happen?*

**IH:** Oh, some of them would go to jail. They were ready for that. But that the party would be ripped apart, you see . . . and Jimmy Weinstein argues in his book that the party grew, but it grew in a disastrous way. There was a tremendous change of social opposition.

**TG:** *I understand some people have contested his way of understanding.*

**IH:** Sure. But by and large what happened is that the American basis of the party was destroyed to a large extent. And there was a great influx of immigrants.

**TG:** *Right. And Bolshevization.*

**IH:** Right. [For] whom what was going on was only a mirror image of the revolution [that] was coming.

**TG:** *How long did they think the war was going to last? Did they ever talk about that?*

**IH:** No.

**TG:** *I wonder if that's another point of comparability.*

**IH:** It didn't matter.

**TG:** *It didn't matter. You just did what was right.*

**IH:** That's right. It's a matter of raising the flag. And there's something very attractive about that. It's not just to be dismissed.

## Notes

1. See Joseph Dorman, *Arguing the World: The New York Intellectuals in Their Own Words* (Chicago, University of Chicago Press, 2000).
2. See Todd Gitlin, "Who Will Lead," *Mother Jones* (October 14, 2002). Available at http://www.motherjones.com/commentary/gitlin/2002/10/we_175_01.html, accessed March 2008.
3. Written by Tom Hayden and others, the Port Huron manifesto was a foundational document for the SDS, concentrating on racial issues, nuclear weaponry, and the ideal of participatory democracy.
4. The Economic Research and Action Project (ERAP) was an SDS program to organize unemployed white youths in the inner city. Begun in September 1963, it promoted various community action projects, including rent strikes and activist neighborhood associations.
5. Paul Potter was an SDS activist in Cleveland who became president of the national student organization in 1964.
6. The Narodniks were a Russian nineteenth-century populist progressive group that opposed the czar but were not Marxists. Gitlin is referring to a prerevolutionary phase.
7. PL was movement shorthand for Progressive Labor, a hardline Maoist group.
8. The Moncada Barracks, the site of an armed attack on July 26, 1953 by Cuban revolutionaries led by Fidel Castro, is regarded by historians as the watershed event that culminated in the 1959 Cuban Revolution.
9. Dick Flacks was an SDS member who helped write the Port Huron manifesto.
10. Nat Hentoff was a *Village Voice* writer and jazz critic.
11. Zbigniew Brzezinski is a Polish expatriate and national security hawk who served as National Security Advisor under President Jimmy Carter.
12. William Lloyd Garrison was a staunch abolitionist and editor of the *Liberator.*
13. Elinor Langer is a journalist whose article, "Notes on Next Time" appeared in *Working Papers for a New Society,* Fall 1973.
14. Rennie Davis was an SDS leader, one of the Chicago 7, who around 1972 signed up to work with an Indian Guru called Maharaj Ji and never returned to politics.
15. David Dellinger was a New Leftist activist who was arrested in 1968 as one of the Chicago Seven.
16. A. J. Muste was a pacifist, anarchist, and supporter of Dorothy Day. He was on the *Dissent* board but left over philosophical differences.
17. David Horowitz, formerly a prominent writer for New left publications in the 1960s, is a vocal American neoconservative. He is founder of the right-wing activist group, Students for Academic Freedom.

18. Peter Collier, a close associate of David Horowitz, is a former New Left writer and (along with Horowitz) former co-editor of *Ramparts*. He and Horowitz have also co-organized a series of conferences ("Second Thoughts") for ex-leftists who have turned rightward.
19. Charles Krauthammer is a syndicated, Pulitzer Prize-winning columnist and political commentator. He is a frequent contributor to *Weekly Standard* and *The New Republic* and is usually associated with neoconservative positions.
20. Ron Radosh is a *Dissent* editorial board member who moved to the right.
21. Jerry Rubin was an American radical social activist during the 1960s and 1970s. His best-known book is *Do It!: Scenarios of the Revolution*, which was introduced by Black Panther Eldridge Cleaver.
22. Martin Peretz became publisher of *The New Republic* in 1974 when he purchased the magazine. He sold his ownership rights between 2002 and 2007, but he remains Editor-in-Chief. Under Peretz, the magazine has generally adopted liberal or neoliberal positions on domestic issues and taken hawkish and strong pro-Israel stances on foreign affairs.
23. Frantz Fanon, a black intellectual from Martinique, was an influential anticolonialist and political revolutionary during the 1950s and 1960s. In *The Wretched of the Earth* (1961), Fanon analyzed how racist cultures oppress black men.
24. James Weinstein was an American historian and journalist. A lifelong Socialist, he was also the founder and publisher of *In These Times*. Although Weinstein supported the 1948 campaign of Henry Wallace and was sympathetic to Stalinism, he repudiated his "third-party" strategy by the mid-1950s and thereafter urged the American Left to work within and influence the Democratic Party.
25. The Spartacists, or Spartacist League, is the popular name for The International Communist League (Fourth Internationalist), a U.S.-based Trotskyist international organization. The group originated as a faction within the Socialist Workers Party, from which it was expelled in 1964. It is known for aggressively polemicizing against both capitalist parties and other Marxist-Leninist groups.
26. Judy Clark was a Weatherman activist who helped to hijack a Brinks truck in a 1981 incident in which a guard and two police officers were killed.
27. Tom Nairn is a Scottish Socialist theoretician.
28. Joseph A. Schumpeter was an Austrian-born economist who taught at Harvard University from the 1930s to the 1950s. In works such as *Theory of Economic Development* (1911) and *Capitalism, Socialism, and Democracy* (1942), he argued that falling profits and fierce competition spur entrepreneurs to devise financial innovations that lead to economic growth.
29. George Kateb is a liberal political theorist.
30. Ray Brown was a radical economist who shaped SDS labor policy in the early 1960s. In an essay published by SDS in 1964, he predicted that massive unemployment would soon send the U.S. into a depression. His forecast of an economic crisis was incorrect, but it spurred SDS leaders to launch numerous experimental organizing projects such as ERAP to fight the "war on poverty."
31. Stanley Aronowitz is a sociologist, labor activist, and environmentalist.
32. Jeremy Larner is a writer and occasional *Dissent* contributor, best known for the screenplay of *The Candidate* (1972).
33. A member of the American Communist Party during the 1940s and 1950s, Howard Fast was a popular fiction writer and the author of such novels as *Freedom Road*

(1944). When Nikita Khrushchev delivered his famous "Secret Speech" in March 1956 that exposed the crimes of Joseph Stalin, Fast resigned from the Party.

34. Frank Manuel was an historian of European intellectuals and colleague of Howe's at Brandeis.
35. Victoria Bonnell is a professor of sociology at University of California, Berkeley. When Gitlin met her in 1961, she was a peace activist student at Brandeis.
36. Allard Lowenstein was a lawyer who challenged President Lyndon Johnson and was elected to one term in Congress.
37. Julius Martov was a leader of the Mensheviks who attempted, but ultimately failed, to mediate with the Bolsheviks.
38. A leading left-wing economist and a fierce critic of corporate bureaucracy, David Gordon devoted his main attantion to economic public policy, specializing in such areas as discrimination in labor markets and the role of social institutions in long-term investment and growth. He taught at the New School for Social Research.
39. Daniel Aaron is an American historian best known for his pioneering study, *Writers on the Left: Episodes in American Literary Communism* (1961).
40. "Pishers" is Yiddish for naïve youth.
41. Morris Hillquit was a Socialist and labor lawyer in the early twentieth century.

# Chapter 10

**Neil Jumonville, "Socialism, Communism, and the New York Intellectuals," 6 June 1985.**

## Introduction

This unpublished interview was conducted by Neil Jumonville while he was still a graduate student gathering material for his dissertation, which would become his first book, *Critical Crossings: The New York Intellectuals in Postwar America* (1991). Jumonville had taken an indirect route toward his academic career, working a series of manual jobs and traveling around the U.S. and Europe before college. Later he was an activist with Ralph Nader's Oregon Public Interest Research Group and an intern for *The Nation* before attending graduate school. In 1987, he received his Ph.D. from Harvard's History of American Civilization program. Jumonville has gone on to a productive academic career marked by a strong interest in Socialism, liberalism, and the public intellectual tradition. He currently chairs the history department at Florida State University in Gainesville. In 2007, he co-edited, with Kevin Mattson, *Liberalism for a New Century* and also published *The New York Intellectuals Reader*, featuring cultural and political selections from Howe, Daniel Bell, Irving Kristol, Dwight Macdonald, and many others.

*Critical Crossings* argues that the group of left-wing New York Intellectuals affiliated with *Partisan Review* divided into two camps: the affirmers, who believed in the basic goodness of American society—and who formed themselves into the neoconservatives by the mid-1970s—and the *Dissenters*, who stayed on the liberal-Left, maintained a vision of social equality, and considered oppositional criticism essential to the public intellectual. With the affirmers increasingly dominant during the Reagan years, Howe makes just a cameo appearance in Jumonville's study. Instead, the central presence is Daniel Bell, who first aligned himself with neoconservatives yet whose intellectual and temperamental bias toward complexity and contradiction soon led him toward a more independent route. Jumonville's emphasis here is not surprising given both that he was a Ph.D. student of Bell's at Harvard University and that Bell was a chief source for the book. The study covers the early development of the elder generation of neoconservatives before their positions had hardened. Still, the book's orientation matches the spirit of a time just passed—the cultural turn rightward since the early 1970s—when intellectuals became increasingly conservative and struggled to forge new identities. Jumonville also stresses the role of Sidney Hook, arguably the senior member within the elder generation of New York Intellectuals, whose anti-Communism induced him to shift increasingly rightward. Indeed, although a Socialist on numerous domestic issues throughout his career, Hook was also a progenitor of neoconservatism.

Hook is a focal point of Jumonville's interview with Irving Howe, who clashed with Hook on issues ranging from the economic redistribution of wealth to the desirability of democratic Socialism. Howe discounts Hook, claiming that "Hook's moral outrage about oppressed people left him." This reflects Howe's anger toward the complacency of the affluent, especially affluent Left intellectuals within his reference group who had recently emerged from poverty. Howe's dismissal of Hook's conservatized liberalism also reflects Howe's long-standing critique of American smugness about the achievements of U.S. society, a stance most notably associated with his controversial 1954 essay in *Partisan Review*, "This Age of Conformity." Neither in the 1950s nor in later decades did Howe ever want to forget the economically marginalized and desperate.

This interview also discusses the evolution of *Dissent*, which in the 1950s struggled to make clear both its anti-Communism and its continuing support for social democracy. By the 1980s, the *Dissent* group felt free to develop a specific program for social democracy—though, admittedly, it consisted largely of policies that had very little chance of actually being implemented. This collection's *New York Times* interview between Howe and Michael Harrington gives a specific taste of such policies. By contrast, in this interview Howe discusses some of the rocks and shoals of his life's political journey. He discusses the difficulty of juggling his leftist orientation and strong anti-Communism without being pulled to the right, as happened with *Commentary* and *Partisan Review* (and both Bell and Hook, among others). In a modern America that favors mass culture, Howe struggled to maintain his radical ideas together with his respect for nuanced complexity, aims not easily reconcilable.

Howe also ponders here a common paradox faced by the left-wing New York Intellectuals, namely a split between championing elite culture and speaking for the common people. He speculates: "There was perhaps an aspect of snobbism in [the New York Intellectuals'] view of high art, but not necessarily a conservatism or elitism." Indeed, literature with an explicit political agenda risks becoming pandering or condescending. The mature Irving Howe grew beyond the rigidities and limitations of his youthful Trostskyism, resisting such ideology and its tendency to vulgarization. He also remained aware of the reflexive tendency to react against the excessive politicizing of art and adopt a purist, holier-than-thou aesthetics—a danger to which, he argues here, *Partisan Review* succumbed: "*Partisan Review* was driven into an elitist stance by the popular culture of the Communists—such as Howard Fast."[1]

Howe's choice of example had a personal element. He had debated Fast at Brandeis in the late 1950s, not long after the Soviet invasion of Hungary and the revelations of Stalin's crimes by Khrushchev. He made the famous accusation that Fast "had blood on his hands," given his long-standing defense of Stalinism and USSR postwar geopolitical policy. It was no accident that Howe chose Fast, three decades later, as his example of the Communist preference for a kind of kitschy mass culture from which many of the *Partisan Review* writers (such as Howe himself) recoiled.

*Partisan Review* had modernist—and highbrow—predilections from the very first issue, even when it was closely affiliated with the Communist Party. At first it tried to balance, or even synthesize, a modernist and proletarian aesthetic; when it was reconstituted as an independent radical quarterly in 1937, it fully embraced the modernist experiment. Howe himself loved modernism and "high" art and detested mass culture. It is seldom noted, however, that the novels in which Howe steeped himself, from Dickens to Hardy, from Sherwood Anderson to Faulkner, had complex and sympathetic portrayals of working-class characters.

## The Interview

*The following is a collection of reconstructed notes and commentaries from Jumonville's interview with Irving Howe. In August 2005, Jumonville appended italicized reflections for this book that recall Howe in his New York milieu and clarify Howe's evolving attitudes toward* Partisan Review *and* Dissent.

*I first met Irving Howe in the spring of 1985 when he was at Harvard doing the William E. Massey, Sr., Lectures in the History of American Civilization (the program in which I did my Ph.D.), a set of talks which was later published as* The American Newness: Culture and Politics in the Age of Emerson *(1986). When I interviewed him in New York a few months later, I was in the process of interviewing many members of the New York Intellectuals, the group to which he belonged and that revolved around* Partisan Review, Commentary, politics, Dissent, *the* Public Interest, *and similar magazines.*

*We arranged to meet on a street corner on the Upper East Side near where he lived. When he first appeared he looked younger than I recalled and was dressed casually. He showed me to his favorite coffee shop, the Concord on 86th and Madison. I was already part of the way into writing my doctoral dissertation on this group, and thus I came bearing some specific questions I wanted to ask him about both the New York Intellectuals and himself.*

*It was after lunch, so neither of us ordered anything substantial. Howe asked for cottage cheese, and then as we began to talk, he took out the pepper shaker and shook black speckles across the white curds. Although I'd lived in the city from 1978 to 1981, this was a first for me, and I thought the incident was charming. (It's interesting that in the midst of trading big ideas, small matters will still penetrate and remain in the memory longer than they should.) People later told me that peppering cottage cheese is not unusual in New York.*

*I didn't tape record this interview, but I made some notes during and after and got everything down that I wanted to. When the interview was done I returned to Cambridge and typed it up and mailed it to him (as I sent all interviewees their transcript) to correct, mark up, clarify, and then mail it back to me.*

*I began by asking Howe about the group's orientation to mass culture, which, on the whole, had been hostile. This is the issue that framed chapter four of my book* Critical Crossings *(1991).* Had the New York group's defense of high art against mass art from the 1930s through the 1950s, I asked, showed an element of elitism and conservatism? Howe said no, there was perhaps an aspect of snobbism in their view of high art, but not necessarily a conservatism or elitism. He said that *Partisan Review* was driven into an elitist stance by the popular culture of the Communists—such as Howard Fast.

*But it is hard to believe that the group's anti-Communism and hostility to mass culture were connected, except in the late 1930s. It is apparent from essays in* Partisan Review *in the 1930s and 1940s that the New York Intellectuals pulled away from proletarian literature at least as much because of the low-culture tastes of workers as because of proletarian Communist politics. Howe and others were thinkers and cultural critics, and they quickly decided that the mass culture of proletarians was contemptible. Workers, in the Socialist dream, were to develop into noble beings, and when the cultural choices of laborers contradicted that hope then the New York group became disillusioned with them.*

I talked with Howe about the evolution of his politics in the decades after World War II, and about the split in the New York group between what I have referred to in *Critical Crossings* as the "affirmers" and "dissenters," and his leadership of the latter circle. He said that in the Cold War the distinction between left and right anti-Communism became harder to maintain.

*By that comment Howe meant that the New York group's common dedication to anti-Communism, especially after World War II, caused a centripetal force that sometimes brought Left and Right to similar positions—partly because the United States was the primary bulwark against the Communist threat. Even a leftist such as Howe, then, might seem to some observers to be an architect of the country's postwar anti-Communist values. In an exchange between Howe and the sociologist C. Wright Mills in* Dissent *in 1959, for example, Mills wrote, "To dissent is lovely. But Irving, as regards foreign policy, from what, tell me, do you dissent?" Mills's suggestion was wrong, because Howe complained loudly about American actions at home and abroad. But as he said in the interview, in the Cold War the distinction between left and right anti-Communism became harder to maintain.*

Asked why Harold Rosenberg and Paul Goodman[2] appeared rarely if ever in *Partisan Review*, Howe replied that Rosenberg and Goodman were too far to the left. I asked why in that case he wasn't left out, too. Howe replied that he was too young to be resented. He also said that Rosenberg was too intellectually fierce, which Howe meant as a compliment.

I asked him about his view of Whittaker Chambers, especially since Howe's review of *Witness* seemed respectful and he called the book Dostoevskian. He pointed out that *Witness* was a book written by a Dostoevskian character rather than by someone like Dostoevsky himself, an important distinction and hardly as complimentary.

*We talked about the literature of ex-Communist repentance (the chapter of my dissertation that became chapter three of* Critical Crossings*), of which* Witness *was only a prominent example in a large stack of books and articles that emerged in the 1940s and 1950s. It seemed to me that some members of the New York Intellectuals disparaged these writings more than others did, mostly because they thought the veiled intention of them was to enforce political and intellectual conformity on the nation.* I proposed that Hook and perhaps Howe welcomed the confessional literature more than people such as Harold Rosenberg and [sociologist and *Dissent* contributor] Murray Hausknecht. Howe didn't think there was much difference between Rosenberg's response to the literature of ex-Communist repentance and his own response. *In a later interview, Hausknecht agreed with Howe that there likely was no difference between their responses. But Hausknecht did think there was a significant difference between Hook and his own outlook on that literature, and I agree with that.*

Asked what kept the New York Intellectuals together, Howe said that it wasn't so much fraternity but common defensiveness. *It's true that there was much posturing and many genuine arguments on principle, as was natural between people who took ideas seriously. Howe is probably correct that though they fought with each other, they felt they belonged to a common defense league against Communism, absolutism, anti-Semitism, and middlebrow attacks.*

Howe agreed with my suggestion that part of the argument surrounding the Waldorf Conference was the issue of intellectual responsibility: that Communist and fellow-traveling "intellectuals" were not fulfilling the New York group's definition of an intellectual—to think for oneself instead of allowing a party to dictate opinions—a definition that was vital to get right during a time when their definition of the proper intellectual role was in transition (the topic of the "Our Country and Our Culture" symposium in *Partisan Review* in the early 1950s, for example). Howe agreed that the same issue of the proper intellectual function was involved in the New York group's tensions with the New Left. While Todd Gitlin and others were incipient intellectuals, he felt that New Leftists on the whole were anti-intellectual and thus were transgressing the proper intellectual role—as had the sponsors of the Waldorf Conference in a different manner decades earlier. He acknowledged that both struggles were connected by the New York group's common defense of intellectual integrity. Howe said that there was probably some false pride on the part of the New York group in these two struggles—with the Waldorf sponsors and the New Left: that we (the New York Intellectuals) alone stand for truth and that everyone else is tainted by the sociology of knowledge. He suggested that the New York group was forced back into a native American stance in their relation to the Waldorf sponsors and the New Left. That is, they acted like the American independent individual who goes his own way intellectually. The New York group, he said, invoked that tradition perhaps more than they had a right to do: the whole tradition of rectitude and independence. On a related point, Howe noted that even political intellectuals should maintain some distance from their movements.

I was very interested in Sidney Hook, and I proposed that Hook's pragmatism influenced the New York group's Socialism in the 1940s, leading it to be more pragmatic, realistic, mainstream, coalitional, and less ideological and factionalized. Howe disagreed and was a bit irritated because he thought I overestimated Hook's influence. Paring down the scope of Hook's effect, he said that Hook's authority was as the New York group's best anti-Stalinist voice. The group was proud to have Hook deal with that controversy. Members respected him for that, but disagreements with Hook grew. Howe said that both Hook and he were (at the time of the interview) social democrats, but that Hook's moral outrage about oppressed people left him. Still, Howe said that Hook had guts in the 1930s when he fought the Stalinists alone. Hook's attempt to fuse Marx and Dewey was brilliant, Howe said; he was not orthodox.

*Howe and Hook had a rocky relationship, partly because the younger and more leftist Irving regularly lobbed criticisms at Sidney for reaching a greater peace with American society than Howe was willing to make. In return, Hook answered sharply, but he was willing to be patient with this particular firebrand. Hook commented once that, even though Howe denounced his positions, he followed Hook's own political parabola at a remove of ten years. There was a great deal of truth in Hook's observation, especially in the two decades following the beginning of World War II, although in the end Hook gravitated farther to the right (ending up at the Hoover Institute) than Howe was willing to accompany him. Howe remained a committed and prolific democratic Socialist until the end.*

When we talked about *Dissent*, Howe said it was two different magazines in the 1950s and the 1980s. In the 1950s, he pointed out, *Dissent* was involved in Socialist reevaluation, anti-McCarthyism, and civil liberties questions. In the 1980s it addressed theory and practice.

*Later, when I sent him a transcript of the interview, he wrote next to the preceding text, "not clear," which I admit was the case. What I should also have written was that in the 1970s and 1980s* Dissent *published many articles on what democratic Socialism would look like concretely were it to come into power in the United States. What would the public sector look like? What would be done with taxes? To what extent would the market still operate in a Socialist economy? In the 1950s, Dissenters knew that to be taken seriously in America they would have to distinguish themselves from the undemocratic global left. The New York Intellectuals had been doing this, of course, since the late 1930s, but their writings had only been aimed at the Stalinist enemy.* Dissent *first had to prove that they loved America and were American democratic leftists. With that done, in succeeding decades they increasingly were able to offer their concrete vision of a democratic Socialist society that would be authentically American. That's what Howe meant to say about the difference between the magazine in the 1950s and the 1980s, and it is clear when one goes back and reads through the essays in those decades.*

When I talked about the New York Intellectuals, Howe objected to making the group too homogeneous. (This was a lament of all of the members I spoke with.) He said that Allen Tate had felt the same way about his identification with the New Critics, many of whom he disagreed with. Tate, he explained, once wrote in the *Kenyon Review* that to a Mongolian I'm sure I look the same as Babe Ruth (although Howe said Tate was "cadaverously" thin). Howe felt the heterogeneity of the New York group was usually overlooked.

*But Howe and other members of the New York Intellectuals frequently denied they belonged to the group. At least half of those whom I interviewed felt uncomfortable with the perception that they belonged, and it seemed to me it was because it threatened their unique identity. Professionally and intellectually, they wanted to be recognized for their own work and didn't want it to be overshadowed by the larger reputation of the circle. They felt they had nothing to gain by others viewing their individual work as part of the common preoccupation of a group of people who grew up together.*

I was also puzzled by the lack of a personal and political relationship between Howe and Alfred Kazin, as I believed that their basic political outlooks were fairly close. Why hadn't Kazin written for Howe's *Dissent*? Howe said that he and Kazin had a personality conflict and they never got along very well, despite being members of the same generation of the New York group and part of the small number of the crowd who remained left of center politically. Kazin, he admitted, would have thought Howe was too vulgarly political, or perhaps too simply and narrowly political and not involved enough in literary or cultural issues—especially because of the overtly political orientation Howe had chosen to impose on *Dissent*. That is why Kazin didn't write for the magazine. For his part, Howe agreed with the assessment that Kazin had of himself, that Kazin considered himself primarily a writer and not a political person. Thus Kazin didn't fit into the political magazine.

## Notes

1. Like Howe, the *Partisan Review* can be seen to simultaneously embody, and be conflicted by, a European centered regard for high art; a cosmopolitan, international outlook; and an American synthesis. In *The Rise of the New York Intellectuals:* Partisan Review *and Its Circle, 1934-1945* (Madison: University of Wisconsin Press, 1986), Terry Cooney describes how *Partisan Review*'s "cosmopolitan perspective stood opposed to parochialism, whether regional, national, or ethnic" (57). Although American society, particularly the interior parts of the country, is often seen as provincial, with its seas of immigrants finding new opportunities and achieving milestones in education, America can also be seen as a great cosmopolitan experiment. Cooney explains that, "especially for the children of immigrants, an open society held far more promise than one with firmly established boundaries. Belief in the positive possibilities of historical change, in values that were shaped by time and place, and in the fluid power of untrammeled thought allowed the *Partisan Review* intellectuals not only to nourish hope for mankind in general, but also to see in an evolving American culture a positive future for people like themselves" (165).
2. Harold Rosenberg and Paul Goodman were iconoclastic writers who appeared often in *Dissent*'s pages. Rosenberg coined the term "action painting"; Goodman wrote about psychology and urban issues.

# Chapter 11

## Susanne Klingenstein, "Thoughts on Jewish Intellectual Life and the American Academy," 12 December 1988.

### Introduction[1]

Susanne Klingenstein came to America from Germany in the fall of 1987 to do graduate work in American studies at Harvard University. Observing that in contrast to most European countries, where the academic teaching of the national literatures had been and continued to be the domain of a fairly homogenous group of native-born (usually male) scholars, the faculty in America teaching the national literature also included large numbers of Jews whose parents or grandparents had been immigrants. She wondered whether the Jewish literary scholars adapted entirely to the American academic environment shaped by white, Anglo-Saxon Protestants and moved into their precursors' critical mold. Conversely, she wondered whether Jewish literary scholars actually maintained Jewish points of view, honed either by particular social experiences or by exposure to the rich spiritual and intellectual tradition of the European Jews, and brought that point of view to bear on their interpretation of English and American literature. Did America shape the Jews or did Jewish literary scholars reshape our understanding of American literature?

In 1985, Irving Howe went up to Harvard to present his reading of nineteenth-century American literature in the Massey lectures, which were published a year later under the title *The American Newness: Culture and Politics in the Age of Emerson*. By that time, Howe was a professor at the Graduate Center of the City University of New York. But to go up to Harvard to present a series of lectures on the very subject that was at the heart of Harvard's self-definition was an act of defiance, or perhaps of chutzpah, even if Harvard had just hired a fluent Yiddish speaker to teach American literature from the Puritans to the Romantics.[2]

This was the context for Klingenstein's interview. She came to see Howe in his apartment on New York's Upper East Side, in a building featuring a marble lobby and doorman, around the corner from the Metropolitan Museum of Art. The neighborhood was a far cry from the world of Howe's fathers. Klingenstein's key interest was to draw Howe out on the issue of Jewish literary scholars in American academe, the social difficulty of their integration, the potential newness of their work, and the mediating role of Brandeis University, where Howe himself had taught. Klingenstein, as yet unschooled in the niceties of American confrontation-avoidance, was forthright, and Howe seems taken by surprise. The sardonic undercurrent in his answers, however, also reflects his dislike of personal questions.

Howe considered everything "personal" immaterial to his work as a "public" intellectual. He shared with European intellectuals, especially British intellectuals such as Orwell, a certain reserve. Private matters were irrelevant to "serious," "proper" criticism. In his autobiography, *A Margin of Hope*, the reader never learns, for instance, that Howe had four wives. Howe never refers to his first wife, Anne Bader, at all, and only the fourth wife is mentioned by name. Some critics argue that Howe's insistence on foregrounding his public self goes beyond an understandable desire for privacy and verges on an obsessive secrecy.

Nevertheless, in this previously unpublished interview Howe is reasonably forthcoming when asked about his personal history. He explains his concept of secular Jewishness as reflecting a person's ethnic history: "My parents were neither religious nor antireligious. They simply were part of a whole tradition or national community." When the question of Israel comes up, Howe is touchy. The very young Howe, who adored the universalism of Socialism, would have been extremely impatient with any Jewish claims to a national homeland. By 1988, the old Socialist hostility for Zionist ideas survived only as a reflex. As an American Jew, Howe now saw that he needed in some way to relate to the state of Israel, but he linked this to a left-wing concern for the underdog, in this case the Palestinians. Specifically, he saw the issue as involving Israel's legitimacy; its treatment of the Palestinians, he claims, "involves the very future of the Jews [and] what kind of people the Jews are going to be."

That the issue of Israel came up at all was due to an explosive conference in San Francisco, entitled "The Writer in the Jewish Community: An Israeli-North American Dialogue," that both Howe and Klingenstein had attended a month before the interview.[3] Under the auspices of the National Foundation for Jewish Culture, thirty American Jewish and Israeli writers (the latter group included the Arab-Israeli writer Anton Shammas) convened, mainly on the campus of the University of California at Berkeley, to discuss their relation to each other and to the Jewish community. Howe had given a paper at one of the plenary sessions that led to a hostile exchange between him and Yiddish literary scholar Ruth

Wisse. Novelist Cynthia Ozick clashed with Israeli dove Amos Elon and Shammas. The debates were heated and split along political lines. Jewish conservatives were supportive of Israel; Jewish liberals were critical of Israel and supportive of the Palestinians, whom they regarded as a test case for Israel's moral standards.

Howe's own Jewishness was a form of *Yiddishkeit*[4] whose roots he had traced in his seminal book *World of Our Fathers* (1976). As he grew older, Howe felt very strongly that he had seen the passing of a mode of thought (Socialism) and a way of life (Yiddish secularism). He softened toward the Jews as he increased his distance from the kind of dogmatism he had displayed in his younger days. This emerges sideways in his impatience with the scholarly work of Alan Wald, who is critical of the liberal anti-Communism of ex-Trotskyist New York Intellectuals, a group that came to include both Lionel Trilling and Howe. In the interview he is impatient with the dogmatic radical Left point of view: "Wald puts everything into a very narrow perspective. The perspective of Trotskyism and his own particular brand of politics, and it tilts everything in that direction."[5] And Howe is rather accepting of Lionel Trilling, with whom Howe's relationship had been uneasy before Trilling's death in 1975. He argues that Trilling's liberalism "became less combative, less assertive, more modulated, more complicated, more questioning belief." But as always in the aging Howe, there is ambivalence. Self-modulation and self-questioning are admirable, but in excess (as in the case of Trilling), they lead to timidity or even political paralysis. Howe struggles here to balance his desire to assume a firm stance with his aversion to brittle ideology.

His consideration of American values was subject to some change, most noticeably in his attitudes toward Emerson. Like many of the New York Intellectuals who revered European culture, Howe had looked down on Emerson as an example of shallow American individualism and bourgeois accommodation to the rapacious status quo. This European outlook also fit Howe's identity as a Trotskyist, and later, Socialist. Alan Wolfe once said, "Howe strikes me, as he occasionally strikes himself, as a European intellectual cast by historical fate onto the shores of an inhospitable land."[6] In John Rodden's interviews with Howe's *Dissent* colleagues, they often observed that Howe was the last of the nineteenth-century European intellectuals, which may also suggest why he felt such an affinity to the revered Leo Tolstoy. Howe was ultimately a nineteenth-century idealist whose passions found their precursors in both Tolstoy and Chernyshevsky[7] (hence Howe's enduring admiration for Lenin's 1902 pamphlet *What is to Be Done?*).

By the time of this interview on December 2, 1988, however, Howe had grown to admire much about America, including the hinterlands of New York City beyond the Hudson River. Emerson, certainly, had undergone a revaluation by academic critics, foremost by Sacvan Bercovitch who had grown up poor and on the Left in Montreal. Howe, too, began to consider Emerson in an American tradition of dissent that pits the individual seeking renewal and redemption against the entrenched interests of an established society grown stodgy in its material comforts. This tradition, Howe declares in the interview, "is the fundamental basis for the creation of what we call an adversary culture, a culture which is in opposition to the wrongs of society." In his Harvard lectures he had already made clear that he no longer saw Emerson and his more extreme disciple Henry David Thoreau as negative examples of American individualism. In the Klingenstein interview he even contradicts his stance against "moral rectitude" that was so evident in his interview with Todd Gitlin. It is possible that his growing distaste for moralistic, ideological elements in his former self emerges in his very sharp critique of another younger intellectual: Tom Hayden. Yet Howe declares, "I see the value of the Emersonian-Thoreauvian figure of moral rectitude who stands firmly on his own."[8] Indeed, although the figure of moral rectitude can develop into a dogmatic thinker, the Transcendentalists' emphasis on the immediacy of experience and on perpetual renewal—the "American Newness" of Howe's title—ought to keep the mind supple while encouraging the dissenter to stand against the crowd.

As his mature rereading of American literary history showed, Howe's growth, especially his increasing capacity for tolerance and patience, was genuine. He continued to believe in the necessity of individualism in public expression, even as he favored concerted social action and an economic system that privileged equality over individual freedom.

Klingenstein, a European cultural conservative, and Howe find common ground in a critique of an academia that mass produces scholars. Although universities appear to allow free discourse and argument, they do so only within narrow parameters.[9] Howe had always refused to define himself by his standing in academe and continued to consider himself a public intellectual who was doing a stint in the university as a way to make a living. Klingenstein, Howe's junior by nearly forty years and only recently integrated into the American graduate student community, is perhaps more radical, arguing that literary academe produces conformists: "You're sucked into a big machine and you're made to produce stuff, and since you don't know very much about life yet, all the stuff you produce inside the machine looks pretty much the same." Howe does not disagree. On other occasions he had expressed reservations about the cloistered life led by literary academics (even as academe enabled him to live comfortably) and his dislike of the pomposity of much of academic writing, his own straightforward style having been shaped by his years as a freelance writer and editor.

Howe's career, if not his political perspective, represents a mixed form in which the discipline of academic scholarship is fertilized by the necessity of participating in public debates and of remaining alive to social and political developments. Already by the late 1980s it appeared as if this mixed form were dying out, as if Howe and Alfred Kazin were indeed examples of "the last intellectuals," to use Russell Jacoby's phrase in the title of his book lamenting that the intellectual capable of reflecting broadly but astutely on a variety of topics was passing from the scene.[10]

Klingenstein conducted this conversation as part of a series of interviews with Jewish academics that eventually enabled her to write two studies on the integration of Jewish literary scholars into American academe. Three years after this interview she published *Jews in the American Academy, 1900-1940: The Dynamics of Intellectual Assimilation* (1991). This was followed seven years later by *Enlarging America: The Cultural Work of Jewish Literary Scholars, 1930-1990* (1998).

## The Interview

**SK:** *It's pleasure to be here and have the great privilege to ask you questions about your life. Of course you've written about your life. I've read your autobiography and I've also read Alan Wald's book about the New York Intellectuals. I see that you're wrinkling your brow, so let this be my first question. What's wrong with Wald?*

**IH:** Wald puts everything into a very narrow perspective. It's the perspective of Trotskyism and his own very particular brand of politics, and it tilts everything in that direction. And, at least in my judgment, it's totally inaccurate and takes figures who were in the Trotskyist tradition and makes them far more significant in the intellectual world than, I think, they actually were. He is a nice fellow. He is sincere, but I think he sees things in a very distorted way.

**SK:** *Reading Wald's book is somewhat depressing because he is particularly good at chronicling the decline of the critical Left and the attending right turn of intellectuals. Do you feel a bit piqued by Wald's critique of the right turn?*

**IH:** No. I'm critical of the right turn too, though I suppose I also turned right. It depends on what you mean by a "right turn." A right turn can be people who moved from a Socialist to a conservative or neoconservative perspective. Or in his eyes, a right turn can mean moving from a Leninist to a social democratic perspective, which is what happened to me, more or less.

**SK:** *But you've been a social democrat from the beginning, although you did become a Trotskyist.*

**IH:** For a very short time, yes. And for him that's the standard, the standard by which he judges rightness and virtue all the way through, and anyone who deviates from that he thinks is somehow falling off from the standard. Well, when we start with that assumption, then of course nobody passes the test.

**SK:** *I learned from that book that your parents' name was originally not "Howe."*

**IH:** That's right.

**SK:** *Did they change the name? I assume they came from Russia. You talk very little about your parents in your autobiography.*

**IH:** The name I have was adopted as a political pen name in the late 1930s and that's all I want to say.

**SK:** *You speak little about your parents. I was told that you're rather reluctant to speak about personal matters.*

**IH:** Who told you that?

**SK:** *A colleague at the conference in Berkeley.*

**IH:** And what do you mean by personal?

**SK:** *Perhaps to some degree speaking about your parents and about your relationship to them.*

**IH:** My parents came from a place between Russia and Rumania.

**SK:** *When did they came to America?*

**IH:** In 1912. My book was called an "intellectual autobiography" and it didn't deal with my personal life.

**SK:** *Had your parents already been politically active in Europe?*

**IH:** No. My parents were very young when they came here. My father was about seventeen, eighteen years old. My mother was the same age. They came, as it happened, in the same boat, in the same ship, but they didn't know each other. They were too young to have had political lives yet. In this country they were not political people at all, though in the thirties and after they became workers. They were trade unionists. They were members of the International Ladies Garment Workers' Union (ILGWU). They were good trade unionists.

**SK:** *They did not come from a religious tradition?*

**IH:** Ah, you see, these categories are very tricky. They were Jews.

**SK:** *Well, yes, but. . . .*

**IH:** . . . but wait, wait, that was the defining characteristic of their life. Their parents were probably in some sense religious; yes, I'm sure they were religious in the sense that religion covered all of Jewish life, though some people broke away from it. But my parents were neither religious nor antireligious. They simply were part of a whole tradition or national community, or however you want to define it. You see, the categories of religious or antireligious, these are retrospective categories, which later analysts imposed for the purpose of simplification. Now, in the New England world, there were indeed religious minorities and antireligious minorities. Most Socialists would be part of the antireligious minorities. But the great bulk of Jews were neither. The great bulk of Jews were people who in some sense shared a little bit of both. They still adhered to certain religious customs; they kept a kosher house, they would go to the synagogue on Rosh Hashana and Yom Kippur, but they were not intensely religious. They didn't observe all the rituals. But at the same time, they didn't at all share the extreme hostility to religion of the radical Jewish Left.

**SK:** *I remember that in* A Margin of Hope *you speak of being Jewish as something that was simply there, as something that no one made very much of. Your friends were all Jewish and you spoke Yiddish. Was that your only language up to a certain point?*

**IH:** Yiddish was really up to the age of four or five. I learned English in the street when I went out to play, because English was spoken there.

**SK:** *The way you define being Jewish as a thereness, largely constituted by living among Jews (you used the term "national community" to describe your parents' and grandparents' experience in Europe) gets to be a difficult definition of Jewishness a generation on, because your kind of experience of being Jewish, of growing up Jewish, disappeared. So what then does it mean to be Jewish today, if anything at all?*

**IH:** That question is very difficult to answer. It means many different things. It means something different to Cynthia Ozick from what it does to me, and to a young person it may mean something different again. It's only from the outside that all Jews look alike, but when you go on to the inside you see that there are enormous numbers of differences. To me being Jewish means a certain inheritance. It means the Yiddish tradition. It means an inheritance of certain starts in life, norms of life; traditions of Jewish secular culture, in which, no doubt, there are also embedded remnants of religion, of Jewish ritual. It means loyalty to Israel, while being critical of many of the things it does. It means a certain elemental solidarity even with Jews with whom I have otherwise nothing in common. But it does not mean to me . . . it is not a religious persuasion, though for some people it is. For some people it is a nationalistic persuasion.

**SK:** *I think this split emerged very clearly at the Berkeley conference.*

**IH:** It did.

**SK:** *What did you think of the conference?*

**IH:** I think it was a waste of time, because everything that was said was . . . except the literary stuff, the literary stuff was interesting to me, but the political quarrel, which was inevitable when you bring together, say, on the one hand Amos Elon and myself, and Ruth Wisse and Cynthia Ozick on the other, and you put them together under this rubric of Jewish discussion, there is going to be a quarrel. There is going to be a fight. It is absolutely unavoidable. It is nobody's fault. Nobody is wrong in this respect and it is entirely predictable as to what would happen. We had this quarrel before and we are going to have it again. It is part of Jewish life in the present time and it will continue for a good length of time until and if, and indeed if ever, the conflict in the Middle East is settled. Maybe this was interesting for other people, but to me it was not terribly interesting. . . . I found other parts of the conference interesting, the actors and various writers I didn't know yet.

**SK:** *What emerged clearly, though, was the degree to which Israeli politics touched the inner core of the American Jews present at the conference, the degree to which people were emotionally invested in Middle East politics.*

**IH:** Because the question of Israeli policy toward the Palestinians involves the very future of Israel and therefore in some sense the future of Jews. In my judgment it involves the whole moral future of the Jews, what kind of people the Jews are going to be. This is THE central question that Jews have to ask in Israel overwhelmingly, and obviously here in America in a secondary but very significant way. You can barely touch any issue at the present time, any question without this looming up in front of you. Yes, there is a great, very passionate debate, firstly because most of us are passionate people, and secondly because the issue, as everyone sees and understands, is absolutely basic. No matter which side you're on.

**SK:** *It seemed to touch the core of people. It wasn't something OUT there.*

**IH:** It was something IN HERE.

**SK:** *At the conference, though, you were doubting that Israeli politics would make for good literary material.*

**IH:** I was not denying that the question of Israeli policy toward the Palestinians is one that we have very strong responses to. I was simply doubting that it would make a very usable subject for literature.

**SK:** *American Jewish literature?*

**IH:** There is a difference between what forms the substance of a polemic and what forms the material for literature. They are not necessarily the same.

**SK:** *What do you think would be good material for American Jewish literature? Novels, such as Nessa Rapoport's* Preparing for Sabbath, *despite its emphasis on spiritual and physical renewal, do not seem to augur well for the future.*

**IH:** Well, that's a problem. I myself believe that American Jewish writing is moving toward an end, that the great phase of . . . that essentially American Jewish writing will have to be seen as an immigrant literature and that its major phase is over. I could be wrong. There could be a whole new outburst of very gifted writers, but I don't see how this is possible.

**SK:** *You've predicted this while Saul Bellow and Philip Roth were still in the midst of their writing careers.*

**IH:** It's like predicting somebody's death. Sooner or later it happens.

**SK:** *In this context, your own development, your own move away from the Jewish immigrant experience and into classic American culture is actually quite interesting. I mentioned in my letter to you that was I struck by the difference in your assessment of Emerson, by what you wrote about Emerson in your essay "Strangers" (1977)—and you mention in your reply to me that my reading here was "in need of serious modification" and by what you wrote in* American Newness *(1985). In "Strangers" you wrote that Emersonian romanticism and individualism presented an impediment for Jews to move into American culture for three reasons: 1) the celebration of nature; 2) the celebration of the self, and 3) its being ahistorical. While whatever there was in the immigrant experience was urban, community-oriented, and reality-oriented, in the sense that in Judaism transcendence and immanence are kept separate and mortal man always lives in the material, temporal world, hence in history. In* American Newness *you find Emerson rather attractive, perhaps even compatible.*

**IH:** People change their views. Otherwise their would be no point in living beyond the age of twenty-one. But before I continue: Would you like a glass of water? Because I do.

Your question is an interesting one but it requires a fairly complex answer. Look, when people were growing up, like myself and a lot of other people, in immigrant Jewish families in America, we were exposed obviously to one or another version or kind of Jewish tradition through our families, education, etc. But at the same time, and perhaps even more powerfully, we were exposed to the American schools, to the whole culture of America—in the streets, through the newspapers, through the radio, later on television—and there was necessarily some tension, and sometimes a conflict between the two. . . . When I wrote the essay "Strangers" I was describing my responses, say, in the late thirties and forties, when I was young. At that point the left-wing anti-Stalinist intellectuals in New York City were strongly oriented toward European literature, because European literature was identified with modernism, which was for them the dominant cultural style or value. And so there was a tendency to depreciate a good part of American literature. So, for example, if you compared Emerson to Dostoevsky, he [Emerson] was thought thin, lacking in experience, deficient in his sense of the complexities of life, deficient in his perception of sexuality, of political conflict, of social thickness, which defines Dostoevsky. I think that part of it is still true. We grew up in the city. I grew up in a part of the Bronx, which is now called the South Bronx and was then called the East Bronx. Didn't know much about cows or trees. There was an occasional tree, not many. The only time we had a near-experience of nature was in the summer. If our parents were lucky they would go somewhere and take us on vacation to a farm in the country. A sense of nature was not part of our experience, and certainly the exultation and celebration of nature, which is part of the romantic tradition that Emerson and other American writers were trying to establish, was not part of our experience. Thirdly, the idea of extreme individualism, which Emerson explored, seemed at variance with, if not adverse to, the Jewish tradition. And then for those of us who developed an adherence to the Left, to various left-wing groups or styles or traditions, we thought extreme individualism, which by then had already been debased and corrupted and vulgarized in America, so that you went from Emerson to Herbert Hoover, quite a problem. We thought of that extreme individualism as being opposed to the need for collectivist societies or communities. These were among the reasons that some of us didn't, I think now, I'm being retrospective, didn't adequately appreciate the significance of the Emersonian tradition. Now it's possible to hold to all of these criticisms of the Emersonian tradition, which, I think, in *The American Newness* I still mention or should have mentioned, and at the same time to see a positive element in it, which we didn't then see.

**SK:** *What's the positive element?*

**IH:** The positive element is that the Emersonian tradition has been the basis for the strongest voice of internal criticism and dissent in American culture, that the Emersonian tradition at its best, especially that of the early Emerson—as it has gone through a whole line of American literary and social critics—that this tradition is the fundamental basis for the creation of what we call an adversary culture, a culture which is in opposition to the wrongs of the society. This tradition provides the grounds for a deep critique of American capitalism, American materialism, American social values. So, as I see it, what I said in *The American Newness* was in part a continuation, but also in part a complication, a correction of earlier views.

**SK:** *What I see is, to some degree, a shift from a cultural reading of Emerson, emphasizing his view of nature and the individual as alien to the urban Jewish experience, to a political reading of Emerson, perhaps a political cooptation of Emerson that would not always have agreed with him. It is still surprising, though, that you choose Emerson as your starting point, rather than say, Ann Hutchinson or Henry David Thoreau, who lend themselves so much more readily to the politics of dissent.*

**IH:** I try to explain this in my book, so I won't go into it now, but Emerson is the central originating figure, much more than Thoreau. He is a much more original figure than Thoreau. He is also much more flexible. Thoreau tends to harden his thought into a kind of manner, or sometimes a mannerism. But when I speak of the Emersonian tradition, I don't just mean something coming from him, I mean the whole intellectual context. There are still parts of it which don't interest me. The Oversoul leaves me very cold. I'm not interested in the Oversoul. I don't even know where it is. And other things like that. But the feeling of the young Emerson, the idea of looking for a transcendence in society, of a social criticism, the sharp perception, the idea that the American Revolution has not yet come to an end, but must be continued and fulfilled and deepened; all such things, which continue straight through a line of other critics, including Thoreau, the young Melville, John Jay Chapman, Van Wyck Brooks, Richard Chase and just a whole host of writers straight through, this seems to me . . . both cultural and political—you see, in the case of Emerson you can't really separate the cultural from the political. He is not political in the obvious outer sense of parties, movements, and proposals, but his cultural views have a strong political component.

**SK:** *That is certainly true. However, Emerson's thoughts also contain a strong utopian element which is ahistorical—moving the thinker outside history and specific social contexts—and that makes clear he does not view those contexts as political instruments.*

**IH:** But you see, I don't have to accept Emerson wholesale. I can also take him retail.

**SK:** *That's the question, isn't it?*

**IH:** A part here, a part there. It is true that there is a strong ahistorical element in Emerson. It is also true that a good deal of American thought is ahistoric. Historical perspectives have not flourished in this country, to put it mildly. And that, indeed, was one of the reasons why, forty years ago, we, or some of us, were hostile toward Emerson, and that still, I think, would [deliver] a very powerful critique of the Emersonian tradition. And although it is true that the historical sense is not very strong in Emerson, I think one can bring a historical sense to one's understanding of Emerson, that the utopianism, which he has, has to be seen historically as something which is a residue, a strong residual element of the best of the American revolutionary tradition and which happens to continue to have repercussions beyond Emerson.

**SK:** *It has been proposed, though, that dissent doesn't last long in America but gets transformed by the other elements in American culture into consent.*

**IH:** That's [Sacvan] Bercovitch's stuff these days and I don't believe it.

**SK:** *Why not?*

**IH:** You can say that about any form of dissent, not only Emersonian dissent. You can say that about all forms of dissent, then everything becomes assimilated into the dominant culture. And that is not true. Not everything does become assimilated to the dominant culture. In fact there is a continued Emersonian perspective which doesn't have to be assimilated to the dominant culture.

**SK:** *I don't see that.*

**IH:** Well, look at a man like Alfred Kazin, who has always been a kind of Emersonian individualist critic. He certainly has not been assimilated into the dominant culture.

**SK:** *It seems to me that if you'd like to make that case, you'd have to acknowledge that on Kazin's part there may have been an element of defiance because the culture wouldn't have him.*

**IH:** He has been very successful. He's been all over the place. He can hardly claim that he wasn't accepted.

**SK:** *I think he's had a rather tough time at Amherst College and at Harvard where he was briefly.*

**IH:** People have a tough time, but that doesn't mean that they weren't accepted. He's gotten all kinds of recognition, all kinds of honors. He stands where he goes as a critic of the culture from an essentially Emersonian perspective. The fact that some people lapse from the tradition doesn't discredit the tradition. I am not saying that it is the only resource for a dissenting critique of American society.

Obviously it is not. Obviously in the era of monopoly capitalism, multinational corporations would need to have a much more thorough socioeconomic analysis than Emersonianism can possibly provide. What Emersionianism provides is a perspective of adversary dissidence, of cultural rejection, of cultural criticism. To that we need to add many other things, which include Marxism, liberalism, etc. But how is all of this related to your book about the literary teachers?

**SK:** *I thought I should include you and I thought I should try to find out how you think. I've been puzzled by* The American Newness *book and by what I took to be your move from being community-oriented to being a champion of Emerson. But you've put that in perspective now.*

**IH:** I'm still community-oriented. I still believe in communal activity, I still believe in political organization, I still see the need of people to get together in organizations. But at the same time—put it this way, say that it is a dialectical, that it is a complex view. I see certain tensions, I see the value of the Emersonian-Thoreauvian figure of moral rectitude who stands firmly on his own. In my book *A Margin of Hope* I talk about this in the section about the antiwar movement in the sixties where there are figures who were often a nuisance because they didn't understand the need, as I felt it rightly or wrongly, of political maneuver, of political compromise. But it was good to have them, it was necessary to have people who said, here I stand, that's it, I won't move, I take a moralistic position and I don't care about the consequences. There were often conflicts and tensions between such people and those of us who had a more flexible politics. But the conflicts and tensions were perhaps in the long run productive and necessary, and it was good that there should be these, so to speak, latter-day Emersonians who may not even have known that they were Emersonians.

**SK:** *And so Kazin is an Emersonian.*

**IH:** He is a funny mixture. He is a Jewish Emersonian.

**SK:** *Which is precisely the puzzle.*

**IH:** There is a certain tension. And I am not an Emersonian, but I have an appreciation for it and I have tried to assimilate a part of it into my thinking. Say that that's dialectical. That's okay.

**SK:** *Let's up the ante a bit. Think of Alfred Kazin, the Jewish Emersonian, an intellectual position that makes him an outsider to certain Jewish communities and an outsider to certain American communities, and who in his status as independent literary critic is still quintessentially American, while being an outsider, so think of Kazin on the one hand and of Sacvan Bercovitch on the other, whose inner dispo-*

*sition is quintessentially that of the outsider, but whose academic career is quintessentially that of an insider, of one who succeeds by integrating himself into the system and playing it—where would you position yourself in such a spectrum of outside/inside tension? Perhaps one can break this down and ask first: do you think of yourself as an academic, a teacher, a critic, an intellectual activist?*

**IH:** I've never thought of myself in relation to Saki. That question has never entered into my mind. But in relation to Alfred, that's an interesting question, because we are often lumped together by virtue of coming out of the same kind of background. He is a couple of years older than I. Although we are actually very different. We are different in experience, in that I was very active in a number of Socialist groups, in organized politics, and he was not. He was always an individualist; he always went off on his own. His temperament is much more inclined toward romanticism; mine less so. His writing is more, let's say, rhapsodic; mine is drier, I suppose, etc. And yet despite these differences and tensions, on many particular questions, we have often found ourselves, Alfred and I, have often found ourselves together. We're often against the same things, although we are not necessarily for the same thing.

Am I an academic? Yes, in one sense I have been. I have taught for thirty-three years, so I can hardly say that I haven't been in the academy, although I never wrote for the academic journals. I wasn't interested in that. I was really a kind of semi-outsider within the academy. I tried to be responsible as a teacher, to do the job as well as I could. In that sense I was perhaps a little more academic than Kazin, I am not sure, although he also taught in his jobs as well as he could. I felt a little bit—I think, I'm not sure, I've never spoken to him about this—I felt a little more perhaps at ease within the academy than he did. But I never was fully at ease in the academy. It haunted me.

**SK:** *What made you feel ill at ease?*

**IH:** I always thought of myself as someone who was interested in, say, writing for political weeklies and magazines, like *The New Republic*. I never thought of myself as a scholar in the narrow sense of the word. I may know certain things, I may have certain scholarly resources, but I wouldn't define myself as a scholar. I would define myself as—oh, I don't know—a man of letters or literary intellectual, or something like that. And so I suppose I would say I had one foot inside the academy and one foot outside. Which foot was bigger at any given moment is a question and not that interesting to decide. I never thought of myself as simply an academic person. I didn't write like an academic person. I avoided the academic style.

**SK:** *Do you experience this as a minus? Do you regret not being an academic?*

**IH:** Oh, in some ways, yes. Sure. There were certain kinds . . . I never went . . . I never got graduate degrees, for example. So there is a certain kind of solid literary training which I didn't have, a certain kind of knowledge, which the ordinary academic has and which I have not had. That's a minus. For every plus there is also a minus. If you've certain kinds of advantages, that means certain kinds of disadvantages go along.

**SK:** *You taught at Brandeis University, which must have been a crazy place back then.*

**IH:** It was quite lively and exciting.

**SK:** *Would that not have been the kind of place you would have wanted to stay at longer?*

**IH:** I wouldn't have been given a job in most departments. I got a job in the 1950s. I didn't have a Ph.D., and it was only a rather eccentric university, an unconventional one, that would give me a job. You see, in the 1950s there was an enormous expansion of the universities in America as a whole and so a good number of literary people who were outside the academy, like Philip Rahv and Kazin and many others, were allowed in. You see, if they took in fifty new people, they could hire one or two oddballs. Brandeis was different because it was much readier to accept freelance intellectuals. And so I came in and then a few years later Philip Rahv came into the English department.

**SK:** *You came to Brandeis in 1953. I've just written about Ludwig Lewisohn who had been teaching at Brandeis. He died in 1955. Did you meet him? Do you remember him? He had a strong romantic streak and had become oddly religious, which makes me suspect that your relationship was not an easy one.*

**IH:** He was an old man then. When people get old they always feel passed by and neglected. He felt this. He had been quite famous as an intellectual and literary figure. He had been one of the first to turn to Freudian concepts. He had written a number of well-received books and an interesting novel

**SK:** *The Case of Mr. Crump. . . .*

**IH:** . . . which I think is a sufficiently good book and it is very painful to live to see your own obsolescence and that was the condition he was experiencing. Being young and eager at the time and not terribly respectful of my elders, I was not greatly sympathetic toward him, because he struck me as pompous and defensive. But he was a nice man, really. He was kindly. We didn't become great friends, but we didn't clash especially.

**SK:** *I recently spoke to one of your Brandeis students, Barbara Herrnstein Smith, who is now a cutting-edge academic. She had a tough time with Lewisohn. She told me that she came to you angrily complaining: "Why do I have to take that Shakespeare course? I'm not learning anything." And you said, "Ah, you always learn something."*

**IH:** It was probably true.

**SK:** *When you were at City College, Morris Raphael Cohen, who interests me, was still teaching. I think he retired in 1939. You also mention somewhere Abraham Edel, whom I don't know. What was the situation like for Jewish academics when you went to college?*

**IH:** I don't really know. Because I was a student. I perceived the vast majority of students at City College as Jewish. Cohen was a revered and adored figure. He was feared and there are legends about that. With Edel I had an introductory philosophy course. He was then a very close fellow traveler in the Communist movement, but I didn't know him. In his teaching there was no propagandizing whatsoever. He was an excellent teacher, open, fair-minded, decent, a very nice man. He was a minor figure. But Cohen was a great, popular star.

**SK:** *Mark Krupnick*[11] *wrote your entry for the Dictionary of Literary Biography. He mentions that you went to Brooklyn College for three semesters. . . .*

**IH:** One semester and then dropped out.

**SK:** *Why was that?*

**IH:** Graduate school was just boring, terribly boring.

**SK:** *Then you went to work in a factory and became editor of* Labor Action.

**IH:** That's right.

**SK:** *Then you were drafted into the army and sent to Alaska. Somehow you ended up in Princeton in 1948. It's not quite clear to me what you actually did there.*

**IH:** The lady to whom I was then married got a job teaching in a secondary school. And so we lived there.

**SK:** *You were a hanger-on.*

**IH:** Exactly. I was a hanger-on to hanger-ons. There was a group of very brilliant young writers who were about five or six, or maybe seven years older than I—

Saul Bellow, John Berryman, Delmore Schwartz. They were then just beginning to become known, publishing their first books. They had part-time jobs in the creative writing program with Richard Blackmur, the critic, who ran the creative writing program. They wanted to get into the English department as instructors but the English department, being very stuffy and academic, wouldn't have them. They formed an extremely irresistible, brilliant young group, and I was even younger and less known, less accomplished. I was close to them, near them. I was closer to some than to others.

**SK:** *What brought you into the Christian Gauss Seminars*[12] *in 1953?*

**IH:** By then I was publishing. I had published two books, one on Sherwood Anderson, the other on Faulkner, and Blackmur who ran the Gauss Seminars, invited me to give one. He had four seminars a year, which would be taught by major older figures and one younger figure, and in 1953 I was the younger figure. The older people were Paul Tillich, Edmund Wilson, and Quentin Bell.

**SK:** *Let me get the chronology straight here. From 1953 to 1961 you were at Brandeis and, while there, founded* Dissent *in 1954.*

**IH:** *Dissent* actually began a bit earlier, but the first issue came out in 1954 when I was already at Brandeis.

**SK:** *The academic year 1961-62 you went to Stanford and in 1963 you went to Hunter College. How long did you stay there?*

**IH:** Hunter College is part of the City University and I stayed in the City University until I retired two and a half years ago.

**SK:** *During those years when you were establishing yourself as a critic, the reigning star in New York was Lionel Trilling, who is much talked about again today. Why do you think he is so attractive again to younger critics today?*

**IH:** He is not so attractive anymore. He was attractive back then.

**SK:** *People reread his essays and do work on him.*

**IH:** Well, working on him doesn't mean very much. People who do dissertations, as you know, need to find subjects.

**SK:** *One does usually choose something of cultural significance, if not something close to one's own heart.*

**IH:** You may be right. Trilling became a cult figure then for a number of reasons. First of all, he was a very attractive human being. Very warm, clever, humorous, complex, sympathetic. Also he embodied in himself and in his thought the feelings of the 1950s and early 1960s, of what I would call a conservatized liberalism. He remained a liberal; he remained one all his life; but the liberalism became less combative, less assertive, more modulated, more complicated, more questioning about belief. This reflected and, indeed, helped create the dominant intellectual mood of the time. Its greatest influence was in the fifties and early sixties and then maybe throughout the seventies. Also he was an accomplished writer. He wrote winningly, charmingly, in ways that people could respond to. Although he articulated with vehemence the sentiments that he had. He was also just a very good critic.

**SK:** *Did you have much to do with him?*

**IH:** At various times . . . In the fifties he was very kind, very helpful to me, when I was young.

**SK:** *He helped you publish the Sherwood Anderson book.*

**IH:** That's right. He was one of the editors of the [American Men of Letters] series. He was very nice about that. And then we had a quarrel when I published an essay that had its moment of notoriety, called "This Age of Conformity," in which he was attacked. He took offense at that and we sort of separated and didn't see one another for a time. That happened when I had left [New York City]. When I came back to New York after Stanford, we slowly re-established relations, not particularly friendly. When the New Left went to extreme positions in the late sixties, it attacked both of us indiscriminately. They didn't make distinctions very much, and that drew us together. Toward the end of his life we were both unsympathetic toward certain developments in literary criticism. He found himself unsympathetic toward structuralism. He once even asked me to read about it and help him understand what was going on, because he didn't want to do it himself. That was a good joke, although at the time I didn't think so.

**SK:** *Your book* The American Newness *began as a series of lectures at Harvard. What was it like for you to come to Harvard?*

**IH:** Pleasant. It was nice. I enjoyed it. Whatever criticisms some people may have had there, didn't get to me. I didn't hear them. I gave the lectures. Professor Donald was very personable; Professor [Daniel] Aaron was there. They didn't express any disagreement, or, at least, I was never aware of any. But in those days you never knew. Politeness is always a factor in such a place. What people say on such occasions has to be taken with a grain of salt.

**SK:** *Having quite recently arrived in America from Europe, and having left as rhetorically contentious a locale as German studies at the University of Heidelberg and come to Harvard, the exquisite politeness of the place is disorienting. It took a lot of adjusting to. I often have the sense that people are insincere and that they are offended by what they take to be my inappropriate bluntness. I seem to have fewer such problems in New York.*

**IH:** Certainly, the tone at Harvard was not the same tone as the one that would prevail at *Partisan Review* or among the New York Intellectuals.

**SK:** *Would you not have been one of the first to note, though, that such politeness was also a form of dishonesty?*

**IH:** Perhaps you should ask Dan [Aaron] and Saki [Sacvan Bercovitch] about that. Maybe they disagreed with what I had to say in the lectures, or they didn't like the way I talked; but I had no way of knowing. Let's say the audience had consisted of people like Philip Rahv and Lionel Abel and Alfred Kazin, I would have heard very quickly what was wrong with the lectures, even before they were over.

**SK:** *Did that disorient you?*

**IH:** No. I have been around the academy long enough to know what to expect.

**SK:** *Do you see that sort of politeness as a minus; do you see it as a form of assimilation?*

**IH:** As a minus? No. It's different, that's all. [*laughs*] It's what's appropriate in a certain kind of intellectual atmosphere—in the university. There were a couple of people who did quarrel with me after the lectures. And that was all right. They were even right about some points.

**SK:** *I spoke with Barbara Herrnstein Smith two weeks ago. She described having been turned down as a student by Radcliffe College as a class issue.*

**IH:** There is a tremendous difference. When Barbara was a student at Brandeis in 1953-54—that was thirty-five years ago.

**SK:** *True. But she received an offer from Harvard two years ago. She turned it down, she said, because Harvard for her would always be the place where she had not been accepted as a student, and she felt that issues of class continued to play a role.*

**IH:** Look, in 1953, those of us at Brandeis felt that Harvard looked down upon Brandeis, condescended to us, not in a hostile, but in a friendly, patronizing way. Patronizing is the right word. It did. When I came to Brandeis in 1953, a very gifted, distinguished man also came to the department, named J. V. Cunningham. He took over the English department, and one of the things he did was to declare it an independent nation, no longer a colony of Harvard, so to speak. Because some men at Harvard, including Harry Levin, had used Brandeis as a colony of Harvard for their graduate students. Perfectly all right. Cunningham pretty much put a stop to that. Probably Barbara felt some of these feelings. She was then married to a man who was Jewish, but also on the Harvard faculty, Richard Herrnstein. And so she may have had some very complicated feelings, which I don't know about. Actually, Harvard was not as bad in this question as was Princeton. Princeton was much more purely elitist, waspish, snobbish. The big entry of Jews into English departments did not occur until after the war. Yale was one place where they essentially became the dominant figures: [Geoffrey] Hartman, [Harold] Bloom, [John] Hollander—that was quite a powerful trio. At Princeton never quite in the same way. Harvard had a very strong contingent of Jewish professors, though not necessarily in the English department.

**SK:** *There was only one, Harry Levin, for a long time [until 1961].*

**IH:** That's right. Now, of course, there are many more. There probably was a feeling then that Harvard was an elitist school. But you don't have to be Jewish to feel that status distinction between, say, Michigan State and Harvard quite acutely. I would say that those of us at Brandeis felt a certain mild resentment of the attitude that the Harvard people took toward us. I think that by the late 1950s, Brandeis had an English department that was not as good as Harvard's, but interesting in its own way: there was Rahv and Cuningham and myself. But there were those status distinctions. But by 1985, when I gave these lectures at Harvard . . . You see, I never found my main gratifications in the academy. For people like Saki the academy was the natural home. For me it was not. It was essentially a place to earn a living and to do a conscientious job while earning a living. But I thought of myself, rightly or wrongly, as needing another environment as a general intellectual, resembling perhaps more the political intellectuals in Europe who need an environment that is partly outside the academy.

**SK:** *Can intellectuals in America exist outside the academy?*

**IH:** Yes, of course. I learned to some extent to be on the move, to be homeless. But to some degree the various universities where I taught were a home. They were very generous toward me. And I took my work there seriously. The work of teaching. I didn't take the academic stuff seriously, but I took teaching seriously and went about my own business.

**SK:** *That sounds very good and mature and so accepting. But I'm not sure that this is the real Irving Howe speaking here. My sense, before coming here for the interview, was that there was a certain hurt when folks in the academy were not taking you seriously as a critic.*

**IH:** Of course, over the years, when certain academic people referred to me as a journalist, I was hurt by that. Or sometimes, when I was put down as a "social critic," I wasn't hurt by that, I was irritated by that.

**SK:** *You're not a social critic?*

**IH:** No. That's a pigeonhole. I am obviously a social critic. But anyone who'd go to the trouble of describing me, if it's worth the trouble, would have to do it a bit more precisely. One of the virtues, for example, of Mark Krupnick's article is that in addition to calling me a social critic, he noticed something that I think is acute. He noticed that there was another angle, that I was always looking backward to something when I was writing.

**SK:** *The element of coming too late?*

**IH:** That's the personal element. "Social critic"—there are hundreds of them. But this is more distinctive, precise, descriptive of me, insofar as anyone would want to take the trouble and do this. Of course, one always can get hurt. Any snob can hurt you. When Harry Levin was condescending toward Brandeis, it wounded us. We knew all about hurt.

**SK:** *Did it hurt more because Levin was a fellow Jew?*

**IH:** No. It was very complicated. He wasn't only condescending, he was also friendly. He didn't have to invite me to his home, but he did. He may have regretted it, though, but I wouldn't know that. He was condescending toward Brandeis, but he was also interested in it. Life is not that simple. It doesn't fall into simple oppositions and polarities. He looked down his nose at Brandeis, *and* he wanted it to succeed. Because he was aware that he was Jewish and he probably suffered some of the threats, though he had buried that experience. The difference to us was that he had suppressed his feelings and we were much more open about expressing our views. We had other sources of tension, though. I had violently attacked F. O. Matthiessen politically. And he had been a friend of Matthiessen's, sort of sympathetic to Matthiessen's views, I think, to some extent. So he didn't like my attack. There were plenty of grounds for tension.

**SK:** *It's interesting that when we speak of "grounds of tension," there are always grounds that lie in the past. Is it true, then, that you have come to terms with*

*America, as Mark Krupnick surmises, since this is the only home you are ever likely to have? How far are you on the inside now?*

**IH:** I'm on the inside in the sense that I believe in democracy with a small "d" and that I prefer a democratic society to an undemocratic society. But I see myself as a principal critic of this society. And I would not have broken my back, so to speak, all these years in publishing *Dissent*, if I didn't see myself in that way. And in that sense I have *not* come to terms with this society.

**SK:** *But you've come to accept a great part of it, of America, as we said at the beginning of this interview.*

**IH:** Yes. I believe that that tradition enables the criticism of this society. I believe that it is necessary to use some elements of liberalism and some elements of Socialism as a basis for a critique of society.

**SK:** *But you wouldn't go as far as Saki [Sacvan Bercovitch] and say that—once this line of thought gets co-opted in America (dissent become consent)—it loses its effectiveness in bringing about real change?*

**IH:** That's utter nonsense. Unless of course you say it from the point of view of a Marxist-Leninist, which I don't think Saki is. I think Saki is a nonpolitical person who decided rather late in the day to adopt a radical stance, strictly in the academic world and started to find a way to criticize people who have been involved in that world. I don't know if that's a possible way of interpreting this. I haven't seen Saki in years. I really don't know. I don't want to be on record for that.

**SK:** *Your description helps me find my way around.*

**IH:** Saki is not a significant figure for my intellectual orientation.

**SK:** *Who would such figures be today?*

**IH:** Someone like Michael Walzer would be one; Kenneth Galbraith would be another—various people on the democratic Left. I don't take very seriously the politics of literary academics, any of them at Duke or Harvard.

**SK:** *Or Stanford?*

**IH:** Stanford too.

**SK:** *Like Walter Benn Michaels's* The Gold Standard*?*

**IH:** I said literary people. I take seriously some of the scholarly *work* they have done. Yes.

**SK:** *But you object that they have no effect on real life?*

**IH:** Not that I can see. They seem to me not even to *want* to have an effect on real life.

**SK:** *Is that why you don't want to be an academic?*

**IH:** There are other reasons. I don't think academic theories and critical quarrels are very significant. They create a bit of an uproar in the academic world. They don't have any consequences as to who gets elected president or what kind of social policies the government adopts toward the homeless, or an impact on labor questions, or anything of that sort.

**SK:** *Depressing. Would one want to sit at one's desk and write articles all the time?*

**IH:** Well, it's better than punching the clock in a factory, isn't it, or writing ad copy.

**SK:** *True enough, but in Trilling's time it seemed that one could still have an effect as an intellectual writer. One of the elements I liked in Krupnick's book about Trilling was the way in which he developed for Trilling the theme of negotiating uptown and downtown.*

**IH:** Yes, but Trilling's liberalism wasn't very precise. It was a liberal nonpolitics. I was always interested in precise things: Who was the candidate for the Democratic Party? I was interested in many specific elements of politics. I was involved in various specific political questions in a way that most academic people were not. Maybe they are right and I am wrong. But it's a difference. I don't have any respect for so-called academic Marxism. I think Marxism should be a way of changing the world, not a form of academic entertainment.

**SK:** *But you haven't been a hard-core Marxist?*

**IH:** Oh sure, in the thirties and into the forties, maybe up to the early fifties. I'm not a Marxist, not in any precise sense, in any orthodox sense. But it's left its mark upon me, its imprint upon me. You can't go through a certain experience without it having left a residue.

**SK:** *You continue to be a bit of a puzzle for me.*

**IH:** That's very interesting, because people like myself were not considered a puzzle twenty or twenty-five years ago. We were considered quite ordinary people. I should be in a museum perhaps, but there were many such people, freelance intellectuals, intellectuals who were partly freelance, partly in the university.

**SK:** *It seems no longer possible, though, to live like Kazin and you and have an effect.*

**IH:** That's true.

**SK:** *One, alas, has to become an academic now.*

**IH:** But you don't have to write like Derrida.

**SK:** *True. But you're sucked into a big machine and you're made to produce stuff, and since you don't know very much about life yet, all the stuff that's produced inside the machine looks pretty much the same; yet if you don't produce, you don't survive, the machine spits you out and you scramble to find part-time work at a community college. The big machine also dulls your senses as to what social activism is. You come to think that writing some paper overthrowing the theories of your forebears is some kind of revolutionary act. So I can see what you have achieved and what you have done.*

**IH:** Thank you!

**SK:** *Oh, geez.*

**IH:** You're right, though. It's become much more difficult to . . . Paul Goodman, my old friend, once said: in times of depression it was easier for freelance writers to make a living. That's true, although today we have a lot of technology that is helpful. Information is easier to come by and instead of a week, it only takes two days to make $150.

One difference seems to me to be that literary academics seem to have totally lost interest in what I would call the common reader. For me the common reader beats the uncommon reader. The common reader would be the kind of person who reads *The New York Review of Books*, who is interested in literature, but not terribly interested in the quarrels of the great critics. Why should he be? Maybe at one time he read *Partisan Review*, but not *Kenyon Review*. Whether there still is such a reader is unclear. But if he does not exist, we must invent him. What seems to me the most distressing thing about the literary academy is its self-sufficiency. Literary academics seem completely satisfied with writing for one another. Of course, I was happy if Cunningham read something by me, or Barbara, though it seems hard to imagine that anything of mine held up under her scrutiny. But I always thought that there were some people out there for whom I wanted to write and to whom I wanted to talk, and perhaps whom I wanted to influence, and I still have that perspective today. It's harder today. Of course, the common reader could be a professor of physics. He doesn't know about intentional fallacy or Jacques Lacan, and he is better off that way. But he does want to know whether there is a good novel that he should read, or what about T. S. Eliot's biography. He is interested in cultural and literary life, but not in that incestuous, ingrown way. But perhaps what has happened was unavoidable.

## Notes

1. Susanne Klingenstein contributed heavily to the editing of this introduction.
2. Klingenstein, however, believes that Howe's execution was faulty: "Howe didn't carry it through, didn't stick to his political guns. He tried to meet Harvard on its own literary-critical turf. The defiance evaporated and the result was a tepid reading of American literature." Personal correspondence, e-mail to Ethan Goffman, February 18, 2008.
3. The information in this paragraph comes from Susanne Klingenstein's personal recollections, e-mail to Ethan Goffman, February 18, 2008.
4. *Yiddishkeit* is a sense of Jewish identity associated with culture, including folk culture
5. See, in particular, Alan Wald, *The New York Intellectuals: The Rise and Decline of the Anti-Stalinist Left from the 1930s to the 1980s* (Chapel Hill, NC: The University of North Carolina Press, 1987).
6. See *The Worlds of Irving Howe: The Critical Legacy*, ed. John Rodden (Boulder: Paradigm, 2005), 275. Howe's inclination toward European culture was symptomatic of the New York Intellectual milieu, particularly that part associated with the *Partisan Review.* That journal's editors, Philip Rahv and William Phillips, "tended to search for the solutions to problems of American culture in Europe" (117), a predilection that extended to Howe's early negligence of Emerson and other Americans as primary sources for social philosophy. James Gilbert, *Writers and Partisans: A History of Literary Radicalism in America* (New York: Columbia, 1992).
7. Nikolai Chernyshevsky was a nineteenth-century Russian revolutionary democrat and author of the novel *What is to be Done?*, which inspired Lenin's pamphlet of the same title. Tolstoy also wrote a novel under that title.
8. Regarding this quote, Susanne Klingenstein comments that Howe "appears to want to have his cake and eat it too." Personal correspondence, e-mail to Ethan Goffman, February 18, 2008.
9. Susanne Klingenstein goes so far as to exclaim that "the dissenter is subsequently punished by failure in the job market." Personal correspondence, e-mail to Ethan Goffman, February 18, 2008.
10. Jacoby, in *The Last Intellectuals: American Culture in the Age of Academe* (New York: Basic Books, 1987 [2000]), crystallized and popularized the argument that the university had defanged the public intellectual, that "the institution neutralizes the freedom it guarantees" (119). Following Jacoby's general argument, and Howe and Klingenstein's more specific one in this interview (at the time unpublished), Alan Wolfe,

among others, describes how in recent decades "the academic world engaged itself in forms of professionalism so strictly defined that little room remained for those willing and able to reach large audiences with their views" (1). See *An Intellectual in Public* (Ann Arbor: University of Michigan Press, 2003). Edward Alexander makes a similar argument for those in academia whom he considered disengaged from the literature that Howe loved: "These people, ostensibly professors of literature, actually prefer the most purely 'theoretical' kind of literary theory. They show little interest not only in the common reader but in literature itself" (231). Alexander contrasts this phenomenon to a continuing defense of literature and history, in which he and Howe stood on the same side. *Irving Howe: Socialist, Critic, Jew* (Bloomington: Indiana University Press, 1998).

11. Mark Krupnick was a scholar of the New York Intellectuals, particularly noted for his work on Lionel Trilling; later a professor at the University of Chicago's Divinity School.
12. The Christian Gauss Seminars are a series of seminars on literary issues initiated in 1949 and held at Princeton University.

# Chapter 12

**Irving Howe, "The First 35 Years Were the Hardest: Interview with Myself,"** ***Dissent*****, Spring 1989.**

## Introduction

Howe is pensive in this interview with his toughest critic, an alter ego who homes in on his anxieties, albeit in a way that allows him to explain himself. The conversation is in the form of an "auto-critique," the only such chapter in the book. It sums up the history of thirty-five years of work on a magazine to which Howe devoted at least two days per week throughout those decades.

The interviewer here obviously has the keenest "insider knowledge" about his subject and the magazine in the entire book; accordingly, the topics he raises are most revealing. The interview occurs at a crucial transitional movement in the checkered history of Socialism: before the fall of the Berlin Wall, yet during the period when *glasnost* and *perestroika* are in full swing. Howe is evaluating *Dissent* against the backdrop of Gorbachev and in hopeful anticipation for the future (at least internationally, in contrast to Howe's gloomy view of the Reagan years domestically).

Howe opens with a discussion of Victor Navasky, the long-time editor and publisher of *The Nation*, a magazine that had harshly criticized *Dissent* for allegedly supporting U.S. capitalism because it advocated anti-Communism and a reformist policy agenda. This might appear a strange opening gambit for a self-interview, but Howe wants to stress the delicate task of ideological navigation between the Right and the far Left that *Dissent* has steered. He assumes a defensive stance in order to parry criticisms that *Dissent* has been an apologist for the Establishment or for mainstream thinking and prevailing government policies, aiming to show instead that it took tough—and carefully considered—policy stands on numerous issues at home and abroad. Howe distinguishes his magazine from the *New Left Review*, for example, which also emerged from events in the mid-1950s that coincided with the birth of *Dissent*, but which adopted a more Europeanized, Marxist orientation that fully supported the movement. Proud of *Dissent*, and a little amazed that it has lasted so long, Howe recounts the difficult line that the magazine walked. He defends its early anti-Stalinism as necessary to safeguard a decent Left vision and preserve some version of democratic Socialism: "It was the Gulag that helped discredit leftist ideas, not the handful of us on the Left who told the truth about the Gulag." *Dissent* struggled to hold on to Socialism in an atmosphere of skepticism about a collectivist future, striving to oppose the domination of private property while seeking a pragmatic, gradualist course that effectively ruled out expropriation and bloody revolution. *Dissent*'s arduous path is evident in Howe's critique of Marxism, which he believes has failed, at least "as a unified system," an admission that must have been painful for someone who had once subscribed to Marxism as a full-scale *Weltanschauung*, a secular metaphysics equipped to explain virtually all questions. Early in *Dissent*'s history, Howe explains, he had come to believe that "the working class was not the lever of revolutionary change." It is unlikely, though, that anyone in the magazine's formative years would have put the matter quite so starkly, as faith in the working class was central even to diverse factions subscribing to social democracy.

Given that *Dissent* was born in reaction to the excesses of Stalinism, it is no surprise that the discussion moves to theories of totalitarianism, of which Stalinism and Nazism are the two prime examples. Hannah Arendt is the major figure here. Her exalted reputation at mid-century in American intellectual circles, her personal relationship to Howe, and her status as an occasional contributor to *Dissent* established her as a central presence in Howe's thinking even though he regarded her ideas as extreme, particularly on the role of the Jewish people in their own destruction (e.g., in *Eichmann in Jerusalem*, 1963). When it came to grasping the American political scene, she was often out of her element, he believed.[1] Still, "Arendt performed a real service," concluded Howe, for she theorized totalitarianism as a brutal ideology of total domination, "a radical new ethos of blood and terror." Although by the 1950s Howe had cast aside as obsolete his erstwhile Marxist belief that the Nazi regime represented a perverted outcome of capitalism and imperialism, theories of Communist totalitarianism had enabled a resurgent conservative reaction by the 1980s, exemplified by Reaganism in America and Thatcherism in Great Britain. Yet Howe's rejection of the Marxist shibboleths of the early postwar era did not entail dismissing all aspects of his Socialist faith; for instance, Howe continued to exalt Orwell—that other great antitotalitarian visionary—as an intellectual hero. Howe also derides what Communism had become while affirming democratic Socialism, with an emphasis on the need to maintain democratic processes.

Howe thus uses this interview as a chance to grapple with thorny questions, while also advancing qualified praise of *Dissent*'s achievements. In the subhead of the original title, Howe writes: "In which a Founding Editor of *Dissent* Magazine Submits to an Imaginary Interviewer Answering Questions He Likes to Hear—And Some He Would As Soon Not." Howe employs this eighteenth-century mode of address facetiously, yet also seriously, to interrogate the two halves of himself that ponder the history of his efforts.

In this spirit, we might speculate: If the Howe of this 1989 interview were to be magically catapulted two decades ahead, how would he view political and social events of the twenty-first century? Which questions would he "like to hear"? And what are "some he would as soon not"?

We would answer as follows: Irving Howe would undoubtedly be upset by the ongoing growth of tendencies that he hoped had reached their zenith in the 1980s, particularly triumphalist capitalism on a global scale. He would be depressed that the hopes unleashed for a reformed Socialism, or at least for social democracy, in Gorbachev's Russia, whose policies of *glastnost* and *perestroika* seemed a kind of miracle in 1989, have been crushed. Yet even here he would likely find some slender margin of hope, too. For example, regarding the misconceived view that totalitarianism is unalterable, he remarks that history does not stand still, but rather moves incrementally, by fits and starts: "What went wrong was something that goes wrong with most theories—the impulse to transform a historically limited observation, no matter how acute, into a timeless universal."

History marches on. Circumstances alter. Conditions evolve. So when Howe talks about "a sort of 'long march' in and through democracy that is central to the Socialist project," he is referring to the welfare state, the condition of which is problematic today. Yet we in the twenty-first century are arguably living in a less violent world, one more generally egalitarian and democratic than ever. It is a world in which the horrible genocide in Darfur, for instance, may be allowed to continue, but at least is vociferously deplored and relatively isolated. It is a world in which an international ideal of human rights has penetrated widely and deeply. It is a world in which democracy, despite numerous setbacks, has been slowly spreading. Of course, Russia today—now bereft of most of the Soviet empire, and having suffered under a "radical capitalist" experiment that *Dissent* has consistently decried—has stepped backwards, returning to a brutal, quasi-czarist nationalism under the leadership of its "strong man," Vladimir Putin.

This interview, one of Howe's pieces for *Dissent,* appeared in the midst of the euphoric international political atmosphere of 1989-91, when the impending fall of the Soviet Union possessed a double edge for Howe and *Dissent*. Despite *Dissent*'s admiration, "Socialists"—who had paid a heavy price for Stalinism—were once again being derided and discredited for the newly emergent revelations about Communist state corruption and oppression. Howe quite accurately describes a period in which "the idea of capitalism has taken on a sheen of attractiveness among people in both East and West such as it hasn't had for a long time."

So if Howe could be airlifted two decades ahead into the world of today, what would he observe? It is likely he would say that the glow of capitalism circa 1990 has dimmed or gone out. And, despite all the crimes that have been unjustly committed in its name, the idea of Socialism retains its beauty and power. Indeed, whereas extremism rules on the right, leftists—albeit inconsistently and with notable exceptions—seem to be learning from the past and thereby assuming more tempered, pragmatic stances, similar to that adopted by the elder Howe. Yet he might also grant that the path to a more equitable and democratic society remains unclear, that new challenges and strains have replaced the Cold War, and that prospects for a peaceful liberal-radical mass movement remain tentative and doubtful in the present century, as they proved to be throughout the last one.

## The Interview

### In which a Founding Editor of Dissent Submits to an Imaginary Interviewer, Answering Questions He Likes to Hear—and Some He Would as Soon Not

**Q:** *How do you explain that* Dissent *has survived for so long?*

**A:** True grit.

**Q:** *That's all?*

**A:** Also the generosity of a few friends and the self-taxation of our editors.

**Q:** *In a book about the McCarthy period, Victor Navasky praises* Dissent *for its intransigent opposition to McCarthyism—I almost get the impression that you fellows did something heroic in those days. How did it feel in the 1950s to be attacking McCarthyism at a time when a lot of others were taking cover?*

**A:** It felt fine; but really, we had no sense of doing anything especially notable; it just seemed like an elementary obligation. Nice of Vic to say a good word for us (considering the press we get in his magazine, *The Nation),* but I suspect that behind it all is his desire to advance a somewhat melodramatic view of the 1950s, and therefore he casts a pleasant glow over the opponents of McCarthy.

**Q:** *But wait, I've heard old-timers speak about those days as if Fascism were only a step away.*

**A:** There were fascists, there always are. There was repression and intimidation. It was a rotten time—ugly. But not Fascism. Even the Communists, harassed as they were, remained a legal party and issued a legal press. A few old-fashioned

Marxists, their imaginations strained by analogies with Europe, started "going underground." But you have to distinguish between legislative thuggery and a fascist takeover.

**Q:** *OK, let's get back to the time when you started. Some of your first editors had come out of Marxist groups, while others were freelance radicals. What were you hoping to achieve with* Dissent?

**A:** In a sense, just to keep body and soul together. We weren't even sure we could last beyond the first year (and now we don't seem to know how to stop—not that we want to!). Those of us who came out of the Marxist milieu wanted to break from sect life completely, which also led in a few years to a gradual abandonment of Marxism as a system, something that may be regarded as an intellectual equivalent of sect life. As for the freelance radicals, they wanted a home where they could discuss and write. Things were very rough on the left. Organizations were breaking up, morale was low. But somehow we stuck it out and the magazine grew. Or at least, it grew on us.

**Q:** *Now wait a minute, you're being just a little too casual about Marxism. In your younger years some of you were Trotskyists or other sorts of anti-Stalinist leftists. So think: Did you start* Dissent *in order to move away from orthodox Marxism or did you move away because you had started* Dissent?

**A:** Who can be sure? You talk as if people entirely understand their own behavior, or as if the passage of time necessarily makes them wise. I'd say this: Since we had to respond to events every three months, we began to realize that as a politics Marxism just wasn't holding up. The working class was not the lever of revolutionary change; the vexing problem of Stalinism could not be usefully approached through traditional Marxist categories; the choice before humanity could not be reduced to capitalism or Socialism; and the Marxist theory of crisis had, at the least, to be modified. And although we didn't join the anti-Marxist stampede of those years, we could no longer cling to Marxism as a unified system that supposedly coped with all the major problems of politics and society. Still, it would be silly to deny that Marxism has left its mark on all of us, as it has on most reflective people.

**Q:** *But didn't you pay a price for this? Some younger people, including survivors of the New Left, still say that your harsh anti-Stalinism contributed, perhaps inadvertently, to discrediting leftist ideas these past few years?*

**A:** It was the Gulag that helped discredit leftist ideas, not the handful of us on the left who told the truth about the Gulag. One of the damaging realities of the past few decades has been the virtual concord (a pact across ideology) by which the conservative Right and the pro-Stalinist "Left" jointly identify the Soviet dictatorship with "Socialism." As long as people accept that, naturally they won't want Socialism. Why should they? I'm not saying all the troubles of the Left were caused by Stalinism—only that a great many were. Remember: millions of good people were burned out, disenchanted, destroyed by Stalinism—whole generations. And the costs are still being measured.

**Q:** *Let's turn to something else, maybe almost as touchy. How do you explain the fact that whichever way the political wind blows it seems always to blow past you folks—that is, both during the turns to the right and the turns to the left?*

**A:** That's a tough question, but I'll try to confront it. In general, I'd say that this century has been a time of violence, extremism, authoritarian delusions; a time in which liberal Socialists or Socialist liberals aren't likely to flourish, though in Europe there have been some good intervals. Still, what chance did European voices of intelligence and reason have during the decades between wars? As for America, there's something about our culture—a strong inclination toward simplistic postures of rectitude and moralizing that comes down from Protestantism and through the Emersonian tradition. These have value in themselves yet also militate against a politics of reform. So when we do have a Left in this country, it tends to run toward moralistic extremes and then, as in the late sixties, to self-destruct.

**Q:** *One more question about the time of your founding. In the 1950s, the* Dissent *group was, naturally enough, concerned with the matter of totalitarianism. Now, in retrospect and bearing in mind the recent Gorbachev changes, do you think the theories of totalitarianism advanced in the 1950s, theories you more or less subscribed to, were correct?*

**A:** You won't think me evasive if I say yes and no? In those years, as we took in the meaning of the Holocaust, as the Stalin regime consolidated its power in Eastern Europe, and as the possibility of Communist victories in France and Italy seemed quite real, it was only natural that a mood of depression should sweep across us. One totalitarian monster destroyed, another takes its place.

The keenest analysts of totalitarianism—Hannah Arendt, Richard Lowenthal, Franz Neumann—naturally focused on whatever seemed novel in the totalitarian upsurge: terror as an integral part of their movement and their exercise of power; ideology as the mental equivalent of terror; "permanent mobilization" in the struggle against "enemies" real and imagined; the atomization of society and the destruction of social groups, movements, publics. The ultimate end of totalitarianism, if there was one, appeared as either world domination or apocalypse—or both.

Arendt performed a real service by stressing these elements and by insisting, as had become obvious to anyone except the Marxist faithful, that totalitarianism was not merely an extension of monopoly capitalism. What made totalitarianism so powerful and frightening was precisely the embodiment of a radical new ethos of blood and terror.

**Q:** *What, then, went wrong with this theory?*

**A:** What went wrong was something that goes wrong with most theories—the impulse to transform a historically limited observation, no matter how acute, into a timeless universal. There was an implicit assumption that totalitarian society had achieved a mode of stasis, which, in a sense, meant an end to history. The overriding value of the theory was that it forced attention upon what was historically unprecedented in the Hitler and Stalin regimes—as against lazy theorists who kept telling us "there have always been dictatorships" and repression. What the theorists of totalitarianism offered us was not so much a complete understanding—how could they?—as a remarkably vivid description and evocation of a novel experience that had shattered the modern world.

Soon the flaws in this approach became clear: Terror can't be maintained indefinitely; history didn't come to an end, it just dragged on.

**Q:** *But didn't Isaac Deutscher, the Marxist with whom you had some sharp quarrels, see better than Arendt, Lowenthal, and the rest?*

**A:** Again, no and yes. With his stress on economic determinism, Deutscher lent a certain aura of necessity to Stalinism. He was wrong in assuming that because it had a "planned economy" (it might better be called an "ill-planned economy"), the Soviet Union was certain to create the material basis for liberalization. Today it seems the other way round: It is the crisis of the Soviet economy that has stimulated the movement to *glasnost*. But we must grant that Deutscher was correct in stressing the inescapability of historical change. "It would be a striking mistake," he wrote, "to treat totalitarianism metaphysically as a state of society's utter immobility, or of history's absolute freezing, which exclude any political movement in the form of action from below or reform from above." On this our old friend and antagonist was right. Credit where credit is due.

**Q:** *Which leads of course to Gorbachev. How, in terms of political theory, would you characterize his regime?*

**A:** I'm in no hurry to paste a label on *glasnost-perestroika*, having had more than my share of embarrassments over premature categorizations. Let's wait and see. I'd just add that those who say the Soviet Union is going back to capitalism are foolish, though no more so than those who still call it Socialist. Let's say it's a bureaucratic collectivist society in a state of extreme crisis, with strong tendencies toward a modernization that entail an as-yet-unsettled quantity of partial democratization. But it is not a democracy either. So I've done just what I said should not be done. And how much help are these labels?

The recent developments in the Soviet Union are the most important, indeed remarkable, since the Second World War. There are sectarians of the extreme Left and extreme Right, more concerned with clinging to their theories than with responding to realities, who minimize the importance of these events. I think these events are astonishing and offer hope. We have, as Lew Coser writes in this issue, finally gotten out of the era in which the Communist parties of Europe represented a significant force; we can look forward to a moment when a Socialist Left in Europe and elsewhere doesn't have to carry the burden of being (mis)identified with Communism. And the events in the Soviet Union themselves show a culture, an art intelligentsia rising out of decades of enforced silence and falsehood, springing to passionate life and speaking with remarkable candor. When I read the collection of Soviet press excerpts that Josephine Woll put together in our last issue, I found myself exhilarated. To have lived to the time when Orwell's *Nineteen Eighty-Four* is published in the Soviet Union, when people there write about Koestler's *Darkness at Noon*—you think, maybe the struggle of the anti-Stalinist Left wasn't wasted, after all.

**Q:** *Yes, but how does this affect your hopes for a Socialist revival? Is the consequence of Gorbachev's policies entirely positive?*

**A:** Few things have entirely positive consequences. The immediate political-strategic effects of Gorbachev's policies are good. There is a visible winding down of the cold war. There is a beginning of withdrawal by the big powers from small countries they've occupied or "liberated." There are signs of a modest economic linkage between Eastern and Western Europe. All to the good. But the ideological consequences are, for the time being, not so good. Insofar as a few on the Left and many on the right further the notion that Soviet society is "Socialist," the result is clearly a major shift among both intellectuals and the general public toward favoring a "free-market" or pro-capitalist outlook. In some Eastern European countries there are intellectuals who, rather naively, celebrate the "free market" without recognizing sufficiently that a) it has really been constrained in the West by many governmental and social interventions and b) there are grave disadvantages, ranging from unemployment to environmental devastation, that result from "free-market" economies. Still, right now the bourgeois democracies look pretty good when compared to the faltering Communist system, and in consequence the idea of capitalism has taken on a sheen of attractiveness among people in both East and West such as it hasn't had for a long time.

**Q:** *A temporary phenomenon?*

**A:** Hard to say. Let there be a major recession in the West and ideological sentiments could change radically. Let Gorbachev achieve even a few economic successes and people might suddenly discover some merit even in the Soviet system. In the age of mass media, shifts of attitude occur much more quickly and unexpectedly than in the past.

**Q:** *Still, you can hardly deny that Socialism as an idea is, these days, in some disarray; that the social democratic parties, even when still strong electorally, have mainly a symbolic or verbal relation to the original Socialist commitment; that even lifelong Socialists have difficulty in providing a clear, simple description of what they want, that. . . .*

**A:** I get it. You don't really suppose you're the first to fire such questions? It would be feckless in a brief conversation to pretend to offer full answers. I've written a book on this, Michael Harrington has just completed an important book on the same theme, and there's the classic study of Alec Nove, *The Economics of Feasible Socialism.* Still, it would be self-deceiving to say that Socialism as an idea and a politics is now in great shape. It isn't. We continue to suffer the repercussions of the failures and disasters of our century. Once a great movement experiences such traumas, it takes a long time before it can regain clarity of thought and confidence.

But if you look at the decades since World War II there have been some very good intervals for the Socialist movement, especially in England, Germany, and Scandinavia. Important strides forward were taken toward strengthening the welfare state, a modification of capitalism that, while not yet Socialism, has significantly improved the lives of millions of people. The welfare state doesn't stir the imagination of apocalypse or violent extremism, but it is part of that steady process of social transition, a sort of "long march" in and through democracy that is central to the Socialist project.

**Q:** *Well, sure, it's easy for you chaps to polish your rhetoric, to say you want a society of solidarity, etc., but I don't see that you're very much nearer to reaching your ultimate goal than your movement was some decades ago?*

**A:** Fair enough, or almost fair. It's true that for some time now we Socialists have been on the defensive, but I think we've gained something thereby. We have a far more sophisticated sense of what socioeconomic change means and how difficult and lengthy the process is likely to be. We have firmed up our principled commitment to democracy and thereby abandoned entirely some of the more ambiguous aspects of the Marxist past. (Incidentally, one can see some signs of this in even the "leftist" pages of the British journal *New Left Review:* pleasing signs of heresy.) The European Socialist and social democratic parties sometimes thrive, sometimes flounder; they hardly have the animating fire of earlier days;

but there are good and serious people within them, for whom Socialism remains a significant option. In any case, consider the other main political trends, liberalism and conservatism: Are they in such great shape?

**Q:** *Sorry, that won't do. That others are in trouble hardly makes your situation better.*

**A:** Well, wait. Politics isn't a zero-sum game, at least democratic politics isn't. It's a regulated conflict for influence and power. The capacity and aliveness of one political tendency is measured in relation to another. The neocons are rapidly going into eclipse now that Reagan's gone. Liberalism? In France it's having a revival, partly because the French intellectuals, avant-gardists all, are never more than fifty years behind everyone else. But in America liberalism is in bad shape, not only as a movement but also as a current of thought. American liberalism has almost nothing to say about the terrible problem of the underclass. American liberalism is all but helpless before the growth of multinational corporate power, the increasing tendency of modern society toward international economic concentration, and the consequent extent to which vast corporate units dominate political life. About this we Socialists may not have the last word either, but at least we point to the urgency of the problem. American liberals, fearful of being smeared with the "s" word, hesitate to challenge even conceptually the existing property relations.

**Q:** *You Socialists have this curious habit of always looking toward the future. But what is the future except a continuous flow of the present?*

**A:** Very eloquent. But we don't only dream utopian dreams, we also engage with current problems. On some things we have answers close to those of the liberals and we cooperate with them. On other things, we point, so to say, beyond liberalism.

**Q:** *So you really want to tell me that in this rather cynical time you people propose to continue?*

**A:** Yes. I need only walk the streets of New York to be persuaded once more that our socioeconomic system is cruel, unjust. On the one hand, Drexel Burnham[2] and all those *goniffs* on Wall Street—the obscene displays of greed, the replays of the Robber Barons, the reckless and mindless speculations. On the other side, thousands of people freezing in the streets. Or I read the statistics that Mark Levinson[3] has brought together in this issue, figures that show how in Reagan's America the rich got richer and the poor, poorer. Problems multiply, injustices grow more glaring—this is no time for men and women of conscience to give up! Or I read about those splendid women in the Black Sash movement of South

Africa who go out into the streets to fight apartheid, or I talk with my friends of Peace Now in Israel: Why, our difficulties here are trivial by comparison.

As for *Dissent,* we're always in need of money, always searching for new contributions. But there's good news, too. Tell me, do you know of any other enterprise like ours, based entirely on voluntary participation, which has lasted for thirty-five years? And as some of us get older or sick or tired, there's a whole new generation of talented and devoted people coming along.

We believe the current economic relationships of power are bad. We believe they undermine democracy. We believe there can be more humane social arrangements, more democratic and equitable modes of structuring an economy: If our flame springs high, then good; if it flickers, then we tend it so that, with patience and time, it will flare again.

## Notes

1. Arendt had been an important professional influence on Irving Howe. He was acquainted with her in the late 1940s, when she was publishing sections of *The Origins of Totalitarianism* in *Partisan Review* and elsewhere. When she worked as a book editor at Scribner's, he was an assistant of hers and got to know her personally. Because of this connection he was able to get her to contribute to *Dissent*. Otherwise her fame by the mid-1950s after the publication of *The Origins of Totalitarianism* would have rendered it very unlikely that she would have contributed to a magazine that paid nothing.
2. Drexel Burnham Lambert was a major financial company that engaged in illegal activities and went out of business in the 1980s.
3. Mark Levinson is a labor economist and regular *Dissent* contributor.

# Chapter 13

**William Cain, "The Making of a Modern Critic,"** ***American Literary History,*** **Fall 1989.**

## Introduction

Although Irving Howe's first love was the European novel, he wrote pioneering works on Anderson, Faulkner, and Emerson, among others. Through these major works and numerous essays devoted to American authors or literary themes, Howe exerted significant influence on the emergence and shape of the field of American Studies across four decades, from the 1950s until his death in 1993. It is this noteworthy contribution that engages the intense interest of William Cain, an accomplished scholar of American Studies. This conversation spotlights Howe's achievement in that field and furnishes a window into both Howe's literary career and his social and political concerns. It advances beyond the discussions of modernism in the Schulman and Greenberg chapters of this volume, delving into Howe's critique of ideological uses of literature.

At the time of the interview, Cain was a young professor of American literature at Wellesley College in Massachusetts (where he has spent his entire career). He had published books on literary criticism, including one on F. O. Mathiessen, and was also a scholar of African American history. These interests make him an ideal interviewer to explore Howe's literary side, especially his concern for the social aspects of literature. Cain has since gone on to a distinguished record of publication, from writing valuable works on pedagogy to editing volumes on American literature and co-editing *The Norton Anthology of Theory and Criticism* (2001).

Howe begins the interview by reflecting upon his tilt toward European authors, a typical preference of American intellectuals in his New York circle. Europe has occupied a special place as the cradle of contemporary civilization—a role attacked as Eurocentric in recent decades—and Howe elaborates upon the predilection of the New York Intellectuals affiliated with *Partisan Review* for a modernism that originated in Europe. Howe also makes an intriguing connection between modernism and the postwar anti-Stalinist politics of his *Partisan Review* circle. When, a few pages later, he describes a modernism that is international in scope, he hints at saving international Socialism through a global cultural project. Yet Howe also admits that many of the New York Intellectuals regarded American literature as shallow, typified by "the idea of the paleness, the thinness of the Emersonian tradition," a judgment with which he would wrestle throughout his career. In his revaluation of *Huckleberry Finn* and Melville, this same coming to terms with Americanness can be glimpsed, so that individualism becomes not just a narcissistic search for wealth but an existential struggle with morality and society. Here and elsewhere, Howe treats American literature as a rich field of study in its own right rather than as a subset of international literature.

Elaborating on the critique of academia in the Klingenstein interview, Howe continues to deride the isolation, specialization, and obfuscation of the poststructuralists. He also discusses the new role of leftist cultural politics in literary criticism, a development with which one might expect him to harbor sympathy in light of his earlier work, particularly *Politics and the Novel* (1957). Too often, however, he finds that ideologically oriented critics of the 1980s, rather than studying political and social contexts to enrich a work of art, subscribe to predetermined knee-jerk judgments, so that "the canon is being pushed too far and too willfully in behalf of ideological ends."

Still, Howe's reflections here on his friendship with Richard Wright and on his quarrel with Ralph Ellison illuminate his own role in extending the canon. In "Black Boys and Native Sons," a 1963 essay, Howe had argued that anger inevitably plays a primary role in African American writing; this led to a sharp rebuff from Ellison, who responded that Howe had pigeonholed African American fiction, which draws upon an extremely broad and motley array of culture and experience. Ellison emphasized the multiple, variegated sources (including European) incorporated into African American literature. He also proudly drew attention to the universality of his own work, especially *Invisible Man,* which owed its lavish, multivalent complexity both to its rootedness in the loamy European literary-political tradition and its obviously intimate understanding of and engagement with African American society. It seems likely, however, that Ellison would have endorsed Howe's statement here that "from a literary point of view, these writers [e.g., Ellison, Richard Wright, James Baldwin] are quite as American as Faulkner or Hemingway, Bellow or Malamud." They are integral, Howe affirms, to the fabric of American literature and, implicitly, the American way of life. In this regard, it is inviting to compare Howe's attitude toward African American literature to his notable criticisms of Jewish-American writers, including Bellow and Phillip Roth, the latter of whom he chided for propagating negative Jewish stereotypes. Whether Howe had a more expansive vision of Jewish-American fiction than of African American writing is an interesting biographical-critical question.

Howe's similar controversies with feminism receive attention in Cain's interview. Howe grants the historical importance of feminism and its humanistic campaign to combat centuries of oppression of women. Yet for him it was never a central issue comparable to the politics of class or even race; unsurprisingly, in the decades following the 1960s, he was often accused of slighting feminism. Vivian Gornick, for instance, in her review of *A Margin of Hope,* argues that for Howe women "are not 'classes,' and their struggle—without theory, manifesto or party program—is unreal and distasteful."[1]

Aware of such criticism, Cain asks Howe about his treatment, in a 1950s essay, of Henry James' *The Bostonians,* which portrayed early feminism in an unflattering light. Howe points out that it is unrealistic to expect someone to step out of his time: "It seems only natural that, if I were to write the essay today, I would treat the novel differently." He also claims that he has always respected women writers and critics: "I have read some of the earlier women critics and respect them very much—Elizabeth Hardwick, Ellen Moers, Susan Sontag. But they are not the women critics who are usually meant when people speak about feminist criticism." Here Howe makes a distinction, quite common in the late 1960s and early 1970s, between "women critics" (or women writers) and "feminist critics" (or writers). The three writers whom he mentions—along with critics such as Diana Trilling—were among the colleagues and associates with whom he interacted during most of his professional life.[2] He seems to have associated "feminist" criticism with the excesses of the New Left, which he opposed as both ideologically obtuse and mired in trendy abstractions and fashionable sloganeering. His aversion to the doctrinal purities of the New Left or the tenets of radical feminism likely also stems from a rejection in his postwar (and post-Troskyist) maturation of polemic and ideology in literary criticism, practices that reduce literature to a political struggle, and to which he succumbed during his youth in his own literary criticism. The Irving Howe of *Politics and the Novel* and later works distinguished sharply between overtly political literature and more nuanced art that nevertheless reflects and participates in the social conditions of its time. A similar distinction can be used to compare black writers and writers who happen to be black; however in this case Howe took a position favoring overt social commentary that rankled Ellison's refined aesthetic sensibilities. Howe's discussion below also criticizes academic feminism for promoting a narrow, politically correct, select set of women writers who exhibit the requisite ideological orthodoxy. Still, feminists might respond that Howe's more traditional preferences conform to his own ideology.

This interview gave Howe a forum for his critique of contemporary literary academe. In Howe's objection that "the canon is being pushed too far and too willfully in behalf of ideological ends," we witness a tentative, strategic alliance with conservatives who believed that the Western canon was being diluted. Howe also believed in the ideal of the "common reader," for whom the Great Tradition provides guidance, as opposed to what he considered ill-educated, jargon-spewing academics who dominated literary study in the late 1980s (and beyond).

Stimulated in his thinking by William Cain, Howe speaks frankly and with confidence. Cain approaches Howe, properly, as a founding father and major figure in the history of American Studies.

An abbreviated form of this interview was first published in *American Literary History* 1:3 (1989): 554-564, commissioned by Cain, one of its editors, in order to honor Howe for his contribution to the field.

## The Interview

*I interviewed Irving Howe in 1988, when he came to Wellesley College for a lecture. Our session lasted about an hour, and soon thereafter I prepared a transcript which I mailed to Irving and to which he made a few minor changes and adjustments in phrasing. Irving told me that he enjoyed our exchange but wondered whether anyone would be interested in what he had to say. This reflected his sense that most academics in the 1980s had become absorbed in literary theory and that they therefore would not feel any affinity with an old-timer (his term) like himself. I told Irving what was true—that to me he wasn't an old-timer in the slightest, and that I was sure his work would be read and valued long after the work done by the theorists then in vogue had faded from view. Irving's literary criticism was vivid and powerful to me when I first encountered it during my years in college, and if anything I find it even more rewarding now, perhaps because I had the good fortune to meet and enjoy the company of the man who wrote it.*

**Q:** *You have written extensively about American literature, yet I notice that you do not include any American writers, save for the somewhat complex case of T. S. Eliot, in your list of "writers who have meant the most to me."*[3] *Which American writers have mattered most to you? Do you find that they speak to you with a different kind of authority, interest, and power than do writers such as Brecht, Orwell, and Kafka?*

**A:** To really explain why, when I first became involved in literary life, the writers who seemed to matter most were European, would require the most difficult of all things—imagining historical circumstances different from the present. If you put yourself back into the period of the late 1940s, and into the somewhat special literary, political, and cultural milieu in which I then found myself, the milieu of the New York Intellectuals, then perhaps you'll see why it was European literature that gripped our imaginations most of all. This wasn't true for everyone. Alfred Kazin was much more of an "Americanist" even at that early point than, say, Philip Rahv or Lionel Trilling. But we—I use the term "we" quite loosely—then thought of ourselves as committed to literary modernism, and modernism meant, above all, European writing.

We knew that there were American modernists; we thought of Hemingway and Faulkner as in some ways modernist. Stevens wasn't yet an important figure for us, but we knew that Cummings, Williams, and other poets were modernist. But literary modernism meant primarily Joyce, Kafka, Eliot, Brecht, Pirandello.

So there was for us the idea of discovering and championing literary modernism, and it is important to remember that the great European writers were not yet fully accepted. They were honored, but within the literary world in America, there was still a great deal of struggle, of rear-guard resistance against the acceptance of these writers. One of the things that gave the *Partisan Review* people energy was the notion of struggling on behalf of the modernists against middlebrows and academic critics. In the academy, it wasn't until a decade later that the fight was over and modernism accepted, and, as it came to seem, accepted all too much.

Another reason for the European orientation was that our politics was that of the anti-Stalinist left. Now today everyone is against Stalinism; everyone attacks and repudiates it. This common understanding of Stalinism was achieved, however, in a sense, at the cost of our lives. It took decades of struggle, intellectually and politically, for this view of Stalinism to become part of the political understanding of serious people. Because we were concerned to advance a leftist anti-Stalinist position, which we allied, skillfully or not, with modernist literature, we felt a strong kinship with certain other European writers. These writers probably do not figure much for a good many younger readers, though I hope that in time readers will come back to them.

I mean writers such as Silone, Koestler, Malraux, Orwell, Victor Serge, and some others. There was a small, rather beleaguered community of gifted, if not great, anti-Stalinist writers, They were not of the same level or quality as the major modernists, but they were serious figures who merited respect. And we felt a kinship with them.

There's another reason for the orientation toward European writers. Many of us were the children of Jewish immigrants who came from Eastern Europe, and the Jewish immigrants brought with them an enormous admiration for Russian literature. The great heroes of the more emancipated, secularized immigrant Jews were Tolstoy, Chekhov, and Turgenev—the masters of nineteenth-century Russia. For someone like Rahv—though he did write very well on James and Hawthorne—what really absorbed his imagination were the nineteenth-century

Russian writers. For me, this was something that came, so to speak, from the very air around me. I drew it in almost unthinkingly.

Now I also remember along these lines that when I got out of the army, in 1946, I picked up a book by V. S. Pritchett, a critic I've always admired (even if he doesn't have a system!). The book was *The Living Novel*. During the war, Pritchett had [contributed to] the *Tribune*, a Left-Socialist weekly in England, and then, I think, he also worked for the *New Statesman*. There weren't many new books during these years, so he decided to write about old books. He would do a piece every couple of weeks about a writer of the past he esteemed. In *The Living Novel*, he dealt with nineteenth-century Russian writers who were not quite of the very highest level, but still terrifically good—Goncharov and Lermontov, for example. I then went through *The Living Novel* systematically, and read every single novel that Pritchett had written about. I only met Pritchett once in my life—he was a charming man—and I told him that my literary education was partly based on his book.

But it needs to be said, too, that we had a certain bias, a prejudice, with regard to American literature. We associated American literature with a narrow cultural chauvinism. Van Wyck Brooks, by the 1940s in his later, inferior phase, and others too were celebrating American writing as against what they looked upon as decadent European writing. And we accepted a little too uncritically this kind of counter-position. We also tended to take a rather simplistic view of the whole Emersonian tradition. The idea of the paleness, the thinness, of the Emersonian tradition was one that Rahv had picked up from various earlier critics, and it was by and large taken for granted. If you were concerned with Socialist ideas, if you felt that you were living in a moment of historical apocalypse—say, in 1939 or 1946—and were trying desperately to define what Stalinism was and what new kind of society had emerged that had traduced your Socialist hopes, then Emerson's Concord could seem extremely thin, even genteel.

It was only in later years, more recently, when I went back and read Emerson again under the prompting of certain American critics, such as Harold Bloom, that I saw him differently. But a period of several decades elapsed between these two phases of my experience. I should say, however, that even then, some thirty-five years ago, I and some of my friends did read Melville with intense interest. We also read Henry James avidly—Rahv played an important role in stimulating this taste, and Edmund Wilson's essay on James was also important for us. But what I now think of as the central tradition in American letters stemming from Emerson and Thoreau—that was something we were not terribly responsive to. And the scholarly work on American literature—Perry Miller's work on Puritanism, for example—I really didn't get to until later. That was a flaw, a deficiency.

**Q:** *Do you believe it is possible to speak of a distinctively "American" literature? I was struck by a sentence in* World of Our Fathers*: "Bored by the apparent parochialism of native American culture, the sons of the immigrant Jews helped break* *down the whole idea, no longer so enabling for our writers, that there was a peculiar grace or virtue in the 'Americanness' of American literature."*[4] *Could you elaborate upon this point, and explain what it implies about efforts to locate something unique about American writers, books, and literary traditions?*

**A:** I now do believe in a distinctive American literature, but back then I would have been much more skeptical. You must remember that our position was strongly international.

Literary modernism, by its very nature, tended to break down national boundaries. Was Joyce an Irish writer or a European writer? Was Kafka a Czech writer or a Jewish writer? These questions came to seem meaningless. We felt that we had entered a period of international literature. Even Hemingway, while very American in many respects, in the 1930s was probably the most influential writer in the world.

There were people imitating Hemingway's style in Buenos Aires, in Tokyo, in Constantinople—everywhere. We judged that both for political and literary/cultural reasons we needed to see literature from an internationalist perspective.

This was enabling but had its costs, primarily, as I have said, in a certain narrowness in relation to what we saw as American. There was, to be sure, a nativist, American parochialism, but our view of it was in turn parochial. Gradually we did correct this view. Of course there is an American literature! How can you read *Huckleberry Finn*, Cooper's novels, *The Confidence Man*, or even a novel like *The Europeans* without feeling that a distinctive American aura and atmosphere pervades these books? Yes, there has been a tendency on the part of some Americanists—who have developed a professional interest in it—to exaggerate the "Americanness" of American literature. Still, I think one can locate a distinctive American quality, a voice, a tone. Though I would then want to add that those critics who have insisted upon seeing Twain, for example, in relation to English and European ancestors, and who wish to complicate the notion of a distinctive Americanness by showing the roots of American literature in English literature and European culture—they also have an important point. If you'll forgive my using this phrase, you need a certain dialectical sense: there is a distinctiveness about American literature and also a similarity to English and European writing, and they coexist within the same "texts."

**Q:** *In* American Newness, *you keenly examine a number of central writers of the American Renaissance, yet you do not deal with Stowe or Douglass, both of whom suggest interesting (if very different) angles on Emersonian self-reliance and individual freedom. This leads me to ask you to comment on the current scholarly (and often highly polemical) emphasis on "expanding the canon." How would you respond to a reader who judges that your argument in* American Newness *should have taken account of black and women writers?*

**A:** Well, one answer is that *American Newness* is a very small book, really a few lectures where I was trying to stay with the main figures. Perhaps a more cogent criticism would be that in this little book the main figures are by no means adequately treated. Since I did not treat them fully, there would have been little point in diverging still further to other writers. I wasn't attempting to write a history of American literature; I was trying to show certain lines of intellectual development and provide what I thought, rightly or wrongly, was a somewhat fresh view of what Emersonianism meant. The only other person I had ever encountered who had expressed a view similar to mine was the American historian George Frederickson, who had written on this period in his fine book, *The Inner Civil War*, and said some of the kinds of things that I wanted to get at. As for the canon, I would say that there are certain expansions that seem perfectly legitimate. Some of Douglass's writing has a particular American eloquence which is impressive. The first third of Du Bois's *Autobiography*, showing his childhood and youth in western Massachusetts, is wonderful, and there is perhaps as much reason to read that book as Henry Adams's autobiography. But my objection to some of the current trends is that the canon is being pushed too far and too willfully in behalf of ideological ends.

I myself cannot see that it is essential for our students to read *Uncle Tom's Cabin* at a time when they read so little and when we would be overjoyed if they managed to read *Moby Dick*.

**Q:** *Could you also describe here your response to such important Afro-American writers of this century as Ralph Ellison, James Baldwin, and Richard Wright? What did these writers mean to you? Do you regard them as "Afro-American" writers, part of a separate tradition, or does it seem more natural simply to term them "American" writers?*

**A:** Wright, Ellison, and Baldwin, as well as the other black American writers, are part of the American literary canon—they were born here, they have lived their lives here, they write about American life, they write in English. Where else could they be placed?

I don't know what, if any, meaning the phrase "Afro-American" has, other than as a token of a certain kind of black politics; but from a literary point of view, these writers are as much American as Faulkner or Hemingway, Bellow or Malamud. Wright was for a brief time, toward the end of his life, a friend or a friendly acquaintance. We met and got along very well.

I admired the courage with which he broke into the American literary world, and I think of him as an important if limited writer. All the work of later black American writers was made possible by, even if written in opposition to, Wright. He was the first to release the full weight of black anger. And he was also interesting for his political experience, first as a Communist, then as one who had broke from Communism and for a brief time, though not uncritically, approached a sort of African "nationalism." By the time I met him he was a skeptical yet still impassioned man. With Ellison I had a once-famous literary quarrel, in the early 1960s, which almost everyone except me thought he "won." (In America you have to "win" or "lose"). We have since become friendly and agree upon many things. I admire his fiction enormously, and in fact reviewed *Invisible Man* favorably when it first came out. Baldwin I never knew. His fiction seemed very thin to me, but I think he was for a while one of the major American essayists.

**Q:** *Have feminist literary theory and criticism affected your critical work in important ways? I am wondering, for example, whether you might write about* The Bostonians *differently today than you did in* Politics and the Novel. *In rereading your essay on that novel, I noted your powerful, persuasive account of James's "conservative skepticism" and suspicion of public life. But would you also want now—possibly spurred by feminist scholarship—to engage James's mocking descriptions of feminism and women's reform even more directly and severely?*

**A:** First, I should say that for a period of eight or nine years, perhaps a shade longer, I was away from literary criticism and, indeed, from literary life—these were the years I was writing *World of Our Fathers* and doing other nonliterary things. You see, while I believe that literary criticism is very difficult and that very few people do it well, I also think that it is not enough by itself to absorb the energies of a serious person.

I am not saying that literary criticism doesn't matter, is not valuable or interesting. But my impression is that almost all of the critics whom I admire, in the recent past and earlier, did other things as well. For them, literary criticism was ancillary to writing fiction or poetry, to being engaged with ideas or politics or with religious interests. Very few critics that I know of, at least very few of the major critics, have been merely literary critics. At the same time, I do want to emphasize again that criticism is extraordinarily difficult to do well. You can perhaps train yourself to do it, but you cannot find a set of rules or a "method." To get back to your question, for a period of time I was away from literary concerns—I am very much back with them now—and I fell behind. I didn't read a good deal of the material that younger academic people are concerned with. (I have the feeling that if I just hold out a little bit longer, I may not have to read all that much of it!) Some of the French stuff I just cannot read. Maybe it's my fault. Maybe I lack the kind of philosophical disposition needed to read it—that could be. I wrote somewhere that I am lamentably cool to metaphysics. I have read some of the earlier women critics and respect them very much—Elizabeth Hardwick, Ellen Moers, Susan Sontag. But they are not the women critics who are usually meant when people speak about feminist criticism.

The academic feminist critics I haven't read with any adequate attentiveness, and so I cannot comment on them. As for *The Bostonians*, remember that

I wrote that essay a long time ago, in the middle 1950s. It seems only natural that if I were to write the essay today I would treat the novel differently. At that point, feminism was not part of the prevailing consciousness. The question of conservatism was. Not being immune to the pressures of the zeitgeist, I wrote a bit more about the conservative aspect than the feminist aspect. But I did pay attention to Olive Chancellor's feminism and her tacit, or not so tacit, lesbianism. I tried to suggest that James had a rather complex view—it would be a mistake to say simply that he was attacking the feminist and transcendentalist traditions. He is condescending toward Miss Birdseye, but he also admires her. Clearly James is writing from a conservative point of view. But he is also extremely sardonic toward and critical of the conservative Basil Ransom. If Basil Ransom wins out in that book, it's mainly because James thinks that he has "biology" or "nature" on his side. But certainly James does not align himself ideologically with Basil Ransom; he makes fun of his ideology. James is trying to establish himself in the book at a certain distance from all of the dominant ideological figures of the day. *The Bostonians* is the coldest of James's novels, the one book where he seems not to have any quavering affection for any of the characters.

**Q:** *In* A Margin of Hope, *you refer to the powerful appeal of literary criticism to post-World War II intellectuals. It seemed, you reflect, to offer a kind of intellectual freedom and range—an opportunity to examine the most "serious concerns" of the culture—that could be found nowhere else.*[5] *Would you be inclined to use such lofty language about criticism today?*

**A:** I certainly don't think such language applies to the dominant trends in current academic criticism. Today, the whole idea of the common reader—whether an actual reader whom we might specify as part of a social group, or a projected desire of an ideal audience—this idea of the common reader has virtually been abandoned in the academic literary world. A tremendous and, I think, disastrous change. You see, when you had people like Trilling, Orwell, Wilson, Empson, Auden, and William Troy, and also some of the New Critics such as Allen Tate, Robert Penn Warren, and Austin Warren, who were not just formalists but also powerful critics of culture, you had people who seemed to be speaking to the deepest concerns of a cultivated reader. This was especially true at a time when many serious intellectuals and readers were becoming somewhat disenchanted with politics. Such a disenchantment usually occurs in a conservative period and did occur in the 1950s. People read the literary critics not merely because they wanted illumination about various books and writers, but because these critics seemed to be making cogent observations about the nature of our life, at least the life of the educated public. Now whatever the virtues may be of the main trends in academic literary criticism, I don't think that anyone is likely to respond to it as readers did to the criticism of the 1950s. Was this conception of criticism specific to the historical moment of the postwar years? I don't think so. The tradition had already been established in the work of the great English critics—Arnold, Hazlitt, Samuel Johnson, all of whom in part were journalists. While I don't believe that journalism should ever become the dominant component, it should always be there as a possibility, as an avenue and occasion for criticism. All of these critics, as well as many lesser figures, found a way to pay attention to a particular text and also comment on the larger cultural context in which these texts had appeared.

**Q:** *Can you speak even more directly about the impact of the academy on literary and cultural life? Russell Jacoby, in his recent book,* The Last Intellectuals, *laments the disappearance of "nonacademic intellectuals" such as yourself, and objects to the manner in which narrow-minded professionalism and self-isolating specialization now rule the academy. The relation between the academic scholar/critic and the intellectual does seem an issue that has often concerned you. I think, for instance, of your complaint in* Celebrations and Attacks *about the "omnivorous" need for research topics among academics,*[6] *and some of your affirmative remarks in* A Margin of Hope *about "the intellectual as anti-specialist."*[7] *Is there any room in the academy for such an intellectual, one who seeks frequent contact with the common reader?*

**A:** I've been both a professor and a freelance intellectual writer. I taught for thirty-three years, took my work as a teacher seriously, did it as well as I could, and enjoyed a fair part of it. I was not, and am not, a scholar in a narrow sense, though by now I may know a few things. From my association with J. V. Cunningham at Brandeis—a poet-scholar I admired enormously and whom I look upon as a teacher—I learned that scholars need not be the musty, irrelevant sort of drones some of us had foolishly supposed them to be. I learned that scholarship can be as serious, indeed as exalted a calling as the intellectual life—and that often enough the two could unite. (You have to learn something as you get older.) My complaint about a lot of what's going on today in the academy is that it is insulated, seemingly indifferent to the "common reader" who is still out there, lost in a tangle of categories and phrases but not especially scholarly, and, so far as I can tell, not deeply engaged with literature.

**Q:** *This line of questioning leads me also to ask about your admiration for Edmund Wilson, whose exemplary critical activity you have described in* A Margin of Hope *and elsewhere. Do you believe that Wilson can still serve today as a model?*

**A:** I think Wilson was a first-rate critic of prose and a splendid writer. The generation of critics among whom he stood out tried to write with lucidity, force, and wit. People like Robert Penn Warren, Yvor Winters, Harold Rosenberg, William Empson, and others were not only lively critics, but were very good writers in different ways. So the question isn't Wilson himself, as an individual. The question is which kinds of predecessors or contemporaries you wish to emulate. I think my choices are pretty clear.

**Q:** *In* A Margin of Hope, *you state that the* Partisan Review *writers scorned "political contamination of critical judgment."*[8] *What in your view is the relation between political and aesthetic judgment? Isn't there a danger in the position that the* Partisan Review *writers favored? Can such a position impel critics to slight or ignore the political meanings and implications of literary works? I'm thinking not only of an obviously disturbing case like Ezra Pound (whom you comment on in* Margin of Hope*), but also Eliot, Lawrence, and Hemingway. When we read* The Wasteland, Women in Love, *or* For Whom the Bell Tolls, *don't we inevitably make aesthetic and political judgments at one and the same time?*

**A:** This is, of course, a very complex matter and it would be foolish to try to respond to it in a few words. But what interests, and amuses, me about your question is the way you phrase it. For decades, the charge against the *Partisan* critics—and sometimes a warranted charge—was that their politics got in the way of, or alloyed, their literary responses. All through the years from, say, 1937 to 1967 no one thought the New York writers were slighting politics. Quite the contrary. Now, it seems they are to be cast . . . well, in another way. Clearly, our political views influence, sometimes sharpen and sometimes debase our literary judgments. At times, as with Pound, it becomes all but impossible to keep them distinct. But with the great works you mention I for one find it not too difficult—am I using the phrase correctly?—to "bracket" the politics and take pleasure in the poem or novel.

**Q:** *A final question about the postwar years. You, Dwight Macdonald, and others wrote very harshly in the 1940s and 1950s about the evils of Stalinism. Do you regret at all the fierce tone that you employed? How do you respond to critics who contend that your polemics against Stalinist sympathizers functioned to discredit the Left in general?*

**A:** I don't want to pretend that every review or polemic I or my friends wrote had exactly the "right" tone. Of course not. There were excesses, indulgences, outbursts, furies. But I strongly believe that the political and intellectual struggle against Stalinism was an essential, perhaps even the central, moral obligation of intellectuals during my earlier years. We were seeking to rescue the idea or image of Socialism from the horrors of the Gulag, from the lies of the Moscow trials, from the cultural barbarism of "Socialist realism." It was a bitter fight and there are still bruises. But it was something we had to do. If we hadn't struggled, as a quite small minority, within the literary world, and an even smaller minority within the Left, to expose the brutality and foulness of Stalinism—and what we said you can now read in the Moscow press!—it wouldn't be possible for people of your generation to look back "dispassionately" and wonder about our tone. It was the Gulag that discredited the Left, not those of us who told the truth about it.

## Notes

1. John Rodden, *The Worlds of Irving Howe: The Critical Legacy*, (Boulder: Paradigm, 2005), 273.
2. David Laskin discusses the implicit double bind for women of the New York Intellectuals of Howe's generation, notably Mary McCarthy, Hannah Arendt, and Diana Trilling. Intellectually engaged, they could be seen as holding their own with men and being treated as equals. Yet they were expected also to uphold the "womanly" arts of cooking, cleaning, and holding family together. Laskin describes them as "ambitious and, for the most part, skilled at turning their ambitions to their advantage. They lived boldly, winning acclaim by writing better than anyone else, loving freely if not always wisely or happily, shouting down literary and political opponents in a time and place renowned for noisy argument" (16). Yet Laskin argues, "They were emphatically not liberated in the way they conducted their private lives, in their assumptions, in their relationships with men, particularly the men they married" ( 16-17). When second-wave feminism came along, in general these older female intellectuals believed in their own mythology, at least in public, believing that they had attained full status to express themselves as intellectuals and siding with Howe's criticisms of feminism. *Partisans: Marriage, Politics, and Betrayal Among the New York Intellectuals* (New York: Simon & Schuster, 2000).
3. Irving Howe, *A Margin of Hope* (San Diego: Harcourt Brace Jovanovich, 1982), 350.
4. Irving Howe, *World of Our Fathers* (New York: Harcourt Brace Jovanovich, 1976), 603.
5. Irving Howe, *A Margin of Hope* (San Diego: Harcourt Brace Jovanovich, 1982), 147.
6. Irving Howe, *Celebrations and Attacks: Thirty Years of Literary and Cultural Commentary* (New York: Harcourt Brace Jovanovich, 1979), 156.
7. Irving Howe, *A Margin of Hope* (San Diego: Harcourt Brace Jovanovich, 1982), 161.
8. Irving Howe, *A Margin of Hope* (San Diego: Harcourt Brace Jovanovich, 1982), 149.

# Chapter 14

**Jim Holt, "'Howe Now' on Politics, Art, and the Critic," *Thesis: The Magazine of the Graduate School and University Center*, Fall 1990.**

## Introduction

This is the most theoretically oriented interview in the book, reflected in its appearance in an academic journal concerned with conceptual issues that bear on politics and economics. Howe uses the historical moment to congratulate the anti-Stalinist Left, which he believed had been vindicated for decades of fierce and unrelenting opposition to Stalinism and Communism. Yet he also worries about the fate of the liberal-Left and the historical injustice of its continuing, utterly unfair association with the discredited and failed Communist states.

Jim Holt, who conducted the interview, proves knowledgeable, thoughtful, and interested in large issues. Holt has gone on to a successful career as a writer on science and philosophy in such distinguished venues as the *New Yorker*, the *New York Times Magazine*, the *New York Review of Books*, the *Wall Street Journal*, *Lingua Franca*, and *Slate*. He is also the author of *Stop Me If You've Heard This: A History and Philosophy of Jokes* (2008).

Whereas the previous interview with William Cain addressed many literary matters not contingent on a precise historical moment, Holt's political and cultural questions turn very much on the immediate condition of American intellectual life. Prompted by Holt's probing inquiries, Howe assumes a more academic approach here than in other interviews in the collection, most of which turn on policy and even biographical issues.

The year 1990 must have been a bittersweet one for Howe, a period of great hope yet also of shattered ideals for members of the Old Left. Holt opens with the concept of "plastic hours," historical periods when anything seems possible.

Howe responds by celebrating the new promise of the Gorbachev years, which were bringing unforeseen, constructive changes in the direction of liberalization, though Howe also criticizes capitalism's unchallenged status. He explains that "the old theories of totalitarianism as something immutable and unbreakable have been proven to be at least in part mistaken." The planet, he says, is entering *terra incognita*. By 1990, the Berlin Wall had fallen, destroying the vestiges of Stalinism, and a triumphant international capitalism was ascendant.

Howe welcomes the unraveling of totalizing theories of totalitarianism advanced by thinkers such as Hannah Arendt. "The notion that there was an inevitable trend toward the power of the Communist political monopolies," he explains, "has been absolutely destroyed. That's wonderful. The rise of democratic participation in Czechoslovakia, for example, is admirable." Quickly, however, he moves to a stance of critique. His joy about the destruction of Stalinism is offset by his depression over the triumph of unfettered free market ideology in both the United States and Eastern Europe. He also uses this historical crossroads to attempt, once again, to decouple the idea of Socialism from the history of the Soviet Union. The distance from Howe's mode in chapter 12, with Howe in the role of an "imaginary interviewer" just before the fall of the Berlin Wall, is apparent: his attitude here is more bifurcated and ambivalent, expressing both celebratory and cautionary emotions about the sudden change in history.

Howe is all too aware that a period of sustained capitalist experimentation is under way, particularly in Eastern Europe, though he excuses it as merely a passing phase, almost like a teenager going through a maturation crisis: "When you suffer under one kind of excessive regime, there is a natural tendency to go to the opposite extreme; however, there's a great deal of naiveté and illusion about what free markets are and how they function in the West." Both Eastern Europe, the most recent convert to free market economics, and the United States, the country at the pinnacle of capitalism, were enchanted at this time with markets as the wondrous answer to all economic and social problems. Howe decries trends in the United States that he trusts will soon be overturned: burgeoning economic inequality and increasing privatization. Citing the weak economy and social unrest of the Bush years, he expects an eventual return to the ideals of a mixed economy and, eventually, to some variant of Socialist thought, albeit in a new, tempered form. Citing "what Harrington called 'visionary gradualism,'" Howe slightly redefines his ideals, expressing his hopes for an "evolution toward a social ethic of cooperation rather than the mad greediness and destructiveness that we have witnessed in America in the last decade."

Even though pressed by Holt, Howe cannot or will not express esteem for a single contemporary political figure. At most he points to Robert Kuttner, who is a journalist and not a politician, as an exemplary thinker about social policy, but one who does not share Howe's long-term vision. The fact is that no political figure ever replaced Norman Thomas for Howe; he finds neither the liberals nor the neo-liberals of the Democratic Party attractive. The only recent political figure whom he admires, his compatriot Michael Harrington, died in 1989, and Harrington was never any kind of national political force.

From the perspective of the early twenty-first century, we know that the political trends Howe deplored have not receded but rather advanced, both in the United States and across most of the planet. Howe specifies some developments that have worsened in our day, "the disintegration of political life, the ascendancy of money in campaigns, and the reduction of political discourse to these crude and empty thirty-second 'sound bites.'" Corporatization and commodification impoverish public culture.

Making explicit this connection between a fragmented politics and a fragmented culture, the interview closes with Howe's reflections on the artistic and intellectual situation in America. Howe notes that, although young intellectuals and artists may be doing good work, "there isn't very much of an intellectual community. There isn't some strong driving ideal that unites people." Here again, the nascent trends of the 1980s can be witnessed in a more advanced stage in the twenty-first century: the sense of disconnectedness and extreme individualism.

Howe's regret here is related to his dismal view of political and economic trends. As George Orwell might argue, a degraded political landscape leads to a corrupted language and culture, and vice versa. Once again, it is difficult to separate Howe's discouragement from his nostalgia; certainly the situation was dim, at least from the perspective of a radical humanist, but the past had its own bleakness, from World War II to McCarthyism to the danger of all-out nuclear war.

Obviously, the repeated failure of Howe's own vision of an ideal society took its toll on his spirit. Despite his insistence on resisting any tendency to "see the world collapsing, disintegrating," his view of the zeitgeist is somber. Again, as with his verdict on American political figures, he is unwilling to cite even one writer or artist whom he esteems or thinks possesses permanent value: "My sense is that we now have many good writers but few, if any great ones, in America." He implicitly contrasts that assessment with the cultural situation of earlier decades. His one exception within the arts, his new-found love—the ballet—is idiosyncratic and more connected to the idea of individual genius than to any sort of movement. But his mention of ballet here underscores its biographical significance: it was the great cultural discovery of his late years; his enthusiasm for an art form that he had ignored and even derided in earlier decades proved redemptive. It also refreshed Howe, providing sheer, joy-filled relief after a lifetime of stern critical judgments and agonizing political defeats. Moreover, it represented for him a welcome release from his intense focus on language and on verbal art.

Appearing in *Thesis,* the magazine of the City University of New York (CUNY), this interview reached a receptive audience, serious about politics and generally sympathetic to Howe's Left-liberal vision. Indeed Howe had gone to City College as an undergraduate in the 1930s and served as professor at the CUNY Graduate Center and at Queens College from 1963 to 1986. With the *Thesis* audience, as had been the case with Howe's appearance at the 92nd Street

YMCA in chapter 3, Howe feels at home, challenged by his supporters rather than castigated by his adversaries.

## The Interview

*In that "herd of independent minds" known as the New York Intellectuals, it would be difficult to locate a mind more independent than that of Irving Howe. One of America's foremost literary critics and social-democratic thinkers, Howe is the author of more than a dozen books on topics ranging from Thomas Hardy to Leon Trotsky to the United Auto Workers. His* World of Our Fathers, *a historical study of the life and culture of Eastern European immigrants in New York from the 1880s to the 1930s, was a national bestseller. Howe has also edited many volumes, including* Essential Works of Socialism *and several collections of Yiddish literature in translation. His latest book,* Selected Writings, 1950-1990, *was published this fall by Harcourt Brace Jovanovich.*

*Howe was born in the East Bronx, a poor but culturally vibrant community of Eastern European immigrants in which Yiddish was spoken almost everywhere. In the 1930s he attended the City College of New York, along with other future members of the New York Intellectual circle like Alfred Kazin, Daniel Bell, Nathan Glazer, and Irving Kristol. There Howe was a fixture in the legendary Alcove One, a murky horseshoeshaped area off the lunchroom where students of various ideological stripes gathered to argue about Socialist theory. (Alcove Two was the haunt of the more numerous Stalinist students.)*

*After a stint in the army during World War II, Howe emerged as one of the more brilliant members of the New York Intelligentsia. Socialist in politics and modernist in aesthetics, he was known as a formidable controversialist and became a frequent contributor to such publications as* Commentary, Partisan Review, politics, *and* The Nation. *During this time he supported himself by writing weekly book reviews for* Time *magazine. In 1954 he founded* Dissent *as a forum for the reexamination of Socialist ideas. "When intellectuals can do nothing else, they start a magazine," he commented in the inaugural issue of the quarterly which he still edits.*

*Although Howe never did any formal graduate work, his reputation as a distinguished and prolific literary critic led to a faculty appointment at Brandeis in the 1950s. In the early 1960s he was made a full professor at Stanford, but he felt removed from New York intellectual life there. In his memoir Howe recalls the "disconsolate evenings in Palo Alto; where are the sidewalks, the pedestrians, the crowds?" But then, he says, "The providence in which I disbelieved again proved merciful: a job offer came from the City University of New York and I scurried back home, moving into "a ratty apartment in the West Village a few doors from a truculent congressman named Koch." At the Graduate School Howe found "students who still cared to read Jane Austen and Henry James" even during the turbulent events of the late 1960s. He spent the remainder of his teaching career here and is now Distinguished Professor Emeritus of English.*

*The following interview was conducted last spring by* Thesis *editor Jim Holt at Howe's apartment in Manhattan.*

**Q:** *In your memoir,* A Margin of Hope, *you talk about certain moments in history—Gershom Scholem called them "plastic hours," "when sentiments of hope spread across the globe . . . The dead hand of the past will finally be lifted, and once again a journey begun to the shores of light." The present seems to be one of those "plastic hours" for the Soviet Union and Eastern Europe, and perhaps for the entire world. How do you view what is happening in the Eastern bloc? What sort of regimes do you foresee replacing the old Communist order? And what sort of political evolution would you like to see there?*

**A:** The destruction or the collapse of the Communist regimes there is from my point of view very good news. It shows that the old theories of totalitarianism as something immutable and unbreakable have been proved to be at least in part mistaken. The rapidity with which the regimes fell, the ease with which they were toppled, indicates that they never really had any great mass support. What kept them in power was the constant threat of Russian intervention. Once Gorbachev removed that threat, it was clear that these regimes would fall.

So that's a good thing. We've lived to see—and I never thought it would happen—the end of Stalinism as a significant political force in Europe. And the judgments and criticisms of the anti-Stalinist Left have in large part been vindicated, though a vindication that comes some decades too late, and after the pointless deaths of millions of people, doesn't always fill one with joy.

**Q:** *In what sense, exactly, has the anti-Stalinist Left been vindicated? Many American right-wingers are claiming that it is they who have been vindicated.*

**A:** Well, we had always denounced the totalitarian nature of those regimes. We had always said that they were not genuinely Socialist. We had always said that people who gave them support were mistaken or cynical or foolish. And we said this long before anyone heard of the neoconservatives.

**Q:** *And certainly at the "scientific" level, the idea that history is somehow on the side of this sort of system has been scuppered.*

**A:** Yes, the notion that there was an inevitable trend toward the power of the Communist political monopolies has been absolutely destroyed. That's wonderful. The rise of democratic participation in Czechoslovakia, for example, is admirable. People like myself feel joyful about that. On the other hand, there's a heavy price to pay for it, one that we are already paying and will continue to pay for some years to come—perhaps some decades to come. The authoritarian Right, the entire range of dominant opinion in America, and the authoritarian Left, whatever little remains of it, have continued to speak of the Stalinist-Communist regimes as "Socialist."

**Q:** *Which duplicates the usage in the Eastern bloc, even among the intellectuals.*

**A:** Yes, almost everybody accepts the Stalinist self-designation. Now, this means that for the great mass of people in Eastern Europe and possibly in the Soviet Union also, the regimes which they detest, which have given them neither liberty nor material abundance—these regimes they identify through overwhelming popular usage with the label of Socialism. And so those of us who have been . . . democratic Socialists find ourselves in the ironic position that though our criticisms have been largely vindicated, and the totalitarian regimes are collapsing, nevertheless we are being sideswiped by these developments.

**Q:** *There's a fellow in the Social Democrats USA group called Joshua Muravchik who wrote recently in* The New Republic *that "democratic Socialism" was empirically a sort of contradiction in terms, because if Socialism is put to a democratic vote it will invariably be rejected by the people.*

**A:** I think that's absolute nonsense. One can cite occasions where it has not been rejected. And if it is rejected, then you keep participating in democratic politics. Muravchik is not omniscient, and neither he nor anyone else can claim to know that Socialism will always be rejected. That's just a reflection of his own abandonment of the Socialist idea.

But the fact is that for the masses of people in Eastern Europe, the idea or at least the name of Socialism is identified with the detestable society they have had to endure since the end of the Second World War, and if that were Socialism they would be entirely right in rejecting it and being done with it. But we don't believe that it is Socialism. It is a gross authoritarian caricature and distortion of the Socialist ideal. I don't hear anyone arguing that because those regimes also called themselves "democratic" their record constitutes a refutation of the value of democracy. All political labels these days are misused, twisted, and abused, and this is as true for the word "Socialism" as it is for the word "democracy." Nevertheless, in the short run in Eastern Europe and the Soviet Union it is perfectly clear that after the devastating experiences of Stalinism and post-Stalinist Communism, what people want is more in the way of material goods, a little bit of freedom, and above all a good deal of quiet. They're not in the mood for new experiments, for great social innovation, and consequently the general tendency there is likely to be in some sense conservative—not necessarily toward conservative politics as ideology, but conservative politics as a feeling, a tone, a mood. There is at the moment an enchantment in Eastern Europe with the ideology—or delusion, as in part I think it is—of free markets. In *Dissent* we have been writing a good deal about this.

First of all, there is no such thing as a free market; even in this country the markets have always been constrained by limited entry, by government intervention, and by various kinds of state planning. But one can see why in Eastern Europe the idea of free markets has a certain attraction when contrasted with the overbureaucratized, overcentralized, ill-planned economies that they had there. When you suffer under one kind of excessive regime, there is a natural tendency to go to the opposite extreme; however, there's a great deal of naivete and illusion about what free markets are and how they function in the West. Also, the Eastern European nations need to sing the tune of free markets if they want to get financial aid from the West, and the West is the only place where they can get it.

Yet it is perfectly clear that in the coming period the turn in Eastern Europe will be toward one or another form of capitalist or semi-capitalist economy. The best that can be hoped for is a mixed economy. And the role of the Socialists and social democrats in those countries will be to protect the poor and the workers from excessive exploitation and from the effects of economic transition, and to try to maintain a safety net for those who are most likely to suffer in the transition.

**Q:** *So you would like to see these countries evolve toward the model of the Scandinavian social democracies?*

**A:** Well, that would be the very best of the possibilities. But I doubt that it will happen. They don't have the material resources in countries like Hungary, Poland, or East Germany for anything like the Scandinavian model, in which a so-called free economy exists alongside of a highly advanced welfare state, [regimes] superior to those of the other countries in Europe and light years beyond what we have in America.

**Q:** *It has been said that Sweden is the only country in the world where you can't tell what social class a child is from by looking at his teeth.*

**A:** Right. So the likelihood is that the nations of Eastern Europe will go through a period of difficulty. The great danger is that they will become "Mexicanized," that is to say, these countries—which are poor and ill-developed and in many cases only partly industrialized, and which are already falling behind in the world economy—will try to industrialize at the very moment that the advanced economies in the world are moving toward postindustrial technology. The likelihood is that they will have severe social struggle after the initial euphoria wears down—you can already see it wearing down—and the burgeoning social democratic groups in these countries may find themselves on the defensive.

The key question, however, is not Eastern Europe but the Soviet Union. There Gorbachev has made, I think, quite extraordinary changes and transformations. Gorbachev is not, so to speak, my man. I don't know whether he is a liberal or a democrat. But he is moving in what I think is a progressive and attractive direction. Nobody that I know of on the left, right, or center could have anticipated that he would come out in favor, however reluctantly, of a multi-party regime. Once you begin to have a multi-party system you are violating one of the fundamental premises, both structural and ideological, of a Communist society. It begins to look as if Gorbachev knows this, and the people around him also know it, and that there is a kind of nascent, quasi-democratic Socialist sentiment among at least some of his advisors. He has enormous problems. . . .

**Q:** *Let's go to a slightly more theoretical level. Do you see the idea of "market Socialism" being worked out in interesting ways today? The phrase is bandied about a lot, but is there any straightforward way of distinguishing it from the case of a mixed economy with a social market, like the Scandinavian model?*

**A:** Yes, that's an interesting question. There are significant theoretical elaborations of the idea of market Socialism. One of them you would find in Alec Nove's book *The Economics of Feasible Socialism;* another one you'll find in the late Michael Harrington's *Socialism, Past and Future.* The difference between what you have in Sweden and the model of market-Socialist society is that the latter would involve a further extension of social ownership. This doesn't mean a radical, apocalyptic break. We're not talking here about revolution in the old-fashioned sense, which has been proven to be nonproductive and downright destructive. We're talking about an evolutionary change, of what Harrington called "visionary gradualism," in which the social benefits of an advanced welfare state are protected, the market functions but [is placed] under social controls and . . . a degree of social planning, and there is a gradual evolution toward an increasingly egalitarian society, that is to say, toward the realization of Socialist values, which entails at least in some part an increase in social ownership and control of the economy.

This does not necessarily mean a nationalized economy; in many cases a nationalized economy would be undesirable. By social ownership one means a whole variety of possible modes of economic functioning: cooperatives, municipally owned financial or productive institutions, shareholding arrangements in which the workers are the decisive factor, and so on. There's no reason why in a market-Socialist society there shouldn't be a significant amount of individual entrepreneurship, especially in the case of small factories, small shops, restaurants, and so forth, which seem to function better under individual ownership when there's a greater incentive to make them work well, and all that is needed in that domain is the continuation and extension of social controls.

In a market-Socialist society you would have an increasing tendency toward economic egalitarianism. This doesn't mean everyone would receive exactly the same pay or have exactly the same amount of money. But the gross and growing inequalities of income and wealth that characterize capitalist society today would be gradually leveled down. And there would be evolution toward a social ethic of cooperation rather than the mad greediness and destructiveness that we have witnessed in America in the last decade.

**Q:** *Is the motivation for the sort of social ownership you describe primarily to reduce worker alienation? It is often maintained that workers who own shares in the firms that employ them and have a role in management decisions find their labor more meaningful and are less inclined to shirk, and that this makes these operations more productive and efficient and the workers happier. Other proponents of social ownership, however, base their argument more on the idea that socially owned firms would not use a narrow profit criterion in making their investment decisions, but instead would consider the full range of social ramifications that these decisions would have.*

**A:** There are several answers to that. In the first place, in a Socialist society as one envisages it—and it is nowhere near realization at the moment, nor is it going to be realized tomorrow morning—a significant portion of the economy would gradually be "decommodified." We have already seen that happen, for example, in England and Sweden today, where health plans and health institutions are to a considerable extent taken out of the commodity market and assigned a social value that is not measured by gross profitability. There is no reason why this shouldn't happen in other areas of life. It has happened long ago in education. One doesn't ask the schools to make a profit, one asks them to teach literacy.

The question of efficiency is very complicated. It is by no means certain that a worker-owned, worker-controlled economic unit would necessarily be more efficient than one that is privately owned. It might be that its concern for certain kinds of social values would make it in the short run even less efficient. But the argument would be that with the growing productivity of modern economies, their growing capacities to turn out vast quantities of goods, the criterion of efficiency, while not to be dismissed or ignored, need not always be the dominant one. Certainly the idea of participation, of people feeling themselves to be and in fact being significant actors in economic life—that is to say, the whole idea of industrial democracy and economic democracy—is a crucial element of the Socialist idea.

**Q:** *Most of the trends in society that you would like to see are pretty much the opposite of what we're actually seeing in the United States these days. The distribution of more and more goods and services is being turned over to the marketplace, and economic inequalities have been widening for several years now. You've written* *about the dissolution of the political coalitions that once pushed for a democratic-Socialist agenda, and the breakdown of the old liberal-labor coalition.*

*You've also observed that there has been a general turning away from politics and a fragmentation of ideological visions into special interest lobbies. Do you see any hope for a reversal of this, for even a slight movement toward the Socialist idea?*

**A:** This is a very depressing thing about living in America today. The whole world is in ferment. Not all of it is great, but there is life, there is stirring, there is excitement, there is controversy. Even some of the most repressive Arab countries are reportedly manifesting glimmerings of an interest in democracy. The United States by contrast, having been lulled to sleep by Reagan, continues in that state under Bush. And of course we are paying a terribly heavy price for it. There is social decay and economic decline. The living standards of millions of workers have gone down. Poverty remains. Even a horrible thing like child labor, which we were supposed to have put a stop to fifty years ago, has been revived. There is a general sense of malaise and disintegration.

Even in *The New York Times*, which for years has been printing prose poems about the beauties of the free market, one now sees editorials expressing alarm at the deterioration of the economy. And conventional politicians are beginning to feel uneasy about the disintegration of political life, the ascendancy of money in campaigns, and the reduction of political discourse to these crude and empty thirty-second "sound bites."

Will there be a change? All one can say is, there have always been changes in the past. Any time you develop a theory about the immutability or necessary persistence of any social mode, history refutes it. If totalitarianism could be brought to an end in Europe, certainly the social inertia, the social mindlessness that has characterized America these past ten years will also be brought to an end. Do I see any strong and immediate tendencies in that direction? No.

**Q:** *Do you take much stock in the Democratic Party? Do you see the neoliberals as strategic, if not intellectual, allies? And how about that trio of Democratic economic thinkers—Robert Reich, Lester Thurow, and Robert Kuttner—who argue for some of the changes you might endorse in a way that appeals not in moral terms but in an economically pragmatic way that mainstream politicians can understand?*

**A:** The Democratic Party, for better or worse, is the arena in which whatever progressive or liberal action there is takes place. It isn't ideal. It isn't very attractive. At the moment it is half moribund. The liberals today are in even worse shape than the Socialists; there may be more of them than there are of us, but they are demoralized, disorganized, and incoherent.

**Q:** *Can you point to a single exemplary liberal politician of national standing?*

**A:** No, no. But there are exemplary liberal spokesmen. I'm not terribly friendly toward the neoliberals. Some of the others you mentioned—Bob Kuttner, for example—are very close to a social democratic view in terms of immediate, urgent needs like health insurance, daycare, job training, and the reconstruction of the cities. Kuttner's views are admirable. The problem is that there aren't any significant forces within the Democratic Party that are prepared to push for these programs. We can only hope that if the deterioration of society persists, there will be a political response; then these views will take on more urgency.

So as far as the short-run picture goes, people like myself and people like Kuttner are in very large agreement. Where the ultimate disagreement may occur concerns long-range social values and goals. But in America Socialism, or the Socialist movement, is not an immediate option. The role of Socialists in America is first the intellectual and theoretical one of propounding certain ideas and values; and second, to act as a kind of ginger group, a stimulus, a prod to the liberals to get them to become, well, liberals.

**Q:** *Moving on to local topics, how do you feel about intellectual life in New York now? In your memoir you speak of some disenchantment you began to feel with the city in the sixties, saying you "no longer loved the city" but remained "hopelessly attached to it." Do you still feel the same way?*

**A:** I think there was a very sad deterioration in New York while Koch was mayor. Koch symbolized a certain moral coarseness and social crudity that has taken over in New York City, with the dominance of corporate values, the overbuilding in Manhattan, the driving out of the poor, and the prevalence of social contempt for minorities and blacks. The message Koch represented to the poor was "take your welfare and shut up."

**Q:** *What about the cultural and intellectual life of the city? Are you bothered by what Russell Jacoby has diagnosed as the "disappearance of the public intellectual"?*

**A:** Well, it's very hard for me to know what is really going on in the cultural and intellectual life of the city because I have reached a certain age and I'm not always in close connection with things that are going on. As far as I can see there's a great deal of individual talent and good will and serious work, but there isn't very much of an intellectual community. There isn't some strong driving ideal that unites people. My impression is that there's a good ideal of cultural atomization. But I cannot be sure of this. It's entirely possible that there are lively groups of younger people who function quietly, but one won't hear about them until and if they have some major achievements to show.

**Q:** *You were the one who coined the term "postmodernism," weren't you?*

**A:** I think that may be one of my unforgivable sins. But I really don't want to talk about postmodernism—it's too boring.

**Q:** *When you look at the more influential and trendy English departments in this country, such as the one at Duke University for instance, you see postmodern Marxists like Fredric Jameson reigning there. Does it strike you that there is any merit to the approach to literature that they represent?*

**A:** It's very hard to make a quick assessment of all that. What goes under the category of postmodernism actually involves a complex of many different ideas and impulses. The remnant of Marxism personified by Jameson seems to me a sad affair. It's as though Marxism has come to the academy to experience a quiet death. The tendency toward a depreciation of classical literature is something I strongly object to and deplore. The substitution of popular culture or mass culture for the study of the great literary tradition seems to me a way of short-changing the students and impoverishing culture. Every once in a while I try my best to read the type of stuff that you refer to, but I find myself seeing a blur of print and an obscure, hopeless, obfuscating language. I believe myself that literary criticism can be written in English—simple, direct, nonspecialized English—and that it is neither a science nor a theory, but a craft and an art.

**Q:** *How do you feel about the fact that modernism, a movement that you and the other left-wing New York Intellectuals grouped around the* Partisan Review *and other publications once championed, has become a protectorate of the Right? The great bulldog of modernism these days seems to be the cultural conservative Hilton Kramer, and what is seen as its core is the idea that there is a privileged canon of literary works, an immutable hierarchy of cultural values.*

**A:** For me modernism means a great cultural movement of literary innovation, one that stresses the problematic, individual consciousness, a sense of social concern and social uncertainty. The whole vast movement, which I think is one of the great creative impulses of modern history, taking in names like Joyce and Proust and Kafka and Beckett, Stravinsky and Picasso and Matisse, etc.—this was a tremendous positive force.

It is, however, a force that has largely been spent. As with all cultural movements, as with romanticism before it, there has been with modernism an unavoidable rhythm of rise and fall.

This was inevitable. Take the case of T. S. Eliot. I think Eliot was a very great poet who embodied the spirit of the moment, the sense of tension and anxiety and uncertainty, of the hunger for values, for an anchor, for assurance. No poet to my knowledge captured more beautifully and powerfully than Eliot the mood of what life was like forty or fifty years ago. His political ideas, his cultural ideology I never accepted—although I think he was a very great literary critic—and one has to distinguish between his role as a literary man and his role as a cultural and political theorist. The anti-Semitic side of him was deeply unattractive and should always have been rejected. Even those of us who were tremendously moved by his poetry tried to make the distinction between Eliot the poet and Eliot the ideologue.

But just as other great writers have undergone retrospective criticism, in which their strengths are separated from their weaknesses, so will Eliot. I think that the Eliot who wrote *The Waste Land, The Four Quartets,* and the other major poems will always be seen as a giant cultural figure; these poems will speak to people for a very long time to come. The Eliot who wrote *After Strange Gods* and other such political and ideological tracts, on the other hand, will fade away.

**Q:** *Did you happen to read Tom Wolfe's recent manifesto in* Harper's *magazine calling for a rebirth of the American social-realist novel?*

**A:** One of the few principles of economy by which I live is never to read Tom Wolfe.

**Q:** *That seems sensible. Do you try to keep abreast with the output of the latest generation of American novelists?*

**A:** I read some, but not much.

**Q:** *Would you like to be prophetic about the current generation of American or British writers? Are there any of them who you think will still be read in a hundred years? Saul Bellow has made some pretty grand claims for Martin Amis.*

**A:** I'll pass on that. I haven't read Amis.

**Q:** *Do you have any sense of literary decline in this country?*

**A:** There is a tendency for people as they get old—oops, no one in America gets old, they only get older—there's a tendency to see the world collapsing, disintegrating, etc. I want to resist that. What we have in American literature today, it seems to me, is a very great deal of disconnected talent—gifted individuals who are serious, who aspire to do very good work, but who don't have very much connection with one another, who don't gain the sense of excitement and energy that comes from being part of a shared literary movement or idea—even if it's not always a good idea.

Take the Southern Renaissance, for example. The ideology of people like John Crowe Ransom and Allen Tate has by now long since passed by, but it gave writers from the South who were close to them an enormous impetus for several decades, and the achievement of many of these poets and novelists remains very substantial. The same thing was true of the New York writers and social radicalism. But today there isn't that kind of shared energy, and you can't manufacture it at will. So my sense is that we now have many good writers but few if any great ones in America. You can't always expect to live at the crest of the wave. We went through a tremendously rich period in the culture some time back. Even after literary life leveled off a little bit there were very powerful developments in other areas—ballet, for instance.

**Q:** *Are you still a big ballet fan?*

**A:** Oh yes. Of course it isn't the same as it was when you had Balanchine around and you could expect one or two masterpieces every year. Now the New York City Ballet maintains a very high technical level, and it performs the works of the past, but not many of the new things are all that exciting. For some reasons that I don't understand the quantity and degree of talent in choreography is very small and difficult to come by. But it's still a very wonderful thing.

# Chapter 15

## Robert Negin, "Fraternal Dissents on Max Shachtman and American Trotskyism," November 1990.

### Introduction

In this conversation with Robert Negin, a fellow onetime Trotskyist, Howe digs deeply into his own Trotskyist past, offering "second thoughts" on his radical youth that venture much further than does *A Margin of Hope.*

Doubtless because he and Negin shared a similar trajectory, Howe felt comfortable in this previously unpublished interview discussing both Socialism's erratic, problematic history and his own complicated relationship with Max Shachtman. Like Howe, who became a Socialist at age fourteen, Negin joined the Young People's Socialist League (YPSL) in 1938, at the age of eighteen. Although they were members of different wings of the YPSL, Negin heard Howe on the podium and recalls that he was "a superb orator." They fell out of contact after their years at YPSL, and it was not until November 1990, when Negin was pursuing a Ph.D. at the City University of New York, that he reconnected with Howe for this interview. After Negin's advisor in the American History program, John Diggins, suggested that he engage in research on the life and career of Max Shachtman, Negin interviewed Howe about the Trotskyist tribune whom both had once followed.

Negin grew up in Newark, New Jersey. His father was a Socialist from western Russia who took part in the revolution of 1905. When the White Russians were defeated, Negin's father emigrated to the United States in 1907, where he abbreviated the family name (originally "Neginuitsky") and bought a candy store in Newark. During Negin's youth, his father also owned a linen supply story, which Negin began to run himself a few years after his father's suicide in 1933, when Negin was fifteen.

In the 1930s, Negin became a member of the Socialist Workers Party (SWP), which was closely associated with and a strong supporter of Leon Trotsky. In 1939, the SWP splintered when Max Shachtman and James Burnham started a new faction, based on disagreements over U.S. involvement in World War II and their belief that the Soviet Union was no longer a workers' state but a tyranny. Unlike Irving Howe, Negin remained a Party member and did not join Shachtman's breakaway sect. That group would eventually become the Independent Socialist League (ISL), but its membership never totaled more than one thousand. Despite his polemical talents as a brilliant speaker and masterful controversialist—a gift that he shared with Trotksy—Shachtman remained a solitary sectarian infighter, a fundamentalist wielding little influence on the far Left. Both Howe and Negin were the progeny of Shachtman, yet both men broke from him. Negin had no contact with Shachtman after 1939.[1] Indeed, Negin continued to run the family candy store until he was drafted into the Navy in 1943, at the age of 25.

For Howe, Shachtman may be seen as the missing link, the rarely acknowledged bridge figure between the Socialist politicians whom the mature Howe most esteemed, Norman Thomas and Michael Harrington. Howe admired those two unequivocally, but he was more closely connected to Shachtman, both personally and politically, especially in his youth. In Howe's autobiography, Shachtman suffers a similar fate to that of Trotsky. Howe had long since distanced himself from both Trotskyism and from the kind of conservatism to which Shachtman had migrated by the late 1960s; by the 1980s he had no substantial ties remaining to either man. Nevertheless, Shachtman resembled Harrington in certain respects: a skilled rhetorician and virtuoso verbal duelist, a tireless campaigner, and a talented writer. More so than either Howe or Harrington, however, Shachtman remained a leader without followers, a thinker whose grand visions detoured into dead ends. As Howe explains, probing into his roots further here than elsewhere, Shachtman "was never a mass leader. He was always living in the world of the small group, the sect," a condition symptomatic of the Marxist Left in America throughout the twentieth century. Given his growing doubts regarding Trotskyism and his increasingly close associations with the *Partisan Review* circle (some of them former Trotskyists and/or Shachtmanites), Howe came more and more to support intellectual independence. Howe finally resigned from the ISL in November 1952. Shachtman in turn rebuked Howe bitterly, and the two severed ties permanently.

While Howe appreciated his new intellectual freedom, he felt the lack of group solidarity in a common cause. In 1954, he formed *Dissent*, at least partly as an attempt to combine the activist spirit of a small sect with the intellectual independence it typically denied. Ironically, Shachtman followed a similar course, though his anti-Communism became more extreme and all-consuming. Stemming from his beliefs during the 1940s that the Soviet Union was not a workers' state and that a third way must be found between Communism and capitalism, Shachtman widened his distance from Trotsky. Without any firm left-wing commitments or a political base in the late 1950s, Shachtman became a supporter of the AFL-CIO, also embracing its anti-Communist predilections. When the New Left emerged, he responded from the reflexive stance of the Old Left and was appalled (much like Irving Howe) by what he perceived as their brashness and ignorance. Instead of criticizing them from the left like Howe, however, Shachtman moved rightward and reproached them from the conservative side of the political spectrum, as did so many other intellectuals of his generation. His neoconservative shift is similar to that of Irving Kristol, though Shachtman was to remain marginalized and largely ineffectual as a political influence. The former Trotskyist leader ended up much further right than Howe, his erstwhile protégé, culminating with Shachtman's support of the Nixon administration in the Vietnam War. In 1972, Shachtman founded the Social Democrats USA, which held state Communism to be worse than Western-style capitalist democracy; the new party, however, was destined to remain another small sect. Shachtman died that same year of a heart attack.

This interview is the only chapter in the volume where Howe, induced by a sympathetic interviewer, discusses in depth his connection to Shachtman, a relationship critical to Howe's intellectual identity and evolution. Howe had broken with Marxism, with "Maxism," and with Trotskyism, the trio of movements associated with heroes from his young adulthood, even though he still maintained a sentimental attachment to these figures who had once fired his imagination. Indeed, Howe defends Shachtman, who by the 1980s was marginalized, scorned, or merely ignored, honoring him here as a brilliant and witty individual.

Yet from Trotskyism, Howe avers a total break: "In many ways, I feel now it was a very distasteful kind of movement." By the late 1980s, Howe has reached the endpoint of a long, slow, wavering journey away from the radical Left, rejecting even the central tenets of Marxism. Perhaps the starkest revelation in this interview is Howe's admission that Marxism was bereft of "anything to say about the practical nature of a Socialist society," effectively dooming the movement from the start. "And that is the great weakness in the Marxist position," he explains, "and the reason for some of the great disasters that have occurred." Here Howe unflinchingly attacks the very roots of Marxism.

Yet while many former Marxists, including Shachtman himself, were propelled by the horrible consequences of revolutionary actions toward an opposite reaction of fierce and narrow-minded anti-Communism, Howe held fast to the core of his Socialist ideals. He also adapted his thinking to the new realities of postwar, post-Vietnam America, becoming interested in process, coalition-building, and reformist economic programs (to a degree that some leftists consider Howe's mature politics indistinguishable from liberalism).

Although Howe's language had changed, with even the word "Socialism" increasingly seldom voiced as a call to arms or even a term of identity, he explicitly refers to himself in this interview as "a democratic Socialist." In many other contexts, Howe disavowed that phrase and instead called himself a "radical humanist." There he emphasized his cultural and literary radicalism, and shied away from identifying with Socialism; rather, he termed himself a "social democrat." These seemingly minor differences in self-description reflect how someone slightly reshapes his identity and orientation depending on his audience and the publications in which his remarks appear. With Negin, Howe felt emboldened to express his doubts and hesitations about democratic Socialism.

Howe also discusses Norman Thomas here, perhaps the greatest American Socialist, for whom Howe confesses envy mixed with admiration, given Thomas' status as the leader of an actual mass movement. Howe, by contrast, found himself in roughly the same political situation as Shachtman, whose ideas never gained strong support beyond a small group.

Yet by leaving behind a huge body of writing, Howe distinguishes himself from Shachtman, who, despite his organizing talents and speaking gifts, "never produced anything of substantial consequence." Of course, young Howe's Marxist god had also failed. In retrospect, his accurate understanding of both the odious nature of Stalinism and the poisonous lure of collectivist idealism was not enough for Howe. In denouncing ideologues of the Left who think only in abstract ideals and self-righteously embrace a fundamentalist radicalism, who are unable to handle "the 'impurity' of the real world," he also implicitly concedes some frustration about his own ineffectual political impact (and his distaste for the ideologically driven self of his Trotskyist days).

This is also the only interview in the book in which Howe discusses at length his Trotskyist past, a topic that received sustained criticism from his neoconservative biographer, Edward Alexander. Howe insists here that he has "outlived the lessons of my mentors." In particular he feels that he outgrew Shachtman himself—and it is indisputable that Howe became a national figure in politics and culture, whereas Shachtman remained a sectarian leader even after his conservative turn. Still, Howe generously pays tribute to Shachtman and acknowledges an immense debt: "But many of the ways in which I moved away from Max, he enabled to me to do. One the things you learn from a good teacher is how to separate yourself from a good teacher." This statement honors the way radical sectarianism taught Howe to argue, to think for himself, and eventually thereby to break from the sectarian straightjacket that "Maxism," like Marxism, had come to represent for Irving Howe.

## The Interview

**Q:** *There are various portraits of Max Shachtman that characterize him as reclusive and petulant. Do you agree with that?*

**A:** No, not petulant. Reclusive? What do you mean by reclusive?

**Q:** *Other people whom I have read about him say that he had no real friends.*

**A:** He was not petulant. He was the wittiest man. I don't know if he had friends or didn't, but he wanted to maintain a private life and he didn't want his political life to overwhelm and totally coincide with his private life. And I think that he did quite a good job on that.

**Q:** *It was said that he wanted to groom you as his replacement. Do you feel that is true?*

**A:** No. Not that I'm aware of. I don't know who said that—if [he wanted to groom] anyone, then it was Michael Harrington.

**Q:** *Did you have any contact with him after you resigned from the Independent Socialist League?*

**A:** Yes. I resigned from the ISL in 1952 and that was a long time ago. And for a while we didn't see one another. Although I can't give you an exact date on this, we gradually re-established relations, friendly relations. He even wrote this little thing for *Dissent*. We became quite friendly and we had friendly discussions until there was sharp political disagreement.

**Q:** *He lived for twenty years thereafter and took an increasingly right-wing view of the past.*

**A:** Yes. He felt that the critical question was anti-Stalinism and anti-Communism. We disagreed, Max on one side and me and some others on quite another side. That was in the sixties. But before then we had many serious and interesting conversations.

**Q:** *When I had been in the Socialist Workers Party, I heard him speak on a number of occasions and I thought he was the best speaker I have ever heard.*

**A:** Yes, a very good speaker.

**Q:** [*laughing*] *Sarah Webber*[2] *remarked to me, "He memorized his speeches to the commas."*

**A:** He wrote them out very carefully. But he was one of the few people around the movement who didn't think that having a sense of humor was in violation of Socialist doctrine.

**Q:** *He also was a bit of a Marxist scholar.*

**A:** No question about that. He was a scholar, however, only in the very narrow sense. I don't think Max knew very much about Marxist economics. But then again, I don't think Trotsky's movement was very interested in economics or economic questions. The kind of things that concern us today—how prices are to be determined in a Socialist society for example—I have no recollection of that ever being discussed. Trotsky's movement only was concerned with problems of strategy and tactics. Especially after Max's group split off from Trotsky's movement in 1939.

**Q:** *1940. The Workers Party was organized in 1940.*

**A:** The Shachtman group arose, in my judgment, in the most interesting historical period because it was engaged in a gradual transition from orthodox Trotskyism to a sort of Left-social democracy, so for about ten years there was a constant process of intellectual reconsideration and growth, change. And slowly there was something that happens in all intellectual life when you begin to adopt new ideas. You still use some of the old language, because you don't yet have a new language for the new ideas. And so, even as we were then moving toward a version of social democracy, we were still using some of the language of orthodox Marxism.

But there were some people in the Shachtman group, who were themselves very much orthodox, such as Hal Draper and a few others, who recognized that this what was happening and opposed it. Max wanted very much to cling to some of the old language and the old notions. I was never quite sure in my mind whether he still remained a defender of Bolshevism in 1917 or renounced his Leninist views.

**Q:** *Alan Wald classified him as the ultimate sectarian. Do you consider that true?*

**A:** Actually Alan Wald was just as much a sectarian, but Shachtman was in the process of changing in a situation where it became clear, at least in my view, that orthodox Marxism and certainly Trotskyism were not working and were not relevant and the expectation of Socialist revolution had not matured and had not come about. The interesting thing about Max in those years was that his mind as a thinker was more fertile than his role as a leader.

If you are the head of a tiny little organization like the ISL, you have to consider the sensibilities of your members and you can't simply announce new ideas all the time, because the membership becomes frightened of you. Shachtman's thinking was always a couple of steps ahead. He was in the process of change. One can make judgments as to whether the changes were good or bad. . . .

**Q:** *How would you compare him with other Socialist leaders?*

**A:** Well, he was never a mass leader. He was always living in the world of the small group, the sect. And even when he moved to the right, he was still a sectarian. He was a right Socialist sectarian or a right social democratic sectarian. But he never had the opportunity or the inclination—I don't know which—to become a mass leader—say, if you compared him to someone like Norman Thomas.

Norman Thomas was involved in mass movements, strikes, and all kinds of major activities in the external world. Sometimes he was the leader of the Socialist Party and sometimes he was an individual figure. That was never true with Shachtman, who was essentially a journalist, a writer, a speaker.

**Q:** *But for a sympathetic audience.*

**A:** Yes, though I've heard him give a general Socialist introductory speech and do it very well. That's true, you see, but this was the training of Trotskyism. The supposition of Trotsykism was that the Socialist idea didn't have to be called into question. You see, I'm sure when Shachtman debated some of the people outside the movement . . . he didn't do very well because he always worked from the premise that the Socialist idea was itself beyond question and that all that mattered was which strategy, which tactics, which politics you use on that behalf. He never had anything to say, nor did [James] Cannon, nor did any of the Trotskyist people, have anything to say about the nature of a Socialist society—what kind of problems might arise, how you would determine prices, how you would organize production or anything like that.

**Q:** *Or, for that matter, neither did Marx.*

**A:** That is true. And that is the great weakness in the Marxist position and one of the reasons for some of the disasters that have occurred. You are absolutely right about Marx. And, you're right, he [Shachtman] flourished essentially within the inner life, the inner milieu, of the Left. And that was a severe limitation. And he's of interest only to leftists.

**Q:** *Incidentally, Shachtman translated some of Trotsky's works. Shachtman didn't know ten words of Russian.*

**A:** He may have translated those from French.

**Q:** *What was your personal opinion of Shachtman?*

**A:** Well, he was the most brilliant man I have ever known in the American Left, which is not necessarily saying much, because I didn't think there were very many brilliant men! I had a great admiration and deal of respect for him. And I learned a very great deal from him. I learned [how to] think, I learned how to speak.

**Q:** *So really he was something of a mentor for you.*

**A:** Yes, and I think I outlived some of the lessons of my mentors. Let me put it this way. I wouldn't think of myself as a Marxist, for example, nowadays. I am a democratic Socialist, but not a Marxist. But many of the ways in which I moved away from Max, he enabled to me to do. One the things you learn from a good teacher is how to separate yourself from a good teacher.

**Q:** *How gifted was he intellectually?*

**A:** He was a very brilliant man, but his range of thought was, in my judgment, too narrow, still confined within the traditional categories of Bolshevism and Marxism even though in the end he veered to the right. But he managed to do this through the use of these Marxist categories.

And he was not productive. He didn't leave very much behind in the way of writing. There is one little book of articles. He lacked discipline. He never sat down to write a book in the way that Harrington did. He never produced anything of substantial consequence. His one theoretical contribution was the "Theory of Bureaucratic Collectivism." In its time it was a substantial work, within the framework of Marxist theory. But he was a man who didn't fully realize his talents. Exactly why is very much a mystery to me.

**Q:** *In that respect, he was very jealous of you, in the sense that you were able to achieve a standing in literature, which he never did.*

**A:** Well, in the outside world. But I don't know if he ever particularly cared for that. I don't know. I split away. I have fond feelings toward him. I don't think he was jealous of me.

**Q:** *What about the fight in 1939 internally in the SWP that led to the formation of the Workers Party over the theory of bureaucratic collectivism?*

**A:** Shachtman and [James] Burnham weren't ready to advance a new theory about the nature of Soviet society, even though they recognized that Trotsky was probably right that it had changed.

**Q:** *Burnham was the political spokesman for the opposition. Burnham wasn't given his due in later years, I suspect, because he became such an ultra-rightist that they tended to play down his role.*

**A:** The loss of Burnham immediately after the split was a very serious loss. I think it upset Max very deeply, very personally. As far as I know, Burnham gave no advance notice that this was going to happen. Burnham was a man whom I admired for his intellectual capacities. I never liked him. He was a cold fish and a bit of a snob.

**Q:** *Shachtman said that he [Burnham] would never come down to the headquarters to do any writing or anything of that nature. He maintained his distance.*

**A:** Robert, did you remain in the SWP?

**Q:** *Well, until about 1950, and then I became concerned with the Holocaust. And I felt that the ISL and the Socialist Workers Party during World War II had been just out in left field.*

**A:** I think that is true. Shachtman also felt that the . . . Trotskyist position of . . . opposition [to the war] was ridiculous, foolish. We can't today say that the Soviet Union, when it was attacked by Germany, was engaged in an imperialist war, which is what the Workers Party said. That was stupid all the way around. It was an imperialist war, [but] that wasn't the decisive question. The decisive question was whether Nazism represented a kind of barbarism so terrible that it had to be destroyed.

We later took for it granted that the positions we held in the Second World War were totally mistaken and that it had been necessary to take a position of critical support for the war, because it was not just an ordinary imperialist war, because Hitler was something new and different, more tyrannical, and it was therefore necessary to support the war.

In many ways, I feel now it was a very distasteful kind of movement. But the one virtue of Trotskyism, the one contribution was the critique of Stalinism. That was the one great contribution, and for that I honor Trotsky. That was his one great contribution at a time when not many other people were saying this. But beyond that, as far as the United States or other [issues in] domestic American politics are concerned, I don't think Trotskyism would ever have anything to contribute.

It would have been interesting to see whether, if Trotsky had lived longer, he would have changed. I think there were some signs of change in store. He was a very powerful mind and a very aggressive and great figure. It would have been entirely possible that he would have changed, but in any case, his followers remained paralyzed [after his death in 1940].

**Q:** *After 1938, Trotskyism embraced many of the ideas of the [British] Labour Party.*

**A:** I disagree. But once you talk about the Labour Party, you are not talking about a revolutionary perspective.

**Q:** *Evidently to Shachtman, Stalinism represented just as great a barbarism [as Nazism]. And whenever a labor group may have raised its head—like for example, during the war in Vietnam—Max referred to it as "Stalinist."*

**A:** Yes, that's true. The Vietnam thing was very difficult, very complicated. And he was wrong.

**Q:** *In addition, he altered facts to support the Bay of Pigs invasion. For example, it was obvious that there were a number of Batista individuals in the group, which he denied.*

**A:** I don't remember that.

**Q:** *Well, Hal Draper published this discussion between the two of them.*

**A:** I was away from all of that. I was living in California at that time. When was the Bay of Pigs? 1961-62? At that point I really had nothing to do with the Shachtmanites.

**Q:** *To what do you attribute his long and far swing to the right where he began to support Democratic Party candidates, etc.*

**A:** I didn't object to his supporting Democratic candidates, because I do too and I think there is no choice in American politics but to support the lesser evil if you want to participate in politics at all. The liberal, pro-labor side is the Democratic Party.

I think he went too far on the whole question of Vietnam, and he became too uncritical of the labor leadership. It is perfectly all right, in my judgment, to vote for someone on the Democratic ticket but you don't have to apologize the way he and some of his friends did for some of the things they do. Well, there's a momentum in these things when you get going in a certain direction. Just as that momentum led the [radical Left] to support the Castroite dictatorship, so that same momentum led Shachtman to support the Vietnam War. You see, [taking an independent stand] became extremely difficult in a polarized world, in a world which was actually split for decades [throughout] the Cold War; the idea of an independent position was more a wish than a reality, more of a fantasy than a reality.

**Q:** *I suppose there has always been that tendency within left-wing movements to assume positions which leave them apart from the real world.*

**A:** Yes, that's true. And then if they assume positions which get them too close to the real world, they would cease being "Left." That's the dilemma.

**Q:** *Well, for example, I'm told that he was bitterly opposed to the candidacy of McGovern because McGovern was for peace in Vietnam.*

**A:** I think that may be true, I really don't know.

**Q:** *In any event, Shachtman died just before Election Day [in 1972]. But he would have voted against McGovern.*

## Notes

1. Negin's wartime and postwar activities possess continuities with those of his youth. Negin was drafted and shipped out to North Africa as a cadet in the U.S. Navy in 1943. Discontented with several of its positions yet still a member of the SWP, he reestablished contact with the SWP upon his return from wartime service in 1946.

    Negin is very forthright about the mistakes that the Trotskyist organizations made during the 1930s and 1940s, especially with respect to their positions on the war and Holocaust. "We didn't take the Holocaust seriously, and we should have," Negin, a secular Jew, admits. He also notes that he was a highly regarded sailor, and "did my patriotic duty during the war."

    Soon thereafter, Negin purchased an Arnold Bread route and began to sell bread locally. ISL leader George Brightman decided that Negin had become "a petit bourgeois" and "kicked me out of the party" in 1949, as Negin puts it (John Rodden telephone interview, fall 2006).
2. Sarah Webber was the code name of one of Trotsky's secretaries.

# Chapter 16

### Maurice Isserman, "'My Recollections of Mike': Harrington the Thinker and Socialist Activist," 26 March 1991.

## Introduction

Maurice Isserman conducted this previously unpublished interview in the course of his research for *The Other American: The Life of Michael Harrington* (2000). Howe reprises here the recent history of American radicalism, with a different emphasis from that in Robert Negin's interview; largely ignoring Shachtman, he concentrates on the most significant leaders of a wider American Socialist movement: Eugene Debs, Norman Thomas, and Michael Harrington. The first two led the Socialist Party of America during the early and mid-twentieth century, when it verged on becoming a major force in American politics. Harrington (1928-89), the main figure here, devoted his life to resuscitating an American Socialism whose day had never come. Occurring less than two years after Harrington's death, this interview is a fitting—and more in-depth—sequel to the *New York Times* interview in 1984 that featured Howe and Harrington. Howe was Harrington's closest colleague and political comrade, and it is obvious in this interview that Harrington's death induces Howe to reflect on his own mortality and legacy.

Isserman, a knowledgeable scholar of the history of Socialism, questions Howe in detail about his relationship to Harrington and his assessment of the latter's achievements. Isserman's book *If I Had a Hammer . . . The Death of the Old Left and the Birth of the New Left* had appeared four years earlier, and it had included material from his 1982 interview with Howe. Between this interview and the study of Harrington, Isserman would publish books on homelessness, Vietnam, and social activists Dorothy Ray Healey and Jane Addams. The Harrington biography reached print near the same time as his critical study on American politics and culture in the 1960s.

This is a follow-up interview, conducted almost a decade after Isserman's two interviews of the early 1980s. Some of the information that Isserman gathered here found its way in revised form into his intellectual biography of Michael Harrington. In that book, Isserman explains that Harrington "was part of what he would call the missing generation on the American Left, those who came of age in the 1950s; I was part of the succeeding generation who came of age in the 1960s, the New Left."[1] Malcolm X had initially been a stronger influence on Isserman than had Harrington, but the latter grew in importance. Isserman interviewed dozens of people who knew Harrington for the book; this conversation with Howe possesses special value because little from it appears verbatim in the text. Isserman seeks, through examining Harrington's role in American Socialism, to facilitate historical continuity on the Left.

Because Isserman is writing a biography of Harrington, he is much more concerned here with Harrington himself than with the sort of issues that governed his two previous interviews with Howe, such as the history of the American Left and the role of *Dissent* magazine. This interview, which addresses the intellectual history of American Socialism up to the 1990s, is informed by rich historical knowledge. The Socialist movement led by Debs in the early years of the twentieth century faltered, largely due to the Socialist Party's unpopular opposition to World War I. Revived by the Great Depression, the Socialist Party under Thomas again disintegrated due to its unpopular and exclusive positions, opposing the New Deal reforms of Franklin D. Roosevelt as merely a palliative for an essentially sick capitalist system. The purity of these positions led to political disaster, which helps explain Howe's increasingly moderate positions after his youthful radicalism.

Given Howe and Harrington's postwar moderation, the term "liberal" would have been easy to fall back on; nevertheless, Harrington (more so than Howe) continued to insist on the term "Socialism." Prompted by the memory of Harrington, Howe returns, despite some digressions and doubts, to embrace the term: "But Mike wanted, and here I entirely agree with him, that what we were doing had to be Socialist or it wasn't worth the trouble. Even though we knew that the term Socialist had been misused and led to endless confusion, etc. and all that." For the two men, the term "Socialism" represented a banner of an ideal society, albeit one with no hope of realization except in some distant and indefinite future.

One aspect of Socialist analysis that Howe maintained was the emphasis on economics and on class to the exclusion of other forms of analysis (as discussed particularly in the introduction to chapter 10). Another fascinating leitmotif here is Howe's discussion of the dynamic among male intellectuals during this period. They simply did not discuss their personal lives. Despite their strong political alliance, Howe notes that he and Harrington never had an intimate conversation: "I never knew about his domestic situation, how well or badly he was getting along with his wife and children." Indeed, Howe and Harrington behaved quite similarly: the New York Intellectuals divided public and private spheres, and Howe himself was also quite guarded when it came to sharing disclosures about his domestic or love life. That is also why he published an "intellectual biography" that excludes almost all mention of his personal life. The extreme personal reserve of white male intellectuals during Howe's heyday, then, seems to have borne a heavy cost.

Politics was all-consuming for male intellectuals of Howe and Harrington's time and place. It became a way to connect and a reflection of social dynamics, fulfilling the same role that sports still does today in many male circles. This interview furnishes an insider's view of the major players in democratic Socialism and radical humanism in the latter part of the twentieth century, with Harrington as the focal point. Toward the end of the interview, Howe mentions Harrington's reputation among Socialists in Germany and Sweden. (Elsewhere in Europe, Howe himself had similar status among certain literary and cultural figures on the left.) Howe also suggests numerous other possible interviewees for Isserman's biography, and shares anecdotes about it that illustrate the force of Harrington's presence in the DSA.

Yet when Isserman asks how Harrington will be remembered "fifty years from now," Howe grieves that he may be largely forgotten: "If there is any kind of continuing Socialist tradition, which is a problem, problematic, yes, he will be remembered. If not . . . people will be writing dissertations and books about social thought in America and he will have a chapter or a section of a chapter." This potential requiem for Harrington represents also a fate that Howe may have feared both for Socialism and for himself.[2] Instead of standing as trailblazers for a great movement, it is conceivable—indeed perhaps likely—that the two of them will be reduced to the status of scholarly footnotes, historical sideshows, and political curiosities, possessing no more than a ghostly presence in the kind of scholarship, removed from activism, that both men resolutely avoided.

## The Interview

*Note: The opening question is missing from the tape.*

**A:** The thing you raise is interesting. If you look back at the three major Socialist leaders of the twentieth century in America—Debs, Thomas, Harrington—one of the things that happens is that there is an increasing intellectuality. Debs, a remarkable figure, was not an intellectual. Thomas was quite intellectual in a general way, but not in the sort of professional, narrow sense. And Mike really was an intellectual, although sometimes his political commitment kept him from doing intellectual work. But the interesting thing is, and I think a sad thing too, is the decline of involvement in mass activities and public affairs, in a way. Debs was the great trade union leader, a great figure, a man with a tremendous popular following, thousands and thousands of people. Both in his trade union phase, which is brief, and then in his much fuller Socialist phase, [when] he is the leader of a mass movement. When he speaks, thousands of people come. . . . Thomas did have some mass involvements, strikes, and he was wonderful in going down to the Southern Tenant Farmers Union in the early thirties at a time when no one else was paying attention. He got involved in the struggle against Mayor Hague, etc.[3] But he was the leader of a declining party, and he got caught in what I now think, rightly or wrongly, was a sectarian Socialist view of the New Deal, which forced him into a position of isolated rectitude or righteous isolation in the thirties and then the SP gradually disintegrated and at the end he was really quite alone with just a tiny handful of followers, and he knew this.

Mike came along at a time when there was virtually no movement left, and he pulled together a few of the pieces, and he did hold it together . . . without any great illusions. Sometimes he would give way to what I at the time regarded as excessive optimism. He thought, for example, that the union of DSA and NAM[4] was going to create a really big group, when in practice it didn't. Most of the NAM people, although they thought they were to the left of DSA, dropped out of politics entirely after the merger. And it really didn't achieve very much at all. But what he [Harrington] did do was hold together a few thousand people and within that very loose, unstructured organization. A cadre of a dozen people, maybe a few score, kept the group together and constituted as much as anyone could, a Socialist presence in America. This was for him a very, very heavy burden. He was not really by nature an organizational person. And here he is completely in the tradition of Debs and Thomas. Debs was no good at organization and Thomas was no good at organization, although Thomas tried very hard to be responsible, as Mike did.

My first recollections of Mike were when he was very young and I was in the Max Shachtman group. And he had . . . a decidedly charming bohemian streak and you would have thought of him as being invaluable, in many respects, for the Socialist movement, for the Socialist idea, but you wouldn't think that he would be a good organizational person. But . . . he not only was in the tradition of Thomas, but also of Shachtman, who also not very good at organizational things either, but who was simply forced [to handle organizational matters] by the circumstances of being the leader—the person to whom everyone looked for guidance and solutions and maybe magic, since that's what followers do, they want the leader to provide some kind of magical solutions and answers; always you have to provide answers, but you yourself don't have them, if you had them, you'd let the world know in a hurry. And Mike took on this burden. And he became in DSA the chief fundraiser, the main writer of resolutions and articles, the main provider of speeches, . . . sort of the father figure, the guru. And mostly the membership was young and they became terribly dependent upon him.

**Q:** *Debs comes into the movement at a time when everything seems to be expanding and reaching its greatest influence. Thomas—his own moment of greatest influence is in the middle of the Great Depression, when again things seem like they're all coming together for the Left. Harrington, however, comes into the movement at its nadir. He really has to reinvent this kind of movement.*

**A:** Absolutely.

**Q:** *In some ways he's more organizationally involved than either of his two predecessors.*

**A:** Right. The burden on [him], I think I'm probably the only one who knows how heavy a burden that was, partly by analogy, from the burden of *Dissent*. Which, however, has been probably easier because you have a smaller group, you have fewer *nudniks*,[5] you don't have the member in south Illinois, who writes in, why don't we make a revolution or why don't we form a labor party or whatever nonsense. In a sense, *Dissent* is a self-chosen group, whereas in DSA, anyone who wants to can join and feels that he or she has an equal right to speak up, which in fact they do, and also to bother Mike and to go after him. Well, like Thomas, and here again there's a certain similarity, he developed a kind of instinctive method of self-protection. He knew how to isolate himself a little bit from the day-to-day life of the organization. He kept in close touch, but his personal life was not involved with the organization. I say this, not as criticism, not at all, but as description. It was necessary, otherwise he would have gone completely crazy. And he began to learn the skills of organization. The skills of organization are not mysterious. They essentially require application, patience, detail, etc. And he became the most extraordinarily disciplined person I have ever known. He was, in the beginning when I first met him, quite undisciplined. That went with the charm. He lost some of the charm, but he became extremely disciplined. And if Mike promised an article for *Dissent* by say, December 2, and if you didn't have it by December 5, you could assume there was something wrong. He was extraordinarily self-disciplined . . . [But with regard to] the three or four books before the last one, there was a real decline.

**Q:** *Where would you date that from?*

**A:** I don't know exactly, Maurice, I'd have to check it out. But there were several books . . .

**Q:** *From* After Socialism, *would you say?*

**A:** Yes, probably. But I would have to check it. Several books which seemed to me . . . there was one book about American social economy, for example. It had a great deal of material, but was quite poorly put together and sloppily written, and it is not as if Mike didn't have craft or pride in writing, although he never did learn to spell. But he was simply so pressed, so hurried, that he simply didn't give it enough time. And a couple of times I offered to go over his stuff and edit it, since I edited for a lot of people for whom I cared a hell of a lot less than for Mike, I would certainly do it for him. The last book I did go over it and I think played some role in the fact that, as it seems to me, it is written considerably better than the previous several books.

**Q:** *Do you think he was conscious of the choice he was making?*

**A:** Yes. Yes. I don't think he would have said it to very many people, but I believe he was conscious of this.

**Q:** *Did he say it to you?*

**A:** Yes. And it bothered him. He knew it, he didn't say it, but when I said it to him, he didn't argue, he acknowledged it. So, in some sense, you see, you could argue that he might have, from a certain point of view, been more effective without DSA than with it. But this is an old argument as to what the value of organization is, even for a small group. If he didn't have DSA and if he didn't have to go around begging money from trade union leaders and old ladies and whomever else he got the money from, various people—he was not a very good fundraiser because he was too self-effacing, he didn't have enough chutzpah. You need to have a lot of gall to be a good fundraiser, you have to have a thick skin, you have to [be able to be] be rejected, etc. He found it difficult. I find it difficult, too. I wasn't much better than he. If he hadn't had DSA as a burden, he wouldn't have had all those chores, all those endless routine meetings, all those foolish little squabbles, which you can't even dignify with the name of "faction fights," but the squabbles in DSA didn't even warrant the dignity of clear or decisive or significant political differences. They were often about hurt feelings, or a lack of dignity, or a failure of recognition. For people who are involved in small sectarian groups, small groups in general, sectarian or nonsectarian, it becomes their only form of gratification, and it is therefore very, very important to them whether they get elected to the national committee or don't get elected to the national committee, or whether Mike answers their telephone calls or doesn't answer their telephone calls, and things like that. And there were a number of people who were in the DSA leadership and who dropped out for completely nonpolitical reasons.

*[missing question]*

**A:** Just personal pique, personal hurt, etc. and Mike wasn't good at that. He couldn't bring himself to stroke. He wasn't good at all on that. He expected people to fulfill their obligations—[to possess] the stoical fortitude. I guess that's the phrase, "the stoical fortitude." He fulfilled his obligations and when he saw—I'm not saying that he was a man without vanity or pride, he was a human and he had his share but he kept them under very stringent discipline. And when he saw that people behaved as some of them did, he couldn't take it—he just pulled away. And I guess he felt, well, it was a small group one person more or one person less is not going to make that much difference. And I suppose that was right.

**Q:** *Well, you're not the first person to tell me this.*

**A:** Yeah.

**Q:** *He was both organizationally involved and yet not an organizational man by nature.*

**A:** Yeah, but that's—it confirms . . .

**Q:** *But it's a paradox that unlike Debs or Thomas coming into the movement at full tide—or even unlike someone coming out of a Jewish trade unionist background for whom this was mother's milk, he almost wills this Socialist organization into existence, which is personally what he doesn't need.*

**A:** "Wills" is a good word. Well, you see, suppose he didn't need or have the organization. He would have been freer to speak and he might have achieved a wider recognition but he would not have achieved it as a Socialist. He would increasingly have achieved it as that vague American term progressive, or liberal or radical or whatever. But Mike wanted to be, and here I entirely agree with him, that what we were doing had to be Socialist or it wasn't worth the trouble. Even though we knew that the term *Socialist* had been misused and led to endless confusion, etc. and all that. So that if life would have been easier for him without the organization, he wouldn't have felt the sense of mission that being the head of DSA gave him.

So it's a complex thing, it's not as if it's all on one side. He got certain benefits and gratifications out of it and he liked being the one who was applauded at conventions and meetings and, of course, he was an extraordinary speaker. He was one of the best orators that I have ever heard. The only people that I knew in the movement who were as good as he or better were Thomas and Shachtman—they had very different styles. Mike inherited a little bit from both in oratorical style. Sometimes I would hear him and I would be amused and I would hear an echo of Shachtman's dialectical twisting or Thomas's eloquent oratory, but he developed—he had his own manner too his own style, he was able to speak, he was extraordinary. He could speak virtually without notes—oh, he had two or three little scribbles—as I got older I couldn't do it. I used to do it for hours when

I was a kid—young—but the more I became thoughtful (or thought I became thoughtful), the harder it became just to get up and make that impromptu speech that Mike could do. And he had the gratification of knowing that these people looked up to him and adored him, and looked to him for guidance. But as I say, it was also a terrific burden. I guess this is in general one of the costs of leadership and especially in a small organization. What he did not succeed in doing, I think, was in creating a sufficiently vibrant ambitious and competent group of heirs. It is something that I don't understand—that I puzzle over—there is a whole group of what was then the secondary leadership of DSA. Very nice young people—very serious, very dedicated, with clear competence of various kinds. But it is as if they became so dependent on Papa. Mike would do this, Mike would do that, and I understand this because I do the same thing in *Dissent*. Sometimes it takes less time and trouble to do something yourself than to delegate it and then you have to correct it and discuss it with the other person, [so] you just do it and get it done. And that's one of the things Mike did—it was a necessary economy—but in some sense he, well, . . . crippled may be too strong a word, he disadvantaged, created a handicap, for some of his followers.

**Q:** *You and Mike were both protégés of Shachtman. Shachtman was, of course, the master at creating lieutenants who would then be able to do things independently.*

**A:** Well, by rebelling against him. That was part of the deal.

**Q:** *But he trained very competent political people—some of them did rebel against him.*

**A:** Not too many. There were just a few, I think. A lot of the leadership in the Shachtman group was very mediocre. I won't mention names but the few really competent people [include] a man named Joe Carter, who goes way back into the past; Hal Draper, although he was very rigid and sectarian, was a learned and gifted man; and Mike, you know. And I rebelled against Shachtman though we had a partial reconciliation later. The same thing was true of Mike. Mike inherited another of Shachtman's bad traits. He tended to hold his cards too close to the vest. He often didn't tell some of his people, some of his lieutenants, what he was really thinking about. That is, he would speculate. This is always a problem with a small Socialist group—their ideology replaces everything else of importance. If you don't have a mass activity all you have is ideology and with Shachtman this was a disastrous characteristic. He was thinking very boldly. Boldly in lines that often I didn't agree with, but boldly. And he was always afraid that if he spoke out and told his people what he was thinking that it would create disputes and differences and splits. But by virtue of not telling them . . .

**Q:** *I know you told me about this before in terms of his own [Shachtman's] ideas about foreign policy.*

**A:** Mike wasn't quite as bad because Mike didn't really engage in as many theoretical innovations as Shachtman did. Shachtman really made a journey from Trotskyism to right-wing social democracy. And I dropped out before he got to right-wing social democracy. When I was around it was still left-wing social democracy. But in any case, there was the same habit and it didn't lead in the case of DSA to splits because DSA in a sense wasn't, in the old-fashioned sense of the word, wasn't as "politicized" a group. It was an organization based more on fellow-feeling, fraternity, comradeship, etc. And the trauma of having gone through earlier splits. We didn't want . . . none of us had any appetite for factionalism any more. We had had it, boy, with that.

**Q:** *Can you give me an example of where Mike was thinking more ambitiously than he was speaking?*

**A:** It wasn't exactly ambitiously. Well, for example, he would be reading the European Socialist theorists—some of them. It never came out in what he wrote for DSA or spoke through DSA. When he spoke for DSA there was sort of a professionally optimistic tone. In private he was decidedly more skeptical though later on toward the end of his life he was more—I wouldn't say honest—he was more candid.

**Q:** *I was going to ask you about that, because, from 1958 on, when you read Mike he is always seeing the progressive majority just around the corner if such and such breaks out . . .*

**A:** And it doesn't come . . .

**Q:** *It doesn't happen.*

**A:** But I'm even thinking about the idea of Socialism. Namely that he began to see Socialism as increasingly problematic. As a possible historical option but further and further off, not as an immediate possibility. He began to see in it what Kant calls a norm, a regulated norm. Something which helps you in your behavior. With that vision in sight, it helps determine your particular, your immediate behavior. So he did not leave a good enough legacy, I think. He left a nice legacy. The atmosphere in DSA is far—has been and is, by and large—far better than any other Socialist group that I was ever in. It is less intellectually challenging. It's not terribly challenging at all intellectually. There are people in the group who are intellectually challenging but the group as a whole is not. And somehow if you think who were the neat people who had achieved any public standing or recognition on the left—you don't think of any DSA people, you think of someone like Bob Kuttner.[6] So that was one difficulty. On the other hand the great positive achievement, in my judgment, which I admired enormously, was that he set about to do, under very trying circumstances amidst all those lectures and speeches—which he had to give both for DSA and to earn some money—and teaching, and meetings—he set about to do serious intellectual work. And he read with extraordinary breadth and part of the self-discipline was to make himself read things which in my judgment were not totally fascinating, things about social policy in the United States. He really became an expert on social policy in the way that no Socialist before him to my knowledge, with a partial exception of Thomas. . . . Thomas knew certain of these things, but Mike knew about poverty. He knew about trade, he knew about industrial policy, he knew about all these kinds of things. The kinds of things, for example, that I don't know. I mean, I know in a general way, but I can't get up and cite figures and examples and provide a detailed argument.

**Q:** *Where did that come out of? For someone who has a literature degree from Chicago . . .*

**A:** It came out of necessity. It came out of the fact that he began to see, which is something that I had been trying to hammer away at with his disciples, he began to see that politics was increasingly a matter of political intellectual debate. That everything in America had become ideologized. That he had [to address] the ads on the Op-Ed pages of the *Times* by Esso [subsidiary of Exxon Mobil] and other corporations which were being ideological. That you had, for example, to be able to get up and debate Charles Murray on welfare policy. Now I knew Murray was wrong, or I thought I knew that he was wrong, but I couldn't have done what Mike did . . . and that is to say, to know all of the details, to work up all of the details. So he would not only read the *Wall Street Journal* and *Business Week* and stuff like that, in detail, but he really read the literature. He read the sociological and economic literature. He also followed the considerable, to me less interesting but that doesn't matter, the considerable post-Marxist or semi-Marxist writings out of Europe. He in a sense outstripped his group. Maybe even too much. It couldn't be helped. But that distance—that distance was created.

**Q:** *I was just rereading* The Accidental Century *again. What's interesting about the book is his first public statement of his Socialist beliefs,* The Other America *not having mentioned Socialism . . . but he does it within the framework of literary criticism. He is looking at novels and he is looking at . . .*

**A:** Yeah, Mike began with certain literary ambitions. He did . . . an early essay on [André] Malraux, I think in *Partisan Review*, it was quite nice. He did a review in *The New International* of my book *Politics and the Novel*— quite generous about it at the time when the Shachtmanites were furious with me. One of his most endearing qualities, and he had many, . . . was—he really was not a hater. He couldn't bring himself to hate people in the way that was so prevalent in the old Marxist milieu, in all its branches, in all his groups, from Stalinists to right-wing social democrats. That . . . gentle Christian side of him was very attractive and very lovely. And it made in our own personal relationship for a certain, a certain tenderness, a certain gentleness. We never wanted to get into a fight. For example, we disagreed about Jesse Jackson. It wasn't world shaking. Socialism continues as best it can even after that . . . and we handled it, I think, pretty well . . . we disagreed and we each said our piece and went on. We remained very good friends and there was no particular tension even about that. Partly because I had made it a policy not to get involved in DSA affairs though I was a member, and so in trying to oppose Mike inside DSA the differences came out in the pages of *Dissent*. But still people knew about the differences and there were a few people who wanted to magnify them almost. But both of us tacitly, without it being said, agreed to not do that. Many of the things that I am talking about, I think it's interesting to note, were not made explicit in our relationship. We didn't say "Let's have an agreement not to get involved in a harsh or nasty dispute." It was sort of a common impulse. We had both been burned enough over the past with the other way of doing things. So that was the attractive side of DSA, which I think kept a lot of people in the organization who had various criticisms or doubts about it. That is the decent atmosphere and Mike has to be given almost total credit for that. Because there were people who were ready to, not because they were old-line political, factionalists fighting for or against the permanent revolution or what ever, but who, out of temperament and vanity, were ready to create [rivalries and animosities]. . . . There was so much frustration in being in this kind of a group. . . . You know, you are always banging your head against the wall. Such people were ready to create a soured tone and Mike somehow always was able to elevate it into a tone of fraternity.

**Q:** *Was that interest in literary criticism that was evident in* Accidental Century, *was that a bond between you? Did you talk about literature?*

**A:** No, not much.

**Q:** *He gave that up pretty much.*

**A:** He gave it up. He gave up the interest in writing criticism. . . . He would occasionally ask me about things to read. He continued to read some literary things—as much as he had time for.

**Q:** *Was that a conscious sacrifice or just a shift in interest?*

**A:** I think it was a conscious. . . . I don't know really, Maurice, but I think it was a conscious sacrifice. I never asked him that. I guess I should have, but I think it was a conscious sacrifice.

**Q:** *The feeling I'm getting is that there were a lot of things he didn't open up about . . . that he didn't share. He was a very private man.*

**A:** We never . . . in all the years of our friendship . . . the friendship must have gone for what, close to forty years, we never had what would be called in a certain sense a personal conversation. That is, I never knew about his domestic situation. How well or badly he was getting along with his wife and children. One heard rumors, but I never heard anything from him and he didn't know anything about it from me. In part this is a carryover from the movement, from the earlier aspects of the movement and also from the style of New York intellectual life, where such conversations are . . . at least among men . . . have been quite rare. I remember once talking about it with Lionel Trilling and he said, you know, we really ought to talk about some of these things, but we never did.

**Q:** *So, it wasn't just Mike then? This was . . .*

**A:** No, oh no, it wasn't just Mike at all. With all the people I knew around the *Partisan Review* group, it was very seldom that I would hold what I would call a personal conversation. Now maybe it was different with others. Maybe it had something to do with me. I can't say. But my sense of it is that this was a prevalent style, the kind of style of impersonal closeness. But on the other hand I don't think that in the case of Mike and myself it was impersonal. I think there was a great deal of mutual concern about the other . . . when one was sick or something . . . but maybe there was a certain shyness. Something like that.

**Q:** *Well, you understand I'm not trying to be Kitty Kelly here, but there is a personal side to the man which I want to understand and he did seem to go through depressions.*

**A:** Yeah, he had a great down at one point.

**Q:** *You were close in that period?*

**A:** No, I don't think . . . what were the years?

**Q:** *1965, 1966 was the most intense period.*

**A:** No, because at that point I was deeply embroiled in disputes with people on the New Left. That New Left thing became for me a crucial matter. Mike also was, but that was amusing in a way, at least in retrospect. We had essentially the same political views and yet we had a different kind of treatment from the New Left. Maybe deservedly. And I got knocked around pretty hard but I also gave a few blows, and Mike would say the same things that I said politically but in a far less polemical style, and I was in my youth a pretty fierce polemicist. They [the New Left] felt friendlier to him. Some of them at least. Those who were inclined to feel friendly to any of us. They felt friendlier to him than they did to me. And so the experience in those years was tougher on me, I think, than it was on him.

**Q:** *You were increasingly linked together?*

**A:** Yeah, sure, we were linked together, but I was more on campus in those days, you see. I spent more time on the campus than Mike, and so I would run into SDS groups and SDS attacks and debates, etc. I may be wrong about this, it may be that he felt it pretty hard too. For us these fights or separations from the New Left in its better . . . well, once the New Left had declined into the Weathermen, we didn't care. That was, we felt they were just sort of fascists. But when we were arguing with SDS people in mid 1966, 1967, before it had turned totally bad, it was a very painful experience because we felt these were the people who should be our friends and yet political differences made it impossible. I think Mike took it hard. I think I took it harder but I can't measure it. It was a difficult moment.

**Q:** *So Mike goes through the breakdown in 1965, 1966, which in some way actually pulls him out of the [intra-Left fighting] . . .*

**A:** Yes, right, so he was less engaged with that stuff. Yeah.

**Q:** *But in subsequent years you would also see some sort of cycle within him. Or you said he was prone to depression. I'm not trying to lead you into anything.*

**A:** No, no, no. It's an interesting question. I would sometimes hear that Mike was depressed. You see, say in the seventies and eighties, when we worked together closely, we might see each other once every couple of months. We didn't see each other day by day or that often. He did not come to *Dissent* board meetings except once or twice when he spoke and I didn't go to DSA meetings, except very occasionally. We would meet here and talk for a couple of hours . . . exchange ideas, impressions. I heard that he had bouts of depression, but who doesn't? And I didn't see much evidence of it. He was really a steady worker, you know he was in there all of the time, as far as I could see. Part of the problem is that he was running around so much. I never understood how he got so much work done. It still is a mystery to me.

**Q:** *Your first organizational link was through the LID in the mid-sixties.*

**A:** You mean after the Shachtman group?

**Q:** *But you didn't really overlap then?*

**A:** No, no. He sort of came in as I was going out. Yeah, the LID thing . . . was ill fated.

**Q:** *What was the idea? What was it supposed to be and why . . .*

**A:** Well, the LID was supposed to be a kind of way of bringing together people of the Left with people from the labor movement, ex-Socialists, semi-Socialists, potential Socialists, progressive unionists, etc. To establish some kind of a link which no organization having the name Socialist in it could possibly do. And it may have worked if not for the differences, you know, which I described in that correspondence you showed me, and the differences became very blunt and crude and Shachtman was really behind some [of the clashes and breakups] . . . behind Tom Kahn and the rest. Kahn was a very talented fellow. One of the most talented fellows around this milieu, but he went hook, line and sinker for [Shachtman's line] . . . well, Shachtman decided evidently that the only hope was the labor movement. Bad as it was, you had to accept it as it was. There was nothing else in his view. And so that was their position. Essentially, they repeated the experience of the Lovestonites. That's one of the interesting oddities of the history of the American Left. I guess you know something about that. [The Lovestonites] also went completely into the labor movement, became quite influential, as a kind of Fabian intervention and well, I guess they left their mark in a way and perhaps the Shachtmanites will have too. They are still close to [Lane] Kirkland.[7]

**Q:** *Was* Dissent *actually affiliated with LID in some way?*

**A:** No, not in any formal way.

**Q:** *Well, at least on the masthead.*

**A:** Was it? I don't really remember.

**Q:** *Well, at least in the sixties . . .*

**A:** It didn't mean very much. We were trying to create sort of a small popular front in what was then the fading Left and there were still some trade union guys who had a nostalgia, partial commitment, [and] whatever their motives, were interested, were willing to do this. Not many, but a handful.

**Q:** *We were talking about Mike's organizational albatross in the DSA but at least that was an organization where he was the leader and basically set the tone. The Socialist Party, which was a much smaller organization in the sixties, and Mike was getting nothing but abuse in it by the late sixties, was even more of an albatross, it would seem to me, yet he was so reluctant to give it up. And here he was trying to recruit you into it in 1971.*

**A:** Well . . .

**Q:** *Was it his tie with Shachtman that was so [hard to break]?*

**A:** Well, that probably was one thing. . . . Shachtman had a great deal of personal force and a curious kind of charm. A lot of people couldn't stand him. You either liked him very much or you couldn't stand him at all. And he had been a kind of mentor and then there was a sense of the futility and tragedy of splits—there had been so many of different kinds—one wanted very much to avoid any more and there wasn't all that much left to split anyway. But once the Vietnam War came along it was inevitable. That did it. You see the labor thing might have been smoothed over or brushed under the carpet for awhile because it didn't take any very visible, dramatic form, but on the Vietnam War there was no way out.

**Q:** *And [Eugene] McCarthy*[8] *and McGovern and the question of who to support within the Democratic Party [forced a confrontation] . . .*

**A:** Yeah.

**Q:** *That began one of the centers of debate between the two . . .*

**A:** Right. That whole party thing was, I guess, blotted out in my memory until it doesn't seem very important anymore. When did DSA start? What was the year?

**Q:** *Well DSOC started in 1973.*

**A:** 1973—so that's been around for a long time. I remember the first convention of DSOC. We had a slight disagreement. Maybe not so slight. I was in favor of forming an organization which would not pass resolutions, not take any line, etc., etc., and I said this at the convention and I was going against the dominant trend. Americans have to pass resolutions. They can't live without them. Even if they mean nothing. Even if no one ever reads them and no one pays any attention to them. And in DSOC and DSA there had been resolutions passed, you know, there's no discipline—nobody has to adhere to them—it just means that there was a vote taken and . . . I thought that was a futile, time-wasting and sterile activity. Mike, I think, probably agreed but he . . . you see, part of being a leader in that kind of a group is . . . is like running the welfare state. There are constituencies, different groupings, and especially in DSA as it went along one of the things that became boring was you had a feminist constituency and you had the Hispanic, black, and the environmentalists, etc., etc., and regional constituencies, and those that felt that New York was getting too much attention, etc. This has been going on since 1903 and it's not over yet, Mike's position was very strong within the organization, and he really could have achieved pretty much anything he wanted. But because he had to satisfy this group and that tendency and this personality, the net result would sometimes be that he was rendered ineffectual.

**Q:** *We were talking about his relationship with Shachtman. What about Thomas? Thomas played a very different role in the Socialist Party by the end . . . He [had his independent activities and spheres of concern], then there was also the Socialist Party. . . .*

**A:** In the thirties, Thomas was very involved in the organization and he was a member of the national executive committee and he really was [involved] . . . when there was a real party . . . let's say through the first part of the thirties he was very closely involved. Put it another way, all of the great leaders of American Socialism have been tribunes. Debs was a tribune, Thomas was a tribune, Harrington was a tribune. They were great public spokesmen in that almost Emersonian tradition. And for all of them organization was a problem in different ways. Also in somewhat similar ways.

Thomas was a big influence on Mike because Thomas for one thing consciously saw Mike as his inheritor, and he was right. And he liked Mike very much and Mike adored him and there was the sense that Mike had that he was carrying on the line and the tradition of Thomas. And also the attention to domestic American things. On domestic American things, Shachtman wasn't worth a nickel. He was great on Bolshevism and the Russian question and all kinds of esoteric history of the movement in Europe, but toward the end he developed this laborite position for whatever it was worth. Not much I think. But he really didn't have a close knowledge of what was going on. He never could have coped with Charles Murray except through ridicule. He probably would have ridiculed him out of existence, beaten him in debate hands down. But he wouldn't have been able to answer specific arguments, because he wouldn't have known about some of these things. Thomas would have been able to do a good part of that. He did follow these things pretty closely. Mike, even more. Mike—the only one in my judgment who is the equal to Mike on this or who carries on his tradition is Kuttner. Kuttner knows this stuff cold.

**Q:** *The role you call the tribune—that was a well-known role, there had been Debs and Thomas. Was Mike consciously crafting a public role for himself in that tradition?*

**A:** Oh, absolutely. He was very, very aware, very conscious. Yes.

**Q:** *Did he say that to you? Or is that your observation?*

**A:** Well, look, he would go out and give lectures, say in San Francisco. He would give a lecture for a university and then he would give a talk for a trade union, and then he would meet with the DSA group of an evening for a talk or two. But the real thing there, as a rule, would be the public lecture. And he was the only one—none of us could compete at all on this—who could get a large crowd on a campus. Or who would be invited by a union to speak at a convention. You see, a lot of the money and help that he got from the trade unions was not really for DSA per se. They [trade unionists] weren't committed to Socialism but they were committed to the idea of Harrington. And they were right because they saw that in terms of the ongoing struggle to defend some of the benefits of the welfare state that were being chipped away, in terms of the social struggle in America as it was actually taking place, which didn't involve Socialism, that Mike was tremendously valuable . . . I'm very grateful that I got to this—I had forgotten.

One of the things that Mike felt, and I still feel about *Dissent* in a way which shapes the magazine, is that because of the failures or the . . . the lapses of liberalism, . . . there are very few new spokesmen for liberalism in America. They have the same problem that we do. It's still [Arthur] Schlesinger and [John Kenneth] Galbraith and maybe [Robert] Kuttner, but Kuttner is really a social democrat. That one of the things that we had to do was to take up the slack and make the liberal arguments for the liberals who were not making them. And so . . . and also there is a political view involved there of a closer coordination, close alignment between Socialism and liberalism in the current situation. And so, for example, Mike was a member of the board of ADA.[9] I don't know if he ever went to meetings but nobody thought this was any kind of heresy. In 1950 it would have been looked upon as a terrible thing. And liberals also saw it in the same way and they welcomed him because he was more skillful than most of them at making the argument and being more energetic too. That is very important. I think you ought to stress that . . . I think it's a very important side of Mike. And so in the eyes of many people, if you would ask them who is Mike Harrington, they would have said he is a liberal. Now, of course, the word in America includes more or less Socialists or left-wing radicals or whatever. But he was also being a liberal in the traditional sense.

**Q:** *I'm not asking the question very well because it is still hazy in my mind, but in some sense Mike was an institution, and I'm just curious as to how he became an* *institution. He certainly had more institutional weight in America than the DSA did or than many people on the Left did.*

**A:** That's correct. And that is why his death was such a terrible loss . . . why there is no possibility of its being filled.

**Q:** *But people . . . someone can become an institution, I guess, by indirection.*

**A:** He became an institution first because of the poverty book. The poverty book made a tremendous impression. Well, you know about all of that and Macdonald's review, Kennedy reading it etc., etc. And it is as if he struck a note, where the hell are all the liberals . . . why haven't they noticed that there was still a lot of poverty in America. And they hadn't. Now Mike didn't rub it in polemically, but I think this played an important factor. He sort of took over that role and the Kennedys, especially Teddy, were very shrewd about this. He had a certain respect for, connection with Mike. They saw each other occasionally. Teddy liked Mike. You know, they were both Irish and all of that. So he filled a gap, a very important gap, of liberalism. He was doing for liberalism what in the thirties people like Harold Ickes[10] and some of the left New Dealers would have been doing. Leon Henderson and others like that.[11]

**Q:** *So there is an element of accident in this. If it hadn't been for* The Other America *at that particular time . . .*

**A:** Well, I don't know. Maybe. It's hard to say. Certainly that facilitated it. And then, of course, there was this tremendous energy, and he became an institution in the sense that he would give, I don't know, forty to fifty lectures a year, [at] various universities and places like that. He ran around like mad. How he did it is a mystery.

**Q:** *You were at the [Norman] Thomas conference at Princeton, I remember, and Mike made a speech there . . . very interesting . . . it was reprinted in* The New Republic.

**A:** Yeah, very powerful speech.

**Q:** *And he talked about Debs and Thomas being part of this same tradition and really saying that that may no longer be possible. That today politics is answering a computer-generated letter that comes in your mail rather than going down to the union hall to hear a speech for three hours by an individual, and I got the sense that he was also talking about himself . . . kind of an anachronism.*

**A:** Well, that could be. That's a very, very painful and interesting question. I mean, when I was a kid, the street corner meeting was a big institution in New York during the warmer months . . . hundreds of street corner meetings . . . not only the radical parties [but also] Democrats and even occasionally Republicans. That's all gone. The big meetings in the halls when the SP, well CP too, but when the SP was running a campaign and I was a kid in the thirties. I remember in the Bronx where I lived, Huntspoint Plaza, which is now the worst neighborhood in the borough, at the climax of the campaign we would hold a meeting at Huntspoint Plaza and 4 or 5,000 people would come and pack the place and various *nudniks* would drone on until Norman [Thomas] came and made the great speech. So . . . and then there was the Madison Square Garden rallies and Roosevelt speaking . . . all that is almost gone. Well, television has changed all of that decisively, enormously. You didn't need that much money to rent a hall, but to get on television now . . . it may be that the popular tribune has passed away. If so, it would be very sad. God knows it's needed. But I don't see anyone playing that role today.

**Q:** *Well, there is certainly no one in the wings to take Mike's place.*

**A:** Or even say in the Democratic Party. I was stunned by his capacity to just get up and speak. I guess he had these things clear in his mind in an impromptu way.

**Q:** *One of the reasons Mike could play the role he did was because he was from the Midwest, he was Irish.*

**A:** Yeah, he wasn't Jewish. . . .

**Q:** *And he was Catholic, or had been anyway. How important was his Catholicism to him? Was that something that you discussed?*

**A:** A little bit. I don't know. I never took that side of him too seriously. I didn't think much of the book that he did on [religious belief] . . . what was the name of it?

**Q:** *The Politics of God's Funeral.*

**A:** Yea, something like that. I didn't think that was one of his better performances. But I'm such an ingrained secularist that I wasn't receptive, open to some of that. Obviously the experience with Dorothy Day played an important role. I don't know. Are there are survivors of that?

**Q:** *Yeah, when I was at the Socialist Scholars Conference I interviewed someone who was his roommate at the Catholic Worker. It was much less an ascetic experience than I had assumed. They went out drinking and they had girlfriends and got their clothes out of the old clothes bin.*

**A:** Well, Mike was interested in women, don't kid yourself about that. He was very handsome, very attractive, very winning and charming.

**Q:** *Of course, his mother wanted him to be a priest.*

**A:** But I don't think he had a genuine religious vocation. Maybe in some . . . well there are people who try to subsume a political idealism under religious categories, but if you do that, then everything becomes religious.

**Q:** *Well, I might be overcompensating a little bit because I have no knowledge of the Catholic side of him other than having talked to his relatives. I know the Socialist side and I don't know the Catholic side. His relatives say that he was still very much culturally a Catholic.*

**A:** What does that mean?

**Q:** *I don't know what that means. But they saw it.*

**A:** Well, maybe the belief in community. Do you know John Cort?[12]

**Q:** *Yeah, in Boston.*

**A:** Is he still around?

**Q:** *Yeah, he is someone I want to talk to.*

**A:** Also talk to Peter Steinfels who is a very intelligent man.[13] The *New York Times*'s gain was *Dissent*'s loss on that one. And he knew Mike fairly well and he is a serious Catholic and he could talk about that in a way that I could not. But he is not a fanatic. I mean he is realistic. He would give you an honest view.

**Q:** *When I think of someone like Shachtman, it's relatively easy to say his contribution to the movement was the theory of bureaucratic collectivism and a number of other things.*

**A:** Right, right.

**Q:** *If you were to say the same thing for Mike, what would the list include?*

**A:** It wouldn't be a particular theory like the theory of bureaucratic collectivism, which has been bruised by historical changes anyway. It's a question as to how useful it still is. I don't know. I would say that Mike's achievement was the effort and the at least partial, maybe complete success, to make the Socialist idea serious and respectable again. To pull it out of that narrow, little-sect grouping. I would say [that feat is reflected in] the atmosphere that you find very often, at least in parts of the Socialist Scholars Conference. When Mike spoke about and for Socialism, there were people in America, serious people, who though they may not share his views, took him seriously. And that was, I think, a major achievement. And also, I think in his books that there is a much more sophisticated version of what Socialism is or could be or what the Socialist idea is and had been. See, Thomas left nothing that I know of on this. Although, it's interesting, I've been reading [Steven] Fraser's book on Sidney Hillman,[14] which is an impressive book in some ways, and he discusses the different approaches to the New Deal. What was the New Deal? All the way from those who thought it was semi-fascist to those who saw it as social democracy and bureaucratic statism, etc., etc. And Thomas in a series of speeches . . . I think I have this in my little book on American Socialism . . . in a series of speeches in the thirties keeps shifting from one view to another. And it was hard at that time, maybe even today, to come to a fixed understanding of it. With Mike I think people could feel that the Socialist idea, even if it wasn't immediately applicable, even if you felt it might never be applicable, that it was passé, etc., . . . was not just something to be dismissed as nostalgia. It was serious thought, serious ideas, serious options. I think that is an extraordinary achievement.

**Q:** *But is it in the realm of theory or is it in the realm of presentation where his strength was?*

**A:** I wouldn't make the distinction. It's the two together. It's the presentation of theory. Not high theory in the traditional Marxist sense but what I call middle-level thought. Not just pragmatic empirical observations and not . . . the law of value, or dialectical materialism or whatever, but in middle-level social theory. Social thought.

**Q:** *So his gifts as an intellectual lay in that realm of middle-level theory, of social thought.*

**A:** Yes, yes. That's what I think.

**Q:** *And he would be remembered fifty years from now as, what?*

**A:** Who knows. Fifty years from now! Look, people who seemed at one point to be absolutely world-shaking figures, does anyone remember Trotsky today?

A few, yeah. Those who, so to speak, it's their business. But in general, I don't know if Mike will be remembered fifty years from now. If there is any kind of continuing Socialist tradition, which is a problem, problematic, yes, he will be remembered. If not, . . . people will be writing dissertations and books about social thought in America and he will have a chapter or a section of a chapter.

**Q:** *And he will be remembered as the end of the Debs/Thomas/Harrington tradition?*

**A:** I hope not, but it's certainly possible.

**Q:** *As my questions may have indicated, the real question, I think, people are going to have when they read this book is, why did this guy stick with these organizations when he could have been Daniel Patrick Moynihan . . . he could have been C. Wright Mills.*

**A:** Yeah, he could have been a congressman. So what? We talked about that a lot. As a matter of fact that question came up with Norman Thomas toward the end of his life, when he was in his seventies. I talked to him often about this and he would laugh about it, and Mike and I laughed about it too. And some people would say after the SP collapsed, why don't you run for Congress? Probably the Democrats would let you—give you a slot—and elect you so you could be in Congress. And Norman would say "What the hell would I do there, what will I do when I get there? So I'll make a speech to which nobody will listen and it won't mean very much."

And it was the same idea with Mike. There were some of his more enthusiastic followers, I remember at some point some of them wanted him to run for president. We knew that was a ridiculous idea . . . I remember back to my youth when we used to knock ourselves out in the SP getting on the ballot. By the time we had collected enough signatures to get on the ballot we had no energy for a campaign. And then the idea came up about his running some place for Congress. That might have been a somewhat more realistic idea but Mike didn't, and I think he was probably right, didn't take to it. I mean it's like the Israeli joke, what do we do if we win.

**Q:** *Well, I guess the larger point I was making is the question of why someone with his many talents stayed with the movement.*

**A:** Well, because he believed that, in order for the Socialist idea to survive or to grow and prosper, there had to be an organization. There had to be a group of people. It wasn't something that could be advanced just by one person alone. There I think he was right. If that's what you believe, then you have to accept the albatross of an organization or for that matter the magazine.

**Q:** *Are there other people in general that I should be thinking of, talking with? People who were extremely close to him or would be good observers?*

**A:** Let's see—some of the people around DSA—there is a fellow in Boston named Jack Clark. . . .

**Q:** *Oh, Jack, I've already spoken to him and I will again.*

**A:** You've spoken to him? He's not a theorist but he ran the group for awhile and he's very levelheaded and sensible and honest and he worked well with Mike. It wasn't easy to work with Mike.

**Q:** *No?*

**A:** No.

**Q:** *Even though he was disciplined, you said, and delivered the article when he was supposed to.*

**A:** But then he would go off on a trip and you couldn't reach him. And because he didn't give out enough to these people. They felt somehow . . . I don't know if Jack Clark said this . . . I think they felt somehow deprived. Well, maybe they wanted more than he could give. Maybe they wanted more than anybody could give. Are you going to see Joanne Barkan?

**Q:** *I'll see her later.*

**A:** She's very bright.

**Q:** *Did she know Mike well?*

**A:** Toward the end. Not all along. She came from NAM but she became devoted to him. She knew him pretty well.

**Q:** *Well, how about figures not in DSA?*

**A:** Not in DSA? [Ask] Peter again.

**Q:** *Stephanie mentioned some people on the* Village Voice, *for example, [associated with] the Village side of his life.*

**A:** Yeah, that was an early point. Not really very important in terms of a political biography. I assume that's what you're writing.

**Q:** *Yeah, but even so he was politically involved from 1950 on.*

**A:** Yeah, yeah. You mean with the *Voice*?

**Q:** *Well, the* Voice *comes along later but he's [residing] in the Village from 1950 on.*

**A:** Well, I never cared that much for that side of it, but I don't think there was much brain power there. . . . Who did she mention?

**Q:** *Oh, Dan Wolf and just other people. I guess they had met when she was working for the* Voice.

**A:** Sure, you might get some insights from them.

**Q:** *Oh, that reminds me of another question. In* Fragments, *Mike writes very lovingly of the Village experience and also of New York. Was he . . . although he was originally a St. Louis resident . . . was he a real New Yorker?*

**A:** Yeah, he became one, absolutely.

**Q:** *What do you think New York meant to him?*

**A:** Well, he liked the cosmopolitan side of it. He liked the intellectual life . . . There is somebody you might talk to, she will give you a completely different slant, . . . Diana Trilling. She and Mike were quite friendly.

**Q:** *Is she still in New York?*

**A:** Yeah, she's in New York. She is old and she is almost blind, but she might agree to . . . see you, yeah, Diana Trilling. He liked very much mixing with intellectuals. He had a little group of personal friends but I don't believe . . . he had one guy, a photographer, and they did the book together . . . Something about New York. Yes, about poverty in New York but it was never published. . . .

**Q:** *Mike would joke that his religion was Labor Zionist, and that he had a feeling for Jewish life and also a feeling for Israel. What, where, did that come out of?*

**A:** Hanging out with all the rest of us. Now you see we all began, not Zionist in fact, for a time anti-Zionists, but gradually that changed and while we didn't become ideological or dramatic Zionists, we became friendly toward Israel and, of course, became critical. But say, in the fifties, sixties, that was a considerable, strong feeling.

**Q:** *But for an Irish Catholic graduate of Holy Cross . . .*

**A:** Well, he was open, fluid. I think it would be interesting for you also to speak to Tom Kahn. I think you had better do that quickly. I gather he's not well. Tom is very smart. He may very well be a little nasty. For a time they were very close. Then it got to be pretty bad. I think that's worth doing because he will give a totally different view of him.

**Q:** *And Rachelle?*

**A:** Rachelle, too. She will be . . . well I haven't seen Tom in many years . . . we were once very close . . . she will be less . . . he'll give you a hard line view. Unless he's changed. People do change. She will be more generous, whereas he will be brighter. He will tell you about what he felt were certain deficiencies of Mike's behavior. I think he will speak about . . . a tendency on Mike's part to sort of drift through things, not get down to brass tacks. Be a little casual about it. Maybe in that period . . . Tom used to complain that Mike was hard to get hold of or pin down . . . something of the bohemian thing was still there. It's interesting that like Shachtman he really didn't become very responsible until he had the burden of being the leader of the small organization, which is nothing I would wish upon my worst enemy. Well, there are a few I would. . . .

**Q:** *One other question. The Socialist International was obviously very important to him.*

**A:** That was something that I never . . . well, I could understand it but I never entirely shared it. I've never had any interest in the Socialist International as an organization. Well, look, here he was the leader of a little group with all of the troubles, etc. He went there . . . those guys they knew he didn't have any following . . . but they liked him, and they admired him, and he spoke on a higher theoretical level than most of their people . . . Just as, alas, probably *Dissent* is the best Socialist magazine in the world, which isn't saying very much. All it tells you is how little there is elsewhere. Maybe there is something as good or better that I don't know, but there isn't very much.

And so, he would go there and he got a great deal of gratification out of it . . . being friends. I don't mean this in any critical way. I didn't share it but I understood it . . . being friends with Willy Brandt and some of the others . . . especially the Swedes. The Swedes loved him. And he admired them. The Swedes are more sophisticated and they were more of what we could call Socialists than some of the other guys in the International. Michel Rocard, who has an interesting history going way back to a left sectarian group, . . . knew Mike and he admired him.[15] Well, Rocard was a pretty sophisticated operator. With some of the others, I don't know—I never went to a meeting of the Socialist International, but to Mike it was an absolute necessity. And it was an important part of his life. He got recognition there. He was working on writing a program for them toward the end. I don't know what happened to that, but it would be interesting to find out.

**Q:** *So, he was really being treated as a peer with [European Socialist leaders]. . . .*

**A:** Absolutely.

**Q:** *And in the role that, had he been born someplace else, he might well have played.*

**A:** Yes. Well, that's something we often talked about. I'm glad you mentioned that. We used to joke . . . say, well look, suppose we were living in England? If there was a Labour government, Mike might well be a member of the cabinet. He was at least as competent as most of those guys, probably more so, and I might be in the House of Commons and maybe be the party whip or something or other, or running a Socialist paper, but who knows? And it was just an accident, fate, that we were in this country where the Socialist prospects weren't very good. On the other hand, we compensated ourselves with the idea, whether accurate or not, that we led a richer Socialist intellectual life than most of the people in Europe. Because we weren't saddled with large organizations and responsibilities. Mike had friendships with some of the Socialists in Europe. I think he was friendly with Anthony Crosland.

**Q:** *He was personally friendly with Crosland?*

**A:** I think so. I'm not sure. I don't know who would know.

**Q:** *Where would he have met Crosland?*

**A:** In Europe. I don't know if he knew Crosland, but Brandt was an important figure for him. I don't think they took him seriously when it came to practical arrangements about governmental politics in Europe. But these people, perhaps for whom Socialism was a residual belief, it's hard to know how seriously they still take it . . . I used to ask Mike, are they really still Socialists or is it just Sunday rhetoric. He used to answer, it's very hard to say. With some of them, with Scandinavians, certainly still serious. The Italians, of course, more or less—probably more. The Spaniards had become complete pragmatists. With the French the whole range. The Germans . . . some of them still take it somewhat seriously. But they want to give up the language, the rhetoric. That in itself is of some significance. It was in the realm of language and theory of oratory that he figured there, and it gave him a lot of satisfaction.

**Q:** *Who would know about that in the DSA or anywhere else?*

**A:** [Joanne] Barkan . . . have you spoken to Barkan? Barkan would know about that sort of thing. I don't know whether Brandt would answer a letter and I don't know that it's worth going to Europe unless you had to go for other reasons. Brandt is getting on.

**Q:** *The Swedes maybe?*

**A:** There is a fellow named Pierre Schori, he's now Undersecretary of Foreign Affairs in Sweden and he was close to Mike and an admirer of his. Ask Joanne [Barkan] tonight about Pierre Schori. I think if you write him he will answer you. Don't ask just in general, ask specific questions. He speaks English perfectly. Write him a letter, ask specific questions or otherwise he will tell you what a great guy Mike was. . . .

**Q:** *Anything else you can think of that I should be thinking about?*

**A:** It would be interesting to talk to some of the trade union leaders. Maybe. . . .

**Q:** *Was that a world Mike was comfortable in, the trade union side of it?*

**A:** They might claim so. Talk to Jack Scheinkman of the Amalgamated who is one of the best of the current trade unionists. Talk to Victor Reuther. He's in Washington. What is it that they felt about him? Why did they respond in [that] way to him? There is a very interesting guy in Texas, lives in Waco, named Bernard Rapoport. He runs a union insurance company. He would help Mike out financially in some projects. He loved Mike. He would come into New York and Mike and I would have breakfast with him at 7-8 in the morning. Poor Mike would have to get up in the middle of the night and come down for this. It would be interesting for you to get a spectrum of responses outside of the narrow little circle. That's why I suggested trade union guys. What would [Arthur] Schlesinger say about him? I think I know what he would say.

**Q:** *Did they know each other?*

**A:** Yes. Arthur would say . . . well he was really a liberal, but he still hung on to the Socialist vocabulary and nostalgia . . . The trade union guys, that's interesting. Because he was able to make a bit of a dent [with them], not greatly, but a bit of a dent. People like that responded to Mike.

**Q:** *Is there anything about Mike and* Dissent *that wouldn't be apparent to me from his published writings in* Dissent?

**A:** He was actually marvelous in this respect. I don't think in all the years we worked together that he ever said no. For the magazine, the loss of Mike and Bob Lekachman, who was not quite of the same stature but a gifted economics journalist, a good one, has been a very serious loss because with the two of them social policy was a strength of the magazine. Now that they have gone it's become a problem. The only one who really can deal with it is Kuttner, who has his own magazine but still is willing to do one piece a year for us . . . All magazines need a stable, people who . . . write on demand, and most of these damn professors who we have around the magazine . . . if you ask them to do something, you will get it a year later. They [Harrington and Lekachman]were tremendously reliable, and it made a big difference, in my life at least, to have them around. I feel every day that it is a great loss.

## Notes

1. Maurice Isserman, *The Other American: The Life of Michael Harrington* (New York: PublicAffairs, 2000), viii.
2. Gerald Sorin describes how in his later years, feeling that he was treading water, Howe lost some of his lust for political and intellectual engagement: "His discouragement arose [partly] from weariness over having to fight the old struggles over and over again in a country where memory is always in short supply" (246). *Irving Howe: A Life of Passionate Dissent.* New York: New York University Press, 2002.
3. Frank Hague was the Democratic mayor of Jersey City, New Jersey (1917-47). Hague's powerful political machine gave him a well-deserved reputation for corruption and the status of the top political boss in the state for decades.
4. NAM was The New American Movement, a splinter group of the Students for a Democratic Society (SDS).
5. *Nudnik* is Yiddish for a boring, annoying person.
6. Robert Kuttner is a prolific writer on political and economic policy. A liberal thinker, he is cofounder and co-editor of *The American Prospect.* His main focus has been to explore how capitalism and the international market system can better serve the public interest.
7. Lane Kirkland was a prominent AFL-CIO organizer and president from 1979 to 1995.
8. Eugene McCarthy, Democratic senator from Minnesota (1959-71), ran on an anti-Vietnam War platform in his campaign for the Democratic nomination for president in 1968.
9. Americans for Democratic Action (ADA) champions liberal values and progressive policies. Founded by Eleanor Roosevelt and other prominent Democrats in the late 1940s, it has served as a leading organization for the liberal wing of the Democratic Party.
10. Harold Ickes was Franklin D. Roosevelt's Secretary of the Interior and helped implement much of the New Deal.
11. Leon Henderson was an economic advisor to Roosevelt.
12. John Cort was an active member of the DSA and a prominent figure within the Catholic Worker movement. He was a close associate of Dorothy Day and served on the

editorial staff of *Commonweal* during the 1940s and 1950s. He regarded himself as a Christian Socialist and was a long-time acquaintance of Michael Harrington.

13. A prominent Catholic journalist and editor, Peter Steinfiels served as editor of *Commonweal* for more than two decades and as a religion editor of the *New York Times* for many years. He is a liberal Catholic and the author of *The Neoconservatives: The Men Who Are Changing America's Politics* (1979).
14. Sidney Hillman was the Amalgamated Clothing Workers of America founder and its president from 1914 to 1946. Steven Fraser wrote his biography, *Labor Will Rule: Sidney Hillman and the Rise of American Labor* (1993).
15. Michel Rocard, a member of the French Socialist Party, served as Prime Minister (1988-91) during the administration of François Mitterrand.

# Chapter 17

**Joseph Dorman, "Irving Howe, New York Intellectual," Selections from interview conducted in 1993 and published in *Arguing the World* (New York: The Free Press, 2000).**

## Editors' Introduction

This interview, compiled from Joseph Dorman's 1998 documentary film, *Arguing the World* (and reprinted in the 2000 book of the same name), contextualizes Howe's thought among and in opposition to certain prominent fellow New York Intellectuals of his generation and subsequently. Dorman, who was born in a Detroit suburb in 1958, had been senior producer for the Public Broadcasting series "Media Matters," and would go on to produce documentaries on the San Francisco gold rush, an expedition to the Antarctic, John Kerry's role in Vietnam, and the Yiddish writer Sholom Aleichem.

Although only Howe's remarks are excerpted below, the movie (and book) juxtapose them with remarks by Howe's contemporaries Nathan Glazer, Daniel Bell, and Irving Kristol, among others. The effect is quite different; while *Arguing the World* conveys the context of Howe's positions and illustrates the argumentative style and interpersonal dynamics of the New York Intellectuals, the version printed here is more faithful to the actual interview, which was conducted just a few months before his unexpected death and done in a single sitting with Howe alone.

Howe is the sole left-wing voice of his generation in *Arguing the World.* Glazer and Bell had moved to the right and were at times associated with the neoconservatives, although both have also maintained an intermittent liberal identity and taken unexpected positions that straddle ideological lines. Kristol, by contrast, is considered the "godfather" of neoconservativism, and has remained a strong presence in the movement as it has evolved from its early criticism of radicalism and aspects of liberalism to its recent advocacy of an aggressive American foreign policy with a strong military component.

The interview addresses Howe's formative poverty and immersion in a culture of ideological critique: "There was a sense of chaos, of disintegration. And so the Socialist view, the radical view, seemed to bring to young people a total understanding." The interview shows once again, this time against the background of clashing intellectuals from his own generation, how Howe's beginning shaped his entire career; he would castigate the particulars but never stop working against poverty and for egalitarianism.

This interview highlights Howe's ongoing disagreements with the neoconservatives. Once again a relationship goes back to the beginning of their intellectual journeys and continues through their reflections late in life.[1] Irving Kristol is the key contrasting figure against whom Howe's journey—which is personal, political, and moral—is chronicled. As Kristol explains in *Arguing the World*, while the two were students at City College, Howe recruited him to Socialism, although only briefly: "He also expelled me, about a year later, for coming to the conclusion that, in fact, there was an organic connection between Leninism and Stalinism." Ironically, the later Howe would largely agree with parts of this analysis, which casts Communism, in essence, as an unworkable system willing to use brutal methods to justify its abstract dogmas. Not surprisingly, Howe sees himself as far less authoritarian in his early personal relations with Kristol. "When he called me the party boss or the chief ideologist," says Howe, "he is perhaps transposing his own experiences in the Republican Party in recent years to an earlier time." The implication is that Kristol is now the rigid apologist for an immoral system, in this case an unbridled capitalism, a kind of inverse caricature of the early ideologue that Kristol considers the young Howe. Nevertheless Howe continued to respect Glazer and Bell, despite their notable political differences, and valued their strong commitment to uphold argument as a process of intellectual engagement and learning.

This 1993 interview was Howe's last, as heart trouble would take his life in May 1993. It includes a new introduction by Dorman written especially for this book explaining the circumstances of the interview.

## Joseph Dorman's New Introduction

The following interview was conducted on videotape with Irving Howe for the documentary *Arguing the World* (1998) about Howe and his fellow New York Intellectuals, Daniel Bell, Nathan Glazer and Irving Kristol. The film traces the four men's political evolution from the Great Depression to the Age of Reagan against the shifting landscape of twentieth century American politics.

While Howe agreed to be interviewed, he was, like my other subjects, skeptical that such a film could be made on men who were essentially writers, and perhaps even more skeptical that such a film would ever find an audience. Some thirty minutes into the interview Howe asked me point-blank why I would make a film on the New York Intellectuals. "Won't it be boring?" he asked. And yet Howe's interview was anything but tedious. Despite his rumpled dress and demeanor, as he dipped into his old political battles—his several triumphs and more numerous losses—he spoke with a kind of searing, superheated energy.

In all he spoke for about three hours that morning and the interview took on a certain rhythm. As long as the camera rolled, he produced a torrent of words and recollections. Each time we stopped to change tapes, he would become self-conscious, often uttering some vague complaint or worry.

Somewhere near the two-hour mark, he mentioned wearily that Woody Allen had needed only ten minutes to interview him for his film *Zelig*, in which he had brilliantly parodied historical documentaries such as the one I was making. After the next tape ran out in the midst of one of several tirades against his old political nemesis Irving Kristol, he grew anxious that he had grown too harsh (Howe had developed a reputation as a particularly savage debate opponent over the years) and wanted reassurance that I would edit the material fairly. I assured him that I would. The camera rolled again and Howe lunged into yet another slashing attack on Kristol as if he had never said a word to me. I tried to hide my smile.

By the end, Howe had given me a remarkable interview, by turns heated and mournful, assertive and self-critical. I was fortunate because it was the only interview I would have a chance to do with him before he died suddenly in 1993. (Though he had been suffering for some time with serious heart disease—evident in his sometime labored breathing during our interview—at the time of his death he appeared to be, at least temporarily, on the mend.)

So I was left rather nervously with this single interview while I was able to spend many hours with my other three subjects over several different sessions. Interestingly, whenever I mention this to those who have seen the film, they are taken aback. Some have even tried to argue the point with me. But the film contains just the one interview with Howe.

Why people's surprise? No doubt it is due, in part, to the many photographs of Howe that litter the film and give one a sense of seeing him over the course of his life. But I think it's more likely the result of the power and depth of Howe's responses over those three hours, the result of his own emotional and intellectual grasp of his past in the last decade of his life. Howe had made a rather remarkable journey from his beginnings as the son of poor Jewish immigrants. It was that journey—portrayed in his autobiography, *A Margin of Hope*—that informed his interview.

Most people are at their most emotional when they talk of their childhoods and Howe was no exception. He spoke with great feeling about the trauma of the Great Depression, the seedbed of his future political life. His parents' loss of their small grocery store to bankruptcy tipped his family "close to destitution," he recalled. "It was like having everything fall out from under you." The fall—the sense of loss and the fall in status—left a far greater impact than the poverty itself. It made him a life-long man of the Left, constitutionally incapable of relinquishing his Socialist ideals long after much of the hard architecture of Socialist politics and economics had been left in ruins.

The Socialist ideology that he adopted at just fourteen served as a bridge beyond the smallness of his life. By the time he entered City College two years later, that ideology had also hardened into a kind of protective carapace for a young man who was still shy and awkward and deeply self-conscious. Even among his impassioned friends on the anti-Stalinist Left who frequented Alcove One in the City College cafeteria, Howe was known as especially rigid and hard-edged in his beliefs. There was a great risk for Howe, as happened to many caught in intense political movements, that the need to believe—and to protect that belief—would ultimately overshadow its quality and substance.

That it didn't owes very much to Howe's years in the army during World War II. Stationed in Alaska far away from the fighting and with little to do, Howe pored through world literature from the army base library. The young man who entered the service a would-be revolutionary emerged from it a nascent literary critic. Most who had known him before the transformation were surprised at the new Irving Howe capable of grasping literary nuance as readily as he wielded the cudgels of Marxist polemics. This was the true beginning of Howe's adult intellectual life. In literature he found a safe place for the intense reflection that made him the voluble, wry, and self-critical man I encountered in my interview.

Of course, Howe never stopped his fierce political engagement, but in time, literature's subtleties could not help but undermine the icy certainties of his political life, if not his passionate belief that politics mattered. He once remarked that literature provided a refuge from the aridity of politics for him, but it's notable that one of his best critical works, *Politics and the Novel*, is a brilliant synthesis of his two overriding passions. Literature provided the lens through which he could explore the complexities of political life as it revolves around the axes of hope and despair, and, not so incidentally, offered a means through which Howe could covertly explore and relate parts of his own political autobiography. This gives the book an emotional and intellectual urgency that remain fresh even today.

As he matured, Howe's engagement with literature would steadily widen beyond political concerns, but his criticism continued to be informed by a deep moral engagement that had grown out of his life in left-wing politics. That almost obsessive concern with morality and social justice also left him with a Socialist politics that, over the years, exhibited an often maddening disregard for practical politics.

I felt the same moral commitment, the same urgency of purpose, throughout my interview as Howe recalled the political battles which had, in the deepest sense, defined his life. Whether it was his fights with the Young Communist

League in the alcoves of City College, with the Communist Party during the age of McCarthy, with the radicals of SDS during the sixties or the resurgent conservative movement in the last decade of his life, Howe's answers often teetered between soft bemusement and full-throated war cry. Perhaps that's because literature tempered Howe's political passions without defusing them, just as politics energized his literary engagement without vulgarizing it. This tension made Irving Howe a more interesting literary critic than he would otherwise have been and a wiser student of politics. It also gave a spark to almost everything he said that morning. Try as the aging critic might to defer from entering political battle once again, to steep his words in the calm of literary detachment, he simply couldn't help himself, couldn't suppress the exuberance—even impetuousness—of his political youth. Thank God.

## The Interview

*Irving Howe grew up in the political and economic cauldron of the Great Depression in New York's Jewish immigrant neighborhoods. The searing experience of poverty would indelibly shape his future political and intellectual life.*

My folks had a grocery store; it went bankrupt and they had to move in with my grandmother in a cramped apartment with many people. For many years I didn't have a room of my own. We were very close to destitution. We moved from the West Bronx to the East Bronx. That may seem like a trivial thing but it was a drop in social ascent. The West Bronx was the middle-class area, the East Bronx was the working-class area and for a kid of eleven or twelve the transition was very difficult and perplexing and painful. It was like having everything fall out from under you.

The thought of getting a job was something which no one really expected to be possible. The thought of a career or future was not something which one could live by. The expectation that one's parents could bring in enough money next week by which to live was very small. There was a sense of chaos, of disintegration. And so the Socialist view, the radical view, seemed to bring to young people a total understanding. It wasn't fragmentary. It seemed to suggest a conceptual frame by which one could structure and give meaning to these very difficult experiences.

And so it was a very normal thing for a kid with some sort of introspectiveness and intellectuality, such as it was, to turn to politics. And there was a group of Yipsels, Young People's Socialist League, a few blocks away from where I lived.

In the immigrant Jewish neighborhood where I grew up in the east Bronx, politics was meat and drink. The political campaigns of 1932 and 1936 were very vigorous, very active. The Socialists mounted within their limited means a considerable campaign. The first time I heard Norman Thomas speak it was a thrilling experience. There was something pure and beautiful about this man's voice!

In 1932 Norman Thomas—heir to the great Socialist leader Eugene V. Debs—won nearly a million votes in the presidential election, thanks in large part to strong support among Jewish immigrants and their children. "The answer to unemployment," he proclaimed, "is nothing less than worldwide Socialism. The answer to the troubles that beset us is worldwide Socialism. But on that road to that glorious goal, there are means we can employ now, now to break the back of this misery, which rests like a curse on people in every hamlet, in every city and every town of America."

*During the Depression, political street corner speaking became a common activity in the highly politicized and left-wing Jewish immigrant neighborhoods. Street corner speaking not only offered a way to recruit adherents but provided an entertaining form of "street theater" to anyone willing to be harangued for a few moments—or hours.*

These were meetings which required no money, you just got a little stand and an American flag and you went to a corner—there were certain corners in the Bronx that we habitually used—and you would set up shop. We would try to sell a little bit of our literature, sometimes we would take up a collection. One would begin talking about the terrible conditions of life—unemployment, the threat of war, the problem of Fascism—and from there you went on. But mostly, it was a form of propaganda.

The essential thing for a street corner speaker is to work the back-and-forth relationship, the give-and-take, because the audience in a street corner is not one that just stands quietly. It participates. It joins in. It heckles. There was no great requirement that you be entirely coherent or that you have an organized structure. Those of my friends who spoke well, and some were quite brilliant at this, were able to achieve an emotional tie with the audience, were able to strike some chord in the feelings of the workers and the people who would gather around a street corner meeting. A good street corner speaker could go on for three quarters of an hour. I rarely lasted more than twenty minutes, even if that long. I had a certain gift. I could lose an audience in about three minutes.

*Like thousands of other sons of poor immigrants, Howe went to the City College of New York. Free and open to smart Jewish students barred by quotas from Ivy League schools, it became a kind of "Harvard of the Poor." There he met future New York Intellectuals Irving Kristol and Daniel Bell.*

I went with anticipation, and fear. Anticipation that it would be very exciting, that I might even learn something, though I didn't learn terribly much—that was my own fault—and fear. The fear that these professors would put one down, the fear that it would be more than I could cope with or manage. You must remember I was a kid; I was sixteen years old when I went to City College. On the one hand, I had visions of great political activity. On the other hand, I was afraid of differential and integral calculus—and as it turned out I had very good reason to be afraid of it.

The atmosphere was dingy—the place needed a paint job, the teachers were overworked, many of them were mediocre. It wasn't a very distinguished faculty at all. There were a few brilliant teachers like the legendary Morris Cohen, [but among the students] there was an atmosphere of perfervid, overly heated, overly excited intellectuality, because the radicalism of the moment was essentially abstract.

*The City College cafeteria, ringed by a series of alcoves, became an informal headquarters for the college's fervent political life. Alcove One became home to the anti-Stalinist Left that included Howe, Daniel Bell, Irving Kristol, and a few years later, Nathan Glazer.*

The alcoves were little divisions in the lunchroom, sort of shaped like a horseshoe, in which students could sit and eat their lunch and there was a table on which we could put political literature.

I had a device of checking in at the beginning of a class when a teacher took attendance, if you could imagine, and then slipping out to go to the bathroom and coming back at the end of the hour and meanwhile spending that hour in the alcove.

Anyone who was an anti-Stalinist on the left was a natural ally for our beleaguered group, because we were distinctly—in the left-wing world at City College—a quite small minority, and we felt, in fact we were, beleaguered. I would say in Alcove One, which was the hangout of the various anti-Stalinist Left groups, there may have been a total of fifty students. In Alcove Two, which was the hangout for Communist students, I would guess that they had upwards of four hundred to five hundred members, which was of course a very good deal.

We were raising some of the most fundamental ethical and moral problems of politics, though we wouldn't have put it that way. We had no awareness that we were engaged in such lofty enterprises.

We thought we were discussing revolutionary or Marxist strategy. At that point we thought of ourselves as anti-Stalinist Marxists, anti-Stalinist leftists. But as I see it now, we were often engaged in more fundamental, ethical questions. The whole problem of the nature of Stalinism. I put it now in abstract terms, but that was really what we were talking about. The anti-Stalinist groups, which meant in those days mostly the Trotskyist youth group and the Socialists and a few other left-wing groups, the main contribution they made politically, intellectually was in the fight against Stalinism and the fight against the totalitarian perversion that we saw Stalinism to mean.

Some of the particular theories we had about Stalinism have proven to be questionable, but in our insistence that any Socialist value that was worth preserving had to be based on democracy, that Socialism and democracy were indissoluble, there I think we were right.

*Irving Kristol, Howe's fellow Trotskyist at City College, would go on to become his lifelong political antagonist. Kristol has claimed that Howe, as an informal leader of their group, "expelled" him for his political views then beginning to diverge from more orthodox Marxism.*

I made a big mistake with Irving Kristol, and that was recruiting him to begin with. He wasn't, let's say, good material, but he wasn't expelled ever. He was part of a little group which developed different ideas, dissident ideas, and they left. When he called me the party boss or the chief ideologist, he is perhaps transposing his own experiences in the Republican Party in recent years to an earlier time. I suppose I and one or two others were the leading spokesmen, the most articulate figures around Alcove One. But the organization of these groups was very loose. There was no effort at any kind of political or intellectual discipline. People spoke freely. We were democrats, without recognizing it or acknowledging it, I believe. There was no effort to conform to a party line. If I was a party boss, I don't know who I bossed around.

*During the years before the Second World War, America's Communist Party executed a series of infamous political about-faces at Stalin's direction in regard to the United States and Fascist Germany. After years of excoriating Franklin Roosevelt and American Democracy, the Communist Party suddenly burst out of its sectarian shell to inaugurate the era of the Popular or United Front in which they embraced the New Deal.*

You had constantly during the Popular Front a difficulty that some of the things the Communists were proposing [like the united opposition to Hitler] made sense intrinsically, but their own manipulative demagogic authoritarianism alloyed and destroyed these policies. All the way through in the Popular Front period, the question of Communist manipulation and Communist domination—Communist bad faith—was a central problem.

*At the same time the Communists developed a populist cultural style scorned by Howe and by the young group of writers who had begun* Partisan Review, *then a small anti-Communist literary journal.*

The Stalinists were middlebrow, the Trotskyists were highbrow, because they thought in the kind of terms that you had when *Partisan Review* started coming out, the union of two avant-gardes, a political avant-garde and a cultural avant-garde. We prided ourselves on reading Joyce and Thomas Mann and Proust, maybe not completely, but at least dipping in, whereas they were reading palookas like Howard Fast.

*The pact between Hitler and Stalin occasioned yet another Communist about-face in America and sickened those on the anti-Stalinist Left.*

I can remember the most terrible few days of my life, intellectually speaking, came after the Hitler-Stalin Pact in 1939. And my friends and I walked around, and we felt in one sense we had been confirmed since Trotsky had predicted a Hitler-Stalin pact, but we also felt that we were at a terrible historical point. That the two main totalitarian dictators, the two monsters, had come together, that a war was certain to follow very soon.

Many of the ideas that we had at the time—ideas of social revolution—seem now half-baked or irrelevant to American conditions. But then you must remember that the situation in the thirties was so utterly different from what it is today; there really was a feeling of apocalypse. That I think is the essential thing. There was the feeling that we were living at the end of the world, and in a way, we were.

*After graduation, Howe, like countless other young men across the country, was drafted. His war years, however were spent in Alaska, giving himself a literary education. Before the war, Howe had been an admirer of* Partisan Review, *the small but influential journal whose influence was destined to grow in the forties and fifties. Upon his release from the service, he longed to enter the New York Intellectual world of which* Partisan Review *had become the nucleus.*

I had been partly transformed by my experiences in the army. I spent two years in Alaska. It was like a graduate school for me. During that time I read a good many books. There was nothing else to do up there. I began to develop incipient literary inclinations, to move away from being just political, and I began to contribute a book review here, a book review there.

On the one hand, I was still involved in the little left-wing group although more and more uncomfortable in it, and at the same time I was involved in this world of New York Intellectuals, though not entirely at ease there either. And then that began to change.

I worked for a while as an assistant to Hannah Arendt at Schocken Books, which was then a very distinguished publishing company, and I would meet with her every two weeks presumably to do business but actually to engage in intellectual discussion and that was very stimulating. And one thing led to another. And so my horizons widened.

I began to meet some New York Intellectuals, like Lionel Trilling and Harold Rosenberg, Philip Rahv, and most importantly for me, Meyer Schapiro, who was sort of my idol and guru. I remember going up to the offices of *Partisan Review* and being received by Philip Rahv in a rather gruff but friendly manner. And he handed me the chance to do a review and that was a big opportunity, it seemed, and in fact it was.

*After the Second World War, the Soviet Union spread its tentacles across much of Eastern Europe and Berlin became a divided city. The U.S. and the Soviet Union, opportunistic allies in wartime, soon became ideological and military foes destined to play out a Cold War across five decades and much of the globe.*

The expansion of Stalinist power was a very alarming thing. One totalitarian monster had been destroyed in the war, and for a moment afterward there was a sense of exhilaration, of relief, and now there was another one and it seemed we would never be done with it. The initial event was the Russian invasion of Czechoslovakia and the overthrow of the democratic society there. That was in 1948. When that happened, we felt that it was a dark night again. That darkness was descending over Europe.

*In 1949, the Communists organized a Conference on Peace and Scientific Progress at the Waldorf Astoria. It was one of many such propaganda conferences organized by both sides as the Cold War was beginning.*

The Communists made a major effort at the Waldorf Astoria conference to bring together intellectuals and people from the Soviet Union on behalf of their views in regard to the Cold War. They brought [Alexander] Fadayev, a literary hack; they brought Dmitri Shostakovich, a great composer. Shostakovich was a pitiful sight. He was clearly terribly unhappy, wanting to be any place else but there. But I guess he had to come. At this conference, the anti-Stalinist intellectuals from around *Partisan Review*—like Mary McCarthy, Robert Lowell, myself—were present and some of us spoke up. They couldn't keep us from speaking.

*With the Cold War anxieties came the rise of "McCarthyism." Though Howe, like his former City College classmate Irving Kristol, remained staunchly anti-Communist, he was angered by his old antagonist Irving Kristol's attacks in* Commentary magazine *on liberal "blindness" toward Communism, which seemed to almost exonerate McCarthy's excesses.*

Kristol knew that McCarthy was a thug. He knew McCarthy didn't use nice methods, and McCarthy wasn't someone with whom Kristol would have wanted to associate personally, but the anti-Communism of the moment was becoming so uninflected, so coarse, that it even found a kind of backhanded apology, if that's the phrase to use, for McCarthyism.

My friends and I had no fondness for the American Communists. Politically, we were bitter opponents, but we took, in the 1950s, a strict civil libertarian position. We were against all the persecutions of the Communists. We felt it was playing into their hands. We felt it was a violation of American traditions and principles. We looked upon McCarthyism as a thing of ugliness.

*In the early fifties, several years after his friends had left the sectarian politics of their youth, Howe, too, deserted his Trotskyist sect. But Howe, unlike his friends, felt more comfortable on the margins of American politics, choosing to remain a "democratic Socialist" and a man of the Left rather than become a Democrat as they had.*

We had been raised, it seemed, with our mother's milk with the idea that the function of the intellectual was to stand apart from the governed institutions of society. To be a critic, even if it meant being marginal in the world. Even if it meant not being part of the elite . . . Even if it meant writing for journals with small circulations. To be consistently a critic and to cry that the fish stank since many of the fish did stink. In the fifties, this whole impulse, which had been the animating values of the whole of *Partisan Review* since the middle of the 1930s, began slowly to weaken.

In 1954 I published an article which had its fifteen minutes of notoriety. It appeared in *Partisan Review* and was called "This Age of Conformity." It was a kind of scattershot attack on the whole intellectual world in New York for becoming too socially complacent, for losing its intellectual independence, its social radicalism, its passion for criticism. It was not met with great fondness on the part of many of victims of the article.

The tendency in the intellectual world in the 1950s was toward conformity, was toward making peace with the status quo, the status quo of American capitalist society, and I was against that. And in 1953 we started a magazine called *Dissent,* which would be a voice of independent Socialist thought but not affiliated with any organization.

In 1952 I and a few friends left a group called the Independent Socialist League, which had been steadily moving from Trotskyism to social democracy. We felt the day of the sects was over. It was over as far as we were concerned. The old formulas of the Marxist Left no longer sufficed. We felt that Socialism—the whole Socialist idea—was in a very deep crisis, and has remained so over subsequent decades. It was necessary to enter into a new kind of experience, sort of freelance individual, in terms of starting a journal or magazine which would not have any organizational discipline or any party line.

*Howe and his colleagues at* Dissent *watched the rise of the New Left on college campuses in the early sixties with enormous hope. The young radicals seemed natural allies after the* Dissent *group's years in the political wilderness in the fifties. Soon, it became all too clear that differences in political style and thought between the two generations of radicals were larger than their joint political sympathies.*

In the early sixties, relations between my gang, the group around *Dissent*, and SDS were quite good. We were sympathetic to the idea of participatory democracy and the idea of participatory democracy still has a certain force to it. [It reminded one] that representative institutions tend to rigidify, become formalized, and you go through these elections every four years, you pick a candidate, but that most people don't really have any share in the actual decision making in the country. In participatory democracy there was an effort, a little naive to be sure but an effort, to find ways to allow people to participate more actively and steadily in political life. They had a fraternal, liberal, Socialist view with which we could easily be in harmony.

We quarreled over Cuba, the Castro regime which they defended, I think foolishly. They had romantic notions about Castroism as being a better form of Communism than that in the Soviet Union and I think history has shown they were totally wrong. Some of them seemed to us very authentic and idealistic, and sincere.

We also sensed important differences among some of the SDS people. Perhaps the most gifted among them, Tom Hayden, was someone we felt had a very strong authoritarian, manipulative streak. We could see the commissar in him. And that put us off. Probably we made a lot of tactical blunders. Some of the criticism they made of us now and even then, we saw, had a certain validity. We tended to seem to them people who knew everything or thought they knew everything. We had become a little fixed in our views, a little rigid in our postures. It's something that comes with age the way your bones and muscles become rigid. We were impatient; we scolded. At the same time we wanted to influence them. And we were hurt by their assaults upon us. There's an inevitable conflict between generations, but I think that to reduce the differences between them and us to a generational conflict is a superficial way of looking upon it. The most tragic consequence of the New Left was what it erased. There was a very great deal of idealism among tens of thousands of young people. Some of it remains, but a lot of it has been destroyed. A lot of it has died out and gone sour. It also, I think, created a very bad series of political backlashes. These kids had an extraordinary gift for knowing how to use and manipulate the American mass media. They were probably responsible in some sense or to some degree for the election of Richard Nixon. The New Left were the ones who created an atmosphere in which people reacted strongly against it and ultimately turned to the right.

*At the time of our interview a resurgent conservative movement was in power and Howe had braced himself for what would prove his twilight battle against the American Right. At the same time, behind the strong reaffirmation of his evolving Socialist vision there remained the sad realization that the country seemed to have little use for these principles to which he had dedicated his life and an uncertainty on his own part that they might be practically realized.*

In the coming decade or so the political struggles will no longer be between the East and West or between democratic capitalism and Communist totalitarianism. It will now be a struggle between conservatism—Thatcherite conservatism or Reaganite or Kristolite conservatism—on the one hand and social democracy on the other.

We continue our criticism of the injustices and inadequacies of a society which allows thousands of people to be homeless in the streets, an affluent society in America where there is still a vast amount of poverty, social dislocation, social pathology.

The crucial lesson of the last fifty years, one crucial lesson, is the absolute indissolubility, the absolute organic connection between democratic practice and Socialist hope. The great tragedy of the last half-century has been the enormous waste of idealism and energy which the Communist movement represented and its malappropriation of the Socialist vocabulary, the Socialist idea. It will take a good deal of time before the consequences of this are undone.

But Socialism means a greater social ethic, a concern for the needs of human beings, economically and culturally—a gradual transformation from the ethic of accumulation and me-ism to social sharing. All of this may sound vague at the moment, I guess it has to be.

Our goal is toward the continuous extension of the welfare state, toward greater social provision in the hope that there will be an eventual transition—not guaranteed but desired—toward social fraternity and social equality.

To me, Socialism is no longer a dogma or ideology, but it is a vision, a hope, an expectation for the world in which there will be greater equality and a common ownership of major industries. Not nationalization, not government ownership, but shared ownership by the people who work in those industries.

*In my final question, I asked Howe to look back on his political-intellectual history and his City College friendships.*

A lot of American intellectuals made fun of us for being so oriented to Russia. They were partly right. But they were largely wrong because the essential question which dominated our generation .was the question of Stalinism. This has been the essential problem of political-intellectual life in the twentieth century. That may be a simplification, but I think it's true.

Here was this terrible, brutal, horrifying dictatorship which had risen out of Socialist sources and which used the Socialist vocabulary, which appropriated Marxism to itself, which was a kind of travesty, a parody of our hopes and desires. How could we cope with this? How could we understand it and what could it mean? Is there a tie that binds all the people that fifty years ago were in Alcove One at City College? With people like Danny Bell and even someone like Nat Glazer, even though he's quite a bit to the right of us, I do feel very strong ties. I have various disagreements with Bell, but I feel a strong tie with him. With Kristol I feel no longer any tie whatever. He has gone way over to the other side. He's a spokesman for corporate interests, for the Republican Party. I look at him as a political opponent. And the fact that we were together fifty years ago doesn't stir the faintest touch of sentiment in me. I wish him well personally, a long life—with many political failures, I hope.

## Notes

1. See John Rodden, *The Worlds of Irving Howe: The Critical Legacy,* (Boulder: Paradigm, 2005), 10-13, 187-93.

# Postscript

## Interview with Robert Silvers on the Death of Irving Howe, CBC Radio, "As It Happens," May 5, 1993.

### Introduction

Irving Howe died on the morning of May 5, 1993, at Mount Sinai Hospital, at the age of 72. The death, of cardiovascular disease, came after a sudden collapse at home. Ironically, this occurred during the early days of the Clinton administration, a time of new hope for a qualified form of liberalism, although not for democratic Socialism.

Still Howe, in his last months, had soldiered on. "Two Cheers for Utopia," his final essay in *Dissent,* celebrated in muted tones what remained of his democratic Socialism: a misty, distant ideal that could serve as a guide to concrete decisions.[1] In that final essay in spring of 1993, he wrote that "utopianism is a necessity of the moral imagination. It doesn't necessarily entail a particular politics; it doesn't ensure wisdom about current affairs. What it does provide is a guiding perspective, a belief or hope for the future."

For liberal humanism even less firm a foundation was apparent. In "A Second Opinion," one of Howe's last *Dissent* essays, written just after Bill Clinton's election, Howe expressed a tepid optimism that Clinton might mean something new, albeit in an altered political landscape with little hope for the kind of social transformation that Howe advocated. His description of Clinton as "an extremely able politician but a figure whose deeper commitments seem uncertain" seems increasingly accurate in historical hindsight.[2] That description also casts Clinton as the mirror opposite of Howe, who was no politician at all but whose deeper commitments were firm. Indeed, if Howe can be considered a stalwart man of the Left whose beliefs had crept toward liberalism, then so-called Clintonism, with its triangulations amid a blast of conservative ideology, might be considered as a timid survival mechanism for liberalism.

"A Second Opinion" also advances an argument more important than one about Clinton's character, discussing the powerful union movement that had spurred the New Deal onward. Without a mass movement, a liberal-leaning president will do little of lasting value, little to alter the social and political direction. Howe rightly foresaw that Clintonism could not mean a dramatic change in direction for America. It did little to alter, and in fact even contributed to, the march toward a global capitalism. Socialism could not have been closer to death as Howe faced his own last months.

Yet on the occasion of Howe's death the feeble state of democratic Socialism, and even of liberalism, was briefly forgotten. In tributes to him, idealism appeared rock-solid and eternal, in word if not in deed, and Howe's life was hailed as a moral and intellectual exemplar. The following interview with Robert Silvers gives a taste of this, and would shortly be followed by a memorial at the 92nd street YMCA, where Howe had spoken often, in which a plethora of notable speakers lionized him.

Robert Silvers is an appropriate figure to discuss Howe, the liberal public intellectual. In 1963, Silvers cofounded the *New York Review of Books*, where he remains to this day, having outlasted Howe's forty years as editor of a major left intellectual journal. From the beginning Howe, along with a contingent of the New York Intellectuals, was a regular contributor to Silvers' journal, writing several pieces a year on an array of subjects over a thirty-year span. Something of a polymath like Howe, Silvers has edited a number of anthologies on such topics as the performing arts, literary influence, Isaiah Berlin, India, the history of science, and the Bush-Cheney legacy. Silvers' passion for opera may also be viewed as mirroring Howe's love affair with the ballet—two grand, classical arts that represent a rich alternative to literature and a welcome relief from politics.

## The Interview

*The world of our fathers loses a son. Irving Howe—writer, Socialist, and intellectual—has died at the age of seventy-two. In a career that spanned more than half a century, Howe distinguished himself as a leader of the anti-Communist Left, as a literary critic and one of the founding editors of* Dissent *magazine. His most famous book was* World of Our Fathers, *the story of European Jewish immigrants in America. Robert Silvers is co-editor of the* New York Review of Books, *which often published Howe's work. He's in New York.*

**Q:** *Mr. Silvers, Irving Howe seems to have been that particular, singular New York individual, the intellectual Jewish writer, the abrasive left-winger. He seemed to embody all of those streams.*

**Silvers:** [*laughs*] Well, he was certainly was one of the most distinguished, the most important, the most active New York Intellectuals of his time. And he made a great difference. He was not only a writer of streams of articles, books, anthologies, translations—ranging from literary criticism to biography—but he was also the editor, the founder, of a very important but small magazine, *Dissent,* which is a magazine you have to go back to the 1950s to understand, the early fifties, the time of McCarthyism, of contempt for anything like radicalism, Socialism. And he started a magazine which, first, was strongly and firmly anti-Communist, anti-Stalinist, and secondly, had a Socialist vision, a Socialist vision for America. And many intellectuals in New York who were fed up or very critical of Stalinism, of Communism, saw in *Dissent* the hope for a different kind of politics, a different kind of culture. And he started it, he founded it with his friends, he kept it going, edited it, right to the last issue.

**Q:** *I'm curious about that. How did it manage to survive all these years?*

**S:** It survived mainly because Irving and a small group kept it going by soliciting funds, by holding dinners, by attracting above all an audience of people who shared the same values. Values of deep criticism of the entire Stalinist Soviet Russian, Soviet Communist project on the one hand and its conquest of Eastern Europe and on the other, a desire for a more humane kind of economic life, a commitment to welfare, to helping the poor, to solving the deep problems of the inner city. All those problems were canvassed in *Dissent* in a radical way. For instance, just to take an example, the presentation of the Canadian system of medicine was put forward in early issues of *Dissent.* So these people had practical ideas of a welfare kind of Socialism. But much more than that, Irving Howe came out of, as you said, the New York Yiddish-speaking Jewish world, he came out of City College. And he absorbed a very broad, very wide culture, he wrote [essays] on Dostoevsky, on Thomas Hardy. And he infused *Dissent* with not simply a lot of ideas of a mechanical kind about new ways of planning society, but with large cultural concerns.

**Q:** *To what extent was his politics formed by the extreme Depression poverty of his family?*

**S:** Very much so, and if you read his book *World of Our Fathers* you see that . . . the Jewish immigrants who worked in the clothing industry who had their own Socialist ideas, and during the 1930s these ideas became very much part of radical movements. And Irving from the first was very critical of Soviet Communism.

He was drawn to Trotsky in the 1930s, and was a great expert on Trotsky and his career, and then distanced himself from the Trostkyite movement and became what you would call a left, liberal leader of a kind of pragmatic Socialism.

**Q:** *But wouldn't that put him in the sights of other New York Jewish intellectuals, I mean metaphorically, who were strongly Communist, very left, who wouldn't tolerate any kind of revisionism.*

**S:** Yes. There was a great struggle, a great conflict, between the people who felt that Soviet Communism was a denial of freedom, of liberty, of fundamental values, even while [they were all] struggling to maintain those values, and this was a constant critical concern of Irving Howe and his friends: to demolish the pretensions, the claims to being truly democratic, of the supporters of the Soviet Union. But what I would emphasize about him is that it wasn't merely the positions he took, it was his literary sensibility, his writing about Dostoevsky, about Orwell, about Silone, about European literature and modernism, and literary modernism, which he saw as exciting. He was a man of great frankness, of great directness.

**Q:** *See, that's an interesting, what would appear on the surface to be a kind of dichotomy, the man writing with passion and love about literature, one would think in a rather cloistered environment, yet he's out there in the political stage at the same time trying to change things.*

**S:** Much of his life was engaged in an attempt to bridge the two, to bring the literary sensibility, the insight into society that writers like Faulkner and Silone and Dostoevsky had, to bear on a possible project for a different kind of society, a different kind of world. And he was one of the few people I ever knew who did bring together a deep feeling for literature and great skill at literary analysis with a sensible, strong commitment to political reform, political change. Very unusual in this combination, and they both came out, I would say, of his early exposure to a . . . large vision of radicalism [fostered by] the Socialist groups of his youth.

## Notes

1. Irving Howe, "Two Cheers for Utopia," *Fifty Years of Dissent*, Nicolaus Mills & Michael Walzer, eds. (New York: Foundation for the Study of Independent Social Ideas, 2004), 247-51.
2. Irving Howe, "A Second Opinion," *Dissent* Winter (1993): 7-8.

# Afterword

Nina Howe

Reading this set of interviews with my father, Irving Howe, which have been so kindly and thoughtfully collected and organized by John Rodden and Ethan Goffman, gave me much happiness and, inevitably, some sadness. Hearing my father's voice again, especially the cadence and tone of his public voice as he spoke with such strength and clarity on the wide range of topics that interested him, brought me great pleasure, but also evoked sadness. I realized how long it has been since his voice has been with us, and I was reminded of the loss of my beloved brother, Nick. Initially, Nick had agreed to write the afterword to this book, a task for which he was well suited. He was an English professor and had known many aspects of our father's work better than I, as a psychology and education professor. Unfortunately, his untimely death in 2006 prevented him from doing this task. Although I was hesitant when John Rodden first asked me to write this afterword in Nick's place, once the manuscript arrived my initial reluctance vanished. Naturally, I wondered what I could say that would add to what my father had already said so eloquently. One of the advantages, however, of looking over a set of such engaging and interesting interviews is that one does not need to say very much as the pieces literally speak for themselves.

While outlining the three main currents of my father's work—Socialism and politics, literary criticism, and Jewish issues including the preservation and promotion of Yiddish literature—these interviews reflect a variety of moods and textures and cover a range of insights. Some are more formal, while others read more like conversations. Certainly the audiences of the interviews varied, and this had an influence on the kinds of questions and the topics of the interview. The interviewers had differing degrees of skill in obtaining the information that they wanted, and clearly, my father was more comfortable with some interviewers than others. It is hard to know why; perhaps it was the topic of the interview or the tone of the questions (which cannot be determined from a written transcript). My father was often eloquent in his responses; sometimes he showed flashes of humor or made sardonic comments, but as he was sometimes wont to be, he could also be prickly, especially on some issues that he considered more personal.

If there is a centerpiece to this book, it is the interview conducted by Stephen Lewis for a radio program on the Canadian Broadcasting Corporation (CBC), which took place in the fall of 1983. My father had come to Toronto to be an external examiner on a doctoral dissertation in English at the University of Toronto. At the time I was working on my Ph.D. at the University of Waterloo, and I traveled the short distance to Toronto to see him. He was staying at the Park Plaza, an elegant old hotel, for which he held a particular fondness. My warm and rosy memory of the interview was confirmed in reading the transcript. Lewis asked a range of questions that engaged my father, and he seemed quite at ease and gave lengthy and interesting responses. Somehow Lewis captured the essence of my father's personal, political, and intellectual experiences in his questions and comments in a more complete way than many of the other interviewers. There seemed to be some kind of connection, an understanding, a sympathy for each other's background and life that was evident between the two men. I realize that I must have learned a great deal about my father's life from being present during that interview. It is one of the pleasures of my life that I was present, so I was very pleased to find it included in this book.

The interviews in this book took place over the last seventeen years of my father's life, a time when I was coming to appreciate the breadth and depth of his professional work. William Novak's interview about *World of Our Fathers* reminded me of an interview conducted by Peter Gzowski, probably about 1976, which helped place the importance of this theme of my father's work into context for me. Gzowski was the long-time host of the national morning radio show on the Canadian Broadcasting Corporation. The show was broadcast live into the reception area where I waited for my father. When the interview started, the staff turned up the volume and stopped to listen as Gzowski asked a number of insightful questions about the book and the immigrant Jewish experience. Afterwards, my father said that it was clear to him that Gzowski had actually read the book, which he considered not a small feat given that it was quite long and that he was only one of many guests on a daily show that ran for three hours. But what really seemed to impress my father was my report of how the staff had stopped to listen to the interview. What impressed me was my father's way with words and ability to capture and bring to life a part of my family background about which I had known relatively little until then.

The interviews in the book dealing with my father's literary insights provide another side of his professional life. He was a university professor but of a unique character. Without any graduate degrees, he did not produce typical scholarly work. Nor did he fall into the double traps of dry pedantry and engagement with petty debates that characterize so much of academic writing. Perhaps the lack of graduate degrees freed him to do as he wished, although he always considered the two years he spent reading books while in the army in Alaska as his graduate education. My mother reported that he had kept a list of these books, which included ninety-six titles, but somehow the list and other important papers disappeared in a move in the 1950s. We do not know what books were on his "army canon," but surely they included the classics of European, Russian, and American literature, plus other eclectic choices. His love of literature was one of the overriding themes of his life and no doubt was one motivation for his work on translating Yiddish writers and preserving a genre that might have faded away without his intervention.

Aside from his work on *Dissent* and his other political writing, I had not known much about the details of my father's political origins; thus the interviews in this book and in John Rodden's previous two books have provided a wealth of information about his early political formation and lifetime of involvement in the political arena. In particular, the interviews provide insight into his early dealings with his mentor, Max Shachtman, his evolution during the McCarthy years, and the founding of *Dissent*. I was too young to remember the politics of the 1950s, but I do have some fond memories of his political friends—Lew and Rose Coser, Manny Geltman, Milty Sachs, Bernie Rosenberg, and Stanley and Simone Plastrik. The trials and tribulations with the New Left in the 1960s clearly took a toll on my father and brought out his more prickly side, which as he grew older and more reflective he could discuss with more openness. Reading the interviews by Maurice Isserman and Todd Gitlin, in particular, has placed this part of my father's life into richer context for me and I hope for readers of this book.

During the second interview with Isserman, he asks my father a hypothetical question: if he and Michael Harrington had been born somewhere else, might they have been more actively involved in politics, for example, by running for public office? My father raises the possibility of England, but I have wondered about Canada, given its long history of third-party Socialist politics. Suppose that the boat that brought my grandparents to New York had, instead, turned north and left them in Halifax, the major Canadian point of entry, and they had then been put on a train and dropped in Montreal, Toronto or Winnipeg? These three cities had large Jewish immigrant populations, and Winnipeg in particular developed a lively cultural and political world for these immigrants. Socialism was alive and flourishing in Winnipeg and was very important in the evolution of the New Democratic Party (NDP), at times a major force in provincial and federal politics as a third party. Suppose my father had grown up in cold and windy "Winterpeg" (as Winnipeg is sometimes fondly called) in the midst of a viable left-leaning political climate; would he have devoted his life more to politics and less to literature? Would he have become a leading voice of the Left in Canada? One can only speculate about this possibility. Certainly, he had contacts with the NDP leadership and knew, for example, David Lewis, the father of Stephen Lewis, whose interview appears in the book. He went to Winnipeg several times to speak on Jewish and political issues. But, much as politics was one of my father's first great loves, I think that it was his other great passion, literature, which saved him from a life of only politics. As Joe Dorman points out in his introduction to the interview for his film, *Arguing the World,* literature provided a safe haven from the "aridity of politics." Certainly politics and literature counterbalanced one another for my father, but it was the combination and intermixing of both loves that fed the richness of his intellectual life and were the passions of his life.

It is not my father's voice with me and his friends but his public voice that I hear as I read these interviews. It is not an accident that his autobiography, *A Margin of Hope*, was subtitled *An Intellectual Autobiography.* As he himself discusses in the second Isserman interview, my father was of a generation of men who did not share personal things with one another. Today we might say that these men were not in touch with their emotions or use some other cliché, but I am inclined to think that it was typical of men (and many women) of that generation not to share personal information very readily. My father was a warm and loving parent, but he was not an open person who shared much about his feelings or told Nick and me many stories about his childhood. Yet clearly his childhood experiences had an impact on his relations with others and his needs and desires. My father traces his lifelong love of shirts to the time when his parents started to earn more money after the International Ladies Garment Workers Union went on strike in 1933 and he was given several "grown-up" shirts for his birthday. He particularly favored blue and white striped shirts from Brooks Brothers, one of the few indulgences he allowed himself.

In the last few years of his life, my father talked about writing some personal memoirs of his childhood that would only be for the family and not for publication. Unfortunately, he never did write those memoirs, so I can only search for the little tidbits of personal experience that he drops in some of the interviews in this book and in a few other places. For example, it is likely that several of the chapters of immigrant life in New York City described in *World of Our Fathers* are highly autobiographical. There is one memory that I treasure when my father did talk about his parents, particularly his mother. We were sitting on a bench in the Toronto waterfront enjoying the summer sunshine, and for some reason, he began to reminisce about his parents. He talked about how hard they had worked, how much of life had been a struggle, and how strong his mother had been. I have so many other questions about his early life, but now they can only be answered in my imagination.

I loved reading these interviews for their breadth and depth, their engaging substance and insights, and of course, for hearing my father's inspiring and wise voice. I am grateful to John Rodden and Ethan Goffman for collecting these interviews and for the insights that they provide about the rich, active, and influential life of my father. On a personal note, they have enriched my understanding of my father. I trust that they will enrich others' understanding of my father and the times and circumstances in which he lived. I now invite you to join me in listening to a voice that I and many others miss so much.

*Nina Howe*

# Bibliography


### 1. WORKS BY IRVING HOWE

*The American Communist Party,* with Lewis Coser. Boston: Beacon Press, 1957.

*The American Newness.* Cambridge, MA: Harvard University Press, 1986.

*Celebrations and Attacks: Thirty Years of Literary and Cultural Commentary.* New York: Harcourt Brace Jovanovich, 1979.

*The Critical Point.* New York: Horizon Press, 1973.

*A Critic's Notebook.* New York: Harcourt Brace Jovanovich, 1994.

*Decline of the New.* New York: Harcourt Brace and World, 1970.

*Leon Trotsky.* New York: Viking, 1978.

*A Margin of Hope: An Intellectual Autobiography.* New York: Harcourt Brace Jovanovich, 1982.

*Politics and the Novel.* New York: Horizon, 1957.

*Selected Writings 1950-1990.* New York: Harcourt Brace Jovanovich, 1990.

*Sherwood Anderson.* New York: William Sloane, 1951.

*Socialism and America.* New York: Harcourt Brace Jovanovich, 1985.

*Steady Work: Essays in the Politics of Democratic Radicalism.* New York: Harcourt, Brace and World, 1996.

*Thomas Hardy: A Critical Study.* New York: Macmillan, 1967.

*The UAW and Walter Reuther,* with B. J. Widick. New York: Random House, 1949.

*William Faulkner: A Critical Study. New York: Random House, 1952.*

*A World More Attractive.* New York: Horizon Press, 1963.

*World of Our Fathers,* with the assistance of Kenneth Libo. New York: Harcourt Brace Jovanovich, 1976.

### 2. WORKS OF RELATED INTEREST

Alexander, Edward. *Irving Howe and Secular Jewishness: An Elegy.* Cincinnati: University of Cincinnati Judaic Studies Program, 1995.

______. *Irving Howe: Socialist, Critic, Jew.* Bloomington: University of Indiana, 1998.

Atlas, James. "The Changing World of the New York Intellectuals." *New York Times Magazine*, August 25, 1985.

Bloom, Alexander. *Prodigal Sons: The New York Intellectuals and Their World.* New York: Oxford University Press, 1986.

Cooney, Terry. "The New York Intellectuals and the Question of Jewish Identity." *American Jewish History* 80 (Spring 1991): 344-60.

____. *The Rise of the New York Intellectuals: Partisan Review and Its Circle.* Madison: University of Wisconsin Press, 1986.

Dickstein, Morris. *Double Agent: The Critic and Society.* New York: Oxford University Press, 1992.

Dorman, Joseph. *Arguing the World: The New York Intellectuals in Their Own Words.* New York: Free Press, 2000.

Gilbert, James. *Writers and Partisans.* New York: Columbia University Press, 1993.

Goffman, Ethan and Dan Morris, eds. *The New York Intellectuals (and Beyond).* West Lafayette: Purdue University Press, 2009.

Hook, Sidney. *Out of Step: An Unquiet Life in the Twentieth Century.* New York: Harper and Row, 1987.

Jacoby, Russell. *The Last Intellectuals: American Culture in the Age of Academe.* New York: Basic Books, 2000.

Jumonville, Neil. *Critical Crossings: The New York Intellectuals in Postwar America.* Berkeley: University of California Press, 1991.

Klingenstein, Susanne. *Enlarging America: The Cultural Work of Jewish Literary Scholars, 1940-1990.* Syracuse: Syracuse University Press, 1998.

____. *Jews in the American Academy, 1990-1940: The Dynamics of Intellectual Assimilation.* Syracuse: Syracuse University Press, 1998.

Kristol, Irving. "Memoirs of a Trotskyist." *New York Times Magazine*, January 23, 1977.

Macdonald, Dwight. *Memoirs of a Revolutionist: Essays in Political Criticism.* New York: Farrar, Straus and Giroux, 1957.

McCarthy, Mary. *Intellectual Memoirs.* San Diego: Harcourt Trade, 1992.

Pells, Richard. *The Liberal Mind in a Conservative Age.* New York: Harper and Row, 1985.

Posner, Richard. *Public Intellectuals: A Study of Decline.* Cambridge: Harvard University Press, 2002.

Rodden, John. "The 'Case' of Lionel Trilling." *Society* 41, no. 2 (2004): 59-63.

_____. *Irving Howe and the Critics: Celebrations and Attacks.* Lincoln: University of Nebraska Press, 2005.

_____. "Irving Howe, Triple Thinker." In *The New York Intellectuals*, edited by Ethan Goffman and Dan Morris, 122-41. West Lafayette: Purdue University Press, 2009.

_____. "The Opposing Selves of Lionel Trilling." *Modern Age* 38, no. 2 (1996):164-75.

_____. "The Politics of Lionel Trilling's Reputation." *Society* 36, no. 5 (1999): 80-89.

_____ "The Reputation of Irving Howe." *Society* 40, no. 2 (2003): 58-69.

_____. "The Trilling Family 'Romance': Report of a Psychoanalytic Autopsy." *Modern Age* 48, no. 3 (2006): 241-50.

_____. "The Trilling Files." *Shofar: An Interdisciplinary Journal of Jewish Studies* 26, no. 2 (2008): 109-27.

_____. "Wanted: Irving Howe FBI No. 727437B." *Dissent* 49, no. 4 (2002): 79-86.

_____. "The Worlds of Irving Howe." *Kenyon Review* 26, no. 1 (2004): 157-74.

_____, ed. *The Worlds of Irving Howe*. Paradigm Publishers, 2005.

Rosenberg, Bernard, and Ernest Goldstein, eds. *Creators and Disturbers: Reminiscences by Jewish Intellectuals of New York*. New York: Columbia University Press, 1982.

Teres, Harvey. *Renewing the Left: Politics, Imagination and the New York Intellectuals*. New York: Oxford University Press, 1996.

Trilling, Diana. *The Beginning of the Journey: The Marriage of Diana and Lionel Trilling*. New York: Harcourt Brace, 1993.

Wald, Alan M. *The New York Intellectuals: The Rise and Decline of the Anti-Stalinist Left from the 1930s to the 1980s*. Chapel Hill: University of North Carolina Press, 1987.

Wreszin, Michael. *A Rebel in Defense of Tradition: The Life and Politics of Dwight Macdonald*. New York: Basic Books, 1994.

# Index

35-hour week, 133
9/11, 122
92nd Street YMCA, xx, 82, 85, 258, 324

ADA, see Americans for Democratic Action
AFL-CIO, 81, 116, 131, 133, 272, 308
Aaron, Daniel, 189, 197, 223
Abel, Lionel, 72, 224
action painting, 205
abolitionists, 164, 169, 175, 195
Abruzzi peasants, 97, 98
academia, 84, 209, 231, 244
academic style, 219
Accidental Century, 290, 291
Americans for Democratic Action, 297, 308
Adams, Henry, 250
Addams, Jane, 281
African development, 108
African American history, 243
African American literature, 244, 245
*After Strange Gods,* 268
Alaska, 91, 92, 94, 113, 221
Alcove One, x, 186, 259, 316, 318, 322
Alcove Two, x, 259, 316
Aleichem, Sholom, xi, 25, 310
Alexander, Edward, 4, 16, 22, 23, 24, 26, 33, 41, 43, 51, 231, 273
Allen Street, 103
Allen, Woody, 40, 312
Allies, The, 137
Amalgamated Workers Union, 307, 309
American capitalism, 4, 16, 24, 135, 142, 215
American Communist Party, 52, 81, 196
*American Communist Party, The,* 14, 52, 151
American Communists, 319
American cultural life, 101
American culture, x, xi, 15, 30, 44, 205, 214, 217, 230, 248
American Empire, 33
American exceptionalism, 2
American Jewish Committee, 35, 38, 39, 97
American Jewish literature, 103, 214
American Jewry, 27, 32
American Left, ix, 10, 17, 107, 111, 117, 121, 123-5, 196, 276, 282, 294
American literary history, 209
*American Literary History,* 246
American Literature, 42, 85, 120, 206, 207, 215, 230, 243-5, 246, 248, 249, 329
American Midwest, 87, 160, 192, 299,
American modernists, 247
*American Newness: Culture and Politics in the Age of Emerson,* xx, 15, 24, 84, 140, 200, 206, 209, 214-16, 218, 223, 249, 250
*American Prospect, The,* 308
American Revolution, 216-17
American socialism, xvii, 1, 9, 21, 120, 122, 281-2, 296, 301
American social-realist novel, 268

American Studies, 206, 243, 246
Amherst College, 217
Amichai, Yehuda, 105
Amis, Martin, 268
Anderson, Sherwood, ix, 27, 110, 112, 201, 222
*Animal Farm*, 138-9, 142
Ann Arbor, 185
ANSWER coalition, 153
Antarctic, 310
anti-communism, 6, 34, 54, 56, 125, 140, 163, 199, 201-2, 208, 238, 271-2, 274, 319
anti-immigration movement, 122
anti-McCarthyism, 204
*Anti-Semite and Jew,* 26
anti-semitism, 26, 202
anti-Stalinists, 59, 83, 100, 109, 111, 112, 203, 215, 230, 236, 239, 243, 247, 256, 260, 313, 316, 317, 319, 325
antiwar movement, 154, 167, 218
anti-Zionism, 26, 28, 304
Arab countries, 265
Arendt, Hannah, 26, 29, 65, 72, 143, 233, 237, 238, 242, 255, 257, 318
*Arguing the World,* xx, 152, 195, 310-311, 330
Arnold, Matthew, 253
Arnold Bread, 280
Aronowitz, Stanley, 181, 196
Attlee, Clement, 62, 80
Auden, W.H., 95, 252
Austen, Jane, 259
authoritarianism, 157, 317
auto-critique, 232
*avant garde,* 37, 41, 48-49, 89, 112, 184, 317
*Axel's Castle,* x, 89

Babel, Isaac, 46, 48
Baeck, Leo, xvii
Balanchine, George, 101, 269
Baldwin, James, 244, 250, 251
ballet, xi, 101, 258, 269, 324
Barkan, Joanne, 301, 307
baseball, 58, 88, 89, 147
*Basic Trotsky, The* 142
Batista, Fulgencio, 279
Bay area, 173
Bay of Pigs, 279
Beattie, Ann, 114
Beckett, Samuel, 46, 49, 267
Bell, Daniel, x, xx, 198, 199, 259, 310, 311, 315, 316, 322, 325
Bell, Quentin, 222
Bellow, Saul, xvii, 45, 47, 103, 113, 114, 214, 222, 244, 245, 250, 268
Benn Michaels, Walter, 227
Bennett, William, 43
Bercovitch, Sacvan, 208, 217, 218, 224, 227
Berkeley, 33, 34, 185, 197, 207, 211, 212
Berlin, 71, 136, 318
Berlin, Isaiah, 324
Berlin Wall, 232, 257
Berman, Marshall, xx, 55
Berman, Morris, 35
Berryman, John, xvii, 94, 113, 222
Big Book of Jewish Humor, 33
Big Brother, 139, 140, 145
Birmingham Church, 187
black anger, 250
"Black Boys and Native Sons," 244
Black Sash, 241
Blackmur, Richard, xvii, 51, 222
Bloom, Harold, 225, 248
Bolsheviks, 197
Bolshevism, 57, 59, 138, 142, 160, 175, 177, 194, 178, 275, 277, 296
Bonnell, Vicky, 185, 197
*Book of Laughter and Forgetting,* 99
Booth, Paul, 75, 156, 169
Borges, Jorge Luis, 46
Boston, 61, 167, 300
Bostonians, 245, 251, 252
bourgeois democracy, 140

Bradley-Gephardt, 133
Brandt Commission, 129
Brandt, Willy, 129, 136, 305, 306, 307
*Bread and Wine,* 79, 104
Brecht, Bertolt, 46, 48, 104, 246, 247
*Breira,* 36, 39
British Labour Party, 61, 62, 79, 80, 278
Brooklyn College, 221
Brooks Brothers, 330
Brooks, Van Wyck, 101, 216, 248
Brown, Ray, 181, 196
Brzezinski, Zbigniew, 162, 195
Bukharin, Nicolai, 81
Buenos Aires, 249
Bundists, 30
bureaucratic collectivism, 64, 277, 300, 301
Burke, Edmund, 16
*Burn Down the Icons,* 82
Burnham, James, x, 79, 81, 271, 277-278
Bush, President George W., 19, 109
Bush-Cheney legacy, 324
*Business Week,* 290
Buttinger, Joseph, 70, 71, 77, 156, 160
Buttingers, the, 70-71

CIO, 177, 178
Cahn, Abraham, 8
Cain, William, 84, 243-6, 259
Cambridge, 201
Canada, 107, 110, 114, 116-118, 329
Canadian Broadcasting Corporation, 107, 338
Cannon, James, xi, 81, 276
canon, the, xx, 16, 17, 43, 122, 244, 246, 249, 250, 267
Cantor, Eddie, 31
Cape Cod, 94, 112
Capitalism, 4, 9-11, 16, 18, 24, 55, 96, 122, 126, 135, 142, 180, 190, 215, 218, 232-235, 236, 238-240, 257, 272, 311 321, 324
*Capitalism, Socialism, and Democracy,* 196
Carter, Joseph, 79, 288
Carter, President Jimmy, 162, 195
Carver, Raymond, 100, 106, 114
*Case of Mr. Crump, The,* 221
Castro, Fidel, 13, 152, 157, 158, 195, 279, 320
Cather, Willa, 87
Catholic Church, 111
Catholic countries, 75, 179
*Catholic Worker, The* 300, 308
Catholicism, 299
CCNY - See City College of New York
CCNY Red Book, xv
*Celebrations and Attacks: Thirty Years of Literary and Cultural Commentary, 22,* 253, 255
Céline, Louis Ferdinand, 104
Central America, 116, 119, 125
Chairman Mao, 13, 97
Chambers, Whittaker, 202
Chancellor, Olive, 252
Chapman, John Jay, 216
Chase, Richard, 216
Chavez, Hugo, 21
Chernyshevsky, Nikolay, 208, 230
chess, 88
Chiaromonte, Nicola, 72
Chicago Convention, 153, 180
Chicago neo-Aristotelian school, 103
Chicago Renaissance, 100
Chicago Seven, 195
Chicago School, 104
Chile, 21, 65
choreography, 269
Christian fundamentalism, 19
Christian Gauss Seminars, 222, 231
Christian Socialists, 160, 309
Chronicle of Our Times, xi
Churchill, Winston, 137
City College of New York, xv, xvi, 34, 37, 259, 311, 313, 314-317, 319, 322, 325

City University of New York, xviii, ixx, xx, 38, 80, 81, 206, 222, 258, 259, 270
"Civil Disobedience," 15
civil liberties, 57, 78, 152, 204
Civil Rights movement, 52, 54, 60, 79, 115
Claessens, 91
Clark, Jack, 303
Clark, Joe, 60, 62
Clark, Judy, 176, 196
Cleaver, Eldridge, 196
Clinton, President Bill, 323, 324
Clinton administration, 327
Cockburn, Alexander, 3, 22
Cohen, Freddy, 98, 118, 171
Cohen, Mitchell, xx, 7, 53
Cohen, Morris Raphael, 221, 316
Cold War, 6, 57, 60, 116, 140, 171, 201, 202, 235, 239, 279, 318, 319
Cold Warrior, 140
Cole, G.D.H., 61, 79
*Collected Essays, Journals, and Letters of George Orwell,* 143
Collier, Peter, 171, 196
Columbia University, xi, xviii, 80, 162, 176
*Commentary,* xviii, 3, 4, 11, 22, 35, 58, 67, 109, 115, 116, 142, 199, 259, 319
Committee for Cultural Freedom, 56
commodity market, 264
Communism, 1, 6, 7, 19, 35, 52, 54, 56, 64, 80, 108, 138, 152, 163, 233, 239, 250, 256, 272, 311, 319, 321, 325, 326
Communist Party, 14, 52, 81, 138, 196, 200, 314, 317
communist regimes, 152, 260, 261
Communist vanguard, 138, 139
Conference on Peace and Scientific Progress, 319
*Confidence Man, The,* 249
Conrad, Joseph, 42, 46
Constantinople, 249
contemporary literature, 42, 44, 45, 246
Cooney, Terry, 145, 205
Cornell University, 98, 118, 171
Cort, John, 300, 308
Coser, Lewis, xvii, xviii, ixx, 7, 8, 14, 23, 52, 53, 57-59, 62, 64-67, 71, 77, 151, 183, 239, 329
Coser, Rose, 329
counterculture, 11, 144, 151, 154, 170, 183, 184
CP - see Communist Party
*Critic's Notebook, A,* xii
*Critical Crossings: The New York Intellectuals in Postwar America,* 198, 201
*Critical Point, The,* xi
Crosland, Anthony, 61, 80, 306
Crossman, Richard, 61, 80
Cuba, 35, 56, 152, 156-157, 159, 195, 320
Cuban Revolution, 56
cultural conservatism, 17
cultural conservative, 16, 17, 109, 209, 267
Cummings, E.E., 247
Cunningham, J.V., 225, 229, 253
Czechoslovakia, xvii, 65, 105, 162, 163, 257, 260, 319

Dante, Alighieri, 89
Darfur, 234
*Darkness at Noon,* 239
Davis, Rennie, 166, 195
Day, Dorothy, 195, 299, 308
Dean, Howard, 20
*Death on the Installment Plan,* 104
Debs, Eugene, 9, 151, 178, 193, 281-285, 287, 296-8, 302, 315
Debsian, 67, 192, 194
*Decline of the New,* xviii, 58, 85
Decter, Midge, 3, 22, 44, 136
Dellinger, David, 170, 195
Dellums, Ron, 125
democratic left, 123, 124, 126, 128, 129, 144, 204, 227
Democratic National Convention, 153

Democratic Party, 8, 10, 120, 124, 127, 153, 161, 167-169, 180, 196, 228, 257, 265, 266, 279, 295, 299, 308, 329
democratic socialism, xvii, ix, 4, 5, 21, 54, 120, 124, 135, 138, 139, 141, 199, 204, 233, 261, 273, 283, 323, 324
Democratic Socialist Organizing Committee, ixx, 10, 15, 24, 60, 67, 73, 120, 295
Democratic Socialists of America, xx, 10, 14, 17, 75, 80, 121, 122, 123, 124, 172, 175, 190, 283-291, 295-298, 303, 307, 308
Denitch, Bogdan, 62, 80
Derrida, Jacques, 229
Deutscher, Isaac, 64-65, 80, 238
Dewey, John, 203
Dickens, Charles, 93, 200
Dictionary of Literary Biography, 221
*Die Tsukunft,* 96
Dien Bien Phu, 70, 80
Diggins, John, 270
*Dissent,* xvii, xviii, xx, ix, x, xi, 5-22, 27, 32, 35, 37, 42, 44, 52-73, 76-81, 83, 108, 110-112, 115, 121, 124, 137-143, 151, 153, 155, 161, 185, 188, 195, 196, 199, 202-205, 208, 222, 227, 232-237, 242, 259, 262, 271, 274, 282, 285, 288, 291, 293, 294, 297, 300, 305, 307, 320, 323, 324, 325, 326, 329
Dissenter, 78
*Do It!: Scenarios of the Revolution,* 196
Dollfuss, Engelbert, 80
Dollfuss repression, 70
Dominican Republic, 19, 122, 128
Dorman, Joseph, 152, 195, 313-71, 330
*Dorothy Healey Remembers: A Life in the American Communist Party,* 52
Dostoevskian, 202
Dostoevsky, Fyoder, 99, 104, 202, 215, 326
doublethink, 119, 139
Douglass, Frederick, 249, 250
*Down and Out in Paris and London,* 139, 141
Draper, Hal, 275, 279, 288
Drexel Burnham, 241, 242
DSA - see Democratic Socialists of America
DSOC - see Democratic Socialist Organizing Committee
Du Bois, W.E.B., 250
Duke University, 227, 267

East European writers, 102, 105
East Germany, 65, 136, 262
Eastern Airlines, 131
Eastern Europe, 5, 30, 64, 81, 85, 136, 237, 239, 247, 257, 259, 260-263, 318, 325
Economic Research and Action Project, 155, 195
*Economics of Feasible Socialism, The,* 240, 263
Eckstein, George, 62
Edel, Abraham, 221
Ehrenreich, Barbara, 126
*Eichmann in Jerusalem,* xvii, 26, 29, 143, 233
Eichmann trial, 29, 143
Eliot, T.S., 46, 48, 90, 92, 230, 246, 247, 254, 267-268
Ellison, Ralph, 43, 244, 245, 250, 251
Elon, Amos, 208, 213
Emerson, Ralph Waldo, ixx, 2, 15, 16, 18, 24, 84, 101, 112, 153, 200, 206, 208-209, 214-218, 230, 243, 244, 248
Emersonian, 2, 9, 15, 18, 19, 21, 75, 84, 101, 102, 175, 209, 214-218, 237, 244-250, 296
Empson, William, 252, 253
England, 75, 129, 140, 179, 240, 248, 264, 306, 329
*Enlarging America: The Cultural Work of Jewish Literary Scholars,* 1930-1990, 210

"Envy, Or Yiddish in America," 96
Epstein, Joseph, 3, 21, 24
ERAP - see Economic Research and Action Project
Erich Fromm, 115
*Eros and Civilization,* 185
*Esquire,* 69
*Essential Ilan Stavans, The*, 24
Esso, 290
Establishment, The, 97, 151
Eurocommunism, 64
Europe, 5, 12, 16, 42, 54, 62, 71, 72, 75, 80, 153, 164, 192, 198, 206, 212, 224, 225, 237, 239, 244, 260, 262, 265, 283, 290, 296, 306, 319
European conservative, 209
European culture, 208, 230
European intellectuals, 2, 7, 143, 207, 208
European Jews, 27, 37, 86, 109, 206, 324
European literature, 215, 244, 247-249, 326, 329
European novel, 102, 105, 240
European refugees, 186
European socialism, 7, 9, 15, 289, 306
European tradition, xv
*The Europeans*, 249
*Every Intellectual's Big Brother: George Orwell's Literary Siblings,* 140, 145
ex-Communists, 56, 202
"Ex-Maoist Looks at an Ex-Trotskyist: On Irving Howe's *Leon Trotsky*, An" 23, 145
ex-socialists, 294
Exxon Mobil, 116, 290

Fabianism, 79, 126, 294
Fadayev, Alexander, 319
Fanon, Frantz, 173, 196
Farrell, James, x, 112
Fascist Germany, 317
fascists, 65, 80, 98, 104, 185, 235
Fast, Howard, xvii, 182, 186, 196, 200, 201, 317
Faulkner, William, xx, 102, 110, 200, 222, 243, 244, 247, 250, 326
federal government, 130-132
federal income tax, 130
Federal Reserve, 181
Fein, Leonard, 27, 32
Fellow, Mike, 159
feminist criticism, 245, 251
feminists, 17, 252, 296
Fiedler, Leslie, 56-57
Fields, W.C., 94, 113
Fitzgerald, F. Scott, 42, 102
Flacks, Dick, 160, 168-169, 172, 181, 195
Florida State University, 199
folksmassen, 110
Fonda, Jane, 172
*Fontamara,* 79, 98, 104
football, 88
*For Whom the Bell Tolls,* 254
Ford, Ford Madox, 46
Ford, Henry, 90
*The Four Quartets,* 268
France, 71, 80, 112, 179, 237, 241
Frankfurt School, 18
Frankfurt, 72
Frederickson, George, 250
*Freedom Road,* 196
free markets, 239, 257, 262, 265
Freedom Riders, 60, 186
Freudian concepts, 220
Friedman, Joseph, 81
Friends of Peace Now, ixx, 242
full employment, 129-132

Galbraith, Kenneth, 227, 297
Gandhian position, 158-159
garment unions, 87, 110, 211, 330
garment workers, 108, 110
Garrison, William Lloyd, 164, 169, 175, 195

Gasset, Ortega y, 68
Gatsby, Jay, 87
Gaza Strip, 36
Geltman, Emanuel, xi, xvii, xviii, 59, 62, 67, 71, 77, 79, 157, 158, 329; as Emanuel Garrett, xvi
Genovese, Eugene, 43, 52
Germans, 306
Germany, 7, 80, 81, 91, 136, 206, 283, 317
"Gimpel the Fool," 113
Gilbert, James, 23, 230
Gitlin, Todd, 13, 19, 20, 24, 35, 55, 75, 84, 151-4, 195, 197, 203, 209, 329
glasnost, 232, 238
Glatstein, Jacob, 28, 95, 96
Glazer, Nathan, x, xx, 58, 259, 310, 316, 322
globalization, 19, 122, 154
godfather of neoconservativism, 310
gold standard, 228
Golden, Harry, 30, 37
Goncharov, Ivan, 248
goniffs, 241
Goodman, Paul, 54, 97, 114, 202, 205, 229
Gorbachev, Mikhail, 232, 234, 237-240, 257, 260, 263
Grade, Chaim, 95
gradualism, 12, 257, 263
Graduate Center of the City University of New York, xviii, 206
Grand Concourse, 89
Graubard, Allen, 66
Great Britain, 139, 233
Great Depression, x, 4, 83, 110, 122, 126, 196, 282, 285, 311, 312, 314, 315, 325
Great Society, 2, 18
Great Strike, The, 87
Great Tradition, 246
Greenberg, Eliezer, xviii, x, 25, 28, 85, 96, 113-114, 243
Greenberg, Sandra, 41, 43
Guevera, Che, 173
Gulag, the, 8, 233, 236, 254, 255
Gzowski, Peter, 328

Haber, Alan, 74, 81, 174, 175
Haber, Barbara, 182
Hague, Mayor Frank, 284, 308
Halifax, 329
Handlin, Oscar, xvii
Harbord Collegiate Institute, 108
Hardwick, Elizabeth, 93, 245, 251
Hardy, Thomas, ixx, 104, 110, 200, 259, 325
*Harper's*, xviii, ixx, 140, 143, 268
Harrington, Michael, ixx, 9, 10, 12, 14, 21, 24, 74, 77, 78, 79, 81, 120-123, 136, 173, 181, 188, 199, 240, 257, 258, 263, 271, 274, 277, 281-283, 284, 285, 296, 297, 302, 308, 309, 329
Hart, Gary, 128, 129
Hartman, Geoffrey, 225
Harvard of the Poor, 315
Harvard University, ixx, 15, 84, 140, 196, 198, 199, 200, 206, 207, 209, 217, 223, 224, 225, 227, 230
Hausknecht, Murray, 76, 202
Hawthorne, Nathaniel, 247
Hayden, Tom, xviii, 13, 55, 74, 75, 151, 155, 156, 161, 162, 167, 182, 195, 209, 321
Hazlitt, William, 253
Healey, Dorothy Ray, 52, 281
health plans, 264
Hellman, Lillian, 70, 80
Hemingway, Ernest, 102, 244, 247, 249, 250
Henderson, Leon, 298, 308
Henry Adams's autobiography, 250
Hentoff, Nat, 161, 195
Herrnstein, Richard, 225
Herrnstein Smith, Barbara, 221, 224
high art, 199-201
Hillman, Sidney, 301, 309

Hillquit, Morris, 194, 197
Hirsch, E. D., 43
hispanics, 17, 296
historical amnesia, 108
History of American Civilization, 198, 200
history of science, 324
Hitler, Adolph, 7, 85, 91, 137, 143, 158, 238, 278, 317
Hitler-Stalin pact, 190, 317
Hoffman, Abbie, 184
Hofstadter, Richard, 72, 80
Hollander, John, xx, 93, 225
"Hollow Men, The," 90
Holocaust, the, 1, 26, 29, 39, 96, 237, 278, 280
Holt, Jim, 256, 260
Holy Cross, 305
Homer, 49
homosexuality, 184
Hook, Sidney, x, 199, 203, 301
Hoover, Herbert, 113, 215
Horowitz, David, 171, 172, 195, 196
Howe, Irving: and American Friends of Peace Now, xi; and Anna Bader, xi, 208; and Arien Mack, x; and *Axel's Castle,* xv; and Essence of Judaism, xvii; and Ilana Wiener, xi; and Jewishness, 26, 27; and Leon Trotsky, 2; and literature of the Holocaust, 1; and Partisan Review, xvi; and Ralph Waldo Emerson, 2; and Sholom Aleichem, xvi; and *The UAW and Walter Reuther,* xvii; and Thalia Phillies, xvi; and the Depression, 4; and the Independent Socialist League, xvii; and *The Old Country,* xiii; and utopian faith, 3, 10; and William E. Massey Lectures, xx, 15, 87, 201; and Yiddish literature, xv; as bourgeois liberal, 151; as Fangs, xvi; as Hugh Ivan, xvi; as Irving Horenstein, xv; as literary critic, x, 1, 41, 92, 95 110, 313,314, 324; as MacArthur Fellow, xx, 1; as R. Fangston, xvi; as radical humanist, 5, 44, 122, 258, 273; as secular Jew, 35; as the American Orwell, 5, 17; as Theodore Dryden, xi, 1137; as Trotskyist, xi, 6, 25, 54, 61, 62, 84, 108, 137, 138, 140, 208, 270, 273, 317, 319; at Belmont, 147; at Brandeis, xviii, xvii, 59, 61, 64, 73, 182, 184, 200, 207, 220-222, 225, 253, 259; at Fort Dix, xvi; at Hunter College, xvii; at Montreal, 149; at Princeton, xvii; at Stanford, xviii, 148; at the City University of New York, ixx, xx, xv; at the Graduate Center of City University of New York, x; birth, xv; cardiovascular disease, 323; death, 310, 312, 323, 324, 327; father's death, xi; heart trouble, 311; in Greenwich Village, xvi; in Greece, 146; ; in New England seaport, 146; in the Bronx, xi, 4; in Japan, 148; in Maine, 149; in U.S. army, xi, 248, 259, 313, 318, 329; Israel visit, xi; marriages, xvi-xi; memorial service, xx, 85, 324; parents' poverty, ix, 315; parents, xv; playing baseball, 147; poverty, ix, 86, 87, 311, 313, 314, 325; pseudonyms, xvi; with granddaughter Anna Bukowski, 150; with Nina Howe, 149; wives, 207; youth, xiv
Howe, Nicholas, xx, 331: in New England seaport, 146; playing baseball, 147
Howe, Nina, xx, 331-5: in Greece, 146; in New England seaport, 146; with Irving Howe, 149
*Huckleberry Finn,* 244, 249
Hudson River, 208
humanist literary critic,103-104
Humphrey, Hubert, 67, 78, 191
Hungarian revolution, 64, 65, 185, 186, 200

Hungary, 182
Hunter College, xviii, 222
Huntspoint Plaza, 299
Hutchinson, Ann, 216
Hux, Samuel, 24, 43, 44, 51

I.M.F. – see International Monetary Fund
"I Have a Dream," 79
Iacocca, Lee, 33
Ickes, Harold, 298, 308
"Idea of the Modern," 42, 51
*If I Had a Hammer...The Death of the Old Left and the Birth of the New Left,* 52, 56, 281
"If Orwell Were Alive Today," 140
"Images of Socialism," 23, 57, 63
Independent Socialist League, xvii, 271, 274, 320
India, 324
individualism, 9, 15, 17-19, 21, 54, 84-85, 132, 208-209, 244, 258
industrial policy, 132, 290
*Inner Civil War, The,* 250
intellectual community, 109, 111-115, 258, 266
*Intellectual in Public, An,* 231
intermediary generation, 157
Internal Revenue Code, 133
International Ladies Garment Workers' Union, 87, 110, 211, 330
international literature, 244, 249
International Monetary Fund, 19, 122, 128
International Socialist League, 6, 37, 75, 76
internationalism, 1, 19, 110, 249
*Invisible Man,* 244, 251
Iraq, 19, 20, 22, 153, 180, 184, 181
Irish, 86, 111, 249, 298, 299, 305
*Irving Howe: A Life of Passionate Dissent,* 23, 136, 145, 308
Irving Howe and His World memorial conference, xii
Irving Howe and the Critics, xii
*Irving Howe: Socialist, Critic, Jew,* 22, 34, 41, 51, 231
"Irving Howe: Yiddish Culture and Secular Jewishness," 33
ISL - see International Socialist League
Israel, ixx, 26, 28, 31, 33, 34-37, 39, 121, 196, 207-208, 212-213, 242, 304
Israeli Left, 34
Israeli writers, 105
Isserman, Maurice, 21, 52-6, 107, 281-3, 308, 329
Italian Communist Party, 171
Italy, 75,179, 237
Ivy League Schools, 315

Jackson, Henry "Scoop," 38
Jackson, Jesse, 291
Jacobs, Paul, 97
Jacobson, Julie, 193
Jacoby, Russell, 24, 209, 230, 251
James, Henry, 94, 113, 245, 247, 248, 259
Jameson, Fredrick, 267
Japan, 85, 102
Jersey City, 308
*Jerusalem Post, The,* 36
Jerusalem, 105
Jewish American fiction, 247
*Jewish Daily Forward,* 29, 91
Jewish: academics, 210, 221; culture, 1, 26, 27, 29, 207; experience, 39, 87, 109, 216, 328; ghetto, 88; identity, 26, 35, 37, 231; immigrants, 26, 37, 214, 247, 312, 314-315, 324, 329; intellectuals, 82; 83, 97, 107, 119, 206, 326; life, 35, 38, 103, 212, 213, 304; literary scholars, 206, 207, 210; literature, 214; messianism,; migration,; professors,; quotas,; radicalism,; street gangs, ; trade unionists, 29, 287; writers, 83, 249, 325

*Jews in the American Academy, 1900-1940: The Dynamics of Intellectual Assimilation,* 210
Johnson, President Lyndon B., 8, 18, 78, 121, 126, 171, 191, 197
Johnson, Samuel, 253
*Journey to the End of the Night,* 104
Joyce, James, 42, 45, 48, 90, 104, 247, 249, 267, 317
*Julia,* 70, 80
Jumonville, Neil, 198-200

Kafka, Franz, 48, 246, 247, 249, 267
Kahn, Tom, 77, 81, 176, 189-190, 294, 305
Kant, Immanual, 289
Kateb, George, 180, 196
Kaufman, Adam, 64
Kawabata, Yasunari, 102
Kazin, Alfred, xi, 93, 204-205, 209, 217-220, 224, 229, 247, 259
Kelly, Kitty, 292
Kenazake, 102
Kennan, George, 70
Kennedy, Edward "Teddy," 298
Kennedy, President John F., 8, 60, 66, 67, 115, 178, 298
*Kenyon Review,* 204, 229
Kerry, John, 310
Keynesian economics, 73
Kilroy, 98
King-Reuther 3rd party ticket, 78
Kirk, Russell, 16
Kirkland, Lane, 294, 308
Klingenstein, Susanne, 15, 84, 206-10, 230, 244
Koch, Ed, 259, 266
Koestler, Arthur, 239, 247
Konrad, George, 98-99, 105
Korsch, Karl, 64, 80
Kramer, Hilton, 3, 267
Krauthammer, Charles, 22, 172, 196
Kristol, Irving, x, xi, xx, 3-4, 11, 16, 22, 115-117, 136, 172, 198, 259, 272, 310-312, 316, 317, 319, 322
Kronstadt rebellion, 137
Krupnick, Mark, 221, 226-228, 231
Kundera, Milan, 98-99, 105
Kuttner, Robert, 257, 265, 266, 290, 296, 297, 308
Kyo, 99

*Labor Action,* xi, xvii, 81, 137, 221
Labor Zionist, 304
Labour government, 80, 306
*Labyrinth of Solitude,* 98
Lacan, Jacques, 230
Ladies' Garment Worker's Union, 87, 110, 211, 330
*landsman,* 91
Langer, Ellie, 166, 180
Larner, Jeremy, 182, 196
Lasky, Melvin J., xv
*Last Intellectuals, The,* 24, 209, 230, 253
late capitalism, 135
Latin America, 85, 102
League for Industrial Democracy, 81
Left sectarianism, x, 14, 152
Lekachman, Robert, 131, 308
Lenin, V.I., 123, 138, 141-142, 180, 208, 230
Leninism, 7, 23, 74, 75, 79, 125, 137, 138, 140, 159, 160, 161, 196, 210, 227, 275, 311
Leninism-Maoism, 160, 161
Lermontov, Mikhail, 248
lesser evils, 192, 279
"Letter from London," 137
*Letters to a Young Activist,* 19, 24
Levin, Harry, 225, 226
Levinson, Mark, 242
Lewis, David, 329
Lewis, Stephen, 107-109, 328, 330
Lewisohn, Ludwig, 220, 221

liberal fascism, 74, 173
*Liberal Imagination, The,* 109
*Liberalism for a New Century*, 198
Liberalism, 4, 6, 8, 9, 12, 17, 32, 33, 38, 56, 68, 98, 122, 124, 126, 128, 164, 172, 198, 199, 208, 218, 223, 227, 228, 241, 272, 297, 311, 323, 324
Liberator, The, 195
Lichtheim, George, 72, 80
LID - see League for Industrial Democracy
"Life in a Sect," 6
*Lingua Franca,* 256
Lipset, Seymour Martin, x, 97
literary criticism, x, 28, 41, 49, 82, 85, 89, 95, 97, 99, 103, 120, 223, 243-246, 251, 252, 268, 290, 291, 325, 327
*Little Foxes, The,* 80
Little Rock, 72
*Living Novel, The,* 248
Lord Beveridge, 129
Los Angeles, 98, 118, 171
Los Angeles Times, 154
"Lovesong of J. Alfred Prufrock," 90
Lovestone Group, 77, 81
Lovestone, Jay, 81
Lowell, Robert, 319
Lowenstein, Al, 187, 197
Lowenthal, Richard, 237, 238
Lower East Side, 25, 27, 30, 83

Moncada barracks, 159
Macdonald, Dwight, xi, xvii, 6, 6, 7, 23, 113, 141, 198, 254, 298
machinists union, 125, 131
macroeconomic policy, 154
Madison, 182, 185, 201
Madison Square Garden, 299
Magic Johnson, 33
Maharaj Ji, 195
Mailer, Norman, xvii, 54, 58, 67, 68, 69, 159, 184
Major Z, 92
Malamud, Bernard, 45, 47, 93, 103, 244, 250
Malcolm X, 165, 282
male intellectuals, 282-3
Malraux, Andre, 98, 99, 106, 247, 290
*Man's Fate,* 98, 106
Mann, Thomas, 92, 317
Manuel, Frank, 184, 197
Marcuse, Herbert, xvii, 64, 66-68, 185, 186
*A Margin of Hope,* ixx, xi, 1, 22, 35, 52, 74, 79, 82-85, 86-93, 94-99, 108, 144, 145, 156, 170, 207, 212, 218, 245, 252-255, 260, 270, 312, 330
marijuana, 183-184
market socialism, 5, 18, 84, 263
Martov, Julius, 187, 197
Marx, Karl, 15, 90, 94, 103, 203, 276
Marxism, 8, 28, 54, 57, 66, 74, 80, 120, 179, 218, 228, 233, 236, 267, 272, 275, 277, 317, 323
Marxist: economics, 90, 275; ideology, 3; language, 73, 160; past, 240; sect, 6, 179; theory, 3, 68, 80, 236, 277
Marxists: 3, 10, 195, 236, 267, 272, 316
Mason, Bobbi Ann, 106
mass culture, 48, 65-67, 199-201, 267
mass movement, 12, 14, 22, 55, 62, 75, 76, 126, 152, 155, 159, 164-166, 170, 177, 189, 235, 273, 276, 284, 324,
"Mass Society and Post-Modernist Fiction," 66
Matisse, Henri, 267
Matthiessen, F.O., 226
Mattson, Kevin, 198
Max, Steve, 156
Maxism, 272, 273
McCarthy, Eugene, 295, 308
McCarthy, Joseph, 236, 314, 319, 329
McCarthy, Mary, 255, 319
McCarthyism, 6, 57, 59, 79, 115, 204, 235, 258, 319, 325
McGovern, George, 33, 280, 295

McKeesport, Pennsylvania, 133, 134
Media Matters, 310
Melville, Herman, 94, 101, 216, 244, 245
Mensheviks, 187, 197
Mexicanization, 262
Michaels, Walter Benn, 227
Michigan State University, 225
Middle East, 213, 214
"The Middle-Class Mind of Kate Millett," x
*Midstream,* 32
millenarianism, 180
Mills, C. Wright, 7, 54, 58, 69, 115, 142, 202, 302
Milosz, Czeslaw, 105
Mishima, Yukio, 102
Miss Birdseye, 252
Mitterrand, François, 308
Moby Dick, 250
"Moderate Hero, A," 142
*Modern Age,* 16
*Modern Literary Criticism,* 48, 51
modernism, 42, 45, 46, 48, 49, 100, 112, 200, 215, 243, 244, 247, 249, 267, 326
Modernist movement, 41
Moers, Ellen, 245, 251
*Moment,* 27, 33
Mondale, Walter, 127, 171
Montaigne, Michel de, 49
Montgomery bus boycott, 60
Montreal, 149, 208, 329
Moore, Marianne, 84
moral rectitude, 87, 153, 193, 209, 218
Morton, Brian, 7, 53
Moscow trials, 8, 111, 183, 254
Moses, Robert, 165
*Mother Jones,* 153, 154, 195
Mount Sinai Hospital, 323
Movement for an Independent Socialist Canada, 107
Moveon.org, 154
Moynihan, Daniel Patrick, 134, 302
multiculturalism, 1, 17, 43, 122
multinational corporations, 134, 135, 218
Muravchik, Joseph, 261
Murray, Charles, 290, 296
MX missile, 125

Naipaul, V.S., 98-99
Nairn, Tom, 179, 196
NAM - see New American Movement
*Narodnik,* 155, 195
*The Nation,* 3, 8, 82, 141, 171, 198, 232, 235, 259
National Book Award, ixx, 34, 109
National Foundation for Jewish Culture, 207
*National Review,* 35, 81
Navasky, Victor, 59, 232, 235
Nazism, 238, 278-279
Negin, Robert, 270-273, 280, 281
neoconservatives, 3, ,4, 11, 14, 15, 16, 18, 20, 26, 44, 55, 101, 109, 109, 116, 117, 123, 136, 140, 144, 195, 196, 198, 199, 210, 260, 272, 273, 310, 311
neo-liberalism, 129, 257
"New 'Confrontation Politics' is a Dangerous Game, The," 136
Neumann, Franz, 237
New American Movement, 284, 303, 308
new colonialism, 128
*The New Conservatives: A Critique from the Left,* xi
New Critics, The, 48, 51, 204
New Deal, The, 2, 19, 53, 109, 126-128, 134, 177, 282, 284, 298, 301, 308, 317, 324
New Democratic Party, 107, 118, 329
New Democrats, 108
New England, 7, 146, 212
New International, xvii, 129, 140, 141, 290
*New Left Review,* 179, 233, 240

New Left, 3, 7, 11, 12-18, 22, 34, 35, 39, 42-44, 52, 55, 56, 58, 66, 73, 74, 76, 84, 97, 109, 116, 118, 136, 144, 151-153, 155, 159, 161, 166, 184, 185, 191, 195, 196, 203, 223, 233, 236, 245, 272, 282, 292, 293, 320, 321, 329
*New Politics,* 73
*New Republic, The* 156, 172-173, 196, 219, 261, 298
New School for Social Research, 197
*New Statesman, The* 80, 248
"New Styles in Leftism," 13, 42, 76, 161, 165, 173
New York baroque, 93
New York City Ballet, 269
New York City, x, xx, 37, 107, 109, 161, 208, 215, 223, 266, 269, 330
New York intellectual life, 296
New York Intellectuals, xviii, 3, 14, 15, 22, 83, 85, 92, 139, 140, 145, 195, 198, 199-205, 208, 210, 224, 231, 244, 247, 255, 259, 283, 310-312, 315, 318, 324-325
*New York Intellectuals: The Rise and Decline of the Anti-Stalinist Left from the 1930s to the 1980s,* 230
New York intelligentsia, 259
*New York Magazine,* 31
*New York Review of Books,* 37, 229, 256, 324
*New York Times Magazine,* 4, 120, 121, 123, 136, 256
*New York Times,* ixx, 4, 12, 34, 37, 38, 120, 121, 136, 199, 256, 265, 281, 300, 309
*New Yorker, The,* 256, 304
Newark, 270
Newspeak, 119
*Newsweek,* 113, 172
*The Next Left: The History of a Future,* 121
Nicaragua, 125, 128, 179, 180
*Nineteen-Eighty Four Revisited: Totalitarianism in Our Century,* xix
*Nineteen-Eighty Four,* 65, 118, 119, 138-144, 239,
Nineteen-Eighty Four: Text, Sources, Criticism, xviii
nineteenth-century Russian writers, 248
Nixon, President Richard, 33, 78, 115, 191, 272, 321
Nobel Peace prize, 136
non-Communist left, 14, 55, 74
non-violence, 157-159, 165
North, Oliver, 33
North Carolina, 60, 186
North Vietnam, 152, 157, 164, 166, 174, 192
*Norton Anthology of Theory and Criticism, The,* 243
"Notes on Next Time," 195
Novak, William, 25, 328
Nove, Alec, 240, 263
nuclear war, 258
*nudniks,* 285, 299, 308

O'Connor, Flannery, 45, 47
Oglesby, Carl, 75, 81, 166
Ohio, 133
Ohio State University, 97
Old Guard, 13, 74, 169
Old Left, 43, 44, 53-55, 68, 70, 117, 144, 151, 154, 256, 272
Olsen, Tillie, 45, 47
Ontario New Democratic Party, 107
openDemocracy.net, 154
Oregon Public Interest Research Group, 198
organic development, 14, 74, 156, 165
*Origins of Totalitarianism, The,* 143, 242
Orwell, George, xviii, 5, 7, 16, 42, 51, 66, 93, 97, 105, 118-119, 137-145, 189, 207, 233, 239, 246, 247, 252, 258, 326
*Other America, The,* 10, 121, 290, 298

*Other American: The Life of Michael Harrington, The*, 281, 308
other Irving, the, 91
"Our 'Uncle Irving': Howe's Conservative Strain," 16, 24, 43, 51
"Our Country and Our Culture," 142, 203
"Our Priceless Economy," 181
Oversoul, The, 21
Ozick, Cynthia, 96, 208, 213

Pachter, Henry, 78, 81
Palestinians, 36, 39, 207, 208, 213
Palo Alto, 259
Panken, Irving, 91
Park Plaza, 338
participatory democracy, 14, 124, 156, 165, 177, 195, 320
*Partisan Review, The*, xi, xviii, x, 3, 14, 23, 25, 43, 57, 59, 83, 85, 92, 99-101, 109, 112, 137-138, 140-143, 145, 199-203, 205, 224, 229, 230, 242, 244, 247, 254, 259, 267, 271, 290, 292, 317-320
*Partisans: Marriage, Politics, and Betrayal Among the New York Intellectuals*, 255
Paz, Octavio, 97-98
Peace Movement, The, 34, 36, 160
Peace Now, ixx, 34, 36, 242
*Pentimento*, 80
*perestroika*, 232, 234, 238
Peretz, I.L., xix
Peretz, Martin, 172, 182-184, 196
Phillips, Wendell, 169
Phillips, William, 43, 138, 171, 230
Picasso, Pablo, 101, 184, 267
Pirandello, Luigi, 247
*pishers*, 189, 197
PL - see Progressive Labor
plastic hours, 256, 260
Plastrik, Simone, 339
Plastrik, Stanley, xvii, 6, 7, 59, 61, 62, 67, 71, 77, 141, 170, 329
Plato, 49
Podhoretz, Norman, 32, 58, 76, 115, 116, 140, 144
Poland, 63, 65, 81, 262
"Political Terrorism: Hysteria on the Left," 136
"Politics and the English Language," 119, 139
*Politics and the Novel*, xviii, xx, 57, 71, 85, 104, 105, 244, 245, 251, 290, 313
*Politics of God's Funeral, The*, 299
*Politics of Literary Reputation: The Making and Claiming of "St. George" Orwell, The*, 137, 139, 140, 145
*politics*, xi, 6, 7, 113, 141, 200
Polsky, Ned, 69, 80
Popular Front, The, 193, 204, 317
populism, 13, 21, 72
Port Huron, 155, 163, 164, 175, 188, 189, 195
Porter, Katherine Anne, 47
possessive individualism, 17, 18, 132
postmodernism, 42, 267
post-Vietnam, 272
Potter, Paul, 152, 155, 166, 195
Pound, Ezra, 42, 82, 104, 254, 266
Princeton University, xvii, 71, 95, 113, 221, 225, 231, 298
Pritchett, V.S., 248
privatization, 257
Progressive Labor, 195
proletariat, 68, 83, 128
prose style, 85, 137, 142
protest tradition, 15
Protestant tradition, 75, 178
Protestantism, 237
Proust, Marcel, 48, 90, 104, 267, 317
"Prufrock," see "Lovesong of J. Alfred Prufrock"
Public Broadcasting, 310
public intellectuals, x, 1, 3, 11, 107, 120, 198, 207, 209, 230, 266, 324
Public Interest Research Group, 198

*Public Interest, The,* 109, 198, 201
Puritanism, 183, 248
Puritans, 207
Putin, Vladimir, 234

Radcliffe College, 224
radical humanism, 5, 44, 122, 258, 273, 283
Radosh, Ronald, 172, 196
Rahv, Phillip, 13, 75, 92, 93, 112, 220, 224, 225, 230, 247, 248, 318
*Ramparts,* 34, 196
Ransom, Basil, 252
Ransom, John Crowe, 51, 268
Rapoport, Bernard, 307
Rapoport, Nessa, 214
Reagan years, 9, 55
Reagan, Nancy, 33
Reagan, President Ronald, 16, 19, 22, 44, 53, 108, 109, 116, 119, 120-122, 126-127, 129, 131-132, 171, 172, 199, 232, 241, 265, 311, 321
Reaganism, ix, 1, 17-19, 107, 121, 122, 233
Reaganite movement, 321
Reaganomics, 108, 129
redeeming the enemy, 158
redistributive income, 135
Reed College, 52
Reich, Robert, 65
Republican Party, 153, 164, 311, 317, 322, 325
Revolution of 1905, 270
revolutionary language, 192
revolutionary terror, 139
Rimbaud, Arthur 94
Rise of the New York Intellectuals: Partisan Review and Its Circle, 1934-1945, 145
Robber Barons, 241
Rocard, Michel, 306, 309
Rockefeller, John D., 90
Rodden, John, xxi, 137-140, 208, 327, 329, 330
Rohatyn, Felix, 129
Romanticism, 48, 139, 214, 215, 219, 267
Romantics, 207
Roosevelt, Eleanor, 308
Roosevelt, President Franklin Delano, 53, 109, 110, 126-127, 131, 134, 177, 282, 299, 308, 317
Rosenberg, Bernard, xvii, 32, 59, 60, 63, 67, 72, 78
Rosenberg, Harold, 56-58, 202, 205, 253, 318, 329
Rosenberg, Julius and Ethel, 34
Rosenfeld, Alvin, 26, 33
Ross, Bob, 169
Rosten, Leo, 37
Roth, Philip, 214, 245
Rothstein, Richie, 169
Rubin, Jerry, 172, 196
Rumania, 211
Russia, x, 9, 13, 64, 71, 191, 211, 234, 247, 260, 270, 276, 297
Russian invasion of Czechoslovakia, 162-163, 319, 322, 325
Russian Literature, 247-248, 329
Russian Revolution, 63, 138, 142, 187, 230
Russians, 70, 170-171,
Rustin, Bayard, 60, 79, 81, 190
Ruth, Babe, 204

Sachs, Milton, 61, 78, 329
Saigon, 72
Saki - see Bercovitch, Sacvan
San Francisco, 207, 297, 310
SANE, 78, 81, 160, 191
Santa Cruz, 170
Sartre, Jean-Paul, 26
scab, 87, 110
Scandinavia, 4, 240, 262, 306
Schapiro, Meyer, xvii, 58, 112, 318
Scheinkman, Jack, 307

Schlesinger, Arthur, 297, 308
Scholem, Gershom, 260
Schori, Pierre, 307
Schulman, Grace, 82-85, 243
Schumpeter, Joseph, 180, 196
Schwartz, Delmore, xvii, 92, 94, 103, 113, 222
SDS - see Students for a Democratic Society
Seale, Bobby, 172
"Second Opinion, A," 323
"Second Thoughts," 196
Second World War - see World War II
sectarianism, x, 6, 7-9, 14, 42, 55, 62, 68, 75, 111, 151-152, 160, 177, 178-179, 189, 273
"Sects in the City," 24
*Seed Beneath the Snow,* 79
*Selected Stories: I L. Peretz,* xi
Selected Works of Trotsky, 110
*Selected Writings: 1950-1990,* xx, 5
Serge, Victor, 247
*Seventies, The,* 51
sexual liberation, 185
Shabtai, Yakov, 105
Shachtman, Max, x, xi, 13, 62, 64, 79, 81, 113, 188, 270-273, 276-280, 276, 279, 281, 284, 288, 289, 294-296, 300, 305, 329
Shachtmanites, 6, 7, 59, 61, 62, 77, 79, 137, 138, 141, 142, 271, 275, 279, 284, 291, 294
Shakespeare, William, 49, 221
Shalom Acshav, 36
Shammas, Anton, 207-208
Shapiro, Meyer, 112
Sharansky, Natan, 33
*Sherwood Anderson*, xvii, xviii, 222, 223
Shocken Books, ixx, 143, 318
*Short Shorts: An Anthology of the Shortest Stories,* xi
Shostakovich, Dmitri, 319
*shtetl,* 25
Schulman, Grace, 82-85
Silber, John, 43
Silone, Ignazio, 56-58, 79, 97-99, 104, 247, 326
Silvers, Robert, 323-325
Singer, Isaac Bashevis, 96, 113, 114
*Slate,* 256
SNCC - see Student Non-violent Coordinating Committee
Social Democracy, 4, 5, 9, 12, 20, 107, 118, 180, 190, 233, 234, 275, 289, 301, 320, 321
social democrats, 59, 169, 187, 203, 262, 291
Social Democrats, USA, 261, 272
social Fascism, 74, 91, 173
social ownership, 134, 263, 264
*Socialism and America,* ixx, 151, 178
"Socialism is the name of our desire," 8, 22
Socialism, ix, x, 1-5, 7, 9, 10, 12, 13, 15, 21, 22, 23, 25-28, 30, 41, 44, 50, 53-54, 57-58, 62, 64, 68, 80, 81, 82, 84, 98, 108, 110, 120-124, 126, 135, 136, 137-141, 151, 188, 192, 198-199, 207, 208, 227, 232-235, 236, 237, 240-241, 244, 255, 257, 261, 263, 266, 270, 272-273, 281-283, 289-291, 296-297, 301, 306, 311, 316, 317, 320, 322-327, 329
"Socialism and Its Irresponsibilities: The Case of Irving Howe," 22
*Socialism, Past and Future,* 263
Socialist dream, 201
Socialist International, 305
Socialist Party, 13, 20, 58, 61, 120, 121, 124, 126, 151, 160, 276, 281-282, 295, 296, 309
Socialist politics, 26, 32, 62, 71, 91, 95, 138, 313, 329
Socialist realism, 8, 254
Socialist Scholars Conference, 300-301

Socialist tradition, 8, 9, 21, 30, 54, 57, 283, 302
Socialist Workers Party, x, xi, 196, 271, 274, 278
Solidarity, 81, 171
Sontag, Susan, 245, 251
Sorin, Gerald, 4, 17, 23, 136, 138, 308
sound bites, 19, 258, 265
South Africa, 176, 180
South America, 21, 158
South Vietnam, 77
Southern Renaissance, 268
Southern Tenant Farmers Union, 284
Soviet dictatorship, 237
Soviet society, 64, 239, 277
Soviet system, 240
Soviet Union, 5, 8, 11, 13, 52, 70, 97, 111, 119, 128, 138, 142, 161, 163, 164, 185, 234, 238-239, 257, 260-261, 263, 271, 278, 318-319, 321, 326
SP - see Socialist Party
Spanish Civil War,179
Spartacists, 176-177, 196
Spinoza, Baruch, 103
St. Louis, 45, 304
Stalin, Josef, 2, 80, 81, 85, 138, 142, 143, 190, 197, 237, 238, 317
Stalinism, 6, 23, 29, 64, 96, 98, 111, 115, 124, 138, 142, 151, 162, 182, 183, 189, 196, 200, 233, 236-238, 247, 256, 257, 260, 261, 273, 274, 278, 279, 311, 316, 322, 325
Stalinists, x, xvii, 9, 13, 59, 79, 90, 91, 111, 112, 141, 185, 186, 203, 204, 237, 254, 259, 261, 279, 291, 316-319, 325
Stanford University, xviii, 97, 118, 148, 186, 222, 223, 227, 259
*Steady Work: Essays in the Politics of Democratic Radicalism,* 1953-66, xviii, 24, 55
steelworkers, 132, 134
Steinem, Gloria, 126
Steinfels, Peter, 300
Stern, Sol, 34-35
Stevenson, Adlai, 76
*Stop Me If You've Heard This: A History and Philosophy of Jokes,* 256
Stowe, Harriet Beecher, 249
"Strangers," 214-215
Stravinsky, Igor, 101, 267
street corner speaking, 315
structuralism, 223
Students for Academic Freedom, 195
Students for a Democratic Society, xviii, 19, 22, 13, 34, 55, 73-74, 81, 97, 151, 152, 155, 156, 165, 168, 169, 171, 173, 175-176. 178, 188, 189, 195, 293, 308, 314, 320, 321
Student Non-violent Coordinating Committee, 159
Suckow, Ruth, 87
Sweden, 61, 134, 262-264, 283, 307
Swedes, 305, 307
Swedish Conservatives, 132

T.V.A., 123, 135
Tate, Allen, 51, 204, 252, 268
tax reform, 133
technocratic elitists, 132
Tel Aviv, 34
*Terrorism and Communism,* 142
textile workers, 87
Thatcherism, 233
Theory of Bureaucratic Collectivism, 277, 300-301
*Theory of Economic Development,* 196
*Thesis: The Magazine of the Graduate School and University Center,* 256
"Thinking the Unthinkable About Israel," 31
Third Camp - see Third Way
Third Way, 54-55, 272
This Age of Conformity, xviii, 139, 142, 199, 223, 320

Thomas, Norman, 9, 13, 20, 92, 124, 236, 160, 177, 193, 257, 271, 273, 276, 281, 282-285, 287, 290, 296-297, 299, 301-302, 314-315
Thoreau, Henry David, 15, 18, 101, 112, 153, 160, 209, 216, 218, 248
Thoreauvian rebel, 19
Thurow, Lester, 265
Tikkun conference, 5
*Tikkun,* 152
Tillich, Paul, 95, 222
*Time* magazine, 112, 259
Times Square, 38
tired heroism, 56
Tokyo, 249
Tolstoy, Leo, 8, 45, 80, 208, 230, 247
*Tomorrow,* xvi
Toronto, 107, 108, 328
totalitarianism, 6, 65, 96, 99, 141, 143, 233, 234, 237, 238, 242, 257, 260, 265, 321
TPMcafe, 154
trade union leaders, 77, 286, 307
trade unions, 30, 68, 97, 108, 110, 297
Transcendentalists, 209
translation, xvii, 28, 95, 97, 113-114, 325
*Treasury of Yiddish Poetry, A,* ixx, 102
*Treasury of Yiddish Stories, A,* xviii, x, 25, 113
*Tribune, The,* 248
tribunes, 1, 9, 296
Trilling, Diana, 245, 304
Trilling, Lionel, xviii, xi, 1, 13, 24, 82, 92, 93, 109, 112, 142, 144, 208, 222, 223, 228, 231, 247, 252, 255, 292, 318
Trotsky, Leon, ixx, 2, 6, 7, 23, 59, 63, 68, 79, 90, 110-111, 138, 139, 141, 142, 259, 271, 272, 275-280, 310, 318, 326
Trotskyism, 6, 7, 59, 115, 138, 142, 209, 210, 270-271, 275-276, 289, 320
Trotskyists, X, 6, 15, 137, 140, 144, 165, 236, 271
Troy, William, 252
Truman, President Harry S., 126, 131
Turgenev, Ivan, 247
Twilight of the Intellectuals: Culture and Politics in the Era of the Cold War, 22
"Two Cheers for Utopia," 23, 44, 55, 323
The Ugly American, 70

*Ulysses,* 184
*Uncle Tom's Cabin,* 250
union contracts, 131
union organizers, 177
Union Square, 161
unionism, 37, 87, 121
unions, 30, 35, 68, 81, 87, 97, 108, 110, 123, 125, 131, 134, 297
United Auto Workers, 259
United Front, 91, 317
United Nations, 108
United States Constitution, 11
University of California, Berkeley, 34, 185, 197, 207, 211-212
University of Chicago, 120, 231
University of Heidelberg, 224
University of Iowa, 175
University of Missouri, Kansas City, 162
University of Rochester, 52
University of Toronto, 108, 338
University of Waterloo, 328
University of Wisconsin at Madison, 182
Upper East Side, 201, 207
urban infrastructure, 130
USSR - see The Soviet Union
utopia, 99, 139
utopianism, 1-5, 10, 18, 20, 21, 44, 50, 53, 55, 216, 217, 241, 323

Venezuela, 21
Viet Cong, 192
Vietnam era, 154
Vietnam protests, 52
Vietnam War, 12, 20, 74, 78, 81, 115, 117, 125, 165, 167, 272, 279, 295, 308
*Village Voice,* 195, 303

Village, The, 114, 303, 304
Virgil, 49
visionary gradualism, 257, 263

Waco, 307
Waffle, 1-7, 117
Wald, Alan, 208, 210, 230, 275
Waldorf Astoria, 319
Waldorf conference, 69, 202, 203
*Wall Street Journal,* 256, 290
Wall Street, 127, 241
Wallace movement, 69
Walzer, Michael, 7, 23, 53, 60, 73, 76, 78, 162, 164, 173, 186, 227, 327
War on Poverty, 10, 121, 196
Warren, Austin, 252
Warren, Robert Penn, 51, 252, 253
Warshow, Robert, 142
Washington University, 45
"Wasteland, The" 90, 254
Watergate, 115
Wayne State University, 179
Weathermen, The, 117, 152, 170, 177, 293
Webber, Sarah, 274, 280
Weinstein, Jimmy, 173, 194
welfare state, 21, 61, 116, 126-127, 129-130, 134, 181, 234, 240, 262, 296, 297, 322
Wellesley College, 243, 246
*Weltanschauung*, 233
Welty, Eudora, 45, 47
Wells, H.G., 23
West Bank, The, 36
West Chester University, 140, 144
Western canon, 43, 122, 246
Western culture, 44
Western democracies, 9, 139
Western Europe, 5, 12, 239
Western thought, 88
Western tradition, 44, 45
*What is to Be Done?,* 208
"What's the Trouble: Social Crisis, Crisis of Civilization, or Both?," 49, 51
*Which Side Were You On? The American Communist Party during the Second World War,* 52
White Anglo-Saxon Protestants, 206
"White Negro, The" 54, 68-69
White Russians, 270
Whitman, Walt, 101
"Who Will Lead," 195
Wiesel, Elie, 27
Wisse, Ruth, 208, 213
Wilkins Avenue, 89
Williams, Ian, 23, 145
Williams, William Carlos, 247
Wilson, Edmund, x, xi, 1, 82, 89, 90, 93-95, 112-113, 144, 222, 248, 252-254
Wilson, Harold, 80
Winnipeg, 329-330
Winpisinger, William, 125
Winters, Yvor, 253
Wisse, Ruth, 208, 213
Wobblies, 75
Wolf, Dan, 304
Wolfe, Alan, 21, 208, 230
Wolfe, Tom, 268
women critics, 245, 251
*Women in Love,* 254
women's movement, 123, 125, 126
Woolf, Virginia, 86
worker control, 135, 264
worker participation, 130
Workers Party, xi, 81, 275, 277, 278
*Working Papers for a New Society,* 195
*World More Attractive, A,* x
*World of Our Fathers,* ix, 25-27, 34-37, 53, 82-85, 102, 109, 208, 248, 251, 259, 324, 325, 328, 330
World War I, 41, 192, 283
World War II, 13, 25, 41, 129, 137, 201, 203, 240, 252, 258, 259, 271, 278, 313

*The Worlds of Irving Howe,* xii
*Wretched of the Earth, The,* 196
Wright, Richard, 43, 115, 244, 250
The Writer in the Jewish Community: An Israeli-North American Dialogue, 207
*Writers and the Left,* 189
*Writers on the Left: Episodes in American Literary Communism,* 197

Yeats, William Butler, 47, 90, 97
Yiddish, 27, 28: culture, 41, 88; language, x, 25, 26-28, 37, 197, 210-212; literature, 36, 41, 43, 82, 95, 97, 108, 259, 327; 99; papers, 95; poetry, 102; poets, 95, 113; press, 29, 31; secularism, 208; theatre, xiv; writers, 28, 85, 95-96, 183, 329
Yiddishist, 110
Yiddishkeit, 25, 37, 208, 230
Yiddish-speaking world, 325
Yipsel, 89, 314
Young Communist League, 313-314
Young People's Socialist League, xi, 37, 116, 270, 314
youth movement, 154
yuppies, 127

zeitgeist, 44, 252, 258
*Zelig,* 312
Zionism, 26, 28, 36, 39, 80, 207, 304